Marketing in Practice
2007-2008

 The Chartered
Institute of Marketing

Marketing in Practice
2007–2008

Tony Curtis

ELSEVIER

AMSTERDAM • BOSTON • HEIDELBERG • LONDON • NEW YORK • OXFORD
PARIS • SAN DIEGO • SAN FRANCISCO • SINGAPORE • SYDNEY • TOKYO

Butterworth-Heinemann is an imprint of Elsevier

Butterworth-Heinemann is an imprint of Elsevier
Linacre House, Jordan Hill, Oxford OX2 8DP, UK
30 Corporate Drive, Suite 400, Burlington, MA 01803, USA

First edition 2007

Notice
No responsibility is assumed by the publisher for any injury and/or damage to persons
or property as a matter of products liability, negligence or otherwise, or from any use
or operation of any methods, products, instructions or ideas contained in the material
herein.

British Library Cataloguing in Publication Data
A catalogue record for this book is available from the British Library

Library of Congress Cataloging-in-Publication Data
A catalogue record for this book is available from the Library of Congress

ISBN: 978-0-7506-8433-0

For information on all Butterworth-Heinemann publications
visit our website at http://books.elsevier.com

Printed and bound in Italy

07 08 09 10 11   10 9 8 7 6 5 4 3 2 1

Contents

Preface
welcome to the CIM coursebooks

How to use this book

This element of the CIM programme is an integrated module, needing candidates to see the various activities as a coherent plan rather than a set of uncoordinated activities. Just as in sport, individual brilliance needs to sit within a team game plan to ensure long-term success. Unit 1 provides an integrated view of marketing, a systems view. The most brilliant advertising will not work if other elements of the offering (marketing mix) are wrong.

Not all candidates will be working in advertising agencies for major brands. Issues other than profitability affect how marketing plans can be formulated and implemented. The CIM qualification not only requires candidates to know and understand the relevant theory but also to apply it to case studies set in various contexts, such as not-for-profit and smaller organizations. In Unit 2 these contexts are explored so that the marketing mix tools in the succeeding units can be considered in the range of contexts that might confront a marketer. Specific attention is given to aspects such as service and international marketing.

Having set the scene, the service extended marketing mix is developed using a range of activities to demonstrate application issues and develop skills. Throughout the book, it is emphasized that skills in marketing are not acquired by some quick 'cramming' a few weeks before the exam, but by exploring and using the theoretical tools in a variety of contexts. The questions and activities should not be regarded as interesting elective elements, but as vital to the development of key exam skills. Where possible, the reader should relate concepts to their own experience, both as a professional marketer and also as consumer (a trip to the supermarket or the bank is also an opportunity for observing marketing in action). Specific exam skills can be developed by studying past case studies, questions and specimen answers given on the CIM website (www.cim.co.uk). To develop the marketing mix, information is needed so Unit 8 explores the issue of information. Before deciding how to research an understanding of why the information is needed and will be used is essential.

Units 9 and 10 cover a range of the communications, management and financial skills needed in the day-to-day activities of marketing.

At the end of the book, a return is made to the theme of Unit 1, with an overview of the complete planning processes and how individual elements that form part of this syllabus fit together into an overall marketing plan. This module is not only the integrative module for level one, it also points to the syllabus elements in level two.

An attempt has been made not to see the contemporary developments (e.g. convergent digital technologies) as something special for a few notes at the end of the unit, but something to be considered as being integrated in all aspects of the marketer's work.

Acknowledgments

The models in this coursebook have been developed over a number of years with CIM students; their contribution in refining the models is appreciated. Sharon Heard assisted in the preparation of the draft manuscript. Helpful discussions, to revise and considerably improve the draft, were contributed by Ali Green (University of Exeter) and Lorraine Kirby (University of the West of England).

Tony Curtis
April 2006

An introduction from the academic development advisor

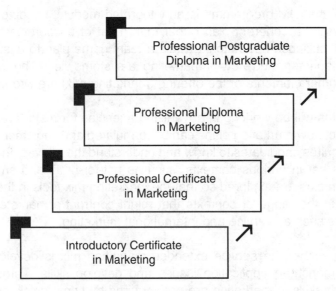

Study note © CIM 2006

The authoring team, Elsevier Butterworth-Heinemann and I have all aimed to rigorously revise and update the coursebook series to make sure that every title is the best possible study aid and accurately reflects the latest CIM syllabus. This has been further enhanced through independent reviews carried out by CIM.

We have aimed to develop the assessment support to include some additional support for the assignment route as well as the examination, so we hope you will find this helpful.

The authors and indeed Senior Examiners in the series are commissioned for their CIM course teaching and examining experience, as well as their research into specific curriculum-related areas and their wide general knowledge of the latest thinking in marketing.

We are certain that you will find these coursebooks highly beneficial in terms of the content and assessment opportunities and a study tool that will prepare you for both CIM examinations and continuous/integrative assessment opportunities. They will guide you in a logical and structured way through the detail of the syllabus, providing you with the required underpinning knowledge, understanding and application of theory.

The editorial team and authors wish you every success as you embark upon your studies.

Karen Beamish
Academic Development Advisor

How to use these coursebooks

Everyone who has contributed to this series has been careful to structure the books with the exams in mind. Each unit, therefore, covers an essential part of the syllabus. You need to work through the complete coursebook systematically to ensure that you have covered everything you need to know.

This coursebook is divided into units each containing a selection of the following standard elements:

- o *Learning objectives* – tell you what you will be expected to know, having read the unit.
- o *Syllabus references* – outline what part of the syllabus is covered in the module.
- o *Study guides* – tell you how long the unit is and how long its activities take to do.
- o *Questions* – are designed to give you practice – they will be similar to those you get in the exam.
- o *Answers* – (at the end of the book) give you a suggested format for answering exam questions. Remember there is no such thing as a model answer – you should use these examples only as guidelines.
- o *Activities* – give you a chance to put what you have learned into practice.
- o *Debriefings* – (at the end of the book) shed light on the methodologies involved in the activities.
- o *Hints and tips* – are tips from the senior examiner, examiner or author and are designed to help you avoid common mistakes made by previous candidates and give you guidance on improving your knowledge base.
- o *Insights* – encourage you to contextualize your academic knowledge by reference to real-life experience.
- o *Key definitions* – highlight and explain the key points relevant to that module.
- o *Definitions* – may be used for words you must know to pass the exam.
- o *Summaries* – cover what you should have picked up from reading the unit.
- o *Further study* – provides details of recommended reading in addition to the coursebook.

While you will find that each section of the syllabus has been covered within this text, you might find that the order of some of the topics has been changed. This is because it sometimes makes more sense to put certain topics together when you are studying, even though they might appear in different sections of the syllabus itself. If you are following the reading and other activities, your coverage of the syllabus will be just fine, but don't forget to follow up with trade press reading!

unit 1
an overview of the marketing system

Learning objectives

By the end of this unit, you will

○ Understand how the various elements of marketing, such as the marketing mix, need to be integrated for success: a systems view of the Marketer's activities.

○ Understand the characteristics of the marketplace and the need for segmentation.

○ Be able to appraise the external and internal environments of an organization and conduct a SWOT analysis.

○ Understand the contribution of an MkIS to a successful organization.

○ Recognize the need for marketing to be integrated fully within the logistic and financial objectives of the organization.

○ Understand the need for segmentation and the development of targeting and positioning strategies.

○ Appreciate the human dimension of marketing teams with successful collaboration among relevant stakeholders both within and outside the organization.

Syllabus references

In the examination setting for this integrative paper, candidates are expected to develop self-consistent (e.g. not suggesting major national TV advertising for a small organization) solutions to case study issues and tasks. The overall objective of this first unit is to provide a systems overview so that answers can be developed that are effective and coherent in the specific case study context. Answers which are correct in format (e.g. a business letter) but lack appropriate context-specific development may only earn a marginal fail grade. The final paper at this level draws upon the three earlier papers and requires candidates to provide an integrated development of the theory and relevant issues in their answers to exam questions or integrated assignment reports. CIM Syllabus references

2.1 Describe the structure and roles of the marketing function within the organization.

2.6 Explain how the organization fits into a supply chain and works with distribution channels.

3.4 Explain how marketing makes use of planning techniques: objective setting and coordinating, measuring and evaluating results to support the organization.

4.7 Explain the importance of the extended marketing mix: how process, physical aspects and people affect customer choice.

5.3 Explain how organizations assess the viability of opportunities, initiatives and projects.

Key definitions

Decision-making unit (DMU) – The group of people who may be involved in the purchase of an item, the buyer may well not be the decider.

Gap analysis – A model for evaluating strategies for moving a company from where it is with its existing strategies to where it desires to be.

Macroenvironment – The general external environment of a company that is explored by a model such as STEEPLE or PEST.

McKinsey 7s – A model for analysing the human and organizational issues within an organization. It is generally considered complementary to the value chain.

Marketing Information System – A Marketing Information System (MkIS) is a continuing and interacting structure of people, equipment and procedures to gather, sort, analyse, evaluate and distribute pertinent, timely and accurate information for use by marketing decision-makers to improve their marketing planning, implementation and control (Kotler, 2000).

Microenvironment – The environment immediately surrounding the organization, including the competition.

Mission – The 'one-page' statement of what the firm is and its position in business from a customer-benefit-orientated viewpoint. It is subject to rare changes when a major change of direction or firm's philosophy is required.

PEST – The analysis of the political, economic, social and technical environment within which the company operates.

Porter Value Chain – A model for the internal examination of the organization and how it interacts with its environment.

Porter 5 forces of competition – A method for the analysis of competitive forces on a company.

Pull strategy – The activities used to directly inform and encourage buyers to go to outlets and purchase a consumer product (e.g. advertising for a detergent).

Push strategy – The activities used to get consumer goods stocked by the retailers and channels.

Segmentation – The division of a large, heterogeneous market area into homogeneous sections to allow more effective marketing.

SLEPT – Social, legal, economic, political and technical environments. A similar version to the STEEPLE and PEST analysis for analysing the external environment.

Stakeholder – A stakeholder is any specific, identifiable group that may have an effect on the organization, either beneficial or adverse.

STEEPLE – A similar version to the PEST (political/legal, economic, social and technical environments) analysis for analysing the external environment.

SWOT – Strengths, Weaknesses, Opportunities and Threats analysis: a way to refocus all the internal and external analysis into key issues for directing management action.

Study Guide

Marketing in Practice is the integrative module of the Professional Certificate in Marketing (Figure 1.1). Some new material is introduced, but much of the content is taken from the other three modules at this level. The major significant difference in this module is its integrative nature. Any single assessment element may need material introduced from any of the four modules.

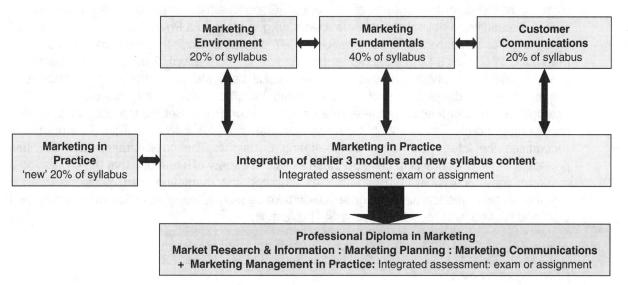

Figure 1.1 Integrated relationship between earlier Professional Certificate in Marketing modules and Marketing in Practice. Bridge to Professional Diploma in Marketing

When studying any new subject there is a potential problem that in reviewing the elements in detail, the overview of the subject as a whole becomes obscured. If you wish to learn to drive a car, you cannot just learn the Highway Code and omit the skill of actually driving the car. To be a safe driver you have to understand all the relevant issues and acquire all the skills. Although a marketing person may work in a specific marketing department such as 'Market Research' or 'Corporate Communications', it is essential to see how each element links into the whole. Marketing Information is considered in Unit 8. The research department collects data (raw elements of observation such as the number of people who buy a product) since managers need information in order to make business decisions. Market research in itself does not make management decisions. Managers have to interpret data and information to make decisions. A marketing professional needs to understand how their role and activities within the organization contribute to its overall success.

Marketing is a 'real-world' discipline in the same way as medicine. When a person visits a medical doctor, they do not want a lecture on molecular biology, they want to be cured. A company does not want to hire a person who can give a lecture on market segmentation, they want an individual who can achieve business objectives such as a successful new product launch, a real link to the practical world. Theory evolves from observing the way marketing has worked; the theory can then be applied to new situations to aid the marketing professional in making better and more successful decisions. To learn and understand theory, it is essential to select practical examples from your own experience. In this way, you will develop not only knowledge but also understanding and the ability to use your knowledge and understanding of theory to develop innovative creative solutions to practical business situations.

In undertaking this integrative module, the CIM expects candidates to be conversant with the content of the other three modules at this level. Also, following the integrative philosophy of this module, learning outcomes such as 'calculate and justify marketing mix decisions' are explored as more than just 'accountancy' and numerical calculations of breakeven points and so on. Clearly, these are important but, increasingly, marketers at every level in the organization are expected to take a more 'balanced scorecard' holistic view of organizations and their objectives. In formulating a profitable implementation strategy, the longer-term objectives of building lifetime stakeholder value must also be considered (hence the relatively early brief outlines of relationship marketing (RM) and internal marketing in Unit 2).

Problems have to be solved and decisions made in a variety of marketing contexts. Marketing a local charity is very different to marketing an international airline. Unit 2 provides a brief review of some of the different contexts of marketing. Good exam answers and integrative project reports demonstrate not only 'mechanical skills' (e.g. a gloss to a PowerPoint presentation) but also insightful context-specific content. Units 3–7 provide a focused review of the integrated marketing mix. Units 8 (The Management of Marketing Information), 9 (Skills for the Marketer) in 10 (Budgets and schedules) cover the syllabus skill elements. Given the integrated nature of this module, the development of skills is linked into the cover of the marketing mix. For example, aspects of finance are integrated into Unit 4 on Price. Setting the price in a marketing-orientated organization should be more than just cost plus a fixed margin. This treatment recognizes the integrated nature of marketing decisions. The case studies and activities provide a range of contexts to develop these skills in a variety of situations that the professional marketer may face. Unit 11 (Bringing it all together: the marketing plan) pulls the threads together to cover the learning outcome: 'Undertake basic marketing activities within an agreed plan and monitor and report on progress' (Table 1.1).

Table 1.1 Learning outcomes/unit guide

Learning outcomes	Study units
Collect relevant data from a variety of secondary information sources	Units 1 and 8
Analyse and interpret written, visual and graphical data	Units 8 and 9
Devise appropriate visual and graphical means to present marketing data	Unit 9
Evaluate and select media and promotional activities appropriate to the organization's objectives and status and its marketing context	Units 1, 2, 6 and 8
Calculate and justify budgets for marketing mix decisions	Unit 3–7 (The Marketing Mix) and 9
Develop relationships inside and outside the organization	Units 1, 2, 6, 8 and 9
Apply planning techniques to a range of marketing tasks and activities	Units 9 and 11
Undertake basic marketing activities within an agreed plan and monitor and report on progress	Units 8–11
Gather information for and evaluate marketing results against financial and other criteria	Units 3–7 (Marketing Mix) and 8–10

This is not a 'linear' book in the sense that if you want to prepare for an exam question 'write a letter', you only have to look at the section on letters in Unit 9. This will give you the framework and cover the general skills issues, but this is only a modest proportion of the marks which can be earned in such a question. The letter must not only have the right structure but also relevant content, drawing upon the marketing context and objectives of the letter. The strategy of this book (Figure 1.2) is to review the issues, contexts and skills, and the professional competence is to be able to integrate these to address a given task.

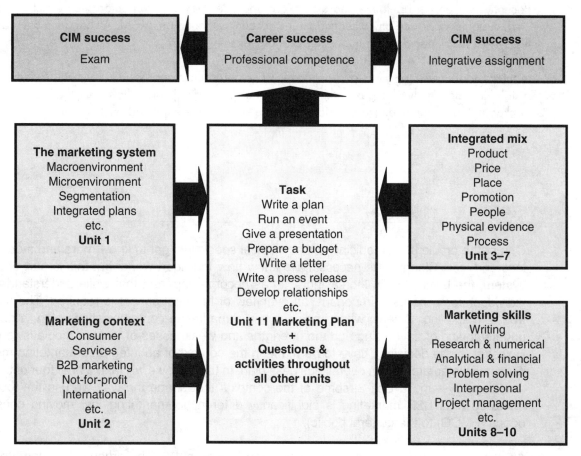

Figure 1.2 Integration of elements to complete a marketing task

In Unit 2 'The Context of Marketing' around 12 'contexts' are reviewed. If the task is to write a marketing plan, this does not imply there are 12 potential marketing plans; more than one of the listed contexts may apply. Thus, one could envisage a small charity wanting to provide medical assistance to a less-developed country. In this case, the contexts 'limited budget', 'not-for-profit', 'international', 'services', 'relationship marketing' and 'marketing ethics' may all apply at the same time. There are relatively few exclusions, for example, in the marketing of consumer goods; it might be thought that business-to-business (B2B) issues were not relevant. However, there may often be a 'push' strategy element that will also imply a B2B aspect as well in the overall plan development. If we take the list of 12 potential 'contexts' from Unit 2, we have a simple yes or no situation for each 'context'. The implication of this is that there are 2^{12} (over 4000) potential contexts for a marketing plan. It is not possible to write a book that provides an example of every type of marketing plan, letter, budget and so on. As shown in Figure 1.2, the need is to learn the elements (in this book for convenience they are grouped into four blocks) and then develop the essential professional skill of synthesis from the elements. The ability to apply knowledge and synthesize solutions for a given marketing problem in context is an essential professional competence at this level. The CIM assessments are designed to test your level of professional competence by exam or integrative assignment. Get the horse in front of the cart; the development of professional competence will enable you to pass the CIM assessments. Passing the assessment provides the evidence of having achieved the appropriate level of professional competence. Success in the assessment (exam or integrative assignment) comes from having previously developed competence.

Why an integrated view?

Recently, an 'online' bank installed a software upgrade. However, an unforeseen effect was that each customer could see any other customer's account without a password. A change in one part of the system had created a bug in another part of that same system.

In integrated marketing, plans and actions must be set in their appropriate contexts. A change in distribution may imply changes in the product (e.g. packaging), price (to cover changed costs of packaging) and promotion (communication of the value of the improved packaging).

A systems view of marketing

One of the problems in medicine is that medical specialists get to know more and more about less and less. Clearly, it is necessary to know how the heart works but this is part of a total system, the human body. Increasingly, it has become apparent that while understanding the individual components is important, an overview of the total patient is required. The same is true of marketing. Clearly, when implementing a marketing communications plan, a depth of understanding of advertising and the strengths and weaknesses of various media is required. However, these decisions have to be made in the context of an integrated marketing mix that itself must integrate into an overall business plan. In this unit, we will take a brief tour of the total marketing system. In Unit 2, some of the contexts that shape the way we use the tools are reviewed (e.g. B2B marketing is significantly different to marketing fast moving consumer goods (FMCG) to the general public).

An overview of the marketing system is given in Figure 1.3. The organization operates in a marketplace, which consists of the buyers and users of the product. Sometimes the concept of 'buyers and users' may need to be adapted for a given situation, so a hospital may consider 'patients' rather than 'buyers'. In the marketplace, buyers and users are influenced by other groups of people (stakeholders); so, even if parents are the buyers in a toyshop, the children for whom they are purchasing the toy are also relevant stakeholders.

The behaviour of the marketplace is influenced by the microenvironment; in particular the competition and their competitive marketing mix offerings. In turn, the microenvironment is influenced by the macroenvironment. In this book, the STEEPLE framework will be used (in other texts, alternative models may be used such as PEST, SLEPT, etc.).

The organization responds to the environment by continually adapting its internal environment. Porter's Value Chain and the McKinsey 7S models give us frameworks for evaluating the internal environment of the organization.

The data from the internal environment, the microenvironment and the macroenvironment is collected and analysed to provide relevant information for the organization's management. A SWOT analysis is one very useful tool for analysing the flood of information. The management team must define the broad mission, aims and objectives and decide the strategic stance to be adopted (e.g. to be a market leader or a market follower). In appraising situations, formulating alternatives and selecting management actions (e.g. selecting new products for development), a range of theoretical tools such as product life cycle (PLC) and portfolio analysis (e.g. Boston (BCG) matrix) are invaluable.

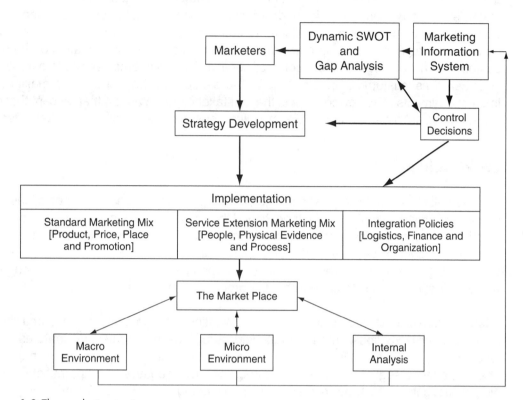

Figure 1.3 The marketing system

When broad initiatives are decided, it is then necessary for the detailed issues of the marketing mix to be developed and amended as required for changing market conditions. The marketing mix is the 'powerhouse' of marketing implementation. The best marketing plan is worthless if the product is of poor quality or does not arrive in time. Marketing plans involve cash flows and so the financial implications are critical. To implement marketing plans, the whole organization must be energized, so marketing plans must integrate with all the other business plans, for example logistics, financial management and organizational development.

In any paper representation of the marketing system, it is difficult to indicate that this is not a linear or 'one-off' activity. It is a continual process; the system is constantly monitored and the organization's plans are adjusted to adapt to changing market conditions, for example, in response to competitors' activities.

 ## Activity 1.1

Select an organization that you are familiar with, such as the one you may work for. Who are its customers? What competition does the organization face? What do you think are the key challenges in the future for your selected organization?

The marketplace and microenvironment

The marketplace consists of the buyers and users of the organization's products and services and the immediate microenvironment in which the purchase and use take place. When mission statements are written, much is made of issues such as customer satisfaction. However, in some circumstances, it is a little difficult to define precisely who the customer is. This may be because the organization is a not-for-profit or social marketing organization or the definition of customer is not obvious for the product or service. Students, employers and parents can all be considered as 'customers' of a college in the sense that they all may be making direct and indirect payments. The key concept is that of stakeholders. We can then accept that customers are a key stakeholder group and that a college has many and complex stakeholder groups.

Stakeholders

It is essential to satisfy or at least manage all the legitimate stakeholder expectations. It is no use marketing a toy to parents only for them to find their child does not play with it. Equally, it does not help if the parents do not buy the toy in the first place. To illustrate stakeholder analysis we shall consider a personal care product – shampoo. Partial stakeholder analysis for this situation is given in Figure 1.4. Note that appropriate interpretation of market segmentation concepts is useful in identifying the structure within the groups that have been identified by the analysis.

Internal stakeholders are vital and staff motivation and commitment are characteristics of successful organizations. Internal stakeholders can be segmented by features such as job level or job function. In internal marketing initiatives, such as during the management of change, attitude segmentation variables (e.g. positive, negative and apathetic) may be useful. No product gets to the supermarket shelf without going through a B2B marketing process. Very often with consumer products, there is a division between B2B customers who use the product for the delivery of a service (in our case it would be the hair salons) and the B2B customers who retail the product to customers for home use.

Clearly, all the normal tools of market segmentation apply to groups of customers, identified for convenience in Figure 1.4 as consumers and customers. Most organizations operate within a framework of law and rules, which are enforced by regulators. For a manufacturer of shampoo, safety in manufacture and in consumer use is subject to regulatory control. The marketing claims made for the product (e.g. 'anti-dandruff') will fall under the jurisdiction of the Advertising Standards Authority. The activity of a firm will be scrutinized by pressure groups with their own specific agenda. In Europe, animal testing of personal care products has been discontinued; however, international companies who operate under different standards in their home market may also come under pressure in Europe. In the fashion sector of the market, consumer pressure groups may consider marketing claims extravagant and products over-priced. A key PR activity is to lobby regulators and address the issues raised by the pressure groups.

In today's Just-in-Time (JIT) environment, close relationships are vital with suppliers who are increasingly being viewed as another sphere of 'internal' stakeholders rather than being 'outsiders'. Firms both compete in the marketplace and will also collaborate (e.g. to lobby regulators when all manufacturers are faced with a common threat such as a poorly framed EU draft Directive). Within the industry, there may be associations such as the Article Numbering Association (industry forum for ensuring the effective and efficient use of bar codes to the benefit of both manufacturers and retailers of consumer products). The media are a significant influence on the brand. Celebrity endorsement in the editorials of the glossy fashion press can be a very positive influence. Adverse reports in the consumer or environmental pages of a paper can have a negative effect. The trade press can be important in maintaining credibility with B2B customers and in attracting the most able staff to join the organization.

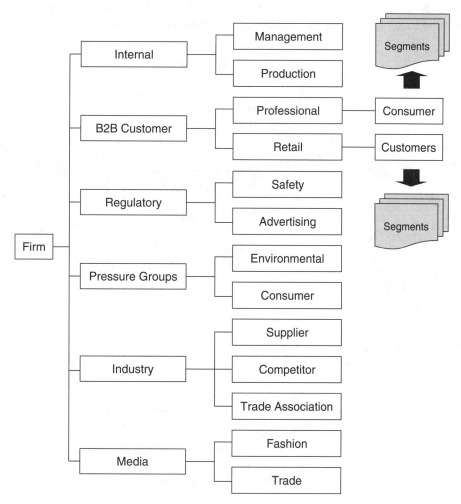

Figure 1.4 Partial stakeholder analysis for manufacturer of shampoo

Activity 1.2

Complete a stakeholder analysis for your local university or college. You should consider both the internal as well as the external stakeholders. Stakeholder analysis is a key skill for a marketer and is often part of a CIM exam question (e.g. 'Kernow Railways micro franchise' June 2005 Question 3a 'Identify FOUR key stakeholder groups of Kernow Railways').

Competition within the marketplace

Porter's five forces of competition model have provided an effective tool for analysing the competition aspects of the marketplace. Figure 1.5 adapted from Porter demonstrates the model for a typical consumer product or service. 'In-segment' competition is what most people would call 'normal' competition: the battle between close competitors such as TESCO and ASDA. There are other companies that compete but not in such a direct way: Boots competes with ASDA in the personal care sector but not in clothing. However, it should be remembered that a large, distant competitor could have a significant impact on a small organization. The supermarkets' move into bookselling has become a major threat to independent and specialist bookshops. By creaming off the sales of the latest blockbuster, the remaining sales of specialist books may not provide enough revenue to keep the small outlet above breakeven sales volumes.

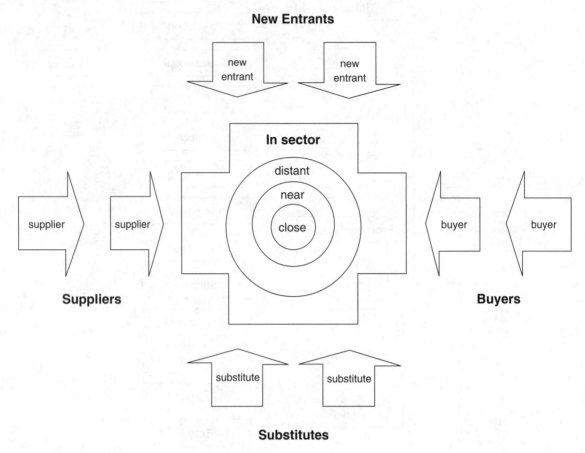

Figure 1.5 Five forces of competition
Source: Adapted from Porter

Buyers can exert power over the organization. Viewing the situation from the point of view of a hotel in a ski resort, it can be seen that in the high season rooms are expensive as demand is high (low buyer power). However, out-of-season prices can be lower as customers can shop around (high buyer power). In general, from the viewpoint of the brand manufacturer of consumer goods, the power of the buyers is twofold. If the supermarkets do not stock the product then the customers are not able to buy it. If the customers select another brand as better value for money, the situation is just as bad. To address these two influences, brand manufacturers use marketing strategies directed at both the retail channels (push strategy) and the consumers (pull strategy). There is also the potential influence of suppliers on the organization. Again, this may be direct or indirect, further down the supply chain. Therefore, a company may be spoilt for choice for a possible supplier of personal computer hardware, but still have to purchase a Microsoft operating system. It is not by accident that Microsoft is one of the most profitable organizations in the world. Further cover of competition is given in CIM coursebook 'Marketing Environment'.

New entrants are also a major potential source of competitive pressure. The air travel microenvironment has been rewritten by the entry of the aggressive, low-cost airlines. The shape of retailing is being rewritten as Wal-Mart enters new markets such as the United Kingdom (purchase of ASDA) and China.

An organization may be integrated to minimize some of the competition forces. The brand manufacturer may own raw material suppliers and also own the retail outlets (managing both supplier and buyer power). This type of vertical marketing system (VMS) can be achieved by other devices.

In the contractual VMS, the same end is achieved not by ownership but by the framework of contractual relationships. The Body Shop developed with the manufacture of its products and many of the outlets working under a franchise system. Here, the outlets are owned by individuals who then operate them under a detailed franchise contract. Co-operatives form a strategy for smaller organizations to gain some competitive stature by working together, to achieve critical mass in areas such as buying power. Large buyers such as Wal-Mart achieve coordination and control (an administered VMS) with their tight supply chain management system and its set of contractual relationships.

Activity 1.3

The market for chewing gum has been evolving. In the past, the product could have been viewed as a confectionery product. More recent introductions have been positioned on 'fresh breath', moving the product into what can be called the 'oral hygiene' market. Complete a Porter competition analysis for chewing gum from the standpoint of a major brand leader.

The macroenvironment

The STEEPLE model (Table 1.2) gives us a framework for analysing the major influences that impact on the marketplace. A sensitive MkIS is required as major changes in the macroenvironment can, at times, take place quickly (9/11). With rapid changes, it is vital to analyse the impact of the event on the organization. Slow changes such as shifts in population demographics are also important, since if the organization is not alert, the change can become so advanced before its impact is detected that major problems arise; even survival may become questionable. For travel agencies, the opening of the Channel Tunnel was a major event, which could be clearly identified. The change in social attitudes to holidays from 'package' to 'à la carte' has been more incremental. However, failure to respond to either would impact on the profitability of the business and service to the customers.

Table 1.2 General overview of selected key STEEPLE issues

STEEPLE element	Selected key issues
Social/cultural	Demographics, society, culture
Technological innovation	Inventions, discoveries, information technologies
Economic issues	Business cycle, inflation rates, interest rates, disposable income, wealth distribution, consumer spending patterns, credit availability, employment levels, exchange rates, taxation
Education/training	Educated consumers, educated channels, education of staff, lifelong training
Political	Stability, attitudes to industry, attitudes to competition, climate for 'free trade', attitudes to foreign investors
Legal	Monopolies and mergers, competition, consumer legislation, health and safety, consumer safety (e.g. strict liability), employment law, environmental law, regulations (e.g. labelling), codes of conduct, self-regulation
Environmental protection	Consumer pressure, volatile organic compounds (VOC), Persistent Organic Pollutants (POP), Ozone depletion/CFCs, global warming, genetic engineering issues, environmental fate, laws, sustainable development, life cycle analysis

Social/cultural

Social influences impact on the consumer decision-making process. Attitudes change quickly; for example, 20 years ago one could smoke on a transatlantic airliner, but now in most countries, the social trend is to want smoking eliminated from public buildings. Social changes can also impact on media habits. The move of the serious daily papers from 'broadsheet' format to 'tabloid' has been in response to commuters wanting something that can be read on crowded public transport. It should be remembered that elements of the STEEPLE model interact. A development in technology (text messaging on mobile telephones) can influence social changes in the population (e.g. the development of 'text speak', now being adopted by Scrabble players). Population shifts can affect the nature of society. Both Europe and North America have become much more multicultural societies, reflecting the global movements of population in the twentieth century. This affects the demand for products and services and this, in turn, generates demand for special communication channels. With broadband technology, TV can now not only be a medium of mass advertising around a soap but also become highly targeted for special social groups.

Technology/innovation

The beginning of the twenty-first century has been interesting for the number of hundredth birthdays including that of the first powered flight and the original development of brands such as Ford. Mass air travel and mass ownership of cars have altered society. In the twenty-first century, convergent information and computer technologies will transform society. The Internet was originally conceived as a technical solution to a military planning problem: how to maintain communications after a nuclear attack? With commercial and consumer access to broadband, this technology has moved far from the uses originally conceived for it. The Internet is rewriting ways of conducting business in both the B2B and the B2C sectors. The development of digital cameras embedded in mobile telephones is adding yet another dimension to people's ability to communicate.

The marketer needs to interpret these developments creatively and imaginatively. For example, the impact of the Internet on book sales is not uniform. Some directories and reference books have, in effect, ceased to exist as people gain this type of reference information directly from the Internet. We may well be happy to buy the latest blockbuster online from Amazon. However, the book addict is looking for a shopping *experience* and specialist shops are adapting to this, hence leading to trends such as coffee shops within bookshops to provide the right atmosphere and give shoppers an offline experience, the real joy of book buying.

Economics

Economics is often seen as a dense and difficult mathematical subject. Certainly, governments employ many statisticians to collect and analyse the figures. However, it is important to realize that economics is at the core of marketing. The Retail Price Index is not a mathematical abstraction. It is an exciting reflection of how people live and how the pattern of spending changes. These reports are excellent sources of secondary data for marketers. In Table 1.2, some of the key issues are listed. Economics is much more marketing orientated than some sources would indicate. The value of a house is what people are prepared to pay. This is a consumer issue involving social attitudes and values. When people see that house prices are rising, they can cash in on this (in late 2006, the majority of mortgages were not new but re-mortgages) to spend on consumer durables and that longed-for world cruise. With the wide availability of credit, it is as much how people feel as what they have actually got (disposable income) that drives the high street (if they do not have it they can borrow it).

Education

In the United Kingdom in the middle of the twentieth century, less than 10 per cent of the population gained a university degree. We are now moving to a situation in many developed counties where 50 per cent of the population have experience of higher education. The educational level of consumers is expanding; this is further levered by pressure groups and the media feeding good information through a flood of channels from Sunday newspaper supplements on wine to pressure group websites. The adoption of thinner, flatter organizations has driven decision-making towards the front line. The implication is that many more skilled and knowledgeable staff are required within companies, for example, to keep up with the development in company IT and communications technologies.

Political

There are a number of facets to 'political' issues. Clearly, a change of government when there are privatization or nationalization policies (depending on their political colour) has an impact on the macroenvironment. Organizations also need to consider not only the national political issues but also regional and local ones. Often the expansion plans of a supermarket are dependent on winning a lot of local political debates in order to gain the required planning permissions. Politics and politicians shape laws, and many organizations see the lobbying of politicians as a key part of their strategic plans. This is not restricted to commercial organizations; social marketing groups have become most active in this area, campaigning to extend smoking bans and to move the healthy living battle lines towards junk food.

Law

Law affects everything we do in marketing. Every aspect of the marketing mix has legal issues that need consideration. When researching, we may well have to take account of data protection legislation. Lack of knowledge is no defence. Therefore, it is vital that a marketer is aware of which aspects of a marketing plan may be affected by laws and seeks professional advice where uncertainty prevails. This is particularly important when implementing marketing plans developed for one country in another, where a different legal system prevails. A competition that is an instant hit in one country may simply be illegal elsewhere. Apart from legal constraints, there may be voluntary codes of conduct imposed by the industry. Thus, much of advertising regulation may not be imposed by government law but by industry codes of conduct enforced within the industry by the industry.

Environment

Environmental issues have become increasingly important as the stark truth confronts society that gross consumption of finite resources cannot continue forever and that, in the long term, sustainable production and distribution is the only way forward for society as a whole. Some of the issues may be rather technical: such as whether genetic engineering is beneficial to society and the economy (largely the view in the United States) or a technical dead end with too many risks (possibly the majority view in Europe). For the practising marketer, two of the aspects of Table 1.2 are paramount. A marketer should be aware of the PLC (in this context we do not imply the traditional PLC concept of introduction, growth, maturity and decline). In this analysis, the impact of the product over its total lifespan is considered: raw materials (e.g. steel, wood), manufacture (e.g. pollution issues), distribution (e.g. energy use), consumer use (e.g. energy-efficient deep freezer) and disposal (recycling targets). This is important, as it is not acceptable to abdicate responsibility. Therefore, a garden centre selling hardwood garden furniture needs to be assured it has been produced by sustainable and legal logging. A car manufacturer may no longer consider that its environmental responsibilities have ended with the sale of the car but build into the vehicle the ability to recycle and now provide facilities for this.

Table 1.2 should not be regarded as something to be learned by rote. Some of the points identified may not always be relevant to a given situation. Sometimes another factor which has not been indicated may be important. The table should be used as a checklist to prompt consideration of issues that may be relevant to the context. The only way to be able to conduct a good environmental analysis is through practice. The suggested activities and case study will give you a chance to apply the framework and develop your skills.

Having explored the marketplace, the microenvironment and the macroenvironment, we need to analyse how effective and efficient the internal workings of the organization are to complete the analysis. The 'traditional' airlines were completely upstaged when the low-cost airlines devised a new business system that provided air travel at a fraction of the price paid previously by passengers. Porter's Value Chain provides a framework to analyse the internal environment of the organization.

Case study

UK Railways

In the United Kingdom, railways are facing major challenges. Customers are complaining about poor services. The government is reluctant to spend vast amounts of public money on developing the decaying infrastructure. The inflated costs of commuting by car (fuel charges and congestion charging in London) are increasing the number of people wanting to use the railways. An outline STEEPLE analysis for railways in the United Kingdom is given below. Non-UK students should consider how this analysis would differ in their country.

Element STEEPLE	Issues
Social/cultural	Increasing concerns about the environment
Technological innovation	New train technologies (e.g. tilting train). These developments also include ways to improve the customer experience (e.g. Internet access, on-train entertainment, etc.) following trends set in air travel
Economic issues	The growth of commuter travel on the rail system means it is working at close to full capacity. This trend is likely to continue with increasing costs of fuel, making car travel expensive. There is a need for investment in infrastructure (e.g. longer platforms, new signal systems). Financing this investment may be difficult
Education/training	Customers – possibly not a major issue for customers
	Staff – New technical systems may require staff training
Political	The balance of public–private involvement in the running costs and capital investments for rail development is a major issue
Legal	The legal framework for the regulation and power of the regulator is a major issue for operators
Environmental protection	Environmental impact of major infrastructure developments is a key issue. Overall, the switch to rail travel is seen to have a positive environmental impact, reducing the congestion and pollution associated with car-based travel
Porter five forces	
In-sector	In certain areas rail operators may be directly competing over the same routes

Substitutes	Other forms of travel such as road and air
Buyers	Severe competition over price with new low-cost airlines on longer city-to-city routes. Online price comparisons make it easy for customers to select lowest cost option
New entrants	New companies may enter the market when rail franchises become available for re-tender (e.g. Virgin a few years ago)
Suppliers	With an increasing number of discrete rail and train operators, the allocation of capacity becomes an issue. This problem is parallel to landing slots at Heathrow Airport. When capacity is full, access to the network is a key issue

 ## Activity 1.4

Consider the impact of STEEPLE as it might apply to an advertising agency being briefed for a campaign for a burger chain.

Case Study

'SMS Cars Ltd' (June 2006 CIM case study)

This case study featured a company holding a franchise for Ford vehicles that are produced in Europe. Below is an outline of an environmental analysis for this situation. Only one item is given under each heading. You should add to these points with your own view of the current situation in the international car market. It is not only important to identify an issue but to evaluate its impact. In the final formulation of marketing plans the need is to find management responses to the environmental pressures. In the 'SMS Cars Ltd' case study the company could be considered to be 'hedging its bets' by also holding a franchise for Hyundai, a South Korean manufacturer with a lower cost base than Ford.

STEEPLE

Issue	Implication & impact
Social/cultural More single females owning their own cars in Europe	Past communications aimed at the male driver may not work as purchase motivation/benefits sought are different for this segment
Technological innovation Broadband access will be in the majority of households by the end of 2006	Easy for customers to shop around for the best price deal
Economic issues China and India: low-cost production areas. The United States: high costs of pensions and medical insurance	Ford and GM may become vulnerable and may have to engage in a 'fire sale' of premium brands. Problems with home US market may limit scope for European expansion

Education/training
New field service requirements with new technologies

Political
Likely to be major political issues about the loss of jobs in the United States and Europe

Legal
Increasing concern about fuel consumption

Environmental protection
Cars will need to be recycled

Need to train field staff in new technologies, for example hybrid cars

Trade unions will lobby politicians

High fuel economy cars will be required

Will need a European mechanism for recycling

Porter Competition analysis

Issue	Implication and impact
In-sector competition Established and emerging manufacturers	Emerging manufacturers may be the major danger
New entrants India and China now, Africa in the longer term	Yet further new low-cost competition could emerge
Substitute products Other forms of transport.	Market for motorcycles and buses might increase
Buyer power High, easy-to-compare prices	High-cost dealerships may not be sustainable
Supplier power In long term not high	Note JIT issues and component problems in the United States

Outline segmentation analysis

Segment/segmentation variable	Implication/developments/impact
High fuel economy sector.	One of the few expanding sectors

The internal environment

Adapted value chain

The marketing-orientated organization is effective and offers goods and services to its customers, which have appropriate market valuation and are affordable. To be profitable, the organization needs to be efficient and to make and market products and services in the most economic way consistent with the required product quality and standard of service. The value chain provides the marketer with a tool to appraise the internal efficiency and effectiveness of the organization. Figure 1.6 shows an adapted version of Porter's Value Chain.

Figure 1.6 Adapted value chain

The primary activities are the day-to-day activities that we need to undertake to provide goods and services to the marketplace. However, just as a car will not go forever if it is not re-fuelled, longer-term support activities are required to ensure that the primary activities can continue successfully. As always with business models, intelligent creative interpretation is required to apply them. The end result of well-tuned, balanced, primary and support activities adds value for the mutual benefit of the organization and its customers. The model is explained below followed by an example demonstrating how to apply it to a given situation.

Primary activities
Inbound logistics
These are the activities and facilities for receiving raw materials with associated storage and quality procedures for a manufacturing organization. For a service organization, this could be ensuring the right number and type of telephone lines, for example, for a telephone-sales insurance company.

Operations
For a manufacturing company, these are the processes used in the manufacture and testing of a product. Typical examples are the manufacture of consumer electronics. Where the product is very expensive and customized, batch assembly might be appropriate. For vast volumes of lower-cost products (e.g. personal stereos), the process may be highly automated. For a service such as insurance, it may be the complex calculations undertaken to evaluate the risk for a new customer and set the appropriate premium.

Outbound logistics
For the manufacturing organization, this is the packaging and the physical distribution of the product. This aspect of the value chain clearly links up with the marketing place (physical distribution) of the marketing mix. Different approaches may be appropriate for the same product under different outlet conditions. In a bar, soft drinks such as cola may be dispensed from a multi-dispenser that uses mains water to dilute concentrated flavoured syrup. This is effective and appropriate as there is a relatively high volume of consumption and the product is consumed immediately on the premises. For home consumption, however, the dilute product is manufactured and packed in non-returnable bottles or cans. For a service such as insurance, the outbound logistics involves the efficient delivery of documentation to the client.

Sales

For the manufacturing company, the cycle is customers order, the product is manufactured or taken out of stock, delivered to the clients and, most importantly, payment is made. Slow payments damage cash flow, which is bad. Non-payment and bad debts are disastrous! The sales cycle involves a number of functions. Sales plans drive the production schedule and stocking requirements. For a supermarket, the sales system can be considered as the checkout. Remember this is not just the laser reader and payment system (Electronic Point of Sale – EPOS), but also involves efficient and friendly operation by a person. The best information and communications systems will not provide a quality experience if run by an unfriendly or poorly trained operator.

Service

Here we have to take care how we define service. This is not the overall efficiency of the value chain but should be taken to cover value-added service for the product or service. As an example, for a car manufacturer this might include maintenance servicing (and spare parts) and financial services such as insurance and a loan to buy the vehicle. For an insurance company, it might involve providing emergency advice (e.g. where to find a plumber at midnight when a pipe bursts). This aspect of the value chain interacts with the service extension of the marketing mix. In a competitive world, one strategy to differentiate a product is to augment its value with added and distinctive service elements.

Support activities

Strategic stance and strategy

Companies need to ensure they have the relevant approach to their operations and markets. Thus, low-cost airlines are ruthless in cost-cutting with a very basic 'no frills' strategy. Their proposition to the market is that no one will get you there more cheaply and their value chain is tuned to move people at the lowest possible cost to selected low-cost destinations (often at less fashionable or less convenient airports). The leading airlines provide a 'value-for-money service' with a different proposition: to fly people round the world in comfort. This implies a complex interconnecting system of hub and long-haul routes to be operated with comparatively lavish facilities such as 'club' lounges and operating from favourite airports such as Heathrow. Other issues that need to be considered include whether the organization wants to be a market leader (implication: heavy investment in research and development) or a market follower.

Safety, environmental, quality and ethical policies and procedures

With customer expectations continually rising, companies have to move beyond ISO 9000 not only to satisfy but also to delight customers. Environmental issues are now so important that they have their own standard, ISO 14000. With strict liability and higher costs of compensation, not only are high standards of safety ethically necessary but also good business sense. Fair treatment of all relevant stakeholders and general corporate behaviour again is not just to make the management and owners feel good, but also to make good business sense. Failure to be considered a good corporate citizen can result in very active disruption of the business by pressure groups (e.g. animal rights campaigners for companies perceived to be conducting unnecessary animal tests). This aspect has been added into the amended value chain both to reflect the major importance of the issues to the success of organizations in the present business environment and because they all have a common linking theme. That is, they all depend on the aggregate culture of the company's internal stakeholders. All employees must be committed to safety, quality and environmental issues.

Physical and financial structure

If the organization's buildings are dilapidated and machinery outdated then poor products and services will be produced, often expensively. The financial structure may affect how the value chain is tuned. In the case of a public company, the shareholders want good share growth and good dividends *now!* Failure to deliver may leave the firm vulnerable to hostile takeover. If an individual wholly owns the business, a longer-term view can be taken, with, say, more invest-ment in research and development resulting in profit further in the future. Similar issues apply to small start-up firms: too often, reliance is placed on bank overdrafts that can be called in at any time, when a different framework of finance requiring longer-term lending would be more appropriate. The wrong financing for an organization can be just as disruptive as marketing the wrong product or manufacturing using the wrong technology.

Information systems, structure and technology

Information and communications systems have been added to the traditional value chain model, as an appropriate framework is vital for most companies, and for some e-based organizations it almost *is* the whole organization. In knowledge-based industries, the ability to lever knowledge and skills internationally with Internets, Intranets and others is vital. For the modern company, it is just as bad for the computer to crash as for there to be a total power-out. In both cases, all operations come to a shuddering halt.

Human resources and organizational structure

No organization can be better than the people in it. Even with the most effective equipment and the best facilities, customers will not be happy if front-line staff are not well trained and empathetic. Roles and responsibilities must be effectively defined by job descriptions and organizational structures. The nature of people (e.g. recruitment processes and procedures), their skills (e.g. effective training) and motivation (e.g. appropriate reward systems) are key. This aspect of the value chain also interacts with the marketing mix in the element P = People.

Technology development

To remain a market leader, attention must be paid to developing the product (new product development), the manufacturing operations and logistics (the first three elements of the value chain primary activities), sales (e.g. Internet sales systems) and marketing (e.g. new methods of market research). Any element of the value chain can be improved and needs development for a successful organization.

Marketing

In the traditional value chain, marketing is considered with sales as a primary activity. However, marketing involves longer-term issues than the day-to-day operation of the sales system. The longer-term needs are to determine where the market is moving and what products the customers will require. Marketing then works through the new product development process to ensure that the organization produces the right products at the right time. Then, with commu-nications, consumers are informed of the availability of the product and persuaded to buy it or adopt the service. The efficiency of the MkIS and the quality of the existing marketing mix should be continually evaluated.

Procurement

Procurement, the purchase of the inputs to the value chain, is vital. For a supermarket, the greatest percentage of costs is the price it pays for the items on the shelves. Getting the right products at the right price is vital. Marks and Spencer at one time found that its clothing was perceived to be unfashionable and over-priced. Urgent attention had to be focused on buying products that appealed to customers at prices that were competitive. Procurement not only covers the purchase of the materials for manufacture, but also covers all inputs to the opera-tion. An extra £10 000 of sales may give you £1000 profit. The £10 000 saved in purchasing is £10 000 straight into profit. In marketing, it is vital to get the best prices for printing and media space to get the most out of a limited budget.

Fresh Foods' value chain

A group of young entrepreneurs have decided they want to set up a business called 'Fresh Foods' to provide a wide variety of freshly prepared speciality dishes both to be consumed on the premises and to 'take away'. Below is a value chain analysis for this situation with some comments on the creative interpretation of the model and some discussion. The value chain can be used to audit an existing business or as a tool to examine the issues, which need to be considered in setting up a new venture.

Primary activities
In evaluating this situation, it is helpful to consider two aspects of the business: food preparation and serving customers.

Inbound logistics
In catering, the utmost attention must be paid to food hygiene with fresh meat and fish clearly segregated from, for example, salad. Food must be stored under temperature-controlled conditions. These facilities will come under the strictest scrutiny. Another key issue is parking. For takeaway service, convenient short-term parking needs to be available with longer-term parking for 'eat-in' customers. Some 'upmarket' city centre restaurants without this facility will use 'valet' parking, where the car is parked in a multi-storey city centre car park and returned at the end of the meal. 'Storage' in terms of seating needs to be provided for people waiting for their 'takeaway' orders or waiting for a table to become free. Many such outlets have a bar area with current magazines so people are comfortable.

Operations
In catering, this covers all the kitchen activities. To see how well organized this can be, look behind the counter of a burger bar into the kitchen area. In the customer area, it is the effectiveness and efficiency of the delivery of the food and drinks to the table in a responsive but unobtrusive fashion. Even this aspect of a restaurant can be developed creatively: for example, the 'sushi' train – customers sit at a counter and the various dishes move past on a miniature railway track. Customers just help themselves to the dishes they want as they pass by and pay the appropriate amount on leaving the restaurant.

Outbound logistics
For 'takeaways', appropriate packaging will be needed so that people can get their order home safely without spillage and still warm. When dining out it may simply be getting the car back at the end of the evening. In the United States, some restaurants will provide a 'doggie bag' to take away uneaten food for later consumption.

Sales system
Even in a small outlet, the till point is usually intelligent enough to allow for sales to be analysed for market development. Most outlets will need a credit card payment facility; however, for some 'no frills' value-for-money formats cash only may be acceptable to keep transaction costs down. The value chain you develop needs to reflect the market position you want to create.

Service
Value-added services might include outside catering for events (e.g. weddings). Another increasingly attractive service for customers is ordering by telephone for home delivery. You may think this last idea should have been considered under 'outbound logistics'. When using the model it is much more important to identify an issue than to get over concerned with how it should be classified within it.

Support activities
Strategic stance
One of the key issues is going to be the positioning strategy. Is it to be 'upmarket' with high-quality tableware for that special evening or basic, low cost with plastic tabletops for a quick meal on the way home?

Safety, environmental, quality and ethical
Food hygiene and safety has been mentioned above. Catering is a potentially dangerous activity and safety is a critical aspect of facilities' design; staff also need to be trained to follow safe working procedures. For customers, issues such as access to fire exits need to be considered. Environmental aspects include not only consideration of the disposal of solid waste, but minimizing the impact of cooking odours on neighbouring properties. If operating late at night, noise pollution from departing clients may be an issue. There was a signal in the opening paragraph of this case study that there was to be a special quality element to the outlet, 'fresh' rather than frozen food warmed in the microwave. Even in an outlet such as this, there can be ethical issues. Do we want to use organic vegetables and free-range meat and eggs? How strict will we be in the interpretation of 'vegetarian'? Will we keep part of the kitchen and associated tools free from any contact with meat or just ensure that not too many chunks of pork fall into the 'veggie lasagne'?

Physical and financial structure
To comply with the issues identified above (e.g. food hygiene, kitchen safety and appropriate fire exits), the physical structure of the building is vital. Moreover, additional points may need to be considered, for example disabled access. Appropriate loans will be needed for the start-up (remember the danger of a simple overdraft).

Information systems, structure and technology
This business is not going to need a mainframe computer. Simple yet effective systems will be needed to track sales for marketing purposes and to ensure efficient stock control. With the high penetration of broadband access, providing an Internet-accessible menu might be appropriate.

Human resources
With just a small group, a massively complex organization is not necessary, but for weekend shifts and the like, appropriate roles will need to be defined, for example shift manager. Often in such outlets where the marketing-orientated view of motivation is considered, a shift manager may be called a 'team coach' to emphasize that the role is to support and lead and not drive staff. Clearly, good training in food hygiene is needed for everyone, and the kitchen staff will need to be sufficiently skilled to ensure food quality and that potentially dangerous equipment is operated safely.

Technology development
This may not be a multinational electronics company, but new product development is still important to such a venture. This may be the creation of special recipes and/or novel methods of cooking (e.g. smoking pit to produce authentic 'New Orleans' smoked pork).

Marketing
A simple, but effective MkIS will need to be set up. Special promotions will be necessary (e.g. opening night and special times of the year such as New Year, Valentine's Day, etc.). However, good, successful restaurants rely on repeat business and word of mouth. This indicates an active, innovative and effective relationship-marketing approach.

Procurement

The old saying about computer systems is garbage in – garbage out (GIGO). A food establishment is no better than the quality of food that it produces. The daily business cycle starts early in the day with visits to the market to purchase fresh food.

Review

The above analysis is not intended to be exhaustive. There are elements which you may not agree with (you may not consider home food delivery relevant to such an operation). You may believe elements have been missed. What is exciting is that with just a paragraph outlining the business situation, our general knowledge of eating out and by using a model creatively, we can start to develop a penetrating marketing insight into the new venture's internal environment issues.

Activity 1.5

Hot Grooves

'Hot Grooves'* is a specialist shop in a city centre specializing in vinyl, microgroove records. Although long since superseded in mass sales by CDs and DVDs, there is a specialist niche market for enthusiasts wanting 'the old sound' and DJs. Some customers live a distance away and so, for some time, 'Hot Grooves' have offered a telephone ordering, postal delivery service. This business has been increasing and some orders are now received by e-mail, rather than over the phone. The city centre is to be re-developed and 'Hot Grooves' will have to move. The compensation package will provide a capital sum to finance the move. One alternative for 'Hot Grooves' is to move out of the very expensive, city centre location into a much cheaper industrial estate and become a largely Internet-based company. The value chain model may be used either to audit an existing company or to provide a starting point for considering the operations of a future venture. Complete a preliminary value chain analysis for how 'Hot Grooves' might operate as a largely web-based operation.

* 'Hot Grooves' is a fictitious organization for assessment purposes only.

Hints and tips

Much of what is required to complete a value chain analysis does not come from reading textbooks but by linking our personal experience with the marketing world. Every visit to a shop or a restaurant, or journey on an airline should be a learning experience.

Data collection and analysis

The problem with management is that there is too much data and not enough good relevant information.

The MkIS is not just a range of computer programmes. People are needed to collect certain data. You can machine-read a bar code but not a customer complaint. Having collected the data, the system must evaluate the degree of confidence one might place in it (e.g. there may be some reservations about a sample scheme with market research). The data needs to be analysed and interpreted to generate relevant useful information (Figure 1.7).

There are a number of issues to be considered when formulating an appropriate MkIS for a given situation:

- What data needs to be collected?
- How can it be collected efficiently?
- What use is to be made of the information?

The macroenvironment and microenvironment need to be monitored, as does the efficiency of our own value chain and those of our competitors, including the relevant marketing mix issues. Market research may be conducted on an ongoing basis to track market trends (e.g. TV viewing habits) or for specific issues (to evaluate if falling sales are due to changes in customer perception of the brand). The research may be quantitative (how many people take part in an activity) or qualitative (how do consumers feel about the product). If appropriate secondary desk sources do not exist, more expensive primary research will have to be commissioned.

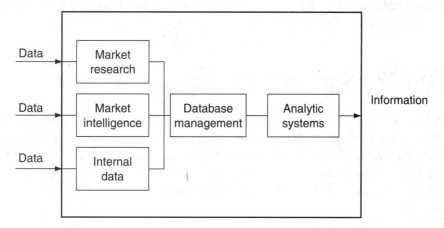

Figure 1.7 Marketing information system
Source: Adapted from Lancaster and Withey (2003)

Marketing intelligence is a critical source of data for the organization. Competitors' websites and annual reports are useful sources. Mystery shopping in the competitions' and one's own outlets can provide useful data for a retail organization. Products can be 'retro-engineered' (e.g. a shampoo can be analysed chemically) and counter-type products developed for a 'me-too' market-following organization. The trade press provides a continual flow of industry 'gossip': who is moving to a new company, new investment plans and product launches, and the like. On a practical note, nobody except the commissioning company takes as much interest in marketing trials as the competition!

Vast amounts of internal data are collected by EPOS systems and loyalty cards. This can give accurate profiles of consumers (the purchase of cat food and pet litter may indicate that you are a ripe candidate for a pet insurance mailshot). Apart from computer data systems (accounts, etc.), care must be taken to capture 'soft' data such as customer complaints and sales visit reports which are not so easily converted into simple numbers but provide vital evidence of not only 'how much?' but 'why?'.

All data needs to be evaluated for accuracy and relevance so should in some way formally pass through the analytical system. If the pound is rising, the cost of imported materials from last year is fine when calculating last year's profits but not when pricing next year's production. Often some adjustment needs to be made to make certain that appropriate comparisons are being made. If we are analysing sales trends, it is important to know if the changes are due to price or volume changes as different corrective action may be needed. In comparing the results for a given week this year with that of the same one last year, care needs to be taken to ensure that there are not odd effects that may distort the figures (e.g. it may be relevant to note that Easter is early in some years and late in others). It is often useful to note not only the physical value but also some appropriate ratio. When comparing the sales from two different sized shops in the same organization, it may be appropriate to calculate the sales per square metre.

Much more sophisticated mathematical approaches such as regression and time series analysis may provide useful information when projecting likely trends. Mathematical models may be built to estimate the impact of price changes or interest rates on sales of a given product group. A little knowledge is dangerous and such techniques should be used with staff or consultants with expert knowledge of the techniques. Techniques such as time series analysis may have, buried deep in the mathematics, an assumption that errors in observations from one month to the next are not correlated. However, if underestimates in one month are 'recovered' in next month's figures then this assumption may be violated and a false prediction obtained. Statistics packages are like a fast mathematical car: only drive one if you have been trained and know what you are doing!

 ## Activity 1.6

The June 2006 case study focused on marketing cars with 'SMS Cars Ltd'. Question 4 was 'Produce a short report, for consideration by the Marketing Department, which (a) identifies what information SMS Cars Ltd would want on their customer database in order to segment the marketplace efficiently and assist with future marketing activity (12 marks) and (b) explains how this information could be gathered (8 marks). Briefly make notes on how you would structure your answer.

SWOT

The strengths, weaknesses, opportunities and threats (SWOT) analysis (Figure 1.8) is a key step in analysing the issues that confront an organization. To conduct a successful, penetrating and relevant SWOT a few rules need to be remembered – care should be taken in defining the firm's platform: the SWOT is specific to a given firm and situation. An attractive prospect for one company may not be so for another. The value of the SWOT is that in considering the macro, micro and internal environments, a vast range of factors are examined and it is easy to drown in a wealth of detail and not see the wood for the trees. A SWOT analysis is drawn up for a given time and some consideration should be given to the dynamic aspects. Is a threat growing or diminishing? How might we convert a threat into an opportunity? In the 'dot-com' introduction period, TESCO might have identified online shopping as a threat. By establishing an online service of its own, it converted a potential threat into an opportunity, which it developed successfully. Strengths and weaknesses are internal to the company but not independent of the external environment. One can only evaluate whether a given standard of performance is a strength or a weakness by reference to external benchmarks. The UK clothing manufacturers supplying M&S considered what they produced to be top quality and that they worked effectively and efficiently. However, their cost structure was a weakness, as they could not match the costs achieved in the low wage production regions of the world. The clear implication is that firms in this situation have little option but to move production outside the United Kingdom. In 2006 this effect was most clearly demonstrated by service organizations such as banks moving their call centres to countries such as India to reduce their costs and eliminate a potential weakness. It is important to see the SWOT not as a conclusion to the analysis but as a bridge from analysis (where are we?) to action (what do we need to do to survive and be profitable?).

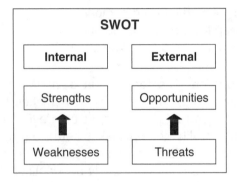

Figure 1.8 SWOT analysis

Hints and tips

When you are completing a SWOT analysis do not do it on paper but use a spreadsheet. Leave column 1 blank and make column 2 wide enough for your SWOT point. Use four tables, one for each element of the SWOT. Do not make any attempt to consider how important an issue is when you enter the points in column 2. Then come back to your list and enter into column 1 a score of 1 – 'critically important' to 10 – 'of very little importance'. You can then use the sort function to classify the issues with the key ones grouped at the top of the list. Having a computer-based copy also allows you to update the analysis as the environment changes.

Introduction to the development of marketing plans

A marketing plan at its broadest level has four elements:

- Where are we? The environmental analysis that we have discussed earlier in this unit.
- Where do we want to be? A gap analysis, shown in Figure 1.9, evaluating where we consider, based on analysis, the organization will be against where the organization wants to be.
- How may the performance gap be bridged? In general, there are two elements to the strategy:

- – How can we improve our internal performance? How can we improve our value chain? Lowering costs by better buying or reducing the costs of distribution are typical possibilities to consider.
- – The second element is to develop the market through Ansoff strategies (market penetration, new product development, new market development and diversification). Further consideration of the Ansoff matrix is given in Unit 11.

o How do we control the process? This is the feedback and control system. Note that though this is most often written as a single heading, this process has three elements:

- – Gaining the relevant information through the MkIS.
- – Analysing what the issues are (e.g. we may note that one line has lost some profitability: is this because costs have risen, product is damaged in distribution, number of units sold is down).
- – The final aspect of control is to have mechanisms and contingency plans to bring the plan back on track. This is just like driving a car and being hit by a sudden cross wind (e.g. new advertising campaign from the competition) and having to compensate to keep the car on the motorway (e.g. we introduce an immediate promotional price to counter the advertising campaign).

This is a brief introduction. The formulation of marketing plans is the subject of Unit 11. Representing and discussing plans in a textbook makes the process appear very linear and that each element of the plan is fully developed before the marketer moves on to completing the next section in detail. In reality, the process is iterative (one cycles around the plan refining it). First, the marketer should complete an outline plan with minimum new research. This is a plan for a plan. Information gaps can immediately be identified and researched. When filling in the gaps, further questions will arise and the marketer will continue developing and firming up the plan cycling around the issues until it becomes clear that either the plan will not work (e.g. product costs are too high for the situation) or the plan looks feasible.

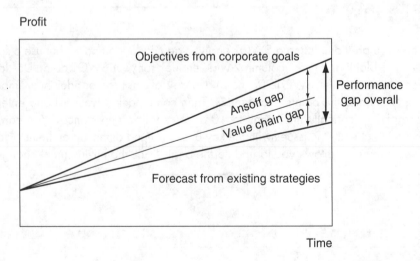

Figure 1.9 Gap analysis

Implementation – the need for an integrated marketing mix

The integrated marketing mix is shown in Figure 1.10. The four traditional Ps enable the marketer to formulate plans for pure products. However, many products have substantial elements of service (e.g. product maintenance for a photocopier) and increasingly, in the post-industrial society, much of our expenditure is on services (e.g. entertainment). Services are intangible and have other characteristics, and to maximize the offering to the customer, three additional elements have to be introduced – the service extension to the marketing mix.

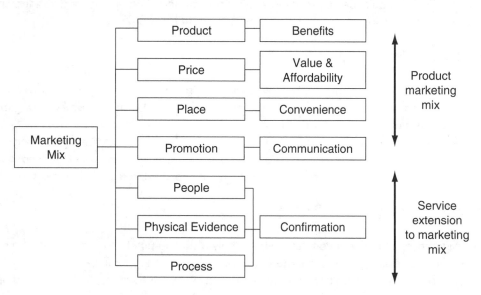

Figure 1.10 The service-extended marketing mix

Customers do not buy products, they buy *benefits*. I do not want a packet of detergent, I want clean clothes. Accountants see price, customers want to experience *value and affordability*. If they do not, there is no sale. Place involves decisions such as the nature of the outlet from which the product will be sold and the physical distribution (delivery) of the product to the outlets and finally to the consumer. However, the customer is not interested in the organization's smart supply chain logistics. They wish to experience *convenience* with the right product, in the right place, at the right time and in the right condition for the customer's use. The firm wants to promote products and make people buy their products. Consumers need to experience *communications* to persuade them that they want these benefits, that they can afford the product which is good value and convenient to obtain. The service extension of the marketing mix (people, physical evidence and process) provides reassurance and confirmation of the quality of the service which, of necessity, is intangible (you do not walk away with a physical object).

Concentrating on any single element of the mix is pointless. The advertising campaign is not going to be effective if the product does not work, is not in the shops or costs more than people are prepared to pay for it. Moreover, the elements of the mix must be in harmony and consistent as they interact. When considering the appropriate communications mix, the marketer needs to ensure that all the other elements of the marketing mix can communicate. Thus, the brand imagery communicated in the advertisements needs to be carried over onto the packaging, an element of product. For luxury and exclusive products, a low price would not sustain the exclusivity proposition. In the same way, if the product were available in every cut-price outlet, it would be difficult to sustain the luxury image. Thus, in developing the detailed plans for one element such as product, it is necessary to consider issues such as point-of-sale ideas. For example, some soft drinks are sold from racks that grip a collar around the neck of the bottle; integrated design was needed for both the product and the point-of-sale promotional stand.

Case Study

SMS Cars Ltd (June 2006 CIM case study)

This case study outlines the sales situation in the marketing of cars. Below is a brief outline of the marketing mix that would be appropriate for Ford in Europe. You should add to these points. More consideration of the detail of the marketing mix is given in Units 3–7.

Product = Benefit

The core benefit of a car is transport. However, all cars provide this and to get an individual to purchase a Ford rather than another make of car additional benefits must be provided. An intangible benefit for premium cars is status. Ford provides a full range of vehicles from town run-abouts (Ka) to premium brands (e.g. Jaguar – owned by Ford) to satisfy a range of benefit needs (i.e. benefit segments). Within each car type there are many variants (e.g. petrol or diesel; manual gears or automatic transmission; range of colours for interior trim and exterior paintwork). Ford operates a full product range and depth.

Price = Value and affordability

The headline price must appear competitive but is only a starting point. In the purchase of a new car, most buyers will have an existing vehicle to trade in. Most buyers do not pay for their vehicle outright but require a finance package. The purchase price is only one factor. A key issue will be the lifetime cost of ownership:

- Cost of purchase
- Cost of running (includes such factors as maintenance/spare parts, insurance, taxation, for some journeys congestion charges (e.g. inner London) and fuel costs)
- Trade in value on the purchase of a new car after a number of years of ownership.

Place = Convenience

A local place to test-drive the vehicle and for servicing and repair later. This implies a need for a network of franchisees.

Promotion = Communication

Mass communication (advertising on TV, radio and press etc) is used to make potential customers aware of the car. Personal selling is needed to close the sale at the franchisee. Relationship Marketing is then used to gain repeat sales after a number of years and make further profits on maintenance and repairs. This was a feature of this case study with Question 5 'Produce a briefing paper to be forwarded to the manager of the Vehicle Servicing Department which (a) describes how the THREE elements of the extended marketing mix (people, process and physical evidence) can be used by the Vehicle Servicing Department to improve customer service, (b) makes recommendations as to how the promotional mix could be used to increase demand for the Vehicle Servicing Department.'

People = Confirmation

As stated above, service forms a significant element of a car franchisee's business, and personal selling is important. Well-trained, attentive staff are vital for the effective, efficient and profitable development of a car franchise.

Physical evidence = Confirmation

Large sums of money are spent to provide high quality selling environments for car franchises. The service department must be clean and welcoming. Documentation must be complete and professional (e.g. service records and invoices).

Process = Confirmation

Cars are a high involvement purchase. Computers must be widely used to provide full records (e.g. to feed the relationship marketing processes). However, this must be 'transparent technology' and the overall impression must be of efficient but personal service.

This is a bare outline and you should review and add points that you think may be relevant. More consideration of the detail of the marketing mix is given in Units 3–7.

Segmentation, targeting and positioning

As soon as the question 'What is the market for a product?' is asked, the first reaction should be 'What is the segmentation structure for the market?' 'How then can the product fit into this structure?' Segmentation is as important for consumers as B2B markets. Consumers can be segmented by demographics, psychographics, geo-demographics and so on. Businesses can be segmented by such variables as size, nature of their technologies and purchasing processes. Segmentation in the various contexts is considered in more depth in the next unit.

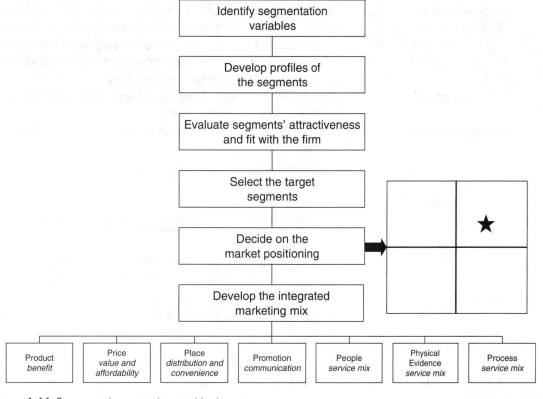

Figure 1.11 Segmentation targeting positioning process

Figure 1.11 gives an overview of the process. The first stage is to develop the segmentation variables of the given marketplace and offering. The starting point for this should be textbook lists of potential variables but it is essential to be highly selective as lots of very small segments, the result of using too many variables, are unlikely to produce a practical segmentation structure. However, care must be taken to consider segmentation variables that are highly relevant to a given situation but not necessarily contained in the textbook listings. Thus, a manufacturer of detergent products will have one product formulated for washing silk and another for heavily soiled cotton. The type of dirt and nature of fabric are vital variables for this given market but they do not easily fit into a standard textbook classification. The process of segmentation needs to be disciplined but must also be creative. Creative segmentation can identify a new market and give an organization a competitive advantage.

Consumer markets can be segmented in a variety of ways including demographics, socio-economic, geographic, lifestyle, purchase occasions, user status, usage rate and benefits sought (Table 1.3). In the B2B sector, industrial markets can be segmented by organization, demographics, geography, purchasing processes, user status, usage rate and benefits sought. Further cover of segmentation is given in the Marketing Fundamentals coursebook.

Table 1.3 Selected consumer segmentation variables

Potential segmentation variable	Comments and examples
Age	Special products for specific age groups, such as baby shampoo
Gender	Different clothes for men and women
Family	Family life cycle. Different packs for single households and large family households
Race	Different cosmetic products to match different colour skin and hair types
Religion	Need to provide different food for religious conformance (e.g. Kosher and Halal)
Socio-economic	Premium products for people with high disposable incomes
Geographic and geo-demographic	Different products for people in different locations. Databases such as ACORN (A Classification Of Residential Neighbourhoods)
Personality and lifestyle	Products directed to consumers with specific attitudes and lifestyles (e.g. 'Fair Trade' coffee, organic food)
Purchase occasion	Purchase for weekly supermarket shop and the emergency 'top-up' from a convenience outlet
Benefits required	People require different benefits (e.g. washing powder: different products for white cotton, benefit – washes whiter; and coloured garments, benefit – colour care, no fading)
User status and consumption pattern	Non-user, light user, heavy user
Activities	Products made for different activities (e.g. sportswear)

It is essential that you understand the customers as well as you understand your products. If you can project yourself into their being to understand how they think, feel and live and how your product will fit into this, you are much more likely to succeed. The marketing orientation is that our product should fit consumers' needs and wants. Only if we deeply understand their needs and wants can we outperform the competition in developing our own attractive and profitable markets for the firm.

Successful marketing starts on two key foundations: the identification of attractive markets for the firm, and only entering those markets if the firm can achieve a sustainable competitive advantage. This is the heart of portfolio analysis using such models as the BCG matrix (discussed more fully in Unit 11. The implication of this analysis is that selectivity is required and not all potential opportunities should be followed.

Once the target segments have been selected, the marketer should revisit the segmentation profiles and develop an even deeper understanding of the segment. Understanding the needs and wants of the consumer for the product leads to better product positioning. The variables to be used depend on the precise situation. Common appropriate variables such as price, quality and performance should be considered. The competitive offerings can be evaluated against the same framework. In some markets such as travel, there is an emphasis on 'value for money' and the communication message may be 'same quality, same experience but lower price' (e.g. booking through a 'dot-com' travel agent rather than through traditional channels).

Case study

The Ship

The Ship restaurant is located on the waterside in an area adjacent to the shopping, entertainment and business areas in a thriving city. The restaurant was not well-run and provided cheap 'fast food' to day trippers. A group of entrepreneurs have acquired the restaurant and are intending to refurbish it and make it into a profitable business venture. A partial outline of the segmentation, targeting and positioning process is given below with some practical comments about the issues that need to be considered. In starting an analysis you need to consider the implications and start to think about potential solutions.

Segmentation variables

- Price (should the Ship go 'upmarket' or go for a quick turnover, value-for-money market?)
- Time of day (this may affect the type of meal and service required): Possibilities might be breakfast, morning coffee and snack; lunch, afternoon snack, pre-theatre meal; evening meal, post-theatre meal (if the entrepreneurs thought that pre- and post-theatre meals were an attractive possibility, this starts to suggest possibilities about potential joint promotions with the theatres)
- Nature of the menu requirements for potential customers such as geographic focus (e.g. Greek, Italian, Indian, Chinese) and nature of food offered (e.g. special focus on fish, vegetarian dishes)
- Location of food consumption: restaurant, takeaway and home delivery
- Nature of occasion such as birthdays, anniversaries and corporate events (implication of this is that it might be desirable in the development of the restaurant to include a separate 'events' space).

This analysis is in outline and not exhaustive (e.g. age may be considered in order to develop a children's menu).

Ship restaurant

Only two segments will be briefly considered given space limitations. In real life, much more analysis would be needed.

The Business Lunch: Lower costs demanded, a more restricted menu might be acceptable and speed of service is critical. This business is potentially profitable with the possibility of developing repeat business and corporate events (relationship-marketing implications).

The Romantic Evening Dinner: Extensive menu, time not so critical, high but unobtrusive level of service required. Ambiance romantic rather than clinical (implication is that need for lighting might change from lunchtime to evening). This segment also gives opportunities for developing repeat business and events (e.g. weddings).

Evaluation of attractiveness and fit with the firm

Segments should be profitable and the restaurant able to offer something special (e.g. competition: no point in opening up the 12th Italian restaurant in the area). Here, decisions are starting to be made. We will consider that the decision is being made to provide an upmarket experience. Thus, inexpensive meals for shoppers might be unattractive but business lunches attractive.

Select the target segments

In this situation, the decision might be to go for business lunches, pre-theatre meals and romantic evening meals. Breakfasts might be rejected as not generating enough revenue and for not being a good fit with the positioning. Post-theatre dinners might be rejected as table availability might be a problem (long leisurely dinners in the evening) and late-night travel might be a problem for staff. There may be logistics issues as well as marketing issues influencing the selection of given segments.

Develop the market positioning

The evaluation that higher margin segments are attractive implies that a premium marketing position with high standards of interior design and service provision are indicated. Evaluation of the competition might indicate that some positioning (e.g. Italian) are well catered for and thus might not be appropriate. Given the waterside location, a specialist seafood/fish focus might be appropriate (if not already populated with competition). The positioning is giving a reason to the target customers as to why they should come here and not to some other eatery. The positioning decisions will have a profound influence on the development of the marketing mix (e.g. the design theme for the restaurant).

Hints and tips

Draw up a list of potential variables to use in the positioning map, revisit the segmentation variables and consider them in conjunction with the service-extended marketing mix. It may be that the competition can match the product quality, but not provide the same convenience as we have better distribution. In the case of a restaurant, price and speed of service might be key variables that could be used to position different approaches; for example, low prices and quick service might be important for lunches for office workers in a city centre and higher prices with slower (but attentive) service for a smart restaurant for a special event.

Activity 1.7

P&G and Unilever market a range of fabric care products. Complete an analysis of the fabric care market. Why do these companies produce such a range of products rather than just one brand/product?

Once the positioning concept has been decided, the full offering can be developed. The term 'offering' has been used in this section to emphasize that the customer does not just see the product but wants to experience a fully integrated marketing mix appropriately tailored by the above process to better meet their desires, wants and needs. The shaping of the elements of the marketing mix is covered in Units 3–7.

Implementation – integration of marketing plans into business plans

In the last section, we learned that the most brilliant implementation of a single element of the marketing mix will not ensure success. This integration extends still further and it is vital to understand how the marketing mix and plan integrates with the overall business plan and the activities of other functions. A marketer does not have the time to be an accountant, personnel manager, product manager or buyer. However, these are all key internal stakeholders, and a relationship must be established so that the bilateral communications in the internal network give all the parties the information they need. Thus, if marketing fails to inform production and purchasing of a large new order early enough, there may be problems in hitting delivery targets. If there is a supply emergency (e.g. dock strike) then the buyer, by keeping the marketing group in the loop, can assist so that priorities for limited short-term deliveries can be agreed with customers. As with the marketing mix, marketing excellence in one element will not lead to success unless it is linked to equally effective performance in other areas of the organization's activities.

Logistics and supply chain management

Clearly, the management of product manufacture is the responsibility of production management. However, with the move from 'conformance to specification' to 'customer satisfaction' with market-driven quality assurance, it is essential to have good links within the internal production chain to ensure customer satisfaction. Specific elements of the marketing mix may be directly affected by other internal stakeholders. Thus a buyer over-eager to purchase clothing at the lowest possible price might award a contract to an overseas producer employing child labour working under unsafe conditions, leading to a marketing and PR nightmare which could damage the brand's value. Physical distribution is normally considered as a function of logistics management rather than marketing management. Clearly, team working and effective communications are vital to ensure that marketing does not give customers unrealistic delivery promises, and once promises have been made logistics must ensure that delivery performance is achieved.

Finance and accounts

Clearly, the marketing mix element 'Price' has a vital impact on the finances of the organization. Again, good relationships and communications are essential. In the B2B sector, it is normal for marketing and accounts to agree a credit limit for a customer. If this credit limit is exceeded there can be a number of reasons, but two typical ones are that the customer is in financial trouble and another that the customer is doing so well that they have considerably expanded their orders without realizing they had exceeded their credit limit. Clearly, an informed decision needs to be made. Mechanical implementation of the credit limit rules may delay an order, miss a customer production deadline and drive an expanding account into the arms of a competitor. The reverse is no better; adding more value to bad debt is not going to help the company's profitability.

Pricing is another area where good communication is required within the internal stakeholders. If the buyer considers that a significant price increase is likely in a key raw material, then finance (will extra working capital be needed to finance the stock?), production (can material efficiency be improved?) and marketing (is a price rise needed?) all need to communicate.

Human resources management

This links directly to the marketing mix element, people. Marketing will have an important input in defining the type of people a company will recruit; for example, to a call centre this depends on how and what the organization wants to deliver through its front-line communications with the customer. Marketing will work carefully with Research and Development (R&D) to define what types of information and questions new customers are likely to request before a new product is launched. Once this is defined, the management and delivery of sales force training may well be the responsibility of the personnel and development function. Marketing output is also important, poor handling of an industrial dispute or a disciplinary hearing may be a potential PR disaster.

In the B2B sector, the greater part of the organization's marketing budget may be devoted to a field sales force. Here, detailed discussions are needed to ensure that bonus payments reward profitable initiatives. A common practice is to pay commission on sales, but this may have problems. Here the sales force will have financial incentives to develop easy sales (possibly by giving away discounts too easily) to current clients and with established products. It is all too easy to milk the cash cow rather than fight to win new accounts or introduce new products that require much more sales effort in the first place.

It is not intended in the above section to make you an instant expert in logistics, finance or personnel. Rather it is intended to demonstrate that relationships and communications between internal stakeholders are vital for marketing plans to be successfully implemented and for the organization to develop profitably.

Marketing orientation

Business may have a number of orientations. With a *production orientation*, the managers consider the priority is making products affordable and available. Customers are considered to be only concerned with price. The management's energy is directed to lowering the costs of both production and physical distribution.

The *product orientation* assumes that the product itself is the primary driver for the consumer. The assumption is that customers want supreme quality and functionality. In the new product design process, this orientation can result in products with features (involving additional production costs) that consumers simply do not want or use. This orientation can occur when senior management have a technical orientation and are more concerned with the product, than the consumer. 'Build a better mouse trap and the world will beat a path to your door' is not marketing reality.

Sales orientation assumes that consumers are reluctant to buy products and all that is needed is heavy promotion and sales. In the past, telesales in the area of home improvements (e.g. double glazing) focused on this type of orientation. It can develop out of a product orientation when the 'product' does not sell itself.

Marketing orientation starts with the philosophy that only if the organization understands the benefit needs and wants of the consumer can it devise products and services that satisfy the marketplace. The word 'marketing' can be used to describe a function (the Marketing Department) or an activity. However, it also describes a culture and orientation where all the people in the organization appreciate their role in delivering ultimate customer satisfaction. In new product development, there is no debate as to if the process should be 'market-led' or 'technology-driven'. Products that do not satisfy consumer benefit needs will not succeed. Products that are poorly designed and poorly manufactured will not succeed. In the market-orientated organization, the satisfaction of customers is seen as central to the development and maintenance of long-term profitability. This implies the integration of all the business functions to arrive at customer-centred marketing performance.

Activity 1.8

Lake View Organic Farms

Some years ago when prices for ordinary vegetables started to drop, a small group of enthusiastic farmers converted their farms to 'organic' status (Soil Association certified) to produce premium organic vegetables. Some 80 per cent of their produce went to regional branches of two supermarkets after packaging. The remaining 20 per cent was sold from a farm shop (next to the packaging plant) run on a co-operative basis. Two years ago, the group bought a small delivery vehicle to deliver to domestic customers and small restaurants that had been making occasional purchases from the farm shop. Part of a successful breakthrough was with the Lake View Veggie box (small, medium and large), which contained a range of seasonal vegetables in an appropriate mix for the average family. A weekly box delivered to the door provided variety and convenience. The members of the co-operative were keen to build on this success but available capital was limited. A contact in the next town perceived an opportunity by linking with the co-operative as a franchisee with a home delivery service (taking products from the co-operative and trading under the Lake View Organic Farms brand). With limited promotional effort and leafleting in selected areas, this new venture has been trading successfully for a year. The members of the co-operative are keen to build on this bridgehead.

With only limited funds, they have approached the local CIM College to see if a group of students might be interested in working with them as a college project. Assume you are the leader of a small group of students who have agreed to provide a student consultancy report to the co-operative. Using the framework below, complete a preliminary review of the situation.

Lake View Organic Farms is a hypothetical organization for assessment purposes only. The information contained in this case study has been taken from public domain sources.

Headings framework for outline analysis of a case study

Social/cultural
Technological
Economic
Education/training
Political
Legal
Environmental protection
Direct competition
Substitute products
Buyer power
New entrants
Supplier power
Logistics
Financial issues
Human Resources
Key stakeholders
Segmentation

In the exam setting, although time is limited, a few minutes spent on analysis and question planning is invaluable in structuring answers and developing context-specific application of the relevant theory to gain high marks. In the integrative assignment, a similar approach is invaluable before developing your report in response to the specific CIM questions. The key question is, 'What is especially significant in the context of the organization I am considering?' The skill for doing this is not gained from simply reading books but actively using the approaches on a range of case studies.

Question 1.1

Complete a preliminary review of 'The Urban Culture Festival 2006', the CIM December 2005 case study.

Question 1.2

Complete a preliminary analysis of 'SMS Cars Ltd', the CIM June 2006 case study.

Summary

In this unit, we have taken a holistic view of the marketing system with an overview of the nature of the marketplace and the macroenvironment and microenvironment. The organization has to understand what is going on in this turbulent context and has to collect information through the MkIS and then formulate policies and action plans to steer the organization to continued success. We noted that key to this was the development of an integrated marketing mix that was not only self-consistent and well constructed but also dovetailed into the logistics, finance and organizational strategies to form an overall successful business plan. We have explored a number of tools and concepts to help us in this:

- o STEEPLE analysis
- o Porter five forces of competition
- o Augmented value chain
- o Marketing information and intelligence
- o Integration of the marketing mix
- o Segmentation, targeting and positioning.

In the next unit, we will examine how the marketing context must be taken into account in tailoring the mix. Social marketing organizations need to use different approaches to those adopted by leading brands in the consumer goods sector.

Further study

Dibb, S., Simkin, L., Pride, W. and Ferrell, O. (2006) *Marketing Concepts and Strategies*, 5th European edition, Houghton Mifflin Chapters 1–3.

Hints and tips

A key skill in marketing is to ensure that every element (e.g. a press release) forms part of an integrated activity. Whenever you answer an exam question or work on a specific activity in a marketing project, take a little time to review how the detailed strategy integrates into the overall plans. This is particularly important for this integrative paper.

Marketers work in a wide variety of contexts. The CIM examination requires you to address issues in case study contexts. In your day-to-day professional activity and when you read the press, make a mental note of interesting examples from different marketing contexts (e.g. not-for-profit, etc.). The next unit examines some of the context issues within which marketing plans are formulated and implemented.

Bibliography

Burk Wood, M. (2003) *The Marketing Plan*, Prentice Hall.

Hollensen, S. (2003) *Marketing Management – A Relationship Approach*, Prentice Hall.

Kotler, P. (2006) *Marketing Management*, 12th edition, Prentice Hall.

Lancaster, G. and Withey, F. (2007) *Marketing Fundamentals*, Butterworth-Heinemann.

unit 2 the context of marketing

The message of segmentation is that the marketing mix needs to be adapted to meet specific market conditions and target particular customer benefit needs and wants. Forces such as consumerism shape this process; selected aspects of such forces are covered in this unit.

Marketing theory has evolved to meet the challenges of a dynamic marketplace. Relationship marketing is one theory and some of its core concepts are presented here. Not all marketing is about major branded consumer products, so we will also examine the adaptation required for other contexts (e.g. not-for-profit marketing).

By the end of this unit you will

- o Understand the forces of consumerism and their impact on marketing plans.

- o Be able to consider how a marketing mix should be adapted to respond to environmental (green) forces and describe the elements of such a mix.

- o Understand how marketing mixes and plans need to be adapted for B2B marketing.

- o Be able to outline the key features of relationship marketing.

- o Be capable of listing the differences between the marketing of services and products.

- o Appreciate the value of internal marketing in the successful implementation of marketing plans.

- o Understand the additional complexity of marketing in an international, multicultural context.

- o Appreciate the different objective sets in not-for-profit and social marketing.

- o Appreciate the specific differences in marketing the performing arts and sports.

- o Be able to explore how to adapt the marketing mix for modest budgets.

Syllabus references

2.1 Describe the structure and roles of the marketing function in the organization.

2.2 Build and develop relationships within the marketing department, working efficiently with others.

2.3 Explain the 'front-line': receiving and assisting visitors, internal and external enquiries.

2.5 Represent the organization using practical PR skills, including preparing effective news releases.

2.6 Explain the supplier interface: negotiating, collaborating, operational and contractual aspects.

2.8 Explain the concept and application of e-relationships.

3.2 Identify alternative and innovative approaches to a variety of marketing arenas and explain the criteria for meeting business objectives.

3.3 Demonstrate an awareness of successful applications across a variety of sectors and sizes of business.

3.6 Explain how an organization should host visitors from other cultures and operate across national boundaries.

4.8 Explain the importance of ICT in the (extended marketing) mix.

As noted in Unit 1, the CIM examination involves a case study. These case studies cover a range of contexts including service, international and working with limited budgets. This unit provides some necessary context to develop tailored, context-specific answers that gain higher marks.

Key definitions

Buy and re-buy – Segmentation with B2B buying. With new buys there is much more DMU involvement than with a simple re-buy context.

Decision-Making Unit (DMU) – The group of internal stakeholders who influence the purchase decision, particularly in the B2B context.

ISO 14000 – An international standard for environmental issues.

ISO 9000 – An international standard for quality issues.

Environmental Product Life cycle – The analysis of a product's impact on the environment from cradle to grave (i.e. from manufacture to eventual recycling).

Relationship Marketing – A focus on the total lifetime relationship with a customer rather than the individual transactions.

Study Guide

It can be argued that much of marketing was initially developed for the consumer goods sector. It is not surprising that techniques used to sell confectionery will not work for an aircraft manufacturer selling airliners. Many definitions of marketing contain the word profit. Charities and social marketers have other aims such as improving the health of the nation. Here again, some adaptation of the concepts is needed. The move from customer catching to customer retention has seen the evolution of relationship marketing (RM). A key aspect of RM is a rigorous approach to stakeholder analysis. Given changes in management philosophies along with more diffuse, flatter organizations, managing the internal stakeholders is key in achieving the organization's objectives. Some of the concepts of internal marketing are outlined. All of these developments are in the context of a more global framework of business, so within a given country, a multi-cultural dimension is needed.

Throughout the unit, there are activities that will help you build your confidence and insights into the subject. However, in addition to the formal activities, it is suggested you augment your notes with your own examples. Marketing is not just a theoretical subject, it is an activity and practising the activity under a variety of conditions improves your level of skill. The CIM syllabus element 3.3 'Demonstrate an awareness of successful applications across a variety of sectors and sizes of business' implies not only textbook reading but also being alert to developments. The web-sources given in this coursebook and keeping up with current affairs by reading the marketing press will enable you satisfy this CIM requirement.

The completion of a CIM marketing task (report, letter, memo, presentation, budget etc.) for the exam or integrative project is an intellectual project. However, it has its parallel in the challenge facing an Engineer asked to build a bridge (Figure 2.1). Faced with this situation, the Engineer does not say, 'No problem just send me down 20 000 tonnes of steel and 100 000 tonnes of concrete and I will have it sorted'. There are reasons why the Sydney Harbour Bridge is different to the San Francisco Bridge in construction. Some research and planning is needed. It is the same with an integrative project or a CIM exam answer (you may only have a few minutes for this but without this your answer may not gain the grade you need). One of the first questions is 'What is the purpose of the bridge?': nature of traffic (road, rail) and volume (e.g. how many thousands of cars a day – so we have the right number of lanes). In the marketing situation, 'What are the marketing objectives?' (e.g. to attract 2000 more customers a week by the end of the campaign etc.).

The next question is 'What are the characteristics of the river to be bridged?' (width, depth, rate of flow, tidal and flood levels, nature and volume of river traffic etc.). In the marketing task, 'what are the characteristics of the marketing problem' (e.g. Are they elements of B2B and/or services and/or international?)?

The nature of the bridge will be affected by the ground conditions (clay, sand, rock, frequency and intensity of earthquakes etc.) and the weather conditions (frequency of hurricanes, typhoons and temperature extremes to be expected etc.). In the marketing task, the shape and content of the output will be affected by the macro and microenvironment.

The way in which the bridge is built will depend on the development of building theory and materials of construction (e.g. the replacement of steel reinforced concrete with carbon fibre composites reducing weight and reducing maintenance. This can be viewed as parallel to the arrival of the Internet. The one making new forms of construction possible, the other making new marketing strategies viable).

In many major cities, a sign of expansion and regeneration is the forest of cranes involved in construction projects. To build a bridge scaffolding and cranes are needed to help in the construction. When the bridge is completed, these are removed and there is no sign of how the bridge was constructed (just as we do not know how the pyramids of Egypt were built). Preliminary analysis and planning is needed both for the integrated project and for exam questions. The intellectual scaffolding and cranes may not form part of the answer but without the framework to assist with the creative process the result is likely to be a badly constructed submission lacking in depth and strength to gain a good grade.

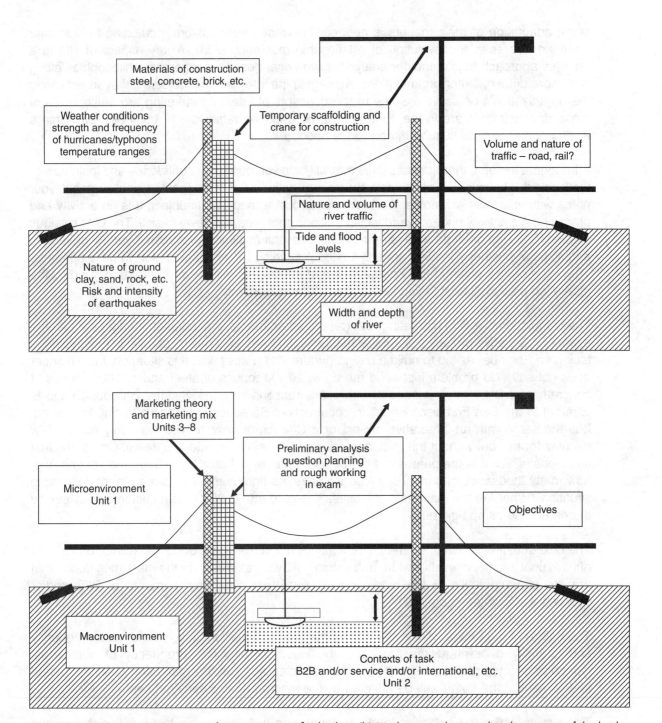

Figure 2.1 (a) Engineering issues in the construction of a bridge. (b) Marketing task viewed in the context of the bridge building model

The contexts of marketing

In the succeeding units, we shall consider how to develop and implement a tailored, integrated marketing mix for a given marketing situation. To do this one has to consider all of the issues in the macro and microenvironment discussed in Unit 1. However, the issues of consumerism and ethics affect all marketing plans and a brief overview is given in the first two sections of this unit.

It is useful to consider the application of marketing, as specific strategic approaches are more relevant for given marketing arenas. Possibly the most important is service marketing. Services are intangible and new elements of the marketing mix (the service extension) are needed in order to ensure service quality. In the post-industrial society of Western Europe and the United States, services form a larger segment of the market than physical products. Moreover, products often have a service element that gives added value. The nature of service marketing is outlined in this unit and the full service extension to the marketing mix is given in Unit 7. Consumer marketing is something we all experience, for we are all domestic consumers. However, nothing gets into the supermarket without being marketed through a B2B process. Special areas of marketing – such as entertainment, sports, social and not-for-profit – also have special characteristics and this unit concludes with a review of some selected special contexts.

Consumerism

Increasingly, consumers want to make informed choices. Not only in the selection of FMCGs, but in other areas such as health care. A given illness may have a variety of potential treatments, each with advantages and potential disadvantages. Patients no longer expect to be told what will be done to them, but want to be involved in a process of informed choice and consent within a mutually agreed treatment process. No matter what the decision is, from buying a camera to selecting a mortgage, there are publications and help pages from various stakeholders providing information. Key stakeholder groups, such as Greenpeace, will not only provide data, but also provide an informed critical argument if it is considered that an organization's policies are not appropriate from their viewpoint.

Rachel Carson and Ralph Nader, mid-twentieth century pioneers of green and consumer issues, changed the world's perception of these issues. John F. Kennedy provided four key rights, which, to this day, guide the ethical marketer into an appropriate appreciation of the issues and direct ethical action. Taking this view, PR is not an activity of 'spin' (rightly a term of contempt for attempts to distort reality), but of ethical behaviour where PR can be defined as 'the truth told well'. The 'Kennedy Rights' are

1. The right to safety
2. The right to be informed
3. The right to chose
4. The right to be heard.

The right to safety

People have been smoking for over 100 years. Increasingly, accumulated evidence demonstrates the link between smoking habits and certain diseases resulting in premature death. In some court actions, the case was advanced that producers of cigarettes became aware of these risks but did not fully and appropriately inform consumers. This has resulted in liability cases. More recently, the law has tended to move further. There is no longer a defence of 'best practice' (i.e. at the time of the event, the risk was unknown to science) but strict liability (i.e. 'I used the product, it harmed me, the court will find in my favour').

The case for smoking restrictions is overwhelming. However, other circumstances are more complex. In the field of consumer products, key areas are allergies and sensitization. In these circumstances, a material that is safe for the vast majority of the population may cause a severe reaction and, in extreme cases, death for a very small proportion of the population (e.g. some people have an allergy to nut products and many products in the United Kingdom can be found with a safety warning 'this product may contain traces of nuts'). Here, information is clearly not just desirable for the small 'at risk' proportion of the population, but a matter of life or death. The recent controversies about long-haul flying and deep vein thrombosis have warranted a similar response from some airlines to give travellers information and advice on the risks and how to reduce them.

The right to be informed

In the above section, people need information to make an informed decision about their safety in using a product. This right extends beyond this to other areas. Some religions such as Judaism and Islam have dietary practices which are a daily part of observing their religion. Thus, it is perfectly reasonable for a person to make a decision to become vegetarian. They then have the right to be informed whether a given product conforms to their needs. To exercise their right to choice and/or safety, people need appropriate amounts of information that is easily accessible and clearly understandable. This is an area where there are no simple mathematical rules. One can fix weight limits on luggage for a flight but how do you measure truth in advertising: what do 'fat free', 'organic', 'free-range' and 'eco-friendly' really mean? Are they terms providing useful information for consumers to make informed decisions or simply some 'spin' to promote a product that is 'unhealthy', for example a product may be 'fat free' but be very high in calories and provide little nutritional value; the so-called 'empty calories' described by the pressure groups.

The right to choose

The principle here is that people may have valid lifestyle values and wish to buy products that conform to these. Above we have discussed the need for information to make choices about safety and more diffuse issues. Product claims are another important ethical issue. Creams that appear to claim to provide everlasting youth are stretching reality somewhat. With truth in advertising claims, product performance must be supplemented with verifiable evidence in support of the claims made. In many ways, the rules for this have become clear for products; determined by many years of use within the industry and companies that transgress the guidelines are quickly disciplined, not least of all by the competition. Services are a more complex area. These days a PhD in Marketing, Economics and Mathematics is required to decide which mobile telephone service is really going to provide the best value for a specific usage. With more than a thousand different mortgage products, the consumer has a hopeless task in attempting to find completely useful information to estimate 'real costs' over the lifetime of the borrowing. Another area of concern to consumer groups and regulatory authorities is the minefield of real costs for the various types of credit cards. 'Borrow £5000 for less than £100 a month' might appear a bargain, but the interest rates might be much higher than in some other forms of borrowing.

It is vital for the industry and statutory authorities to provide a framework so that consumers can obtain real and useful information, not a smokescreen for 'sharp practices'. It takes many years to build up trust in a given brand but a mis-selling scandal can destroy that in a few days; the public resent the violation of their trust in the brand.

The right to be heard

With better-informed consumers and active pressure groups, consumers will want to debate with companies the acceptability of their activities. This may be a well-considered and well-argued campaign, say by an environmental group about the impact of operations on the environment. In India, Coca-Cola encountered problems with the extraction of ground water as the local population considered this was affecting the supply of water they needed to irrigate their fields. In a free society, we can describe this as 'fair comment' and appropriate. However, with the spread of uncensored information on the Internet, companies now face an almost desperate task combating 'rogue' websites. The wildest allegations can be made and it is not fully clear how the law can be effectively applied. Where should the law be enforced, where the site is located or where the information is downloaded? At the moment, definitive answers are not available. However, when faced with wild and unfounded allegations, a company, which has in the past been open and truthful, is much more likely to have its view accepted than one that has been perceived to be secretive and evasive.

Insight

Current trends indicate that consumers are moving away from carbonated drinks to more 'healthy' options. In the United Kingdom, sales of mineral water have expanded greatly over the last decade. Reading this environmental social trend, Coca-Cola launched Dasani (pure, still water). Close reading of the label revealed the product was, in effect, purified tap water, 'state-of-the-art reverse osmosis process that precisely delivers pure still water'. The press noted that this product was not a 'pure natural mineral water' (it had not claimed to be that). The product's fate was sealed when analysis showed that processing introduced minute traces of a potentially poisonous chemical. Dasani was not re-launched. A decade ago, Perrier water (a natural, bottled at source, mineral water) suffered contamination when there was a process failure. The product was withdrawn on a global basis and was subsequently successfully re-launched. There is no suggestion that Dasani was mislabelled but the proposition 'pure (tap) water' was difficult to defend in brand image terms against 'natural mineral water'. The processing problem during the launch, contaminating the product, just proved too much in the end.

Right to be informed: the labelling of Dasani was entirely correct but some people did not understand the difference between 'pure water' and 'pure natural spring water'. The press were able to quickly fill the gap on being alerted (Right to be heard). When the choice was between an apparently 'industrial' product against a 'pure natural' product, consumers started to exercise 'Right to choose'. The contamination problem was the end, as the product appeared to have 'safety' issues in some customers' perceptions.

 ## Activity 2.1

In 2006, there were growing fears about the quality and nutritional value of school meals. Medical authorities were expressing concerns about obesity in children. A campaign was developed for rethinking school meals. TV programmes featuring celebrity chef Jamie Oliver created awareness of the issues in the general public and move the issue up the political agenda. Many schools do not prepare school meals but outsource the function to contractors that specialize in catering in such situations. Consider yourself in the role of a marketing assistant for a company providing catering services for a number of schools. The head of a school has telephoned your Area Manager inviting him to a parents' meeting to discuss the quality of school meals. In the call, it was indicated that some parents had concerns about healthy living and the dangers of 'junk' food. Prepare briefing notes for your Area Manager as background preparation for this meeting.

Green marketing

Increasingly, key stakeholders are examining organizations' products and operations to evaluate their impact on the environment; ISO 14000 provides a parallel framework to ISO 9000 (quality systems) for environmental auditing. Porter's Value Chain can be used (Unit 1) to audit the internal operations of the organization for their environmental impact. Peattie and Charter's model provides a framework for 'greening' an organization's marketing processes (Figure 2.2).

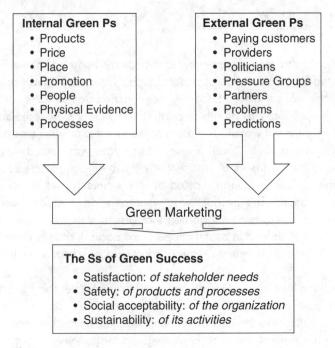

Figure 2.2 The green marketing process
Source: Adapted from Peattie and Charter

The green marketing process

Internal green Ps
The service-extended marketing mix can be used to appraise how green the mix offering is. The issues and questions posed by the model are given below:

Product
Environmental PLC analysis (some companies use the term environmental loading) provides a framework for considering the impact of the product on the environment:

- What is the environmental impact of the manufacture of the materials used in the construction, are they from finite resources (e.g. oil) or from potential renewable sources (e.g. wood)?
- What is the impact of manufacturing the product? For example, is the process energy efficient? What effluents result from manufacture?
- What is the impact of distribution? For example, is distribution energy efficient? Is packaging for transportation recyclable? Are the outlets environmentally sensitive (e.g. supermarket location and energy use within the outlet)?
- What is the environmental impact of consumers using the product (e.g. energy and water use for a washing machine)?

○ Can the product be recycled after it has been used? In an ideal world to have total sustainability, all materials should be recyclable and recycled. European legislation insists that for products such as cars and electrical/electronic appliances, manufacturers must ensure that processes are in place for recycling them after their useful life has ended.

All elements of the marketing mix can be affected. In this case, we will consider product. One market area where these issues have impacted greatly is the electronics industry. For instance, there are increasing concerns over the high levels of lead in solder within printed circuit boards found in an ever-increasing number of products, from washing machines to mobile phones. These products have ever-shorter life cycles and are difficult to recycle or dispose of with minimal environmental impact once they reach the end of their life. Moreover, during the twenty-first century, the exposure of workers to toxins during the manufacturing process is now a primary concern for responsible electronics companies. In the industry, this has led to rethinking the soldering process and the development of new chemical compounds with the same function but with lesser environmental impact. The response to these issues must be global; pollution does not respect customs' posts.

Price

What are the additional costs of greening the product? Are consumers prepared to pay these additional costs? Is the greenness of the product reflected in the customers' valuation?

Place

Are the physical methods of distribution energy efficient with minimal impact on the environment? Transport is energy consumptive and not only pollutes the environment with greenhouse gases, but also causes other problems such as noise pollution. Warehouses and sales outlets should be environmentally sensitive in their construction and energy use.

Promotion

Are the messages for green attributes fully valid? Are the methods of promotion green? There is no point in putting sustainable messages onto non-recyclable plastic signs or glossy hand-outs printed on non-recycled and non-recyclable paper. Does the company website provide relevant information to customers on environmental issues concerning the organization's products and services?

People

Environmentalism starts and ends with the values of people, both the employees and other key stakeholders (e.g. suppliers and customers). Are staff trained in environmental issues? Are customers provided with recycling facilities (e.g. printer companies now provide boxes or envelopes for recycling used printer cartridges)?

Physical evidence

It is not possible to tell from external observation if an egg is free range; in this context, environmentalism and green issues are like a service with intangible elements that need physical evidence to provide the consumer with the appropriate cues (e.g. green imagery and packaging).

Processes

Are the company's procedures and policies consistent with green values? To take an internal marketing example, does the organization promote green travel with supporting car share policies and schemes for its employees?

External green Ps

All but the last two elements of this aspect of the model are concerned with the identification of key stakeholders. The last two introduce key factors in the macroenvironment.

Paying customers

Are the customers green-informed and literate? What is their green agenda and how can the organization meet their expectations at acceptable costs?

Providers

Organizations may not export their 'dirty washing'. It is essential to ensure that suppliers of goods and services also implement green marketing policies. For example, a manufacturer of hardwood furniture must ensure that its wood is obtained from appropriately managed forests and not obtained by illegal logging of endangered virgin rainforests.

> The UK government was embarrassed when it was discovered that in renovating part of the Houses of Parliament wood had been used from a non-certified source.

Politicians

Politicians at all levels – international, national and regional – are responding to pressure groups and the electorate by legislating for recycling and other green impact issues.

Pressure groups

Well-informed and marketing-astute pressure groups will provide organizations that do not observe the green imperatives with a succession of PR disasters such as Brent Spar (an oil company misjudged the public view of the disposal of an obsolete oilrig).

Problems

Has the organization been linked to an eco-disaster such as an oil company responsible for a massive oil spill?

Predictions

Certain elements of environmental policies are based on forecasting outcomes such as global warming.

The Ss of success

If all the above Ps are given appropriate attention, the result should be the 4 Ss:

- ○ *Satisfaction* – of relevant stakeholder needs and legitimate expectations.
- ○ *Safety* – of the organization's processes and products throughout the product's environmental life cycle.
- ○ *Social acceptability* – companies that have been perceived to abuse the environment will face adverse publicity and their brand value (and thus shareholder value) will be affected.
- ○ *Sustainability* – possibly one of the most important concepts for the twenty-first century. Reserves of metals and oil are finite and sustainable usage is essential for long-term survival. Failure to recognize this will result in economic failure, for example the European fishing industries' sharp decline caused by over-fishing.

Green issues in fabric care

Below is a life cycle analysis and green marketing mix developed for automatic washing machines.

Preliminary STEEPLE analysis

Social/cultural – More easy-care fabrics (lower wash temperatures), more convenience demanded, smaller households, more frequent washes.

Technological innovation – Electronic controls, new construction materials, analytical technologies that detect washing residues in the environment.

Economic issues – Higher disposable incomes, increasing middle class in China and India also demanding convenience, costs of energy increasing, move in the United Kingdom from flat water charge to metered charging on volume of water used.

Education/training – Consumers more aware of environmental issues.

Political – Not a major issue.

Legal – EMC and other safety/technical compliance issues.

Environmental protection – Concern for energy and water use, pollution (air and water), life cycle analysis of machine (including disposal/recycling).

Selected stakeholders – Internal to manufacturer (e.g. R&D, Production etc.), manufacturers of complementary products (e.g. detergents, fabric conditioners), distributors, buyers (note that such goods often purchased as part of a package – e.g. home comes with fitted kitchen so buyer is the building contractor not the ultimate owner), users, 'consumers' (wearers of the cleaned clothes), utility providers (water, electricity, sewage), environmental agencies, pressure groups, media.

Life cycle analysis

Extraction and manufacture of the raw materials – Energy and other costs in the extraction and processing of basic raw materials (e.g. metals and petroleum-based plastics). *Note*: this has to be considered in a holistic way. An apparently expensive material (both in costs and energy), such as aluminium, may be environmentally justified as it is relatively easy to recycle and its comparatively high value makes recycling more probable.

Manufacture of the machine – Energy-efficient methods of fabrication, assembly and finishing (e.g. replacement of solvent-based paints with powder-based electrostatic processes). Factories run in energy-efficient lines (e.g. Combined Heat and Power (CHP)) can significantly cut CO_2 emissions.

Distribution of machine – Energy-efficient distribution, for example, ensuring distribution vehicles carry full loads in both directions with strategic alliances. Transit packaging must be recyclable and actually recycled (desirable in all countries but a legal necessity in some).

Use of machine – Inputs: Electricity (low wash temperatures, high spin speed to reduce energy use in drying cycle, low water use, e.g. half load option), Water (high efficiency in water use, note interaction with electricity use), efficiency in use of detergents and so on (e.g. half load option). Outputs: Hot, wet air with fabric dust (efficient filters), water effluent (major concern in amount and environmental impact, e.g. musk fragrance materials found in the environment and phosphate builders used in the past were responsible for lake algae growth).

Disposal of machine – Facilities for return of machine and identification of nature of components (e.g. PVC) to aid segregation for recycling. Failure to ensure this in the past has caused refrigerator mountains (decontamination of the compressor units, containing ozone-depleting materials, needs specialist facilities).

Internal Green Ps

Product – Green product issues identified in life cycle analysis above.

Price – Extra costs need to be built in (e.g. cost of eventual disposal/recycling).

Place – Efficient distribution covered above.

Promotion – Green issues to be promoted. Buyers and users must be made aware of the green issues, along with proactive communications with pressure groups and environmental regulators. RM links with complementary products manufacturers (e.g. detergent manufacturers). Green issues featured on website.

People, physical evidence and process – Possibly not to be considered a major issue with this product. However, note that green attitudes are needed by both internal stakeholders and field service agents (e.g. installation, care in recycling transit packaging).

External Green Ps

Paying customers – Are buyers prepared to pay the costs of recycling?

Providers – Providers of goods and services involved in the manufacture, distribution and disposal of the machine (increasingly, manufacturers of consumer goods will be made responsible for disposal/recycling of appliances). Are complementary products compatible with the new needs of the machine (e.g. low wash temperature detergents)?

Politicians – Covered in discussion of environmental regulators.

Pressure groups – Proactive discussion to demonstrate green commitment of company.

Partners – All partners in the value chain have to be involved.

Problems – Identified above, pollution, energy and water use and so on.

Predictions – CO_2 impact on global warming is a prediction but lowered impact, with new green machine, covered in life cycle analysis.

The Ss of Green Success

Satisfaction – Stakeholders to be satisfied identified above.

Safety – Part of the normal design process (e.g. spin interlock so the door may not be opened while drum is in motion).

Social acceptability – If all the above are covered, this will follow.

Sustainability – Issues covered in life cycle analysis.

Note: Input data does not only come from textbooks but also comes from our awareness of current issues. It is essential for the professional marketer to be aware of general environmental developments through the media. Our day-to-day activities (e.g. a visit to the supermarket) also provide background data.

Activity 2.2

The concepts of green marketing apply to services as well as products. A key environmental issue is pollution by vehicles in congested urban areas. The recent introduction of congestion charging in London is an example of how 'non-green' travel will be taxed. The reflection of this is that transport which is regarded as being green will gain advantages (e.g. bus lanes) and tax breaks (e.g. bio-Diesel). Consider the environmental issues relevant for a regional bus company and formulate a green marketing mix for this situation. Such an analysis would be vital preparation for marketing activities in this context (e.g. influencing media and pressure groups by strategic PR to gain support for introduction of more bus lanes, introduction of more 'Park & Ride' schemes etc.). The June 2005 case study 'Kernow Railway micro franchise' focused on regional transport issues.

Marketing ethics

Sometimes a view is advanced that marketing is unethical, inducing people to buy products they do not need and that may harm them. In addition, people are not able to afford these needless products and these unnecessary purchases drive them into a pit of debt. This view completely lacks any understanding of the nature of marketing. Marketing is a technology and, thus, does not have any ethics. The Internet is an enabling technology. It may open the door to the riches of knowledge allowing students in any part of the world access to a realm of information that was previously only accessible to the privileged. Sadly, one of its major uses (abuses) has been to circulate pornographic images. The technology is neutral; it transmits computer files, lots of 'zeros' and 'ones'. The view is advanced here that marketing has no ethical values, it is a technology, and only marketers and society have ethical values. The Chartered Institute of Marketing Diploma is a stepping stone to full Chartered status where professionals are not only guardians of the 'skills' but also of the ethics as to where, how and for what purpose these techniques may be properly used. In the section on consumerism, some consideration was given to the issues of truth in marketing. In this section, we will also consider some other issues of social acceptability. The legal issues are clearly important. However, merely conforming to the law is not necessarily ethical behaviour or socially acceptable. Often, technologies such as marketing advance so quickly that the law is always attempting to catch up (e.g. Internet law).

Only people in society have values. As people have different religious, cultural and personal values, there are no firm dividing lines and something that would be regarded as entirely appropriate in one context may be totally unacceptable in another. A racy advertisement for a perfume may be totally acceptable to the 'sophisticated' readership of a glossy fashion

51

magazine in Europe but totally unsuitable for a poster display where some sections of the wider audience may find the imagery distasteful. Ethics is a complex and diffuse subject. To provide some structure, we shall first consider a selection of illustrative issues using the marketing mix as a structure and finally conclude with some ethical dilemmas.

Ethical marketing mix

Product

In the section on consumerism, the issue of consumer safety was considered and this will not be duplicated here. People do not buy products but benefits. Therefore, when marketing research demonstrates that part of the benefit set is that some people will gain their benefits by 'abusing' the product, there are ethical issues that need to be considered. Marketing communications for tobacco and alcoholic products should not encourage over consumption or induce under-age use. In a country where the speed limit is 70 mph, what is the point of marketing cars with top speeds greatly in excess of 100 mph, especially when in the United Kingdom over 1 000 000 drivers a year are caught exceeding the speed limits determined by society?

Price

Two key issues are costs and value. A supermarket may have enormous buying powers, as do the manufacturers of major brands. Both make considerable profits in the marketing of processed products such as instant coffee. However, small subsistence farmers in less-developed countries live close to starvation, gaining a small fraction of the value added to the final product. Should this simply be considered as reasonable forces of supply and demand and the harsh impact of neutral forces of economics or is it multi-national companies ruthlessly exploiting vulnerable people in weak economies? The issues are complex. The production of fashion goods in low wage economies has, in the past, involved the use of child labour (i.e. employing children below the legal working age of a Western European developed economy). One view is that, this is clearly wrong and that the same rules should apply in all economies. Another view is that, in subsistence economies the addition to the family income may be vital in providing enough food, let alone luxuries.

Parallel pricing is where an organization takes a view that in one market it can charge significantly more, with a bigger profit margin, than in another market. In general, the price of designer jeans is higher in the United Kingdom than in the United States, even if they have the same cost structure as they are made in the same low-cost production area. The brand owners will argue they are following free market forces and gaining for their owners the best profits possible. The other view is that the brand is 'price gouging' and exploiting its brand supporters.

An ethical and political minefield surrounds intellectual property. It may take a multi-national pharmaceutical company in excess of £1 000 000 000 to research, test and bring to market (e.g. a new drug for treating AIDS). This investment is risky and the products that fail must be paid for by the products that eventually succeed. No government agencies undertake this type of risky drug research and without this vast investment by the private sector, medicine would stagnate. The consequence of this is that the physical cost of producing the drug bears no relation to the sales price, as this has to recover all the vast costs involved in the development and regulatory process. This is the pharmaceutical company case. Many developing countries in Africa have a significant AIDS problem. These drugs are too expensive for the majority of affected people who then die as a result. In these circumstances, should less-developed countries allow or disallow the local manufacture and supply of the drugs at cheaper prices? Should the drug companies supply the drugs at actual production costs to less developed countries? Would local production by another company, in contravention of international patent law, cause the whole world trade in intellectual property to collapse? In this context, the issues facing the World Trade Organization (WTO) are far from simple.

Place

In the fashion industry, brand leaders may wish to be selective in their distribution policies to support their exclusive image and high profits. Thus, such a brand owner may refuse to supply a downmarket supermarket, as the product appearing in such a location would be perceived as damaging the brand's exclusive image. Where, as discussed above, different pricing contexts may result in different prices in international markets (e.g. lower prices in the United States than the United Kingdom), the supermarket may enter the 'parallel trade market' (sometimes called the 'grey' market) and buy goods in the cheaper market from wholesale suppliers and import on their own account. The brand owners may then attempt to block this by legal action. Who has the moral high ground? The brand manager defending the value of the brand for its owners (the job he or she is paid for) or the supermarket attempting to source goods at the lowest prices to provide the best value for its customers?

Promotion

Promotion is about communication, a subjective area that is very sensitive to people's culture and social values. Therefore, in one country it may be acceptable to show a naked body in advertising a luxury bath product, whereas in another social context such an image would be outrageous and cause great offence. In the not-for-profit sectors, the limits of social acceptability are stretched. Thus, in a drink driving campaign violent, disturbing imagery may be used but is only considered socially acceptable given the seriousness of the issue. However, just because the objective is considered to be good, it does not imply that the marketer has free licence to use any imagery he or she may choose. A hard-hitting campaign from a charity wishing to increase awareness and social concern about child abuse depicted an image of a child with a cockroach leaving its mouth. This image was considered unacceptable and this element of the campaign was withdrawn.

Apart from the imagery, the tactics and targets for communications may cause ethical controversy. Is 'pester power' (the communication of messages to children) a legitimate form of a 'pull' strategy for a computer game or is it exploiting people too young to be exposed to such pressures and messages? In the past, the tobacco companies claimed that advertising of these products was aimed at brand switching and did not induce young people to start smoking or that smoking was an essential part of the 'high life'. Similar dilemmas face the advertisers of alcoholic drinks. Most recently, the medical authorities have become concerned about risks of premature death from unhealthy eating habits and the heavy promotion of so-called 'junk' food. Again, some advertisers claim that such advertisements just support the brand and do not induce over consumption. One view is that, if it is legal to sell the product then it should be legal to advertise the product. The contrary view is people, especially the vulnerable in society, should not be encouraged to indulge in behaviour or products that may affect their well-being.

People

In the selection and recruitment process, there are ethical issues about equal opportunities. Many organizations will now have explicit equal opportunities policies and insist on a transparent process to ensure compliance with both the law and company policy. In this area, there is strong guidance from laws and pressure groups representing special segments (e.g. employment and access for the disabled). However, other issues such as reward systems may have ethical dimensions that may not be covered by legislation. A major problem has been the mis-selling of financial service products (mortgages, investments etc.). One of the main causes of this massive regulatory problem was a commission system that rewarded front-line staff for total sales and not for appropriate sales (i.e. staff might have been 'rewarded' for mis-selling a product). Is 'hard selling' a legitimate tactic for banks and other financial institutions in a competitive market with such massive choice for prospective buyers? Conversely, with complex financial products, are inexperienced people being duped by financial organizations to buy inappropriate products to gain fat commissions?

Physical evidence

In the shopping experience, the store ambience is a critical factor. Clearly, a poorly lit, cold shop is not good for either customers or staff. However, other factors such as sounds and smell may have subliminal effects on our mood and modify our pre-disposition to spend. Is this simply a logical extension of store design or a sinister method for manipulating customers?

Process

Modern electronic transactions leave a comprehensive audit trail of our lives. Should these databases be used to seduce people with additional goods or services or should the process be neutral, simply used to draw up a profile of people to legitimately predict their needs and wants, so suppliers can surprise and delight by exceeding customer expectations by anticipating their desires and wants? Security, privacy and civil rights will become an increasingly complex and contentious area as technological advances make correlative research easier. Clearly, in the event of an accident, it is desirable to have access to a mobile phone. Is it right to use this technology to text a message as a person passes a given sales outlet or is this a gross intrusion of personal privacy?

Selected marketing issues with ethical dimensions

Convergent technologies are reshaping the marketplace. Images, sound and data can freely be exchanged between systems such as mobile telephones, computers and home entertainment systems. The Internet, wireless LAN and Bluetooth technologies allow this connectivity to be truly global. However, these advantages come at a cost. It is great to have instant access to e-mails but we soon find the inbox filled with unwanted spam. In many ways, this can be viewed as just irritating, but civil rights and privacy present key dilemmas to the emergent technologies market. A bar code is simply a machine-readable number and for all its apparent sophistication, the product bar code does not contain many bytes of information. Yet, this modest invention has transformed supply chain logistics. The next generation 'bar codes' remove two of the key problems, the amount of information stored and ease of reading. The 'new bar codes' are very small, very low cost microchips which need no independent power supply. They have sufficient information density that it is not only possible to identify a product but each individual item. The information is read by radio signals, thus, getting around the problem of laser scanning. It is therefore possible to identify every individual garment made for a fashion manufacturer and then track each garment through every stage of the supply chain from the factory to the designer shop. However, the chip remains in place after the sale. We can already microchip our pets so, if lost they can be identified. Each item of clothing could, theoretically, act as an electronic tag and with appropriate radio sensors a wearer could be tracked around the shopping mall and around the city. If people have in the past been concerned about the intrusion of junk mail into their life, this is as nothing compared to the intrusive possibilities of these convergent technologies. As with genetically modified food products, society will have to make an informed decision as to what is legitimate commercial development and what is considered to be beyond acceptability. In the case of genetically manipulated food products, the decision may not be the same in all countries. The arguments may be finely balanced.

Another area of ambiguity is in medical diagnostics and genetic profiling. To obtain certain financial services such as a mortgage or life insurance, a provider has in the past asked for information such as age, gender and lifestyle (e.g. smoker or non-smoker). As frontiers move, it is likely that genetic testing could identify people at high risk of certain diseases. From the point of view of medical care, it is clearly an advantage to have early warning. However, such people could become 'non-persons'. They could become un-insurable, unable to gain a mortgage and become an under class. Society may have to place limits on what information may be held on an individual, who may have access to such data and what use might be made of it. Thus, in English law, it is not possible to discriminate against a person on grounds of disability. However, if medical evidence is available that a person will become incapacitated in some way in the future, the individual is in a twilight zone and may not have the protection of law.

Insight

Issues in this area are widely debated in the marketing media and general press. At the start of 2006, a hot issue in the United Kingdom was whether smoking should be allowed in enclosed public places. There is an accumulating body of evidence linking passive smoking (inhalation of other peoples smoke by non-smokers) to respiratory diseases in workers subjected to smoky environments. Two ethical issues associated with tobacco products are

○ The right to chose: Should the state in a free society stop people doing things that could damage their health? People engage in other activities (e.g. mountain climbing) which carry an element of risk and society accepts this.

○ The marketers' dilemma: One view is that if something is legal then the marketers should be free to promote the product. The alternative view is that marketers as professionals should exercise social responsibility and not promote products that cause disease. It is of the nature of ethical issues that different people and organizations may have opposing views.

The CIM syllabus demands that candidates should be aware of current marketing issues.

Activity 2.3

A multinational chain of 'designer' coffee shops has plans to expand into your country and has announced plans to open its first outlet in a local town centre. There has been some initial opposition from local residents to the proposed plans expressed in the local paper. The company has learned the value of using local expertise in its international expansion. It has appointed a local PR/Advertising agency to assist it. Taking the role of an account manager in the agency, write a report on the ethical, green and consumer issues that might need to be considered in this situation. The December 2004 case study 'Danum Chocolates' featured the opening of 'The Chocolate and Coffee Café' in Middleton.

Consumer marketing

Marketing can be said to have evolved out of the need to improve the sales of consumer goods to mass markets. This process is so ingrained within society that it has become embedded in our culture and language so we will call a television series, such as 'Eastenders', a 'soap'. The name originating from the fact that these programmes were first devised to promote the sale of detergents.

A major sector is FMCG. These are the range of day-to-day products that we frequently buy and use. The category includes food, drink, personal care and household products (detergents, cleaners etc.) that fill our shopping basket each week. Branding and mass marketing communications are key, with advertising often being a major spend. A relatively simple message, for example 'A Mars a day helps you work, rest and play', needs to be given to a comparatively large group; often many millions of people. TV, radio, press and poster advertising are all important in this area.

Insight

Hair care market

Major brands have to continue to re-invent and rejuvenate their product lines. The category managers (people responsible for managing a line of products such as 'fabric care') in the supermarkets are always seeking new innovations to freshen up the range and provide value-added benefits to customers (i.e. provide increased margin over product variants that have become commodities). As part of the interview process for new marketing employees, candidates may be requested to make a brief presentation. This serves two purposes to the company. It allows an evaluation of the person's presentation skills (important for marketing roles) and also gives a chance for the interview panel to assess the amount of understanding the candidate has regarding the product they will be working on. Below is an outline of the segmentation analysis that would be appropriate before preparing such a presentation.

Potential segmentation issues for shampoos and conditioners: price (e.g. premium branded, low-cost generic); size (e.g. larger family, normal, small for travel), male and female variants, products with additional functional benefits (e.g. anti-dandruff); nature of hair (e.g. dry, normal, greasy, damaged and coloured); place of use (e.g. special products and packs for professional use in hair salons), age (e.g. special products for babies). Some of the variables are not listed in standard textbook listings. Some standard textbook variables may need interpretation: for example, type of hair may be considered as an interpretation of benefit need segmentation. Some variables are not so relevant in a specific context. A core skill for a marketer is to be selective and appreciate what is key in a given case and other factors which do not greatly influence the decisions. A key issue would be to identify trends (e.g. products needed for new emerging hair styles). Secondary sources can help and a visit to the supermarket is vital (there is no substitute to first-hand experience where it can be easily achieved).

The above consideration is in the context of FMCG. However, some other issues in this unit also apply: due in part to consumer pressure groups, labelling of cosmetics products has now become subject to new EU Cosmetics Directives which aim to standardize labelling of cosmetic contents.

Always remember, more than one of the contexts considered in this unit may apply in any single situation (e.g. B2B context needs to be considered here as well as the 'push' element of the strategy to get the channels to stock the product).

Consumer durable and white goods (refrigerators etc. so-called as they were usually white in colour) pose a slightly different problem, as purchases are infrequent. Here there is a much more explicit buyer decision-making process. The 'I feel hungry, I will have that bar of chocolate' is an almost instantaneous decision (conditioned by long-term brand building). However, 'the TV is getting old maybe I will replace it with a flat screen plasma display' follows the steps: problem recognition, information search, evaluation and purchase (Unit 6). Brand building is just as important for world leading brands such as Philips and Sony as it is with FMCGs. FMCGs have to sell off the shelf. With white goods service elements such as installation and breakdown services become more relevant. Personal selling may become important and demonstration of the equipment may be vital. The ultimate consumer durable might be considered to be the car; here the test drive and personal selling stages are critical to close the sale. With such products, the marketer is presented with a challenge in building a relationship with the brand, even though the purchase is infrequent.

Consumers in advanced economies spend a large proportion of their income on services ranging from entertainment, eating out, communications and financial services (insurance, mortgages, etc.). For some services, there are some similarities with consumer durables, in that one does not buy a broadband service every day or re-mortgage the house every month. However, there are, as stated earlier, the special issues of intangibility associated with service and consumer services (fully covered in Unit 7).

Activity 2.4

Fantastic Fragrances* are about to launch their 2007 season's cosmetic range 'Vibrant 2007*'. This will be launched with TV and cinema advertising, full pages in the fashion press and local in-store promotions in the opening launch month. Consider yourself in the role of a Marketing Assistant working in a major local department store. The local promotion will involve a free makeover from an international consultant with a free gift and a £5 voucher off the next purchase for purchases from the new range over £25. You have talked to the IT Department and from the analysis of the store loyalty scheme, they can provide a database of customers who have purchased similar products in the last year. Draft a letter to be used in a 'mail merge' process to invite potential customers to the store to take advantage of the promotion. The format of business letters is covered in Unit 9.

* Names for assessment purposes only.

Business-to-Business marketing

This is the hidden facet of marketing. If consumer marketing is the visible tip of the iceberg, then the web of marketing through the supply chain of components, raw materials and services is what is hidden under the water. As previously stated, in consumer marketing, the B2B strategy is important as the 'push' element of consumer marketing, it supports the channels and feeds the consumer 'pull' strategy elements with mass advertising and communications. B2B advertising may be restricted to the narrowcast trade press rather than national newspapers or TV. Other elements of the communications mix will be adapted and the balance of the spend may be rather different. In many situations, such as the marketing of pharmaceuticals to medical practitioners a major cost will be in personal sales. Sometimes marketing can be viewed as simply support (brochures, planning exhibitions etc.) to the sales force.

There tend to be fewer customers in the B2B context and their purchases tend to be larger so personal selling tends to be relatively more important, especially in gaining new sales. Often the buyer will have an expert knowledge of the product. Major supermarkets have extensive technical support laboratories that may collaborate with a brand manufacturer or an 'own label' contractor to jointly develop a new consumer product. The DMU concept is important. The supermarket buyer will not make the decision to purchase a new product line alone. The new line will have been identified through marketing to fill a gap in the product range or to replace a product in the decline phase of its life cycle. Supermarket technical staff will evaluate the performance and likely customer acceptability of the product, collaborating with marketing in consumer trials. Quality assurance will want to access the product to test for consumer safety in use and compliance with legislation (e.g. food labelling regulations, which are complex and differ from country to country). Logistics will be concerned with how and where the product should be delivered (fashion clothing is a completely different issue to chilled food). The buyer will be involved in the detail of the ordering process, which may involve a fusion of stock-control systems to provide a seamless chain from the laser checkout to the manufacturer of the product and the supplier of raw materials. To drive down inventory costs the supply chain must be smartly managed. The supplier's account manager will not be the only person communicating with the company. There might be direct linkage between the technical staff in the joint development of a new product. The key issue for the B2B marketer is to identify all the relevant decision makers in the target organization and consider what their needs and objectives are. Then they must ensure that these are satisfied not only for a one-off sale, but also to develop long-term relationships for continued profitable collaboration. Aspects of relationship marketing are considered in the next section. The acronym DMU used in many texts can be viewed as a term for industrial customer stakeholder analysis, within the client organization. Sound stakeholder analysis is the key foundation skill for the marketer.

Large purchases are often made in a context of risk aversion. Failure to deliver the product or service on time to the required standard may put the client organization at risk and even threaten its survival. Clearly, the actual and perceived risk is greatest when the product or service is new to the company and the supplier has no established track record – the new buy situation. A small company purchasing a stock-control system will be most concerned about this initial purchase with a number of people involved in the decision-making process. A stock-control system that fails to work could wreck a manufacturing or retail company. If, after a few years, new improved system software is released then it will be carefully considered, but not as much as with the initial purchase – the so-called 'modified re-buy situation'. If it is just the addition of a single new terminal, identical to many others already in use, this is the simple re-buy situation. In many situations this type of re-buy, for restocking a supermarket or supplying components for JIT manufacture, may be effected automatically by the organizations' computer systems; reducing errors and driving down costs.

The Internet provides a vital function with customers having secure access to information via a private virtual network. For modest transactions, Internet ordering and electronic payment may minimize costs. A typical example is the purchase of company travel, where authorized employees may book their own hotel rooms online and pay by corporate credit card. This provides high efficiency in service and flexibility and drives down transaction costs to benefit both parties' profitability.

Brand building can be just as important in some circumstances in the B2B sector as with consumer marketing. Major global companies such as IBM will have heavy advertising spends supported on a product-by-product basis with targeted sector specific initiatives, for example, to support the introduction of a new line in payroll systems with advertisements in the specialist trade press. Moreover in many sectors, organizations may have both a strictly B2B segment (e.g. Ford commercial vehicles and fleet sales) and a consumer segment supplied directly or by distributors or retailers (e.g. Ford family cars).

Insight

Computer sales to the B2B sector

Consider the situation of a person moving from the retail sector to the B2B Marketing group in a computer company. Their first involvement in a project is to assist in the preparation of the literature for a major computer B2B exhibition. Below are a few of the points that this person's manager might make in explaining what is different about the B2B sector when compared to FMCG marketing.

Selected segmentation issues

Size of company – Global (e.g. Ford), national (e.g. UK health service), regional, local and small- and medium-sized enterprises (SMEs): these are important issues since each account will be managed on a different basis. Global companies will have a structure of international account management to provide global service in all localities. SMEs may well be serviced by agents and retailers with some focus on B2B (e.g. Staples).

Method of purchase – Many companies may place an order, whereas public sector organizations (e.g. the Police) will often put projects out through a tender process. Some organizations may not wish to purchase but lease or have a service contract (e.g. complete outsourcing of computer services such as payroll). Some companies may not buy from the computer manufacturer but from a Value-Added Reseller (VAR) providing a 'turn key' (hardware, software, installation, training, etc. to provide, just like your car, 'turn key and it runs') solution.

End-use situation – Air Traffic Control is a very different market to SMEs' accountancy use (system failure with an accountancy package is a nuisance; in air traffic control it could be a catastrophe).

Level of service required – Do they just need hardware or do we supply complete 24-hour hardware/communications/software service with onsite staff working in customers' premises on a global basis?

Decision-Making Unit/Buying centre

Various roles have been identified – Initiators, users, influencers, deciders, approvers, buyers and gatekeepers. In the case of a substantial organization, the initiators might be senior management needing technology to reduce costs. The users are the operators and the like. Influencers would include technical staff such as maintenance technicians. Deciders in this case might well be a small committee that advise the board on the purchase decision. Approvers would include senior financial staff (e.g. financial aspects of contracts including penalty clauses for late delivery). The buyers in this case will be strongly influenced by the control of the deciders, with little flexibility to switch vendors or change the contract. Gatekeepers would include such functions as safety (compliance of equipment with local and company safety policy, e.g. VDU use). The reason for this DMU analysis is that not all the DMU participants will visit the exhibition and so the literature and the rest of the integrated communications must carry the company message to them. The term DMU/buying centre is just a specific RM/stakeholder focus. The members of the DMU are key stakeholders with whom the selling organization needs to build strong links/relationships. This is particularly important for the VARs who may have many individual clients and thus provide access to many contracts if a successful long-term partnership can be built.

 ## Activity 2.5

'Clean Sweep*' has grown well since it was founded 3 years ago. The company provides cleaning and maintenance services for commercial premises such as offices and the like. Though a small company, the owners strongly believe that 'people are our major asset' and the company has just been awarded the coveted 'Investors in People' designation. The Managing Director (John Smith*) has arranged for the award to be presented at an event, which will take place at the Imperial Hotel. Consider you are the Account Manager in a local PR agency and as one of your tasks you are to write a press release. Draft this press release. How might this fit into an integrated communication plan for this company? If possible, before you start this activity look through the business pages of your local paper to see how your local companies are covered in your regional press. One of the key issues, in this context, is to get cover that will create awareness in other small business that could be users of the firm's services. How to write a press release is covered in Unit 9.

*Clean Sweep and John Smith are fictitious names for assessment purposes only.

Relationship marketing

In traditional marketing, considerable emphasis is placed on closing the sale. Increasingly, marketers are deepening their conviction that closing the sale is only one of the important milestones in an ongoing relationship. Thus, a car dealership is not only interested in selling you a car but servicing it and, in a few years' time, supplying you with a replacement. This is building a relationship between the client, the staff at the local distributorship and the manufacturer's brand. Viewed in this context, the 18 000-mile service is not only seen to be a chance to make a sale (the income from the service), but a marketing opportunity to maintain and develop the relationship. Thus, the reception team and the motor technicians are involved in building the relationship through their contact with the customer (Figure 2.3). Another key concept of relationship marketing is the part-time marketer (e.g. customer-facing staff). Much of the relationship building does not take part with the full-time marketers. In supermarkets, the full-time marketers may be comparatively remote. How the shopping experience feels will be greatly affected for better or worse by the interaction between customers and front-line staff at the checkout and others in customer contact roles – the 'part-time marketers'.

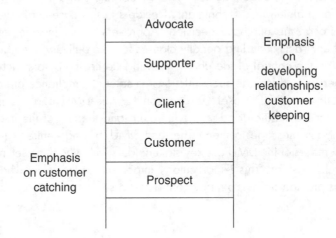

Figure 2.3 The relationship ladder

Although relationship marketing is important in consumer marketing, it is critical in B2B marketing. As discussed in the previous section, organizations do not do business with organizations. People in one organization do business with other people in client organizations. Thus, a key strength of an advertising agency is the quality of the relationships between the creative staff and the key personalities in the commissioning organization.

This often involves many people interacting with many other people in the linking organizations. A network of interacting relationships is formed between the organizations, which then have to be maintained and sustained both internally (internal marketing) and externally. Thus, in considering the marketing action plan, the impact on all the relevant stakeholders is important. Relationship management focuses on how these relationships may be positively sustained and developed.

Marketing is not seen as a mechanistic set of actions, intellectual cogs in an industry machine but as an activity that depends on a network of human relationships to support the organization's mission and objectives. The move to relationship marketing can be seen as the leading edge in developing from a production orientation (any colour you like as long as it is black) to sales (all we need to do is push harder) to developing long-term relationships of positive benefit to both parties. In traditional sales negotiations, you could end up with winner–loser outcomes. In a relationship-marketing context, only creating and sustaining win–win outcomes will nurture and develop the relationship and future profit opportunities.

Relationship marketing is in harmony with the marketing orientation. Companies can have other orientations. The production orientation has a focus on the manufacturing process and cost reduction. If it is cheap enough, people will buy it. Product-orientated organizations are focused on product design and product quality. These organizations take the view that there will always be sales for the top quality product. With the sales orientation, the organization takes the view that customers will buy as long as the organization pushes them hard enough with activities such as sales promotion and personal selling. The marketing-orientated organization takes a customer focus and views the marketing mix offering from the customers' benefit view. In this context, organizations often view 'marketing' not only as a function but also as a philosophy. This is a way of looking at the organizations' activities and products from the view of providing customer satisfaction and relationship building. This view is in harmony with the relationship-marketing concept of the 'part-time marketer'.

Case study

New Town Arts Theatre

New Town Arts Theatre is a charitable trust with the objective of making multicultural films and stage productions available to a regional audience. The organization is not-for-profit. The aim is to bring a diversity of multicultural films, plays, dance, opera and so on that would otherwise be inaccessible to a regional audience. It should be remembered that such organizations have to have a strict budget focus since a charity can become bankrupt. To achieve the required income, relationships must be built with a range of stakeholders. A few key stakeholders are identified below with initiatives that would assist in building relationships.

Loyal customers – Use of database marketing to profile their interests and wants so that tailored communications can be sent. Given the need to contain costs, this might be by getting such customers to sign up to an e-list to get up-to-date news and information on future performances. A 'Friends of the Arts Theatre' scheme with advantageous booking facilities and special members' events (e.g. a 'backstage with the cast' event).

First time customers – An information pack to attract them to become mailing list subscribers.

Local arts groups – A framework for such organizations to enter into partnership arrangements, for example, to co-sponsor events of special interest to given groups.

Local organizations – A framework for commercial sponsorship from local companies. Acknowledgment could be given in the monthly programme mailings and preferential facilities offered for corporate hospitality for sponsoring organizations.

Media publics – Personal invitations to briefings and the provision of facilities for meeting and interviewing performers.

The above is just a selection of potential relationship activities for a selected range of key stakeholders. It is worth mentioning that a well-designed and well-maintained website would support all the above initiatives.

Activity 2.6

Discuss with other members of your group or colleagues, the extent to which relationship marketing is applicable in the development of their customer relationships.

How might an Account Manager in a PR agency develop and maintain relationships with key clients? What other relationships would a skilled PR professional need to develop and maintain? Networking and the development of stakeholder relationships featured in the June 2006 CIM case study 'SMS Cars Ltd': Question 3b 'You have been asked to represent SMS Cars Ltd at a business networking event run by your local Chamber of Commerce (Chamber of Commerce – an organization of business people designed to advance the interests of its members). Your Manager has suggested that you use this as an opportunity to raise the profile of the organization and to promote the launch of the event. What personal objectives would you set yourself to ensure that you achieve your aims? What networking skills would you use?'

Services marketing

Services account for more household expenditure than products in post-industrial society. It is over simplistic to consider the marketing of products and services as separate areas of marketing. It is true that services have certain characteristics that need special consideration by the marketer. However, many products have a large service component (e.g. cars). The provision of value-added service is often not only a much-needed source of profits, but also builds relationships and brand loyalty (Figure 2.4). Equally, many services have products involved at the core of their service. Many airlines, for example, will highlight the excellence of the in-flight food (a product) as part of the total quality of the service experience. Most marketing is best seen not as service or product marketing but as existing in a spectrum of product and service, where balanced consideration is needed. Thus, a supermarket is best viewed not as a pile of products in an out-of-town field but a buying service offering a pleasurable shopping experience. Clearly, the product range and depth is important but may often be matched by competitors, so the added dimension may be convenience and the pleasure of the experience rather than the physical nature of the goods. After all, most goods are made by the same range of brand owners or contract manufacturers.

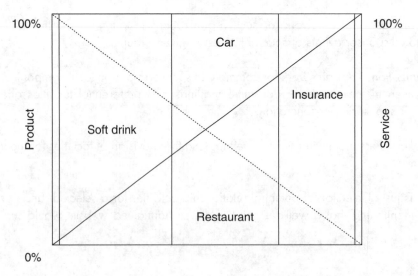

Figure 2.4 Percentage of value as 'product' or 'service', product–service continuum

Services are said to have four characteristics that differentiate them from products:

1. Intangibility
2. Inseparability
3. Heterogeneity (sometimes given as variability)
4. Perishability.

The service extension of the marketing mix provides the marketer with the tools to tailor the mix for service offerings.

Take care with the service-extended mix. All seven Ps are needed, not just the additional three. In an exam setting, take care to note if the context is that of the 'service-extended mix' (all seven Ps) or the service extension to the marketing mix (just the three additional Ps).

Intangibility

When you buy a packet of sweets, there is a physical product. If you have been to the theatre or made a telephone call after your transaction you have nothing physical to show for your purchase, nothing physical to demonstrate the quality of the consumed service. Thus, one of the key purposes of the service extension of the marketing mix is to make the intangible tangible, for example, with physical evidence. The service extension provides reassurance and communicates the quality and acceptability of the service.

Inseparability

For many services the provider and customer have to be brought into contact, however, care should be used in interpreting this element in the context of Internet services (where this is not so). If you stay at a hotel or travel by train, you have to be present at the site of delivery of the service. The customer and the service provision must be in the same place at the same time. The service extension element Process provides a framework for analysing the issues to ensure appropriate delivery of the service.

However, the Internet is now rewriting some of these rules. I do not have to visit the shop and I am not constrained by trading hours if I shop online which is a 24/7/365 service (24 hours a day, 7 days a week and 365 days of the year). The effect is to remove time and distance from the service provision equation.

Variability

Many services involve a person-to-person interaction. In a restaurant setting, what might be perceived as quality service by one customer might be perceived as pretentious affectation by another. Both the provider and the consumer are subject to variability and thus there may be considerable variation in the perceived level of service quality. The *People* element of the service extension considered both the provider–customer person-to-person interactions as well as the potential issues of customer–customer interaction. One of the advantages of service automation (e.g. ATMs) is to take the variability out of the service experience. However, this only removes one end of the uncertainty, that of service provision. The quality of service perceived by the customer will be dependant on their acceptance of the automation.

Perishability

A restaurant does not make money by serving customers on a Saturday evening but by remaining full on a wet Thursday lunchtime, when business is much lighter. Last night's unsold hotel room is worthless today. It does not matter if you are selling telephone services or entertainment; the management of demand is critical to successful service marketing. At peak time, demand can be lowered and profits maximized by charging higher prices. Peak holiday travel will be at premium rates. A city centre business hotel will charge premium rates during the week and may offer bargain weekend breaks for two to attract customers at the weekend when there are fewer business customers. The astute management of demand by promotion and pricing structures is a key success factor for the service business.

Insight

Small Business Banking

A common CIM question is 'in the context of ... outline a relevant service-extended marketing mix'. Sometimes the question is implied rather than asked directly when tasks such as 'Write an outline marketing plan for ... ' are given. Small business accounts are an important and profitable sector for high street banks and the segment needs more than personal accounts with a business name. An outline marketing mix for a high street bank targeting the small business sector is given below. The elements of the service-extended marketing mix are covered in more depth in Units 3–7. It should be noted that this situation has implications in addition to 'service marketing'. The context is also B2B, with implications of RM working with organizations that have limited budgets. The small business sector is highly segmented with everything from manufacturing, farming, fishing, retail and so on.

Product – Range of business banking products such as special 'reserve' deposit accounts; companion range of financial products such as insurance.

Price – Competitive pricing with other high street banks; customer concerns that charges should be transparent with no hidden extra charges at the end of the month.

Place – Even in the Internet age, some services may not be provided remotely (e.g. banking cash); therefore, a convenient high street location is required with easy access and parking along with convenient opening hours.

Promotion – Through marketing to SMEs, banks have big budgets; so, the following are possible: advertising (TV, press) in areas likely to appeal to SME owners, posters especially in areas such as exhibitions attracting SME visitors (e.g. agricultural shows for farmers). Personal selling is key – see below under people.

People – Specially trained staff with a range of experience and skills to provide understanding of various sectors (e.g. business advice for small companies exporting). The product is not only banking, but also business and financial advice (added value to the client). A key RM issue is people who understand the clients' business sectors and the need to work with limited budgets.

Physical evidence – Separate facilities (e.g. 'Business Centre') for meetings with clients.

Process – Range of services. Increasingly, Internet-based but with good provision for those services that need to be delivered on a face-to-face basis. Key issues are flexibility, dependability and security. The development of a marketing mix to fit a given case study context is a frequent examination question, for example December 2005 'The Urban Culture Festival 2006' CIM case study Question 4 'Compare how the THREE elements of the service marketing mix (people, process and physical evidence) might differ in application between the UCF and a financial services provider.' and in the June 2006 CIM case study 'SMS Cars Ltd' Question 5a and 5b 'Produce a briefing paper to be forwarded to the Manager of the Vehicle Servicing Department which (a) describes how THREE elements of the service extended marketing mix (people, process and physical evidence) can be used by the Vehicle Servicing Department to improve customer service; (b) makes recommendations as to how the promotional mix could be used to increase demand for the Vehicle Servicing Department'.

Service quality

As services are intangible, measuring quality is more difficult than with products. In selling a bottle of fruit juice, it is easy to check that the volume is correct and that consumers are not being short-changed. How can you measure the quality of service given by a restaurant? Is it just the amount of time the waiter spends at the table, or does it also have more diverse elements such as empathy with the clients and knowledge of the menu? The issue of service quality is more fully covered at the end of Unit 7.

Activity 2.7

Successfully arranging memorable events (e.g. openings, launches, sales conferences, etc.) requires much effort and marketing skill. Consider that a friend of yours, who has only recently started work, has been given the task of organizing an event to launch a new food product manufactured by a small regional company. The launch event is aimed at owners of local delicatessens and specialist food shops. Using the concepts in this section, write brief notes on issues your friend should consider in arranging this event.

Internal marketing

An organization's internal stakeholders are the key to success or failure. In the smaller organization people can know each other and their management as individuals and develop working relationships. In larger organizations, with a broad geographic spread of operations and many thousands of employees, a more structured approach is required. In the relationship-marketing view of organizations, individuals outside the sales and marketing function are still considered part-time marketers. Individuals will only perceive this if they are brought into the extended marketing team in an inclusive way.

In the past, a problem has been that internal stakeholders were considered as a uniform group. We segment customers, but previously, less attention was paid to 'segmenting' within the organization. The principle is the same. If we want effective communications, the process must address the agenda of the target group. A 1-year work experience intern has a very different outlook to a shift process operator with 25 years service, yet motivating both is essential for the successful implementation of the organization's strategies. Some selected possible variables are given below:

- Role: front line, technical, managerial and so on
- Level of stake holding: high (e.g. sole owner), considerable (e.g. institutional investor with large holding), low (e.g. shareholder with a broad investment portfolio)
- Function: Manufacturing, Finance, Marketing and so on
- Geographic location
- Age
- Length of service
- Condition of employment: part-time, full-time (fixed contract, permanent contract etc.)
- Hours of work: day, shift and so on
- Attitude to issue: against, passive/apathetic, supportive
- Depth within the organization: core (full time – long established), close (immediate family of the employee, part of the extended community), peripheral (friends of the employee). The boundary of the organization should not be seen as a prison wall, but more diffuse and graduated.

The above list is not intended to be exhaustive, but to indicate that just as the process of customer segmentation requires creativity so does segmentation within the company. Some of the failures of company's internal communications in the past were due to a 'one-size-fits-all' attitude. Senior management would present financial projections of great interest to senior and middle management. Front-line staff might be much more concerned about changes in working practices and shift patterns, with the introduction of a new computer system, than the impact on the cash flow. Communications must be relevant to the audience and the word communications implies a two-way process. Internal Marketing is not just keeping staff informed but listening to people.

The Internet provides a very powerful tool for this. As with most powerful tools, some care must be exercised. Information that is intended to be company confidential could be leaked. Discipline and etiquette as to what is acceptable and unacceptable in e-communications need to be established. This is part of establishing the corporate culture. If the organization is not able to build its brand values from within, what chance does it have to project them outside the organization?

Case study

Internal marketing at a motorway service station

Motorway service stations are a 24/7/365 operation providing retail and refreshment facilities to travellers. Given below is an outline analysis of internal stakeholders.

Head office staff (outside the service station but part of the organization): Downward communication on policy and operational matters (e.g. daily update of stolen credit cards and other security issues). Upwards communication on operations matters (e.g. customer complaints). The staff working at the service station might be classified in a number of ways. Hours of working: day, shift, full-time, part-time (e.g. care needs to be taken to ensure good communications with shift staff working, not so easy as with full-time day staff). Nature of work: administration, catering, retail front line, security and so on. (e.g. changes in food hygiene regulations will not need to be communicated to all staff, communicating everything to everyone just dilutes impact and gives data overload). Length of service and nature of contract (e.g. pension issues not relevant to part-time vacation staff but do concern full-time permanent staff). Internal marketing issues featured in the June 2005 case study 'Kernow Railway micro franchise': Question 5b 'Write a letter to the employees of Kernow Railways informing them of the takeover of the services by Kernow on 1 July, highlighting the benefits for them'.

Activity 2.8

Across the world, attitudes to smoking have been changing and many countries are now banning smoking in public places. Consider you are the marketing manager for a chain of restaurants. The past policy has been to have designated areas for 'smokers' and 'non-smokers'. It has been decided that in 2 months time the chain will move 100 per cent to a non-smoking policy. Draft a general memo to all staff to inform them of the change and how the policy shift should be implemented. How to format a memo is covered in Unit 9.

Marketing in an international context

An organization is said to be engaged in International Marketing when it markets its goods or services in more than one country. The implication of this is that at least three macro/micro-environments have to be considered: the home country, the destination country and the relevant international trading environment (e.g. conditions set by the WTO). However, the title for this section has been deliberately drawn more widely than this; the international business environment may still critically influence a sole trader in a single country. A sugar beet farmer in Europe will be critically dependent on decisions on EU subsidies and attitudes to the import of sugar from tropical cane production. A shift in international policies may indicate a move into other crops; even though the business is essentially domestic, it is still connected into this one world system.

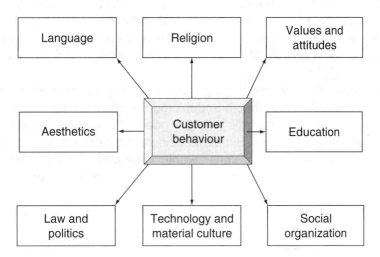

Figure 2.5 Components of culture
Source: Adapted Carter/Terpstra/Hall

One crucial aspect is the successful delivery of products and services to markets with greatly differing cultures. However, in many countries (e.g. United Kingdom, United States, Europe, Malaysia etc.), the domestic marketer is increasingly working in a multicultural environment. An understanding of the impact of culture on marketing plans and strategies is thus of importance to most marketers, not just those working in giant multinational organizations.

The Terpstra model (Figure 2.5) provides a framework for examining the impact of culture. In considering culture, it is important to note that cultural multiplicity is a celebration of diversity, not that one culture is better than another. Language is not only a means of expression but is also a reflection and demonstration of culture. Moreover, one should remember that in many countries, the population can be segmented by language, either explicitly in that more than one language is recognized (Wales, Canada etc.) or that there are very significant segments who do not have the 'official' language as their first language and use another in home life (e.g. Spanish speaking population in the United States). With media fragmentation (e.g. cable TV) and the ability to micro market (e-commerce), it is now possible to consider such segmentation variables. One of the key skills of a marketer is to be sympathetic to the needs of target market segments. Religious beliefs can influence what people eat (e.g. Kosher or Halal food), what they wear (e.g. Sikh turban) and how they live their day-to-day lives. Differing cultures also have their own styles of dress and architecture.

In Hofstede's work, the attitudes of societies to 'male' and 'female' values were explored. In some societies, there is considerable difference in how these values are perceived. In the United Kingdom, very few women study Engineering yet this is not so in other countries. Education is not only about the acquisition of knowledge but the development of values. The education systems in England, Scotland, France, Germany and the United States are all different. They are not only different in the ultimate levels of attainment, but also in the ethos of education and curriculum. The way in which society works is different too, in the United Kingdom context the family is becoming a more diffuse unit with children disappearing with their microwave meal to their computer games. In other societies, the family meal is one of the pivots of daily life. The acceptance of technology is a social phenomenon, with some societies being fascinated by electronic gadgets and others more conservative.

Legal differences are not restricted to minor idiosyncrasies such as the legal driving age, but the systems as a whole are totally different, so that a lawyer expert in one legal system might not be at all competent in another. Scottish, English, French and Islamic law each differ in the very foundations of how law is administered and cases argued, often due to the religious background of each country.

Once it has been decided that the organization should begin international operations the next decision is where. Relevant macro and microenvironmental aspects may be used to segment international markets. For the sale of luxury goods, the number of people with high disposable income might be appropriate. Simple consideration of the average gross domestic product (GDP) per head may conceal considerable variations, for example, although India is, on average, modestly wealthy, there is a significant and growing market for luxury and designer goods. The GE Matrix approach to alternative strategy selection is discussed in Unit 10. For the moment, we need only to consider the two key factors used in the model: market attraction and competitive advantage. Market attraction is relative to a given organization and context. A publisher of French literature would find the Australian market unattractive as a market for its type of books. American and UK publishers would find this an attractive destination market. The decision about long-term competitive advantage needs considerable research when exploring the environment. The Porter Five Forces of Competition model we explored in Unit 1 is most useful. The identity and nature of the competition in a distant market will be very different and if the process is not carefully conducted, the company may attempt to enter inappropriate markets resulting in failure. M&S found problems in attempting to expand in the United States; it did not have the power to buy into critical mass and never became a serious player there. Conversely, Wal-Mart did achieve critical mass in the United Kingdom with its acquisition of ASDA. Wal-Mart was able to use its global buying power to lever ASDA ahead in the United Kingdom in a way that just was not possible for M&S who had a small bridgehead in the United States and a much smaller international buying base. However, Wal-Mart found local competition much more difficult in Germany where its market entry strategy was much less successful.

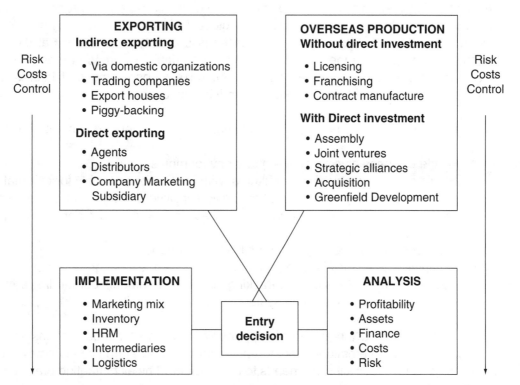

Figure 2.6 Market entry alternatives
Source: Adapted from Carter

Once a target market has been identified, the precise method of entry has to be decided; this is shown in Figure 2.6. The first aspect is to decide if it is best to export or manufacture abroad. If the product is heavy and of relatively low value (e.g. soft drinks), then local manufacture is required. If the product is light, high value and has to be made in high volumes (e.g. consumer electronics), then exporting from a relatively few global manufacturing locations is indicated. Companies are increasingly seeking global solutions to sourcing products. Once the decision is made about location of manufacture (home or destination market), the key factor is the level of commitment and the risk that the organization wishes to make. Indirect exporting involves relatively little management effort and expense. However, this comes at the cost of control. If more control is required, then direct exporting is required. This can be effected with partners (agents or distributors) or, for maximum control, by establishing a local sales and marketing subsidiary. With some products, production in the market can be achieved with little capital investment. An owner of intellectual property (e.g. patent, brand or copyright) may license the production rights to a local manufacturing organization. If more control is required with additional costs, franchising may be an appropriate option. Increasingly, companies are reaping the benefits of flexible, international production with close control by working with an alliance of contract manufacturing partners. Where part of the product is high value and other parts lower value and more bulky, local assembly may be the best solution. Where direct ownership may not be possible (e.g. legal reasons), strategic alliances may provide an option (e.g. US restrictive laws about foreign carriers flying internal US flights force European carriers to form strategic alliances with US airlines to provide full city-to-city cover between Europe and US destinations). In developing the strategy, the marketing mix and other business aspects such as logistics need to be addressed. The precise entry strategy selected will depend on issues such as profitability, the amount of capital required, the relative cost structures and levels of risk. If risk is high, then exporting via agents is a possibility. A large, stable, growing market may indicate the building of new production plants (the so-called 'greenfield development').

It must be decided whether the mix needs adaptation or standardization. This should not be seen as an all or nothing situation. Almost invariably, some changes will be needed to labelling

69

and instruction manuals even if the product (e.g. a computer) is largely the same. Other products such as the mix of food offered by a global food manufacturer may need considerable tailoring to the local culinary culture. Financial issues may have a cultural dimension. The majority of mortgages in the United Kingdom are 'variable' whereas in many other countries 'fixed term' mortgages are more common. Attitudes to borrowing and interest rates have resulted in the creation of specific products in Islamic cultures.

For a firm to move from domestic to international marketing, there are a number of implications:

o Single business environment – many environments.
o Single culture – many diverse cultures, with implications not only for external marketing, but also for the organization and culturally sensitive management of the company.
o The adaptation of the marketing mix to accommodate the differences implied in the above conditions.
o More complexity and length in supply chain management.
o Complexity in financial management and risks (e.g. exchange rate movements).
o Vastly increased flows of data tracking all the environments demanding a more sophisticated marketing information system.

E-commerce is both a threat and an opportunity and smaller organizations are now more directly exposed to international trading environments. The international context of marketing is not just for a few specialists but needs to be considered by all marketing practitioners, we do truly now live in a global village.

Insight

International Soups

The food and drink market is very sensitive to the local STEEPLE environment and in particular to the social environment component. A brief discussion of the issues surrounding food and drink is given below with some specific emphasis on ready-prepared soups.

Preliminary STEEPLE analysis

Social/cultural – Given the importance of culture in this context, the full Terpstra headings have been used. Language: packaging will need to be translated; even American is different to English. Religion: many religions have dietary requirements (such as Halal, Kosher etc.). This is a minority market sector in the United Kingdom, but can form a major sector in other countries. Values and attitudes: attitudes to prepared foods differ from the computer games 'geek' (if it takes more than 55 seconds to microwave count me out) to the 'foodie' (if it is not freshly prepared from organic ingredients it is not fit to eat). Education: in some contexts, literacy may not be high and instructions may have to be more visual. Social organization: in some societies we could be said to be in the 'microwave-and-go' society, in other countries, the family meal is a pivotal part of the day and social culture. Technology and culture: different cultures have different attitudes to technology; note that technology does not always imply processed. The trend for freshly brewed, 'real' coffee and fresh fruit drinks has generated a range of consumer appliances to prepare instant fresh real coffee and fresh smoothies at home. Law and politics: food is complicated. Genetically modified (GM) ingredients are an area of major political dispute between the United States (bring the yummy GM food on) and Europe (no way GM, not over a dead butterfly – in the trials of GM crops some researchers reported a drop in the number of butterflies the field supported). At the operational level, the law in each country will proscribe certain ingredients and how they must be declared on the labelling. The issue of salt content has been noted already. Another area of controversy in the EU is the use of 'E number' additives such as synthetic food colours. Aesthetics: good taste and design is a cultural variable. In some countries, a pony steak is fine. Attitudes to whale meat are very different in the United Kingdom and Japan. In some countries, only freshly brewed coffee is acceptable. In the United Kingdom, the market is largely dominated in the domestic sector by instant coffee. Recipes and flavours (e.g. degree of spiciness/hotness) must be market tested in different markets.

Technological innovation – As mentioned above, new methods of cooking (e.g. penetration of combination microwave ovens). In the case of soups, packaging has had some impact with multi-layer plastic packaging being lighter than tins. Innovation is not confined to the specified product but complementary products (e.g. development in 'fresh' coffee makers).

Economic issues – Ready-prepared meals tend to be more expensive and so need international markets with significant segments with high disposable incomes.

Education/training – The issue of literacy levels has been noted above. When novel food products are introduced, it may be essential to educate consumers on how to prepare and serve the product.

Political – Issues of GM foodstuffs has been noted above.

Legal – Legal issues on food content and labelling have been noted above.

Environmental protection – GM issue noted above. The UK aversion to whale meat may, by some, be regarded more as a green issue than a matter of aesthetics. For processed foods, 'excessive' packaging is a factor in countries with high environmental concerns (here the ease of recycling of the packaging may need to be emphasized).

Activity 2.9

Consider that you are in the role of a Marketing Assistant in the Sales Department of a company making medical diagnostic equipment sold to hospitals and clinics (a B2B context). Previously, sales have been restricted to the national market only. However, a 'breakthrough' new product has generated interest from a range of new international customers. Your Managing Director has arranged a meeting to plan for a number of new international clients to come to a series of demonstrations and seminars on the use of the equipment to be held at a local conference centre or hotel (yet to be decided). Your Sales Director has no international experience. You have been asked to write briefing notes for your Sales Director to prepare him/her for the meeting. Prepare these notes.

Case Study

'Fair Trade Coffee'

Consumerism, green issues and corporate social responsibility have become significant issues for consideration by international marketers. Some major fashion brands have had their brand image and value damaged by consumers reacting to past exploitative employment policies in less developed countries. Some major supermarkets are concerned that their fish should be 'sustainably' caught and tuna is 'dolphin friendly'. Organic foods have come out of the cold from being a fad (interesting only to sandal wearing, bearded (only the men!) 'Tree huggers'), to become a significant and growing market sector. Some consumers have become concerned that farmers in less developed countries are not being paid 'fair' prices for commodities such as cocoa, tea and coffee. A sector is growing for 'fair trade' coffee, cocoa, tea, cotton etc. For this case study, we focus on just one commodity: coffee. Consider that you have been appointed by a major co-operative of farmers, located in a developing country, as their international marketing consultant. You have been approached to produce a review of market entry issues. Below is an outline of some selected issues that need to be considered in this context.

Segmentation

In analysis, full development would be needed but two key segments can be identified: B2B (hotel, coffee shops and restaurants) and B2C (home use). Other variables would include type of product required (e.g. instant freeze dried, ready roasted and ground etc.) and flavour strength (e.g. mellow and high roast).

Marketing Mix

As a 'product' only the 4Ps of the 'Product Mix' will be considered.

Product: Differing countries have different tastes in coffee. In the United Kingdom most coffee is 'instant', in other countries fresh ground coffee is preferred. Research would be needed to identify what type of coffee is needed for given national markets (a culture issue). The coffee could not only be 'fair trade', but also 'sustainable' and 'organic'. Would this be perceived as a further benefit by customers?

Price: The production of premium, fair trade and organic coffee will involve extra costs. Can these costs be recovered in a premium price?

Place: Physical distribution for a small operation is likely to be under contract. The nature of target outlets would come from the segmentation analysis.

Promotion: Key stakeholders will include food media, buyers and users. On a limited budget, limited magazine advertising with PR to gain editorial cover about 'coffee to save the world' could be considered.

Market Entry

We are working for a farmers' cooperative and so the coffee will be grown and then exported. However, options exist for processing. The coffee could be processed in the less developed country (providing added value and jobs there) or in the destination market. Given the need to gain more control but with a limited budget, the coffee may have to be marketed by distributors but with some marketing communications support (possibly via marketing agencies).

Not-for-profit and social marketing

Many organizations, such as charities, do not have profit maximization as their key objective but some other non-financial objective (e.g. education or supporting the Arts). Other organizations are not concerned with getting people to buy products but to effect societal changes.

There are two key aspects in not-for-profit marketing for charities:

1. Their major objectives are not monetary but some other parameter that may be more difficult to measure.
2. Charities may often, but not invariably, have social marketing objectives.

Thus, a heritage charity may have as its primary objective the preservation of an historic building (e.g. The National Trust), but also have a secondary objective in changing people's attitude to heritage. However, this does not mean that charities and not-for-profit organizations are not concerned with money – far from it. As the money often comes from charitable donations, these organizations are most concerned that it is used for good purposes. Moreover, when working on limited budgets, cash flow is vital. A charity can just as easily go bankrupt as a commercial organization. Charities are in a competitive marketplace fighting for limited donations and grants. To adapt normal definitions of marketing which talk of 'profit', the marketer needs to substitute the words 'satisfactory financial outcome'.

In this context, a hospital can be considered as an 'ill health' service and what is required is social marketing to change people. In FMCG marketing, we may use the AIDA model to help us move people from unawareness of the product to purchase. In social marketing, we need to consider a slightly different AIDA process (Figure 2.7).

Knowledge developed that drinking impaired driving ability even at low levels of consumption. Advertising and other communications, reinforced by changes in legislation, resulted in action change: only driving after modest consumption of alcohol. The value change is that the concept of drinking at all is not compatible with driving; one simply does one or the other. In this case, the value change battle has been largely won. In the case of speeding, the United Kingdom has still to get off the starting blocks. The weight of evidence is that excessive speed kills, yet more than 1 000 000 are caught doing just this each year! Consider the outrage if 1 000 000 people a year were found over the drink-drive limit.

Figure 2.7 The social marketing process

Social and not-for-profit marketing differ from FMCG marketing. Here are a few examples:

o Issues are more complex.
o There is more public exposure.
o There are sceptical stakeholders.
o There are some novel stakeholders and segmentation variables.
o Negative and uncomfortable messages may be needed.
o Secondary data may be poor or unavailable.

- ◦ Difficult and sensitive subjects are involved.
- ◦ Change of values, not just action, may be the aim.
- ◦ Difficult to modify the mix in many cases.

For the FMCG marketer, the situation is easy, 'eat my brand of chocolate, eat more of it each time and eat it more often'. For a social marketer, the situation is much more complex. All authorities agree that for good health one should eat an appropriate and balanced diet. Then it all breaks down. The Atkins diet has changed eating habits to the extent that sales of bread and pasta are down as people switch to a very high protein diet. However, other authorities claim that whatever the short-term apparent benefits, they may be won at the expense of longer-term health risks. The individual needs a PhD in nutrition to make sense of the competitive claims.

The public exposure and range of sceptical stakeholders issue is a major concern. The traditional response to speeding is to have more speed cameras and more speed traps. 'It is simply an issue of law enforcement; all that is needed is more police and bigger penalties'. At best, this may effect some action change but there are two problems. First that the game becomes 'cat and mouse' ('how can I beat the traps?') and people who would normally be called law abiding become alienated against the law enforcement authorities to the ultimate damage of society. If we take a social marketing view, we need a communications programme (enforcement is an element in this) to move people forward from action change (slow down for a traffic calming hump or a speed camera) to a value change that excessive speed is socially unacceptable behaviour. This argument may not be easy to win for the marketing professional dealing with a sceptical public and the possible traditionalist reactionary element within the law enforcement agencies. This also has an impact on often-limited budgets and an unrealistic expectation of results from people with little experience of marketing (e.g. trustees of a charity).

A special group of stakeholders that are important in this area are volunteers. Many charities would not be able to operate without unpaid workers. In terms of income, a key area is donations, so motivation for giving is a special psycho-demographic segmentation variable of critical importance to charities.

Negative and uncomfortable messages are not easy. 'It is a cold day so I will take the car. One trip will not kill me for lack of exercise or put 10 degrees on global warming.' Yet, the sum of an individual's lack of exercise will damage their health. The actions of millions taking unnecessary car journeys do add to pollution levels.

The difficult nature of the topics can affect the availability of secondary data and make primary research more difficult. Conventional market research might be fine in determining people's attitudes to and use of chewing gum. A social marketer working in the area of substance abuse may have a much more difficult task in gaining data on attitudes to the so-called 'recreational drug' use. However, without understanding the profile of the segment, it is difficult to tailor communications that are relevant and change such people's behaviour and values. Value change is a major additional dimension to social marketing. It is one thing to get a person to switch from a Ford to a Peugeot but another to switch to a green lifestyle and green values and use the car pool or travel by public transport.

In FMCGs, if your target segment does not like some aspect of the product, it is relatively easy to modify the mix (change the pack, modify the flavour, change the style or colour). In some social marketing environments, this is not possible. For instance, nicotine patches or gum are likely to reduce smoking-related diseases, but only if the target users actually give up smoking and suffer some discomfort in the process. Essentially, aspects of the mix are not controlled by the marketer. The biochemistry that makes nicotine addictive is not something that the marketer can change. Ingenuity is required to emphasize other aspects of this product, such as long-term health benefits.

Case study

Safety on the water

You do not need a driving licence to take a boat out and every year rescue services put their lives at risk as the result of people's lack of boating skills and safety awareness. The local water rescue services have approached you to advise on a communication plan to promote safety awareness amongst all users of the water and harbour facilities. Outline three potential communications initiatives. The aim in this context is not to make money but to create awareness and change attitudes to safety on the water and so reduce incidents and loss of life. The stakeholders would include casual users (e.g. holidaymakers on a day fishing trip), regular users (e.g. local sailing clubs etc.), professional users (e.g. local fishermen), local business (e.g. outlets supplying sailing equipment), other safety services (e.g. Police), local politicians (e.g. change in local laws such as speed limits) and the media.

To: Rescue Services Committee

From: CIM Candidate

Date: (exam date)

Communications activities to promote safety awareness

Below are three initiatives that the committee should consider to help develop better safety on the water.

1. Posters: posters around the harbour, beaches and access points to slipways and ferries. These will create awareness to infrequent casual users and remind regular users of the safety issues.
2. Exhibitions and events: a series of exhibitions (e.g. of safety equipment) to be held in local locations such as local yacht clubs. The aim will be to develop awareness and change attitudes to safety on the water with regular users.
3. PR: a series of press releases to the media to create awareness. These could feature the exhibitions discussed above. In addition, these could feature dummy rescues to make the key publics aware of the dangers and change attitudes to water safety.

CIM Candidate

Activity 2.10

Passive smoking has become a hot consumer and health issue. In the European Union, Ireland has followed the direction set by some states in the United States in banning smoking in workplaces (in effect all enclosed public spaces). In some countries, such a full ban is not yet likely but some cities are planning to consider local legislation to ban smoking from all enclosed public places. A local cancer charity has approached you (Ms Smith) for marketing advice on how they might conduct a local campaign in support of a local city ban on smoking in public places. Write a letter (Unit 9) to the group suggesting what they might do. Before starting the initial draft, talk to a few non-smokers and smokers to gain some market feel for how people view the issues.

Marketing Performing Arts and sport

These two areas are service activities and often organizations active in these areas are either Not-for-profit or have extensive not-for-profit objectives. All the comments made in the earlier sections about services and not-for-profit marketing should be taken into account as well. It is helpful when marketing the Performing Arts for, say, a regional theatre to segment the marketing plans into three dimensions: the location, the performance and the stars.

- o The location must be marketed. A key issue is relationship marketing and developing initiatives such as 'Friends of the Theatre' who not only attend performances regularly but also support the theatre with donations and fund-raising events. For international centres, such as the Sydney Opera House, the location must be marketed so no stay in the city is complete without a visit.
- o The performance must be marketed. If there is to be a season of Tchaikovsky ballets, then it is necessary to reach out to both lovers of ballet and the composer in a special segmented communication programme. The implication of this is good database marketing to retrieve targets with special interests.
- o The final element is to market the 'star' quality of the performer(s). The extreme example is popular music concerts, where a major group or star can sell out a major location in a matter of hours. Here the implication is, again, relationship marketing, working in collaboration with the marketers of the group and tour sponsors. Apart from ticket sales, merchandising and sponsorship are often very important income streams.

In marketing terms, sport has many of the characteristics of the Performing Arts. Manchester United is a major international brand. Relationship marketing is key, with the loyalty of football fans being something that most other brand managers in other sectors can only dream about. Again, the location, the sport, the game (e.g. cup final) and, most importantly, the stars must be marketed. Again, relationship marketing is key in maintaining and developing loyalty and in working with a range of partners (e.g. the competing team's marketing group) to achieve the marketing objectives. As with the Arts, sponsorship, TV rights and merchandising are the most important sources of income, far exceeding, for the major clubs, receipts from ticket sales.

Case study

Regional Orchestra

Some years ago, the Sydney Symphony Orchestra was used as the basis for the final Level 3 'maxi' case study. Across the world, regional and national orchestras, opera and ballet companies thrive. In general, they all incorporate the three elements of location, performance and stars. Most have a home base so that the location becomes linked with the company (e.g. 'Royal Opera House home of the Royal Ballet'). Those organizations may have a series of satellite provincial locations for touring productions which become the 'Home of the National Orchestra/Ballet/Ballet in the SouthWest/NorthEast' and so on. The management will ensure a balanced portfolio of performances including popular classics/crossover (cash cows) to support more adventurous productions (question marks and rising stars). To this setting of performances and locations will be added the glittering jewels – conductors and performers of international status – to provide that extra pull for audiences.

There are some similarities in marketing education. The university must be marketed: Oxford and Cambridge are, in their field, just as strong brand names as Manchester United. The course must be marketed (e.g. 'Is there a BSc in Surf Science?') and the research and teaching stars must be marketed. How many Nobel Prize winners does the institution have on the academic staff? The common thread in all these sectors, Arts, Sport and Education, is that one needs not to market a single facet of the product but a number of different facets simultaneously to gain maximum success.

Activity 2.11

It has been reasonably easy to get capital funding for regional arts projects (e.g. museums and theatres) from local councils and charitable funds (e.g. national lottery). However, the business experience after this initial funding has been patchy and some have had to close for lack of sufficient visitors/audiences. In a capital city, the theatre market contains a fair number of 'blockbuster' productions which run for years (the Mousetrap in London has run for half a century!). With many visitors and a local catchment population measured in many millions, it is easy to understand why. A regional theatre may have a local population of a few hundred thousand and just a few thousand visitors a week in the town. To fill the seats, a more complex marketing strategy is needed. Moreover, 'not-for-profit' objectives may come with the charitable capital funding. The capital city has its diverse range of cultural needs satisfied by many theatres and concert halls. The single local theatre/arts centre has to satisfy similar segments in a much smaller overall population. The satisfaction of this diverse range of cultural needs may be part of the 'strings' that come with the charitable funding from local government and charitable sources.

The implication of the differences is that a regional theatre will not survive or satisfy its stakeholder expectations by attempting to run a single 'blockbuster' production all year. A skilled and imaginative, marketing-driven portfolio of productions is required. Consider you are a member of a CIM student group who have been asked to make a presentation to an action committee seeking capital funding for a new regional theatre. Using the 'three threads' model proposed in this exercise, prepare a short presentation on how a regional theatre can succeed in attracting sufficient visitors/audiences. Assume that your contribution will be part of a larger presentation and only 5–10 slides are required. If possible, before you start your preparation have a look at the range of productions in your local area either by looking in the press or by Internet search.

Marketing on a limited budget

Much commercial activity is not undertaken by billion-dollar multinationals, but by a vast number of small enterprises. Many professionals now work as consultants to small partnerships or sole traders. Although the large supermarkets dominate, advertising for many small family firms and shops, craft bakeries and other specialized retail enterprises is widespread. The Internet has added to the communications armoury for these SMEs. From this host of SMEs will emerge the new giants of commerce. Wal-Mart, HP, Microsoft and Body Shop were all SMEs in the not so distant past.

The key issue is the limited budget. A major company may spend much more than £10 000 000 on supporting a brand in a single year. A small family business or consultancy may only have total revenue of the order of £100 000 per annum or less. Such organizations do not usually have a full-time specialist marketing person; they are not able to afford it. Most often, they will have one person, often the owner, with this as one of their responsibilities. If the down side of the issue is the size of the budget, with such a close-knit structure, the fact that all staff are part-time marketers is clearly evident. All elements of marketing are present of course. However, new product development for a craft bakery would be trying out a few new recipes or copying successful products from multinationals – no large R&D laboratory here. Pricing issues will be the same, keeping costs down and creating value for enough customers to be profitable. Distribution is likely to be a local delivery service or contracted out to a supplier (e.g. possibly simply the Royal Mail). For service businesses, such as a small graphic design consultancy, all the normal rules for the service extension apply without the possibility of spending many thousands of pounds on re-fitting and decorating the offices. Two areas need special attention for SMEs: marketing research and communications.

All the elements of the MkIS are present in the small organization and database management in a simple form can also be present. Access databases or Excel spreadsheets (e.g. selective retrieval) can analyse sales and provide output for sales mail shots. However, with a single modest survey costing many thousands of pounds, formal market research is likely to be replaced with less formal approaches such as market intelligence by tracking trends with secondary data, rather than necessarily leading them. If the problem is lack of budget, the advantage is that it is likely that all employees are close to the customer and reflecting on what works and what is less successful can provide key feedback. With a small organization, flexibility is a key advantage. With good 'market-feel' from close contact with customers and skilful use of secondary data sources, an alert SME can achieve much on a relatively limited budget.

In general, mass advertising and similar communications are very expensive and even the local paper may be out of reach for a sensible campaign for a small organization. In the B2B sector (e.g. design consultancy), building up networks and call lists is key. For a small business such as a restaurant or hair salon, word of mouth may be key to building up a loyal and profitable customer base. For companies making specialist products of relatively high value and shelf life, the Internet can be invaluable. The rule here is KISS: keep it sweet and simple (an alternative is 'Keep it simple, Stupid'). On a budget of hundreds, rather than thousands of pounds you are not able to rival IBM's website! Given the very high costs of commercial printing, the advent of low-cost, good-quality colour printers has been an advantage. The set-up cost for a simple colour brochure could be a few thousand pounds which is clearly uneconomic for the small consultancy. It may, of course, be appropriate for a small regional tourist attraction where it may be one of the key mechanisms of communication distributed from hotels and other such locations. Even if the cost of colour printing is rather expensive, the cost of a CD is now pence and these can provide an effective media for business consultancies or small training partnerships. If advertising is too expensive, there is still room for clever publicity. A few mentions in the glossy fashion magazines can make a restaurant the trendiest place to go. Selective use of exhibitions and directories can be appropriate. Collaboration with other small organizations may give critical mass for more expensive communications initiatives (e.g. a group of farmers running a farmers' market may be able to afford local radio spots). Posters can be cost-effective and for the right product/audience local cinema (e.g. cinema audiences tend to be younger) may be cost-effective.

In the exam situation, the case study will often be based in a context, which implies a limited budget. It is essential in marketing communications on a limited budget to take account of three key points:

1. On a limited budget, mass advertising on peak national TV is not going to be possible.
2. With limited budgets, selectivity in the allocation of the budget is essential, for example spreading the budget to buy half a column centimetre in 20 magazines is not going to work. Some practical selectivity is required (see Unit 6). Good answers demonstrate this selectivity with justification.
3. With limited budgets, ways of levering the budget need to be explored: for example, strategic PR with well-aimed press releases can gain media cover.

Case Study

'The Urban Culture Festival 2006' (December 2005)

'The Urban Culture Festival 2006' was the case study in December 2005. A key aspect of this case study is that the marketing communications budget would be limited (this was also true in the 'SMS Cars Ltd' case study in June 2006). In this case, the communications strategy is not 'Mass national TV and press advertising to create awareness.' Limited advertising would be possible in local media and strategically placed posters. Joint promotion would be a useful way of stretching a limited budget (e.g. with the local cinema for the film festival). However, given the 'arts and culture' nature and visiting artists, it should be possible to gain favourable cover in the media (press, radio and TV). The 'Eden Project', a major international visitor attraction in the South West of the United Kingdom, uses this type of strategy to build its brand and uses a very modest amount of direct advertising expenditure. A key communications tool is the website; it does not cost a vast amount to set up an adequate site. Other marketing communications can direct people to the full information on the website. Even on a limited budget, creative approaches can yield good results.

Information and Communications Technology (ICT)

The second half of the twentieth century could be described as the emergence of the digital age. The start of the twenty-first century can be considered as the convergent wireless age. The laptop computer has now become an entertainment and communications centre, just as mobile phones have become media devices with cameras, music and video playback capabilities. Wireless communications can be effected via high-speed, wireless Internet 'hot spots' and 3G mobile phone networks. The TV satellite decoder or other types of 'set-top box' are now commonly equipped with two-way data communication via a telephone modem or direct Internet connection for e-mail or online shopping. The increasing penetration of broadband Internet services into the home enable a multitude of interactive services, such as video on demand, low-cost telephony (VoIP) or group video games across continents. Several communications technologies may be used to provide data links. For example, Internet radio stations broadcast their programmes by making MP3 recordings available for download from file server. The MP3 file could be transferred to another continent over the Internet via a chain of different communications systems, each one using its own unique complex system to a local wireless hotspot, where a customer is able to listen to the programme on their pocket PC, using some Bluetooth stereo headphones. Another user may be listening to exactly the same programme elsewhere, but on a mobile phone, where the final leg of the transfer takes place over a 3G network. Many complex network technologies are in use here (even in the Bluetooth headphones), but the complexity is masked from the user so they enjoy a simple, seamless experience.

Voice over Internet Protocol (VoIP) provides a way to make telephone calls via your PC to another PC or even cross over to traditional telephone networks at no (or low) cost. Internet companies are increasingly offering telephony services and traditional telephone companies are bundling a whole range of new Internet offerings alongside traditional 'landline' services that may well be entering their PLC decline phase. For example, British Telecom's 'Fusion' service combines a 'landline' with a mobile phone, wireless Internet provision and a Bluetooth router. Aside from the usual telephone service and wireless Internet in the home, the Fusion product allows a customer to use their special Bluetooth equipped mobile phone in the home to make low-cost VoIP calls, reverting to the conventional GSM network when out of the house.

Companies such as e-Bay have invented new ways of conducting business. This is particularly important for small and sole trading enterprises that now can bring their goods and services to a global market. Digital downloads of music and video offer entirely new ways for new emerging bands to find an audience outside the traditional record companies. The year 2006 may become recognized as when the dot-com revolution came of age. A key factor is that critical mass has now been achieved in Internet access in most of the developed world, much of this via broadband. Linked to this is low-cost computing with powerful software packages such as Access and Excel which bring relatively sophisticated techniques such as database mailing within the economic capability of the smallest organization. Information and communications technologies are converging. This allows organizations to not only do existing tasks better, but also do business in completely new ways, for example the London congestion charging system is wholly dependant on these advanced convergent technologies.

Information and Communications Technology was featured in the June 2006 CIM case study 'SMS Cars Ltd' Question 7 'Produce a short report to be circulated to Department Managers which explains how ICT can enhance the marketing mix (product, price, place and promotion) to generate sales and encourage customer loyalty to all departments of SMS Cars Ltd.'

Question 2.1

In Unit 1 with Activity 1.8, we began the preliminary analysis of a new case study situation (Lake View Organic Farms). In Questions 1.1 and 1.2, two recent exam case studies ('The Urban Culture Festival 2006' and 'SMS Cars Ltd') were considered. In this unit, we have considered some of the various contexts and flavours of marketing (e.g. B2B and consumer). In the preliminary analysis of a case study, integrative assignment or exam question it is essential to develop the content recognizing what is 'special' and 'different' in the situation. For the above three case studies, what do you think are the contextual issues to be noted?

Summary

In this unit, we have

o Seen how several special environmental forces such as consumerism and green issues have made sufficient impact on marketing for specific theory to be developed to address society's concerns.

o Appreciated that marketing, as with Mathematics has no ethics. However, society expects marketers to develop marketing mixes and plans that are acceptable to society.

o Explored the developments in some selected aspects of marketing theory with an introduction to relationship marketing, internal marketing and the marketing of services.

o Considered how the marketing mix needs adaptation within specific contexts.

o Considered a number of different contexts of marketing such as consumer, B2B, international, not-for-profit, social and small budget marketing.

o Reviewed the approaches to marketing, performing arts and sports.

o Considered how the international environment impacts on marketing activities.

Further study

Dibb, S., Simkin, L., Pride, W. and Ferrell, O. (2006) *Marketing Concepts and Strategies*, 5th European edition, Houghton Mifflin Chapters 3–5, 13, 22 and 25.

Hints and tips

The CIM examinations take questions and case studies from all areas of marketing and so it is essential to be able to consider not-for-profit and service and the like case studies as well as more traditional product-based contexts.

Bibliography

Douglas Hoffman, K. and Bateson John, E.G (1997) *Essentials of Services Marketing*, The Dryden Press.

Ginter, P., Swayne, L. and Duncan, W. (2005) *Strategic Management of Health Care Organizations*, 5th edition, Blackwell Publishing.

Gummesson, E. (2002) *Total Relationship Marketing – Rethinking Marketing Management*, Butterworth-Heinemann.

Hutt, M.D., Speh, T.W. (2006) *Business Marketing Management*, 9th edition, Thomson South-Western.

Jeannet, J. (2004) *Global Marketing Strategies*, 6th edition, Houghton Mifflin.

Kotler, P., and Andreasen, A. (2002) *Strategic Marketing for Nonprofit Organizations*, 6th edition, Prentice Hall.

Kotler, P., and Scheff, J. (1997) *Standing Room Only – Strategies for Marketing the Performing Arts*, Harvard Business School Press.

Sargeant, A. (2004) *Marketing Management for Nonprofit Organizations*, Oxford University Press.

unit 3

the integrated marketing mix: product

Learning objectives

By the end of this unit you will

- Understand the product life cycle (PLC) concept and the need for a balanced portfolio using Boston (BCG) matrix concepts.

- Understand the different levels of product.

- Be able to use a structured approach to analyse product benefits.

- Understand the process of new product development.

- Appreciate the role of branding in adding to product value.

- Set the product mix element in the context of an integrated marketing mix.

- Understand the need for adaptation in the international context.

Syllabus references

2.1 Describe the structure and roles of the marketing function within the organization.

2.2 Build and develop relationships within the marketing department, working effectively with others.

2.5 Explain the supplier interface: negotiating, collaborating, operational and contractual aspects.

2.6 Explain how the organization fits into a supply chain and works with distribution channels.

3.3 Demonstrate an awareness of successful applications of marketing across a variety of sectors and sizes of business.

4.6 Describe how organizations monitor product trends.

4.7   Explain the importance of the extended marketing mix: how process, physical aspects and people affect customer choice.

5.5   Make recommendations on alternative courses of action.

5.6   Examine the correlation between marketing mix decisions and results.

Key definitions

Augmented product – The augmented products are those aspects or elements of a product that add value to and improve or support the core and actual features (e.g. customer service) after-sales service and delivery.

Boston (BCG) matrix for products – A portfolio model used in order to select markets on the basis of market share and market growth.

Cash cow – Cash cows are products that have developed a high market share in a mature market. They deserve the company's full attention, as the revenue can be invested in newer market areas with high growth potential.

Complementary products – Many products are part of a system and can only be utilized with other products, equipment and so on, for example pre-recorded DVDs are essential to the enjoyment of an entertainment centre but are not usually made by the same company and are purchased separately often from completely different outlets.

Core benefit – The main benefit that a product provides for the user, using the example of a car this would be 'transport'.

Decline – A phase of PLC where consumer preferences may have changed or innovative new products may have displaced existing products.

Dogs – A cell in the BCG matrix. Dogs (products) show no growth and have relatively low market share. Although they may not be a drain on the company's resources, they are unable to make a positive contribution to profits.

Environmental/Life cycle – Not to be confused with product life cycle. Analysis of the environmental impact of the product from cradle to grave (manufacture, distribution, use, disposal and recycling).

Expected product – This is the level and quality of product attributes that the buyers normally accept and agree to when they purchase the product. When they exceed the buyers' expectations, we have satisfied customers; when they do not we have dissatisfied customers.

Feature attributes – These are the features that make up the product. Using the example of a car, this could be low-profile tyres, powerful engine, aerodynamic design and quality of construction materials.

Growth – A phase in the PLC. This is where most products enter the market and there is less product distinctiveness. Rising sales generally mean more profitable returns at this stage.

Intangible benefits – Benefits that cannot be measured (e.g. love, security, passion etc.) that a user may gain from the product or service. For example, mobile phones can create a sense of security for the lone female traveller.

Introduction – A phase in the PLC. This is when a new product is launched and the goal at this stage is to create awareness and communicate the product's benefits to the consumers.

Limited life cycle – Some products are only launched for a season (e.g. 'Olympic Games 2004' sweatshirt).

Maturity – A phase in the PLC. This is where most products are situated. Profitability carries on growing but at a reduced rate.

Potential product – This form of the product is the 'potential product' which encompasses all the augmentations and transformations that the product might ultimately undergo in the future. These could be future improvements that might keep the product competitive within the market.

Question marks – A cell in the BCG matrix. These can cause problems for management. While market growth prospects are good, they have a relatively low market share. Substantial investment may be needed to increase their market share and increase profitability. 'Question mark' is called 'Problem Child' in some texts.

Range and depth – The range is the number of product types; hence Ford makes a whole range of cars from small town run-arounds to off-road 4 × 4s. The depth is the variety within each individual type or range; so with cars they might include automatic versions, diesel engine option, colour, paint finish and so on.

Rejuvenation – After a number of years on the market, a product (e.g. an existing model of car) might be re-thought and updated using a facelift and re-launch (e.g. VW Beetle re-launch).

Signal attributes – These are the properties of the product that convey the message that it has other qualities that the buyer or consumer considers desirable.

Stars – A cell in the BCG matrix. Stars are those products that have a promising future. Significant investments of cash are required to develop their full potential. If managed properly, they will develop into a valuable source of revenue as the market evolves.

Tangible benefits – These are measurable benefits the user gains from the ownership or use of the product or service.

Study Guide

Satisfying consumers' needs and wants by providing a well-designed benefit package generates profits. One may regard product as the diamond in the setting of the integrated marketing mix to create the irresistible marketing jewel. The word product is used for convenience but should be taken to embrace the entire product–service continuum. In this unit, we consider the nature of product and explore tools to analyse existing products in order to improve them. These same tools can also be used as a framework for defining the product needs of target market segments in the new product development process. Branding is important for many products and approaches to branding are outlined. Packaging is a support to branding and also has other roles in contributing to customer satisfaction. An overview of packaging functions is given in this unit.

There are a number of activities in this unit to help you build an understanding of the models and develop skills and depth of insight. For products, the best laboratory and library is the marketplace. The more products and services you analyse, the greater will become your understanding of the concepts.

Product life cycle and the product portfolio

Products do not go on forever, they have a life and go through stages (Figure 3.1): the PLC. In the standard PLC, products go through an introductory phase then, if successful, grow. Here, care must be taken; people can think that growth will continue forever. It does not; the market becomes saturated and the product enters the maturity phase. The product then declines and may become totally obsolete, unmarketable and unavailable (e.g. by the end of the decade old analogue TVs will no longer work, the only signals that will be available will be digital).

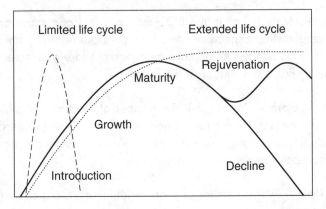

Figure 3.1 The product life cycle

A particular problem faces the manufacturers of classic fragrance brands. There are fashion trends in fragrances and younger consumers may find an established classic fragrance not to their taste. However, just changing the existing product could alienate the existing, still loyal users. The solution is to launch a variant but maintain the brand values. 'Poison' now has 'Tender Poison'. Such brands can also be rejuvenated with limited life products available for a restricted period only (e.g. Jean-Paul Gaultier Summer Fragrance). Coke faced a similar problem as people moved into healthier drinking. Now 'Diet Coke' is out selling 'classic Coke' in the United Kingdom.

However, this outcome is not always inevitable. Some products appear to go on forever. Chanel No. 5 is 80 years young and remains among the top ten selling perfumes in the twenty-first century. This is not an accident; Yardley with English Lavender went out of business after over 100 years in the fragrance industry; they had not appropriately rejuvenated the brand. Chanel's success is built on exemplary marketing. The brand, as well as the individual fragrances, is supported at all times. Every few years, the product is re-launched with contemporary imagery and it exudes timeless elegance. Some products appear to have an almost infinite life cycle, such as tea. We may switch from loose tea leaves to bags, but people still drink tea. This is in contrast to some other products where the life cycle can be measured in months. Computer games are an example of a very turbulent market with many new introductions, but by the end of the year today's top game will be in the bargain bin (limited life cycle). Again, the brand may possibly be rejuvenated by the re-launching of a modified product (e.g. Tomb Raider II). Sometimes a product may decline in the major market yet find an extended life cycle in a specialist sector. The traditional vinyl record has predominantly been replaced by digital technology, except in the nightclub, where DJs still find vinyl the medium of choice.

The PLC is a useful concept, but just as with segmentation its application needs imaginative analysis of market situations. During the introduction phase, competition may be lighter as the product is new. Heavy marketing communications will be needed to support the launch, creating awareness. In this phase, both profits and cash flows are negative.

During market growth, some competition may emerge, but as the market is growing this may not be too damaging. The marketing communications effort may still be high but as there are higher sales volumes, the product should become profitable. However, cash flow may still be an issue, as with increasing volumes, increased funds will be needed to finance stock and work-in-progress. Strong profits do not always result in a positive cash flow if the business is hungry for new working capital; this is a major problem for young growing companies. At maturity, there may be more competition and profit margins may start to come under pressure, but with the stock-build phase complete, little additional working capital will be required and so the result should be a healthy cash flow. During the decline phase, there is even more competition and profit margins may be under even greater pressure. However, if the decline is properly managed (i.e. no obsolete stock write-off) then working capital can be recovered and there should be some cash freed up to support new products.

The implication of PLC theory is that a major brand will need a succession of new products to replace those which are declining. The BCG Matrix concept provides a useful framework to consider the portfolio of products (Figure 3.2). The axes of the matrix are market growth per year as a percentage and relative market share for the product under consideration. The four quadrants of the matrix are then

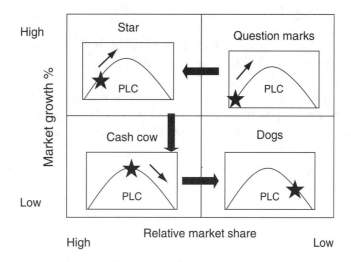

Figure 3.2 Adapted Boston (BCG) Matrix for products

1. High growth and low market share (often a PLC introduction situation), a question mark
2. High growth and high market share (PLC growth situation), a rising star
3. Low growth and high market share (PLC maturity situation), a cash cow
4. Low growth and low market share (PLC decline situation), a dead dog.

The pattern of the BCG matrix reflects the issues in PLC analysis. As with PLC analysis, the model should be used with care. Both market growth and market share depend on making the right judgement regarding segmenting the market. Ferrari are not in competition with the Ford Ka so, in considering a BCG analysis for Ferrari, the appropriate segment is not the car market but the luxury sports car market. It is *relative market share* that is used in the matrix not market share. To calculate relative market share, you take your own market share and divide it by the strongest competitor in the market segment (i.e. the competitor with the highest market share). If you are new or weak in the market (introduction or decline sectors), the strongest competitor will have a greater share and the relative market share is less than one. If we have achieved a strong position as a market leader (growth and cash cow segments), we have the largest market share and the nearest competitor has a lower market share so the figure is greater than one. Setting aside the detailed arithmetic, the message from both PLC and BCG analysis is that a healthy organization needs a balanced portfolio of products; a firm with a simple collection of cash cows might look profitable on paper but may be out of business in 5 years' time. Polaroid cameras had difficulty in balancing their portfolio when the introduction of digital cameras sent their core technology into decline. Kodak and other major companies had to move quickly to embrace the new technologies, moving from analogue imaging (films) to mega-pixel digital imaging. The high ground of their new technology became the conversion of digital images to high-quality, fade-resistant digital prints.

Activity 3.1

For the past 25 years, the video cassette recorder has been an indispensable piece of electrical equipment for TV viewers around the globe. However, in early 2005, Britain's largest electrical retailer, Dixons, announced that they would no longer sell video cassette recorders, instead concentrating on DVD players and recorders. A half-century of cathode ray tubes in TVs is rapidly coming to an end with new, flat screen plasma and LCD technologies.

In the United Kingdom, Digital Terrestrial television has already been widely adopted. The government plans to completely phase out old analogue TV transmissions between 2007 and 2012, making most existing UK TV receivers redundant, unless new digital adapters known as a 'set-top box' are used.

The BBC has already demonstrated a High-Definition TV service (HDTV) and is considering making it widely available via the emerging digital network.

Visit an electrical retailer in person or via the Internet and analyse the products on view. Using a standard PLC framework, such as shown in Figure 3.1, complete an analysis of domestic TV/video equipment for the period 2000–2015 in the market (2000–2007 as historical; 2007–2015 as your projection).

The architecture of product

In Unit 1, the need to segment and target markets was introduced. The financial needs of a student are different to those of someone buying a house and yet again different to those of the 'grey' market, the retired. A large bank will have all these segments in its customer base and will need to devise appropriate offerings for each of them or lose profitable business. However, it is not just the products that need to be adapted, but the whole marketing mix. For example, if we select just one element of the mix 'Place' (convenience): for the young professional working out of hours, access to services may be key (online banking could be a solution). For the less mobile retired client, local access may be more relevant. This may be the physical presence of a small local branch or possibly online banking as well. However, with online banking, the message to the professional is 'services when you need them' and for the retired 'all your financial services from the comfort of your own home'. Thus, it is not sufficient to devise a product and then tag on the other elements of the mix as an afterthought. It is the complete mix that is experienced by each customer. Therefore, each element of the mix needs detailed consideration whilst ensuring a seamless proposition to the target segments when they are brought together – a totally integrated marketing mix.

The augmented product

In marketing a product, more often than not, we do not market the core benefits. These are 'hygiene' properties. If we go to a hotel and find the toilets clean and well kept, we do not rush to reception to heap praise upon the management. If we find the reverse and the facilities are dirty and neglected, we will inform the management and possibly check out and tell all our friends. In a hotel advertisement, you will not see the message 'all of our rooms contain beds'. These core benefits are taken as read, but it is with the higher levels of service/product that we gain the business. This facet of product can be linked in the broadest sense to the general concepts, researched in other contexts, advanced by Maslow (Hierarchy of Needs) and Hertzberg in their motivation theories.

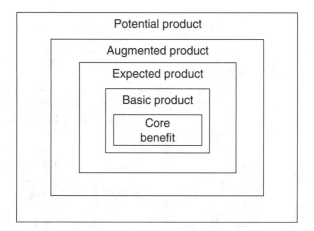

Figure 3.3 Levels of product
Source: Adapted from Kotler (2000)

Figure 3.3 shows the customer value hierarchy framework. At the lower levels, customers are provided with what they expect; all providers must supply this or they gain no business at all. To gain a competitive edge, one must provide something of benefit value to the customer above and beyond the expected benefit set. This target is not static since customers' expectations grow; what delighted them 5 years ago is now taken for granted (e.g. in business hotels 5 years ago Internet access in all rooms would have been an 'extra', now it is expected). The ultimate product is that which satisfies the dream needs of the customer. People do not want detergents; the ultimate product would be self-cleaning clothes that never needed ironing. The core benefit of a car is travel but people expect comfort not just a seat on a chassis. Today, cars are providing an ever-increasing number of electronic features (cruise control, global positioning systems and in-car entertainment systems). The ultimate potential product will be the car that provides total comfort and drives itself.

Pilkington, innovators in glass manufacture

The ideal window glass would never need cleaning. Pilkington have devised a glass with a built-in detergent in the surface of the glass that allows the rain to 'wet' the glass and wash off the dirt. Thus, the customers' desire for a no care product has been translated, by technological innovation, into a commercial reality. We have moved from something basic (that lets some light in but keeps out the rain) to a low-maintenance, high-quality optical product. The ultimate product will be 'intelligent' windows. Moves in this direction are under active development. Boeing's plans for the proposed 'Dreamliner' new airliner will eliminate pull-down shades. The windows will have 'electro-chromatic' controls that will change the tint of the pane from clear to opaque.

Firms need a model that enables them to bridge the gap between marketing and technology. 'Geek-driven' technical ego trip products are likely to only appeal to a minority. Equally well, that wonderful marketing concept is not likely to be a success if it costs ten times more to manufacture than people are prepared to pay. Affordable products are needed which provide value, with benefits that surprise and delight the target customers more than the competitions' ranges. The Plymouth model of attribute analysis provides such a framework (Figure 3.4). Before this analysis is completed, the segmentation and targeting process covered in Unit 1 must have been completed with the development of the relevant segment profiles.

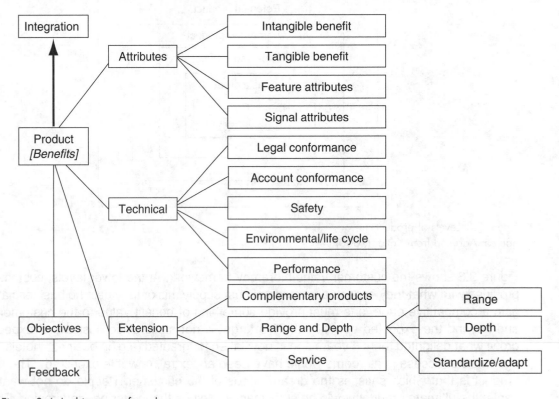

Figure 3.4 Architecture of product

Attributes
Intangible

The most important aspects of our life are not tangible. You may not have 10 kilos of love or 3 metres of security. A glass of water or a can of cola will both satisfy thirst, Coca-Cola claims more. In marketing, we need to move into the areas of intangible benefits; for a natural fruit juice, the intangible proposition may be well-being. For a young man, a car may be considered in some ways to be a sporty fashion accessory. For the young female, the proposition may be more of freedom and assertiveness (e.g. Punto) with style. Thus, for distinct target groups, the same product may satisfy different intangible benefits. The identification of key intangible benefits is part of the detailed profiling of the segments, tailoring the product and the communication of these intangible benefits is an element of the positioning statement for the product offering. One might describe these characteristics as the psychological benefits of the product.

Tangible benefits

To supply the intangible benefits it is necessary to provide tangible benefits. For a car, part of the intangible benefits may be well-being and comfort. Part of this will be keeping engine noise low and maintaining the temperature within a comfort zone (e.g. 20–25°C). These are the physical benefits provided by the product, needed to support the above psychological benefits.

Feature attributes

Having decided what physical benefits are needed, it is then over to the technical research and development (R&D) team to explore technology to find cost-effective, innovative solutions. For a car to be used in tropical climates, the solution may be energy reflective glass (to minimize solar heating of the interior) coupled with a good air conditioning system. For winter use in Siberia, the solution will be a good heater. The delivery of the same intangible and tangible benefits may need different features depending on the conditions of use of the product.

Signal attributes

This area needs collaboration between the marketers, technical staff and designers. A mobile telephone is not simply a hunk of technology; it is also a fashion accessory. A TV is not only a device for viewing moving images, but also a statement of lifestyle through interior design. Products are not silent and passive; they are a powerful means of communication. We see the advertisement a few times; we live with the product! The ability of the product to communicate is explicitly recognized by this aspect of the model. It may be the design for a camera, the packaging for a drink and a fragrance for a hair conditioner. Design and other creative staff must work with marketing to communicate (signal) the features, tangible and intangible benefits of the product. A mobile phone or a watch are, in technical terms, rather un-inspiring sets of microchips (one looks very much like another, give or take a few electrical contacts). Stylish design must be added to functionality to succeed in these fashion-driven markets. Clearly, branding is part of this process and brand quality and values are indicated by aspects such as packaging and design.

Technical
Legal conformance

It is not acceptable to make products that are illegal. What this actually implies varies from product to product and from market to market. Beef reared with hormone growth-regulators may be legal and acceptable in the United States but not necessarily in Europe. This is a complex and highly technical area and even an apparently simple issue such as labelling a fruit drink may need expert advice (orange drink, orange juice drink or fresh orange juice may all have different legal interpretations).

Account conformance

Very often, some B2B customers may have requirements that are over and above any legal requirements. The Body Shop is concerned about the acceptability of animal products and animal testing procedures in product development; these were not legal requirements but nevertheless demanded by that business. Often the major retailers may take a market-driven view about issues (e.g. green packaging) that is responding to the ultimate customer demands, but not yet enacted in law. Breach these requirements and you do not have a saleable product.

Safety

Major aspects of safety may be encoded in legislation (e.g. food quality). However, there is no such thing as absolute safety and all products and their use contain some element of risk. This may not only cover the legitimate use of the product but the potential abuse of the product.

A manufacturer of a product which uses an organic solvent may re-formulate to a water-based product to lower risks to normal users and prevent potential abuse by 'glue sniffers'.

Environmental life cycle

This has been covered in the section on Green Marketing in Unit 2. Clearly for all products, an environmental life cycle impact analysis should be completed.

Performance

Some properties of products are easy to measure. The weight of sugar in a packet or the volume of drink in a bottle is easy to measure. However, with an artificial sweetener the claim may be '400 times as sweet as sugar'. This is not a parameter that is easy to measure with an instrument. It is easy to show that mercury is much denser than water; that is a physical property. Sweetness is a sensation and we do not have a sweetness test meter. It is essential to be able to demonstrate a claim which is to be used in marketing communications. Whenever we are devising a product to satisfy tangible benefits, we need some technical framework to estimate the 'benefits' parameter. For flavour and fragranced products, this will often involve the use of trained panels of assessors (e.g. tea tasters).

Product extension

To use many products, we need other products or services. We must take a systems view of the product.

Complementary products

These are products needed to use the product but not made by the manufacturer of the product. To use a car, you need fuel. There is no point in building vehicles with catalytic converters, if the only fuel available contains materials that damage the catalyst. Engines do not run without coolants and lubricating oils. Washing machines do not run without detergents and fabric conditioners. The user does not care if the poor performance is due to poor design of the car or poor quality of fuel. They do not get the performance and so both brands get blamed. When developing a new product, collaboration with suppliers of the complementary products is necessary. This is yet another example of relationship marketing in action.

Product range and depth

The range is the variety of offerings, so a major supermarket has a very wide range. A specialist shoe outlet may have a great depth of special offerings (e.g. different width fittings) and brands within a restricted range (just shoes). M&S markets a wide range of products including shoes. However, they all fall under the M&S brand. Other supermarkets with a wide range of product types such as ASDA may also have their own brand (e.g. George at ASDA), and also market a range of leading brands. Thus, in the marketing of a single product group (e.g. shoes), vastly different strategies can all be seen operating.

Service

The product–service continuum was outlined in Unit 2. A car without the facilities to service it is not going to be of much use. The manufacturer of kitchen equipment may find that a good quality installation service is not only an additional source of profits, but also gives a competitive advantage.

International dimensions – standardize or adapt

Many consumer products, such as food, are subject to a rich variety of environmental influences such as legislation (any issue in the macro/microenvironment may be important in a given circumstance). For example, culture can greatly affect tastes and preferences; often a significant product modification may be required.

For more technical items, such as microchips, or commodity products, such as sugar, it may well be appropriate to market a standardized product (even if the packaging has to be adapted). The more the product mix can be standardized, the more economies of scale may be gained. This is potentially at the cost of a less acceptable product; a balancing act is required to ensure that the offering is fully acceptable to the market but that the adaptations do not price the product out of the market.

Objectives

Objectives may be needed for any element of the product model, for example, to alter product features to comply with forthcoming legislation on recyclability. To increase acceptability in the marketplace, service may have to be improved. During the planning period, the marketer needs to consider what may be left unchanged and what must be adapted to maintain profitable exploitation of the product.

Feedback

Objectives are of no value without feedback; appropriate information must be collected through the MkIS to evaluate the degree to which objectives have been achieved. The information may be quantitative, such as the number of units sold. Qualitative information must also be gathered to provide colour and depth to the picture; if the number of units sold is down, is this because the product is losing its appeal and needs redesigning?

Earlier in this unit, the need for a balanced portfolio was discussed. The Plymouth model gives a framework for translating a marketing definition of a product in customer benefit terms into a technical brief for the research, development and design team. In the next section, the process of new product development is presented. Without a continual stream of new products, an organization will stagnate and eventually fade away.

Case study

'Lake View Organic Farms: product analysis for the "Veggie Box" '

The market segment may be defined as people who care what they eat ('you are what you eat' factor) and are prepared to pay a premium price for a premium product (with the convenience of delivery). The product positioning is the opposite of 'It looks good. Don't worry what it tastes like. Who cares about the vitamin content?'

Attribute analysis

Intangible benefits – Well-being, healthiness, feel-good 'green' factor.

Tangible benefits – More nutritious products. There is some evidence to suggest that heavily processed vegetables and fruits may suffer loss of vitamins in processing and long storage. Good cooking and eating.

Feature attributes – Fresh products, 'unprocessed', and free from preservatives and pesticides.

Signal attributes – Products come entire (e.g. carrots with mud and leaves) to show that they have not been heavily processed, organic packaging that can be reused and/or recycled (e.g. collapsible cardboard boxes that can make several trips and then they are composted).

Technical – Key area. The definition of what is an 'organic' product is complicated (Soil Association rules and testing).

Legal conformance – Conformance to the Soil Association rules to ensure that product claims can be substantiated (e.g. trading standards and/or Advertising Standards Authority).

Account conformance – Not applicable for direct sales to domestic customers. Remember, do not over-work a model. In some cases, a particular element will not be a major issue.

Safety – Critical as a food product. This issue is considered further, in the section on new product development, later in this unit.

Environmental cycle – Organic grown and no heavy processing. However, distribution may be a problem, a horse and cart might look good but not practical. 'Lake View Organic Farms' might ensure that all fleet vehicles were converted to run on 'bio-diesel'. The packaging, as discussed above, could be reusable and/or recyclable. Non-edible material (e.g. carrot leaves) can be composted.

Performance – Proof of the product is in the cooking and eating. Kitchen trials and taste panels essential as 'a great natural flavour' is an important selling proposition.

Extension

Complementary products – Cooking equipment for healthy cooking such as steamers and woks could be part of the offering (product mix) alongside the food products. Compost bins for composting leaves and peelings. A possibility of a link to a supplier?

Range and depth – Range of boxes and depth of different fruit and vegetables offered, for example, different exciting 'rare' varieties. Products selected for flavour and nutritional value, not for appearance and yield. Could also offer non-fresh organic products (e.g. organic jam).

Service – The delivery service part of the package. Advice on composting. Run 'cook-in' sessions, in the development kitchens, to teach customers how to prepare unusual vegetables. This could link in with relationship-marketing communications activities.

Activity 3.2

The next time you use a washing machine complete a full analysis using the Plymouth model. Then, using the Kotler concepts of augmented and potential product, decide what improvements you might be asking R&D to build into the next generation of washing machines. Build these improvements into your model. Remember before you start to formally use the Plymouth model you need to consider the segmentation and targeting issues.

New product development process

The clear implication of PLC theory and the BCG matrix is that an organization needs to maintain a balanced portfolio. As products slide into decline, there must be a flow of new products to replace them. Although in this section, we shall, for the sake of convenience, talk about new product development, in reality it is the total mix offering that has to be developed. If we are unable to deliver the product at the right price and communicate the benefits, we do not have a product. It is the total integrated mix that has to be developed.

Kotler's eight-stage new product development process is shown in Figure 3.5. As products go through the screening process, some will be eliminated and so, for every hundred ideas originally considered, only one or two may be finally commercialized. It is important that each stage of the process is conducted as well as possible. Generating ideas is not cost-free but the sums are relatively modest. The cost of a failed launch is high. The Persil Power disaster cost more than £100 million when a detergent that not only washed the clothes but also destroyed them entered full commercialization.

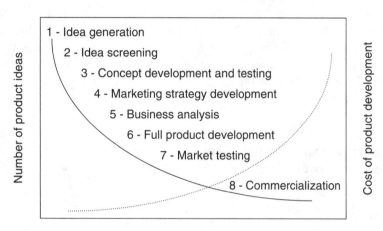

Figure 3.5 Stages in the new product development process

Idea generation

Creative ideas may not be limited to the formal R&D team; the organization should capture ideas from whatever source and evaluate them. A key consideration at this stage is not only to estimate the value of the invention, but also its protection. Microsoft's market value is not in physical objects, but in the ownership of the copyright to computer programmes. Increasingly, in post-industrial society, intellectual property (brands, patents, copyright, design rights etc.) is a key asset. Customers and channel feedback (even customer complaints) can provide insight into how to meet new customers' uses with better products. When all else fails, one can learn from the competition. Supermarkets own brands are rarely innovative but good quality 'me-too' cover versions of the brand leaders. Suppliers can be a great source of new concepts possibly linked with technological development. A manufacturer who develops a super high-speed, high-powered graphics card will work hand in hand with computer games designers to exploit the power of the new capabilities, creating a superb visual experience for the user. The continual assessment of the marketing environment can identify an evolving trend and a product hole that needs to be filled with a new offering. Problem solving does not only lead to a product that solves the problem, but also generates a platform for other product developments. Earlier we noted the Internet was originally conceived as a nuclear attack-resistant communications system, but has now evolved into a worldwide information superhighway.

Case Study

'The Urban Culture Festival 2006' – New Ideas (December 2005)

'The Urban Culture Festival 2006' was the case study in December 2005. With more and more festivals, the market is becoming more crowded and more competitive. Only high quality (in the perceptions of customers) and innovative festivals will survive and flourish in the long term. How could new ideas be generated for the 2007 festival?

The present festival involves a rich variety of local organizations, each of these could be asked for their suggestions for new events. Internet research on developments in other festivals would provide evidence for new successful themes. This need not be restricted to local festivals but to festivals in other countries. The festival attracts international artists and their views should be canvassed. The media could be approached for suggestions and sponsorship (e.g. BBC World service with its programmes on 'World Music'). Feedback sheets could be provided for customers at events such as the 'Film Festival' and include a question on suggestions for new events.

Each situation needs an innovative approach to the specific context. The 'fit all' answer 'Conduct secondary research and then follow with primary research (questionnaires and focus groups).' is not an appropriate exam answer.

Idea screening

This is a difficult area with two potential opportunities for error. The first is to invest vast sums of money in new concepts that never achieve market success. Passenger flight in Concorde may have been an interesting engineering triumph, but in the hard light of commercial day was a total financial disaster. The second error is in the premature rejection of an idea. It was over 10 years from the original idea of the mouse (a Xerox invention) to its first mass commercialization. The Plymouth model provides a framework for fully developing the concept and its technical design specifications. Only where it is considered that a market need has been identified and that an economically feasible method of production is possible do we have a viable new product concept.

Concept development and testing

After initial screening, there is a need for significant investment in development. The product has to be realized in prototype form and tested to see if the concept will actually work and that the technical gremlins can be eliminated. This tends to be largely a technical responsibility, but providing the best start for the technical development team necessitates the best possible definition of the tangible benefits. If the technical team is poorly briefed, the wrong product will result. For consumer products, a key link with the marketing function will be the joint development of evaluation panels (e.g. sensory evaluation of new food products).

Marketing strategy development

Development is not restricted to the product alone, but the full mix. Figure 3.5 and this discussion suggest that the development process is sequential and that marketing strategy development can only start when concept testing is completed; this is untrue. All stages may have elements running concurrently. One of the key factors in marketing new products is 'time to market'. There is a major advantage in being the first to market (as long as you have got it right!) and in some cases there is an opportunity window, miss it and the product is dead (e.g. the 'Lord of the Rings' game would not be a hit if it was launched 9 months after the release of the film 'Return of the King').

Business analysis

In both the business and marketing analyses, the financial viability of the project will be considered, but in the business analysis broader, business issues have to be considered. Many companies no longer make their own products but outsource manufacture to contract manufacturers in low-cost production areas (e.g. for consumer electronics increasingly China; Wal-Mart, TESCO, etc. do not make a single product). Thus, there is much that must be done in identifying partners and considering logistics for the whole supply chain. A product launch with no stock does not go far. In the field, new partners may need to be found to distribute the product or, at the very least, existing channels must be trained and made ready for the new product (e.g. point-of-sale material). The effectiveness of the proposed systems must be continually evaluated (will it all work?) and the efficiency considered (if it works, can we ensure that costs are economic?).

Full product development

Up to this stage, prototypes are likely to have been made in a laboratory. At this stage, products produced by the intended full-scale processes need to be made, ideally by the contractors who will be used in the final commercialization. Then, full beta testing can be conducted. In new product development, products can be tested at three levels:

1. *Alpha testing* – does the product work in the laboratory?
2. *Beta testing* – does it work in the customers' 'in-use' situation?
3. *Gamma testing* – does it do what the customer wants?

Market testing

Given the high cost of failure, the opportunity to fully test the experimental marketing mix is a big advantage. Thus, any minor deficiencies in the intended marketing mix can be remedied before the final, full launch. However, this phase comes with two very heavy costs. The first is 'time to market'; if you wish to estimate the likely success of an FMCG you need to run the time-consuming test marketing for long enough to estimate the likely levels of repurchase, thus allowing the maximum time for the second problem to work against you. Once you begin test marketing in the public arena, it is no longer possible to maintain commercial secrecy (all of the first six stages should be conducted under full commercial secrecy). Test marketing announces to the entire world, including the competition, what you intend to do. Unless you have good intellectual property protection (e.g. copyright and/or patents), you have declared 'open house' and, in some cases, the competition will be alongside you in the market in weeks rather than months. Moreover, the competition may affect the original findings if they react strongly to the test launch.

Commercialization

Here the product is launched with a fully integrated mix. There is only one aspect of the plan that is certain; not all aspects will work as predicted, if for no reason other than it is not possible to predict the likely reaction of the competition. Flexibility and contingency options need, therefore, to be built into the plan. Demand in excess of prediction might sound good news.

However, if there are no contingency plans to increase product availability, the unsatisfied need may let the competition in – you will have built a platform not for yourself but for your competitors. The product needs a rapid response feedback system with clear lines of management control through this dangerous launch period.

Case study

'Lake View Organic Farms: How a new product might be developed?'

Idea generation – Marketing analysis and looking at sales trends in the United Kingdom shows that the 'ready-to-eat' prepared salad market has become a major feature. This market did not exist a decade ago. This is a high-value, premium market. This might prompt the company to consider an organic version.

Screening – How will the new products fit with the existing range's positioning? This product has to be highly prepared. Other products come with mud, and so on, and are not highly prepared. This might be a significant change in direction.

Developing and testing – Checking the year round availability of suitable salad ingredients from organic sources (in the United Kingdom context will involve importing in the winter). Kitchen tests and 'taste panels' to evaluate the final products. Packaging trials (these products rely on 'environmental' packaging, special gas mixtures extend the shelf life). Distribution would be a major consideration as this type product has to be transported in temperature-controlled conditions (just like chilled food). A tricky safety issue would be cleaning. Normal equipment uses heavily chlorinated water. Not the organic style! Salads may be contaminated with faeces from poor hygiene and/or poorly composted farm waste used in growing the product. A proportion of UK food poisoning occurs from eating contaminated 'ready-to-eat' salads. Strict hygiene and cleaning is essential. Ozone or UV light sterilization treatments might provide a 'fix' for this problem. Note here the interplay of market needs 'We do not like chlorine' to a technical quest for a solution that avoids chlorine, without killing the customers with food poisoning.

Marketing strategy development – Should this be part of the 'standard' 'Veggie Box' or a new product in its own right (if so might alternative distribution be used, such as selling through organic food shops in city centres)?

Business analysis – Would all the costs of new equipment, for cleaning, preparing and packing, be justified? New vehicles may be required (see above about temperature control). See Unit 10 for consideration of launch budgets.

Full product development – Complete testing of the final product.

Market testing: Test out the full mix on one round before full launch. Possibly, hire packaging equipment (or contract out) for this period.

Commercialization – Full launch. See Unit 10 for more about launch communications schedules and budgets.

Activity 3.3

The next time you are at display of confectionery, make a note of the range of chewing gums on offer (you will find it helpful to consider the segmentation variables and possibly draw up a perception map for the products). Consider what new products you would introduce if you were the marketing manager for the company. To what extent do you think the eight-stage process would help in this type of situation?

Branding

Branding helps consumers recognize the product and identify it in a competitive marketplace (Figure 3.6). The brand conveys values which the consumer is invited to share. It is a sign of recognized quality and thus branding can increase the customers' perceived value of the product, at the same time decreasing the level of perceived risk in the purchase (customers' risk aversion is covered in more depth in Unit 6).

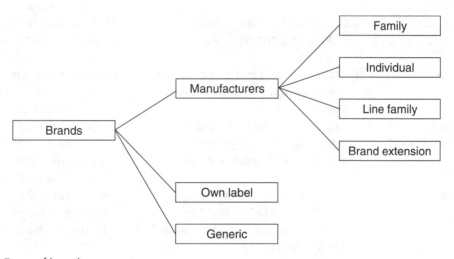

Figure 3.6 Types of branding

Manufacturers use their brand as a badge of quality; thus one does not buy any car but a Toyota *Avensis*. The vehicle type and the manufacturer's brand are intimately linked. Manufacturers may not in all cases use the corporate brand for all products. This is often the case where the company wishes to make several different segmented offerings to the market-place (e.g. Ladybird, Puffin, Rough Guide are all imprints of Penguin). These brands are not competing with each other but are manifestations of specific segmentation policies. Surf is marketed under its own brand name. Jaguar is marketed with its own imagery and positioning, not to confuse it with dramatically different offerings from its parent company. This strategy is called individual branding, where one product (or a small group of products) is marketed under a given brand name and trademark. Line family branding is where a brand name is used for a complete line of products. Calvin Klein fragrances were a brand owned by Unilever and not to be confused with its ice cream or margarine product lines. Brands are like other forms of intellectual property; a publisher owns the copyright to a book but it is the author who sold the copyright (i.e. in effect the brand) who is promoted in the marketplace. Who remembers the publisher of *Bridget Jones' Diary*? Who first published *The Lord of the Rings*? A major brand may have a value on its own and, with care, other products may be badged with the brand's associated imagery (e.g. Harley Davidson apparel and fragrances), the film based on the computer game (e.g. Tomb Raider, etc.).

Manufacturers are under increasing competition from supermarkets with them not only promoting their own brand name and imagery (M&S, TESCO, Sainsbury and ASDA), but also creating their own successful sub-brands (e.g. ASDA, owned by Wal-Mart with George). As mentioned before, one must take care not to confuse the customer with two sets of brand values. Split personalities are difficult to accommodate. With very low-priced, the so-called 'generic' products, generic branding will be used which indicates unbeatable price. In these simple packages, it is the product rather than the brand that is featured. It would be difficult for consumers to identify with 'super value for money, highest quality' with 'lowest price in town, acceptable quality' within the same brand identity. Examples of branding strategies are given in Table 3.1.

Table 3.1 Types of branding

Type of branding	Policy	Example
Line family	Using a brand name only for products in a single line	Ajax is a range of cleaners produced by Colgate-Palmolive. Toothpaste products are marketed under the Colgate brand
Individual	Each product carries its own individual branding	P&G markets its detergents under individual brands such as Bold and Daz
Family	In this case, the company products are marketed under one brand name	The Heinz brand is used for products ranging from salad cream to a range of soups
Brand extension	Attaching the brand name to an additional range of products but keeping the brand personality	A typical example is the addition of a range of cosmetics products to a successful brand name created by a fine fragrance
Own label	Major consumer outlets (e.g. TESCO, Sainsbury etc.) have products produced under contract for sale under their brand identity	Around half of the detergent market in the United Kingdom has been taken by distributors' own brands
Generic	Low-cost generic products with little branding	No frills basic products, largely sold on being lowest in price in their product category

 Activity 3.4

Earlier, in Activity 3.3, we looked at the situation in a confectionery segment. The next time you are in a store, consider the soft drinks on display. Classify the branding strategies using the framework outlined in this section. If you had conducted this exercise for chewing gum (Activity 3.3), would you have obtained a similar result?

Packaging

For many consumer products, the item must sell off the shelf. In a crowded arena with many distractions, the pack must be easily recognizable and communicate the brand values discussed in the last section. The shape of the pack may be part of the branding statement (e.g. the classic Coca-Cola bottle or Marmite jar). The nature of the packaging material may be important so clear glass and plastic allows the consumer to see the product and provide reassurance and confirmation (e.g. whether the olives are black or green). Even when the pack is entirely uniform in construction and shape (e.g. soft drink cans), good graphic design and printing can provide the necessary lift for the product to gain attention and shelf space. Although not so exciting, packs must also convey information. Some of this may be a legal necessity such as the weight of goods in the pack and ingredient listings. Other information may be more general such as directions for use and, of course, the bar code identifying the product.

The original role of packaging – to protect the goods in transit, in the sales outlet, in the home before and during use – is of course still important. Many packs have an additional function acting as a dispenser and/or a measuring device when using the product. The 'roll-on' anti-perspirant/deodorant pack is a good example. An innovative example of packaging being designed for application is the 'Toilet Duck' toilet cleaner which injects the cleaning material at that difficult to get at the bit under the rim. Fabric conditioner caps contain an inner measure devised in such a way that the conditioner remaining in the measure runs back into the container not down the outside of the pack.

Future archaeologists researching the twentieth century will find the majority of household waste in the first half of the century was ash from coal fires used to heat homes (much of the other rubbish was burnt on the fire). At the start of the twenty-first century our bin bags are full of packaging which largely goes to land fill. In another decade, this practice will appear as quaint as coal ash does to us today. Far less than half of the products that could be recycled are being at the present. Attitudes to such profligate waste are changing, partially as a result of social marketing campaigns and partially as a result of changes in the law. Environmental issues will be a key factor in packaging design and technology with packs being designed to be refilled (e.g. fabric conditioner with refill pouches) and eventually recycled.

Activity 3.5

Raid your food cupboard and look at the various types of packaging and products. If you had to select one example, to illustrate as many functions (discussed above) as possible, which one would it be? Draw up a list of its features.

Sodastream

Family consumption of carbonated drinks has increased. Sodastream made a device that allowed people to carbonate drinks at home. It held a small, returnable carbon dioxide cylinder, which could carbonate drinks, made from concentrated syrup and tap water in reusable bottles. With reusable bottles and returnable cylinders, the system was eco-friendly. Why do we not see this product much in evidence now? Customers found the cost of buying exchange cylinders and syrup no better than buying the same drinks in plastic bottles, once they were introduced. Moreover, the plastic bottle could go into the dustbin and you did not have the bother of cleaning out the reusable bottles and returning the cylinder. A change in packing technology created a new product form and resulted in rapid PLC decline for another. The product may have been eco-friendly, but did not offer consumers the same convenience as non-returnable packs.

Note: The same technology is now widely used by restaurants and bars to dispense soft drinks such as cola, lemonade, soda water and so on. Here the system does provide a major cost saving and convenience. Such outlets use a variety of special gases to dispense other products such as keg beer. They already have a weekly delivery service for gas cylinders – no major additional delivery costs in adding one more cylinder. The product is dispensed at the time of use directly into the customer's glass so there are no bottles to display and no empty bottles to recycle. Just because a technology has been superseded in one context, it does not always imply that with creative re-invention it might not be a runaway success in another.

Case study

Persil Power

In 1994, Unilever launched Persil Power. To obtain whiter effects, detergents incorporated bleaches to deal with stains and discolouration of fabrics. However, these were only effective at elevated temperatures, whereas the trend was for washing at lower temperatures to be less harsh on the fabrics and to conserve electrical energy, a major element of running costs. The solution was to incorporate a bleach activator, which would work with the bleaching ingredient, to provide the desired effects at lower temperatures. However, under certain conditions of use, the product was so effective that it not only washed the clothes, but also destroyed them. P&G were able to show two halves of a garment washed in the competing products. The damage was self-evident. Persil were forced to withdraw the product and lost market share. Product testing had not highlighted a problem that only was discovered after the product had been fully launched. Total costs of the problem including lost market share were estimated to be in excess of £100 million.

Over a decade later, it is interesting that the market has moved on into new areas – colour care and easy iron are the platforms, and the old soap advertisements with 'Surf washes whiter' are consigned to history.

Question 3.1

Earlier in this chapter, we considered physical products. However, similar considerations apply to service situations. Selectively, using the concepts outlined in this unit, analyse the conference facilities provided by a major hotel if you were seeking a location for a launch. The December 2005 case study 'The Urban Culture Festival 2006' feature issues in this area with the compulsory Question 1(a) 'Calculate the expected revenue, costs and profit from holding the Celebrity Gala Evening at each of the two venues, stating any assumptions.', 1(b) 'Identify the NON-FINACIAL factors that should be considered before selecting one of the venues.' and 1(c) 'Considering financial and non-financial factors, which venue would you recommend for the Gala? Justify your decision.' The June 2006 case study 'SMA Cars Ltd' also featured a question on venue selection, this time for a product launch: 1(a) 'Calculate the total direct costs of both venues for the launch event and fashion show', 1(b) 'Show your calculations and state any assumptions.' and 1(c) 'Produce a report for your Managing Director (MD) that recommends which venue to select. Justify your recommendation, explaining what criteria you used to come to your decision.'

Summary

In this unit, we have seen that

- o   An organization needs a balanced portfolio of new products to thrive.
- o   The concepts of PLC and the adapted BCG matrix provide a framework for evaluating the product portfolio's balance.
- o   In creating new products, the framework of attribute analysis, given by the Plymouth model, provides a bridge between market-led product definition and technology-driven invention.
- o   Fundamental to success is the understanding that people do not buy products, they wish to enjoy benefits; benefits are derived from a continuum of products and services.
- o   The product or service is of no value to the customer and will fail in the marketplace, if the segmentation and positioning have not laid the proper foundation and an appropriate, fully integrated marketing mix developed.
- o   Branding can increase the customer's perception of product value.
- o   Product may need to be adapted in an international context.
- o   The new product development process.

Further study

Dibb, S., Simkin, L., Pride, W. and Ferrell, O. (2006) *Marketing Concepts and Strategies*, 5th European edition, Houghton Mifflin Chapters 10–12.

Hints and tips

The key to successful marketing is to identify the segments and the benefits demanded by the target. This primary information then allows the positioning strategy to be formulated and then the communications plan. Without this stage, the communications plan will lack a firm foundation. We have to communicate relevant benefits which requires an intimate understanding of both the product/service and the target customers. Marketing is a skill and skills are improved by practice so apply the concepts to typical products/services that are relevant to you to develop your personal skills and insights.

Bibliography

Burk Wood, M. (2003) *The Marketing Plan Handbook*, Prentice Hall.

Crawford, M., and Benedetto, A. (2005) *New Products Management*, International student edition, McGraw-Hill.

Hart, S. (1996) (ed.) *New Product Development*, Dryden Press.

Hollensen, S. (2004) *Marketing Management – A Relationship Approach*, Prentice Hall.

Kotler, P. (2006) *Marketing Management*, 12th edition, Prentice Hall.

Tidd, J., Bessant, J. and Pavitt, K. (2005) *Managing Innovation: Integrating Technological, Market and Organisational Change*, Wiley.

Trott, P. (2004) *Innovation Management and New Product Development*, 3rd edition, Prentice Hall.

unit 4 the marketing mix: price

After this unit, you will be able to

o Identify factors that contribute to customers' perception of value and ability to pay (affordability).

o Identify what factors contribute to costs and appreciate the architecture of costs.

o Appreciate the legal factors affecting pricing.

o Explain how organizations approach price setting.

o Describe the systems needed to deliver the pricing strategy and collect the revenues.

o Understand the importance of budgets (a multi-disciplinary activity between marketing and finance) as control and communication tools.

o Review the issues of feedback and control along with the role of variance analysis in this.

o Appreciate the management of pricing in an international context.

Syllabus references

3.2 Identify alternative and innovative approaches to a variety of marketing arenas and explain criteria for meeting business objectives.

3.4 Explain how marketing makes use of planning techniques: objective setting; and coordinating, measuring and evaluating results to support the organization.

4.4 Analyse the impact of pricing decisions and role of price within the marketing mix.

4.5 Describe the current distribution channels for an organization and evaluate new opportunities.

4.7 Explain the importance of the extended marketing mix: how process, physical aspects and people affect customer choice.

4.8 Explain the importance of ICT in the new mix.

5.1 Demonstrate an ability to manipulate numbers in a marketing context.

5.2 Explain the process used for setting a budget and apportioning fixed and overhead costs.

5.3 Explain how organizations assess the viability of opportunities, marketing initiatives and projects.

5.5 Make recommendations on alternative courses of action.

5.6 Examine the correlation between marketing mix decisions and results.

5.7 Evaluate the cost-effectiveness of a marketing budget, including a review of suppliers and activities.

Key definitions

Breakeven point – In business situations where there are fixed and variable expenses, it is the production volume where the total sales income just equals the total of fixed and variable expenses.

Cost-based price – A method of pricing based on taking a percentage of costs and 'marking up'.

Cost drivers – Those expenses that account for a substantial proportion of the company's expenses. Frequently, Pareto's principle may be applied here and adapted for the type of business concerned. For example, paperclips are not a significant expense for solicitors, but staff expenses are.

Decimal point myopia – Often figures entered onto a spreadsheet can have considerable errors, particularly, if too many numbers following the decimal point are used. If an estimated figure can only be estimated to +/–10 per cent, there is little point in calculating the result to six decimal places!

Depreciation – Items of capital equipment have a productive life of a number of years. Depreciation is the accountancy process where only part of the value is assigned to a given production period. Depreciation affects profits but is a non-cash expense and so it does not affect cash flow and thus does not enter discounted cash flow calculations.

Elasticity of demand – The way in which consumer demand varies with price. For example, fuel prices are elastic; motorists continue to use fuel even if the price rises by a significant amount. On the other hand, other goods, such as restaurant meals are relatively different; a small price rise can result in a significant drop in demand.

Fixed and variable costs – Fixed costs are those such as rent and insurance, tending not to vary with the level of sales. Variable costs are those that vary with the level of sales, such as the cost of raw materials and components.

Learning curve effect – This is the impact that research and product development can have on price. In the mid-twentieth century, computers cost hundreds of thousands of pounds; improvements in manufacture and design means that more powerful computers are available for a few hundred pounds. (Moore's Law – first stated in 1965 by Intel co-founder Gordon Moore – that every new printed memory circuit contained about twice as much capacity as its predecessor, and each chip was released within 18–24 months of the previous chip. If this trend continued, he reasoned, computing power would rise exponentially with time).

Pareto's principle – The rule proving that a minority of the issues drive the majority of the effects (e.g. often around 20 per cent of the customers provide 80 per cent of sales income).

Penetration pricing – A strategy of low prices to buy market share from competitors.

Profit contribution – The sales revenue of a unit less the variable cost of production of the unit. This ignores fixed costs including depreciation and is used in the calculation of the breakeven point. Fixed costs divided by profit contribution give you the number of breakeven point.

Sequential skimming strategy – This is a process where several markets of different benefit and value are skimmed in turn. For example, advanced braking systems were first introduced into luxury cars; now they are standard in all production cars. This is an example of both sequential skimming and learning curve effect.

Skimming strategy – A strategy of entering the market with a high unit price to maximize the profit per unit. This is typical for luxury products during the introduction phase.

Sunk cost – In some textbooks, advertising is given as a variable expense, however this is not so. A perfume company may spend many millions of pounds launching a new perfume; this money is committed or 'sunk' before any perfume is sold and thus is entirely independent of sales achieved.

Value – This is the amount of money people are prepared to pay for an object or service. This need not have any relationship to the physical costs of delivering the product or service. A first edition Harry Potter has a value far in excess of its original production cost.

Study Guide

Before it is possible to discuss pricing strategies for an organization, the key factors affecting price must be understood. Customers will not buy the product if it is priced beyond their valuation. Even if the product is perceived to be of good value, it must be affordable. This is the top end pricing for the product. If an organization does not recover its costs in the sales it generates, it rapidly goes out of business, as many of the 'dot-com' companies found. The difference between costs and customer value is the strategic pricing gap. Within this gap, various strategies can be implemented according to the organization's business objectives. Alternative approaches to costing are needed for different purposes and these are outlined in this unit.

In international business or with promotional pricing for a supermarket, the systems for setting and informing the customer of pricing have to be relatively sophisticated because of the volume of transactions. If the customer sees value and affordability, the organization sees cash flow. The price is only realized when the money is banked and effective, so efficient transaction systems are vital to marketing success. Sensitive feedback and control systems are needed to ensure pricing strategies are on track. Variance analysis on budget will provide quantitative information, but other information sources are needed to complete the picture.

Customer value and affordability

There is, in marketing terms, no direct link between value and costs. The cost of production of one additional copy of Microsoft Windows is zero: it is an electronic download with almost no physical costs to Microsoft. Users do see value in the software and are prepared to purchase it.

Costs represent the floor below which it is not viable for the organization to sell its products or services. The function of marketing is to drive up the benefits for the customer, to increase perceived value and ensure that the sales systems make the product affordable. Efficient value chain management, along the total supply chain to delivery of the product or service to the customer, drives down costs. The overall architecture of price is shown in Figure 4.1. In this section, the nature of value is considered.

The market for houses provides an interesting platform on which to consider pricing. A roof that does not leak and walls that do not fall down are usually considered useful, but as we noted in Unit 3 on Product, it is not the core benefits that sell the house. Status for a 'celebrity address', ease of access to motorways, the sea view and even availability of schools can all have significant impact on a buyer's perception of value. In this sense, each purchaser represents a micro-segment of one, with their own matrix of benefits and values. The result is an almost free market for the purchase of homes. If houses are in short supply and there are many buyers, then prices will rise. If there are few buyers, in depressed and unfashionable locations, prices will fall.

Economists enjoy building complex models of elasticity of demand – how demand may vary with price. The government employs the best economists and statisticians and is still unable to accurately estimate tax revenue. Therefore, we will set aside the complex equations and big computer approach to get to the practical aspects that are really of interest to marketers.

Elasticity is a real effect. The demand for some products does move with price. This is vividly illustrated by the entry of the low-cost airlines that demonstrated that if you made travel costs low enough you could generate a whole new market. If you lower the price, you can encourage existing customers to buy more and new customers, who could not previously afford the cost, to enter this market. Some products do not have a change in demand when the price changes. If table salt costs £0.01 a kilo, we will not increase our consumption to 10 kilos a week.

In modern life, there are two products that have limited supply. With the introduction of congestion taxation in London, that which was free (road space) is having demand moderated by a pricing strategy. Water is a limited resource with consumption rising as people pay a fixed charge, irrespective of the amount of water they use. If society is seriously concerned about the environmental impact of excessive water usage, people should pay for it as they do fuel for the car. As a result, we would consider how many litres of water it takes to wash a few plates.

Branding is a key device for marketers to build value. A single low-cost manufacturer may produce unbranded jeans, own label jeans for a supermarket and designer label jeans. Near the source, a pair might sell for less than £10 and in a premium segment shop, with the latest trendy label, the same type of product, made to similar quality standards, might be priced in excess of £100. The extra value comes from the status and lifestyle associations of the fashion product and the core benefit is the same.

Even if customers see value, they may not be able to buy the product; the product must be affordable. Part of the explosive growth phase for mobile telephones was fuelled by 'pay-as-you-go' type plans. Customers could limit their expenditure to a level that was affordable, and under their control. The provision of vast amounts of consumer credit has caused economists problems with their projections. When credit was scarce and difficult to obtain, people spent what they earned or what they had saved. With credit, there is no longer this simple relationship. Therefore, people spend what they feel they can afford and this tends to more of a subjective 'feel-good' factor that is not changed by a decimal point on interest rates. Payment terms and systems are all part of the pricing package perceived by the customer. Credit cards, store cards and extended payment terms are all ways that retailers can make the purchase more affordable. Use can also be made of psychological pricing breaks: £9.99 is less than £10.00. The marketing aim is the same, to make the product appear affordable and value for money.

Activity 4.1

Have a look at the house prices in the local paper or estate agent's website. What do you think contributes to higher rather than lower prices (e.g. age of the property, etc.)? Are prices increasing or falling in your area? What do you think is driving the movement? When a person is buying a property what are the issues you think they ought to consider in selecting a mortgage type (e.g. fixed rate, cash back option, etc.).

Competition is a key issue in customers' perception of value. Motorists will travel miles to save a few pence a litre. Where accurate price comparisons can be made, consumers become very price sensitive and shop around. For a major purchase, once a consumer has decided on manufacturer and models, increasingly the next step is not to go to a shop and purchase but complete an Internet search for the best possible price. The 'dot-com' companies were not wrong in understanding that the Internet is changing purchasing habits. They often got the timescales and the way the market actually developed wrong. People are also now able to make price comparisons across international borders and can see where companies are operating different pricing policies. Companies have a dilemma in that different markets have differing perceptions of value and affordability so differential pricing may be necessary. However, a flexible pricing policy (the company view) may be perceived as price gouging (consumer pressure groups). Internet research provides the consumers with this international price comparison information.

Purchase cost is not the only concern of customers. Cost of ownership and use of the product is also important. That inkjet printer for under £100 looks a really good buy. Just work out how much you will spend on cartridges over the life of product. For major consumer purchases such as a car, people will take into account running costs and trade-in value. For the B2B sector, accountants will do detailed cost comparisons of value for money over the life of the product or the period of contract for a service.

Marketers sometimes make the comment that accountants know the cost of everything but the value of nothing. Accountants do know the value of marketing; it creates value that results in profits. However, profits are the difference between two numbers: sales revenue and costs. It is important for pricing that marketers understand the issues of costing, the other half of the strategic pricing gap. The consideration of pricing issues is covered below. More consideration of general finance issues is given in Unit 10.

A marketing guide to costing

Fixed and variable costs

Here is a question to ask your accountants. Ask them what is the cost of a product or service produced by the organization. If they give you a figure, never trust them again, as the only thing this is likely to be certain is that the figure is 'wrong'. If, however, the accountant asks you 'What cost do you want?' or 'What use do you need the cost for?', this person is a key colleague who will provide you with invaluable information and advice. Too often, this aspect of marketing is seen as an area for calculators and spreadsheets. It is, but an architect does not have to build the drains, they get plumbers to do this. Let the finance people take care of the spreadsheets, as a marketer concentrates on what the figures are telling you. Concentrate on the message not the details of the financial media.

To consider the issue of costs, we will use an illustrative case study to provide a meaning and context to the discussion; we will do this without any complicated figures. A marketing graduate decides to set up a new eating experience 'New China Delight'. The premises are taken on a lease. The rent, insurance and other costs (such as wages, lighting, heating, marketing communications, etc.) are a fixed cost. These costs do not change if the restaurant is largely empty or largely full.

The restaurant needs equipment, furniture and decoration. Together with the launch marketing costs, this is a sunk cost. If the business never gets a single customer after opening all this money is spent. If the business is to continue in the long term, enough money must be generated to renew the equipment and decorations when required. Accountants make a provision for this and call this depreciation. Accountants have fun by working out the 'best way' to do this. For the marketer, the key feature is that this is a non-cash expense. The money was spent and lost at the opening, it will not come back. It is worth remembering that we are not running a 'real' business if we are not able to recover our investment in equipment and decorations, things which do not have an infinite life.

When the restaurant opens, we incur variable costs. These will include such items as food, drink and laundry bills for table linen and so on. Some marketing costs may also be variable. If you run a money-off promotion, this is a variable cost and depends on the number of people who take up the offer. The advertisement that announces the offer is not a variable cost; the cost of placing it is the same, irrespective of the number of people who accept the promotion. It is important for the marketer to understand the colour of the cash flows. Fixed costs are one colour; variable costs are different and must be considered separately. Different coloured socks are bad dress sense, mixing cash flows in the wrong way is even worse.

At the beginning of this section, a controversial statement was made: Accountants know cost, not value. To illustrate the issue, let us consider the situation regarding lunchtime opening. Often lunchtime meals do not have the same customer valuation as candlelit romantic evening meals so prices are often lower. Is lunchtime opening still profitable? An accountant may calculate a cost based on the variable costs and add a proportion of the total annual costs, which are arrived at by dividing the annual fixed costs by the estimated total number of customers (averaging the fixed costs). If the total cost calculated is greater than the prices that can be charged at lunchtime, the logic here is that 'New China Delight' should not open. The road to bankruptcy is accepting calculated costs without understanding the basis and assumptions on which they were made. What is relevant to the lunchtime opening decision is not the average costs, but the variable costs. Here the concept of profit contribution is helpful. Here we take away from the money paid by the customer the direct costs (food, drink, etc.); if we are left with a positive figure then opening makes sense and we have a contribution to profits and fixed expenses. The danger of using average costs is that we might over-price the lunchtime menu and under-price the evening menu. The objective of the pricing policy should be to maximize the overall profit contribution. We will see in a later section on pricing objectives and price setting that simple 'cost plus percentage' formulae based on average costs are most dangerous, especially for service business with differing demand levels and price acceptability at different times.

If we do not make enough overall profit contribution, we do not recover our fixed costs over the year and we will go out of business, given enough time. If we get lots of customers, we will get a healthy profit and the bank manager will love us. The precise number of customers where we neither go broke nor get a birthday card from the bank manager is called the breakeven point.

Having talked about the issue in words, it is not too difficult to use a spreadsheet or calculator to do the number crunching. Below some simple numbers have been added to the New China Delight lunchtime opening situation.

New China Delight

The accountants have looked at the figures: staff, rent, insurance and general overhead costs for the year have been estimated at £200 000 a year. In addition to the general overheads, decoration, fittings and equipment cost, an initial £150 000 and it is expected that the facilities will last 5 years before needing renewal. This indicates a non-cash depreciation cost of £30 000 a year (the £150 000 initial cost divided by the expected life of the fittings and decorations). The restaurant will seat 60 people at a time. In the evening, it is expected that people will be prepared to pay £25 for a meal and that direct costs will be £8 a person (e.g. food and laundry, etc.). If the restaurant trades 6 days a week for 52 weeks a year, what is the breakeven number of customers for evening business alone, as customers per day?

We need to first calculate the total fixed costs. This is the £200 000 given as the running fixed costs (wages, rent etc.) with the addition of the depreciation of £30 000 a year. This is a total of £230 000 a year.

We trade 52 weeks and each week for 6 days: a total of 312 opening days a year. Therefore, our allocation of fixed costs per opening day is our total yearly costs (£230 000) divided by our opening days (312), that is £737.18 a day.

We expect to be paid £25 for an average meal. The variable direct costs (food, laundry etc.) are given as £8 per meal. We get a contribution of sales price (£25) less direct variable costs (£8) or £17 for each meal sold.

If we divide our daily fixed costs of (£737.18) by the contribution (£17) we get, the number of customers needed to just cover our total average costs, the breakeven number (737.18/17) or 43.3635-ish people! If we get less than 44 people a day, we are below breakeven numbers and if we are not able to recover the numbers on other days, we will go out of business. This implies that we need, on average, 73 per cent of our table space sold for a meal each and every night.

The additional labour costs of opening at lunchtime are estimated to be £100 a day (additional wage costs etc.). With a simplified menu, it is expected that a 'lunchtime special' will be attractive to customers at £12 a meal. With the reduced menu, the variable costs can be contained at £7 per meal. For this decision, we may assume that the evening trade covers all the fixed costs. Now we are investigating how many customers will be needed at lunchtime to add to our evening profits (there is no point in opening at lunchtime if we are unable to cover the additional costs of this opening). How many lunchtime customers are needed to breakeven?

The contribution is the sales price (£12) less the variable costs (£7), that is £5. The additional cost of opening was £100 per lunchtime, if we divide this by the contribution of each person lunching (£5), we will get the minimum (breakeven) number of lunchtime customers (£100/£5), that is 20.

At the start of this section, some concern was expressed about the value of accounts for marketing purposes. The above example starts to demonstrate the complexity of even a simple business. Not only could the prices be different at different times of the day, but also on different days of the week (e.g. Saturday 'shoppers' special' for a business restaurant that might be otherwise empty in a city centre location at the weekend). A good accountant prepared to work with marketing to model various pricing strategies is what every organization needs. Too often, it can be thought that because 10 divided by 3 is 3.333333333333333 that the science is precise. Feeding into the equation, in real life, are assumptions such as: what will be the likely cost of salmon next month? What will be the cost of champagne if the Euro moves against the Pound and so on? How many customers will come in next week? What is required is a team that understands that both financial skills and a marketing orientation are necessary to develop an optimal pricing strategy. The answer to 'What is the cost of a product?' should be 'What cost is relevant to the decision that is under consideration?' Data without context is dangerous, and certainly not information.

The situation is, as one might expect, slightly more complex. If the restaurant in the above example is setting prices for the new menu to be printed for next year, it is not present costs that need to be considered but best estimates of future costs. The profit and loss calculations for tax purposes are past historical costs, and should not be used for the future conduct of a business.

Activity 4.2

Consider that 'New China Delight' has been trading for a year and plans for next year are now being made. Take the figures from above and construct a simple Excel spreadsheet to check out the calculations and form a simple table.

Now perform a couple of 'what if' calculations. If it was thought that the costs of food would add an extra £1.00 to the cost of a meal and that wage and other fixed costs would increase by £10 000 next year, how many extra people would need to eat in the restaurant each evening to still get to breakeven? The alternative strategy would be to assume that the numbers would remain the same and the price would have to increase. By how much would the price have to increase to still breakeven?

Consider the restaurant only trades in the evening.

Cost drivers

Costs are not in real life fixed. In Unit 1, the value chain was introduced as a tool for auditing the internal capability of the firm. It is necessary to maximize the effectiveness of the organization's value chain (make certain it delivers the right products and services) and also to ensure that it is as efficient as possible. In this section, just a few selected value chain issues will be considered but, in appropriate circumstances, any part of the value chain's cost efficiency may be vital to the organization's success.

For many organizations, the added value is relatively modest as a percentage of the sales value. Supermarkets make profits not only by minimizing the cost of their operations, but also by intelligent procurement (buying). One of the key issues in the financial management of a business is cash flow and working capital. In an average supermarket the number of days stock held is just a few days, what you see is what they have got. The customers pay by cash or credit card. The supermarket, in effect, has its money there and then. However, in the B2B context it pays its suppliers on a monthly basis. Thus, an efficiently run supermarket uses its suppliers to finance the business. Products are demanded on a JIT basis and paid for later. Sourcing from high-quality, low-cost producers have made these organizations efficient profit machines. If I generate another £1000 of sales, I need more working capital and may increase profits by £100. If I save £1000 on purchasing, I have put £1000 into profits and possibly reduced the need for working capital. The key role of successful purchasing in most organizations just cannot be overestimated.

Supermarkets pay rigorous attention to forcing down transaction costs. The laser checkout (EPOS) systems not only drive stock-control systems and track customers' buying patterns, but also reduce labour costs. Budget airlines also play this card. Paperless 'e-ticketing' drives down transaction costs. Banks are discovering that the lower transaction costs of 'e-banking' can generate more profits.

A hidden cost can be in covering risk. For goods in transit, this can be insurance. For B2B accounts, it can be the issue of bad debts. In international business, prudence demands that cover should be taken for potential risks, such as exchange rate movements between fixing the contract and payment being received.

Care must be taken when considering the value of an account about the terms of trade offered. If extended credit is offered with volume discounts this, in effect, increases the costs for this account. This is a particularly important aspect of international trade, where it may be months before payment is effected and the costs of covering the risk with, say, a confirmed letter of credit may be significant.

Case Study

'Low-cost airlines'

Airlines provide an example of some key issues in pricing: cost drivers, customer value and elasticity of demand. In 2006, the low-cost airlines were announcing good profits and formulating aggressive expansion plans. At the same time, some major 'traditional' airlines (e.g. Delta in the United States) were in grave financial difficulties.

Legacy of the past: In the mid-twentieth century, many airlines were state owned enterprises with near monopoly trading conditions and fares were held at high levels and a complex series of agreements effectively prevented competition. With this level of profitability and strong trade unions, high wage levels and good pension packages were negotiated. Slowly, the world is moving to an 'open sky' policy with free competition and restrictive pricing has disappeared. The scene was set for the entry of a new business model: the low-cost airline.

Traditional airlines inheritance: As discussed above, with past easy profits employees expected over-manning, high wages and some of the most generous pension rights in industry. Moreover, these airlines operate a complex network of international flights and feeder hubs. This results in their aircraft waiting on the ground for inter-connections to be made.

The low-cost airlines challenge: These airlines had no past history of over manning and adopted less costly employment packages than the traditional airlines. They could run their operations with much lower labour costs; ruthlessly seeking maximum cost advantage, they cut into 'frills' such as four course meals, introduced internet booking (with 'e'-ticketing) and dispensed with individual seat number reservations. If this did not give them a big enough advantage with their 'point' to 'point' strategy they had no need to keep aircraft on the ground to wait for connections and so could keep their aircraft in the air for far longer (aircraft do not earn money sitting on the ground waiting). To reduce prices still further, they often operate from formally less popular (less expensive) airports, such as Stainsted rather than Heathrow in the United Kingdom for London. To back this up, they ruthlessly communicated their proposition with aggressive advertising and occasional 'silly' promotional pricing such as '£1 one way'. The result has been a rapid increase in air travel (elasticity of demand effect) enabling the low-cost airlines to fill most of their extra seats. The picture of air travel is going to look very different in 2010 compared to 1990.

 ## Activity 4.3

A friend has approached you about starting a small business as a photographer taking pictures of events such as weddings. This person has only limited capital. Evaluate the cost drivers in this situation.

Legal issues in pricing

In this short section, we note two key legal issues with price offers. It is often assumed that all organizations can charge just what they wish. However, in the privatization of utilities and other such operations, governments have created commercial monopolies (you only have one source of electricity – that cable from the street). To prevent abuse, such industries are highly regulated and pricing structures and policies are strictly governed by law and interpreted by the regulators.

Price offers, in terms of contracts, may also be subject to special regulations. Offers for certain financial services have 'cooling off' periods that must be built into the contracts. Again, particularly in international contracts, care must be taken to spell out the conditions in detail. A cheque drawn on a foreign bank, even if in your currency, may take weeks to clear and incur a charge far in excess of the same cheque drawn on a local bank. A marketer not only has to make a friend of the accountant, but also the company lawyer. Other hidden costs and risks in contracts are product liability and warranty costs in the event the product is defective.

Pricing objectives and strategies

There are differing objectives and strategies for pricing depending on the business objectives. For a major company entering a new international market, the objective may well not be to make a profit but to establish a foundation of market share to build profits some time into the future. In this section, we shall consider some of the issues in pricing objectives and strategies. We have noted the issue of trade terms and credit under costs and will not cover them again in this section.

Penetration pricing

If the objective is to grow market share and the demand for a product increases with lower prices, the strategy indicated is penetration pricing. The quality of the other mix offerings is maintained and the price is held below that of competitive offerings of comparable value aimed at the same target segment. This strategy is often combined with an aggressive marketing communications programme to inform customers of the exceptional value of the offering. In effect, market share is being bought. This strategy is only sustainable if the cost base can be kept low and, in ideal circumstances, lower than the competition so the strategy can be sustained indefinitely. This is the strategy of the new low-cost airlines.

We noted under legal issues that some laws apply to pricing. The pricing of goods or services below cost is known as predatory pricing or dumping. Such strategies may be declared illegal and damages awarded or, in the case of international marketing, retaliatory duties imposed (e.g. imports of steel into the United States in 2003).

Skimming strategy

This metaphor is taken from the skimming of cream from milk. Where there is some protection (e.g. a patent) or limited supply (e.g. places on the first cruise of the Queen Mary 2 in 2004), then high prices may be charged, thus, maximizing the profit generated from a limited supply. As with the penetration strategy, the communications activity may be high to maintain the interest and demand, thus sustaining the high price set.

For technical products, possibly with patent or other protection, a sequential skimming strategy may be appropriate. Thus, when computers cost £1 000 000, they were only available to the big corporations. When lower costs from improved manufacturing (the learning curve effect) brought prices down to a few thousands of pounds, they could be used by small companies and professionals, such as authors. Now costs are below £1000, every home can have a computer. Each price drop brings a new segment of consumers into the market. Each segment is harvested and then the next price break brings in another group.

The two methods above can be considered demand-led pricing strategies; they start with an appreciation of the value of comparative offerings and then the price is set in comparison to the competition to achieve the intended objectives, for example rob the competition of share with penetration pricing.

Cost-based systems

Here a formula is constructed around costs and, in effect, the price is generated by the software. The advantage of this system is that it does not rely on a lot of competitor market research and is relatively simple to operate, once the parameters are set. If full costs are used in the calculation (not variable costs), and if it is successful and target volumes are achieved, then all costs are recovered. It thus appears to be a safe option, but note all the 'ifs'. This is a simplistic falsehood; there is no such thing as safety in the competitive business arena. If target volumes are not met then costs are not recovered and the business is heading for extinction. Although widely used, the view advanced here is that it could be a symptom of an organization that has not fully adopted a marketing orientation. This process works satisfactorily in a stable marketplace where competition is modest. This is an increasingly rare situation.

However, in the past marketers were not always financially literate and could appear to be attempting to buy volume at the cost of price and profits. In the section on costs, the view is advanced that the marketer must not be a decimal point person but must have sufficient understanding to debate sophisticated pricing strategies with the Financial Management specialists. The aim of maximum total profits is obtained by maximizing the total sum of profit contributions. For services, this can imply charging more than a simple cost plus formula might indicate at peak periods and accepting marginal prices at times of low demand. The classic example of this is first class and standby fares. On long-haul flights, a person pre-booking first class may be paying thousands of pounds. Another person on an opportunistic standby fare may pay just a few hundred pounds. The view advanced here is that price should not be seen as a simple fixed price formula but a complex price mix to be debated between the marketer and the finance functions; just in the same way that service levels and quality are debated between marketing and production.

Online insurance

This is a very competitive market. However, accepting risky customers with low premiums will not provide a stable business. Marketing and financial experts have built sophisticated models of customer profiles and risk so each quotation is bespoke to a segment of one, calculated at the time of the enquiry. To be competitive, the transaction costs must be minimized (e-commerce) and cost of claims managed (good, efficient field logistics support). This sophisticated, elegant process is light years away from the Stone Age average costs mark-up policy, with one-price/size-fits-all.

Perceived value

At the very start of the book it was noted that customers do not buy products, they buy benefits. For these benefits, they do not see price, but value and affordability. Value is not just the product offering, but also the whole value of the mix, for example branding. Convenience in distribution may provide perceived added value. Earlier in this section we noted that value and affordability could be affected by the terms of trade (extended credit terms, volume discounts, etc.), cost of ownership over the lifetime of the product and payment methods (e.g. store card). Comparisons with the competition affect what people consider to be fair and reasonable for a product.

Pricing and sales systems

Too often, the emphasis can be on 'What price should be set?' However, the systems for making this work and ensuring the money is collected and banked (profits are not real until we have the cash) are an appreciable cost. In the insight above, the cost-efficient pricing and payment systems used by e-insurance businesses were highlighted. Supermarkets with shelf pricing and laser checkouts and card payment systems have moved in the same direction. There is a cost to costing, yet customers do not perceive that this has added anything to the value of the offer. It is important to get the price right and bank the money with the minimum of administrative cost overheads. This is especially important for export businesses where every transaction can, just as for car insurance, be an individual calculation of a quotation (transport, insurance, currency cover, etc., that varies with destination and from day to day).

Budgets, variance analysis, feedback and control

Budgets are constructed in either a general spreadsheet package or some more sophisticated financial software packages such as Sage. For non-financial or non-computer experts, the key factor to note is that they are, whatever the complexity of the business and systems, relatively crude financial models. There may be detailed and complex costing systems (e.g. as discussed for insurance), but the final profit comes down from the revenue line and that involves an estimate of how many customers we will get. We may be able to calculate our costs to 1 per cent. Often we are lucky if we can estimate customer numbers to 5 per cent for next year. In this discussion, we shall attempt to avoid 'decimal point myopia'.

All a budget is is a spreadsheet. Normally, across the top runs the time periods that are required (days, weeks, months etc., as needed). Down the sheet, cost and revenue elements are listed. Then, in each cell, estimates for parameters are set, such as number of passengers that might travel. Other elements of the spreadsheet are calculated from input data (e.g. sales revenue will be a calculation based on the number of customers and the price they are expected to pay). The great value of this is that the model is not carved in stone. The marketer should work with the systems and finance specialists to ensure that 'what if' scenarios can be run (e.g. looking at estimated effects of new pricing strategies).

Once debated, the budget becomes the cash-flow plan for the organization. As stated before, only one thing is certain about plans, that is, they will not work in the way expected (e.g. the weather may affect the number of passengers that want to travel). Plans are nothing, planning is everything. In setting the budget, an understanding is shared about parameters and their effect on the budget (e.g. number of customers and its impact on profit). When problems occur, this understanding is invaluable.

Here we are not concerned with balance sheet analysis (best left to the accountants), but with the consideration of relevant financial control parameters. If we are concerned with customer service, a relevant parameter may be overdue orders, rather than simple average delivery time. There are two issues to consider: how good are we and are we on plan?

The major, traditional airlines are some of the most sophisticated businesses in the world. The low-cost airlines have re-invented the business processes so that they have dramatically lowered the cost of selling a ticket and the cost of a passenger mile (not the traditional ratios you find in an accountancy textbook). What is needed is a debate between the marketing group (who tend to track the competition), and the financial staff (who drive the computers) to devise measures (e.g. ratios) that track performance against the performance achieved by the competition (benchmarking). For a supermarket, it can be sales per square metre, sales per employee, sale per customer and so on. If a gap is opening up with the competition then this is an indication that we are losing ground.

Variance analysis looks at how we perform against our plan, the budget. Management time is finite and should be used to maximum effect. If we are on plan, the pragmatic view should largely be that management should be by exception looking where maximum value for intervention can be obtained. Variance analysis can be regarded as a forensic investigation as to what is causing a deviation. If profitability of a given line is down, is it because costs are up or that the number of units is down? If sales of a particular line differ between various outlets in the same organization, is it possible that some better merchandising activity explains the better sales? Can this idea be used to boost sales at other locations? The implication of this is that variance reports need to be timely. Reports which do not result in management action are useless. In a competitive marketplace, the ability to quickly identify a shift in consumer preferences and respond is not simply desirable, but essential to survival. This debate is continued in Unit 8 Marketing Information.

 ## Activity 4.4

A city centre taxi company has approached you. They own a variety of vehicles (e.g. standard taxis, mini buses) and employ all their drivers. The company operates 24/7 and drivers work on a shift basis. The owner has asked you what 'ratios' might be potentially useful in monitoring the profitable operation of the business. What would your recommendations be?

Question 4.1

The New Arts Theatre is a regional arts theatre that seats 1000 people. Of the seats, 400 are sold at a premium price of £20, and 600 at a standard price of £15. On Fridays and weekends, all seats tend to be sold, but in the week only 70 per cent of seats are sold (same percentage for both classes of seats). The marketing manager is considering a loyalty card scheme where clients pay a subscription fee of £20 a year for a 'Friends of the Theatre' loyalty card and are able to purchase two premium tickets each month for £10.

Preliminary market research has indicated that very few people who are not existing customers already will be attracted. However, existing loyal customers who attend on average only six times a year would attend ten times a year under the new scheme. On preliminary research, the uptake appears to come from people who buy standard seats at the moment. The cost of setting up the scheme and administration for the first year is projected to be £5000. How many 'Friends of the Theatre' are required to achieve breakeven on the scheme?

The Catering Manager has noted that the pre-theatre occupation of the restaurant is only 50 per cent on the days that would be covered by the new scheme. Further research suggests that 50 per cent of the Friends would take advantage of a special offer of a 'Friend's pre-theatre dinner' and that the average spend per head would yield a profit of £2.00 a meal. If this factor were included in the breakeven calculation, what would the new breakeven figure be?

International aspects

Any aspect of the price mix may need adaptation, as pricing in the international dimension is somewhat more complex. A brief outline of selected issues is given using the structure of Figure 4.1 Architecture of price.

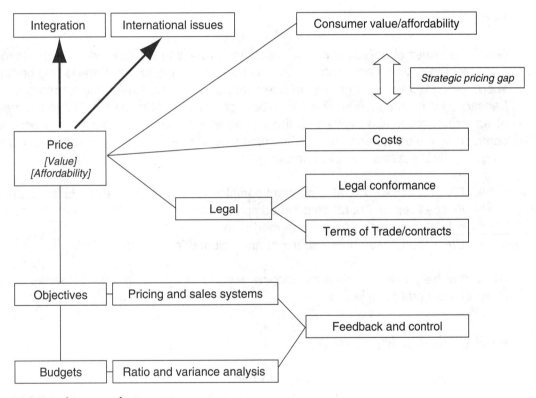

✳ *Figure 4.1* Architecture of price ✳

Customer value and affordability

Four key factors that drive the customer perception of value are brand awareness in the destination market, competition, disposable income and availability of credit. When M&S attempted to penetrate the United States, it had little brand awareness and so this did not confer value in the perception of the US consumer. In the United Kingdom, Wal-Mart uses the established George brand in the ASDA group to good effect. In the same way, UK customers are not overly familiar with the US brand. This neatly illustrates the key aspect of international marketing: 'think globally, act locally'. Competition can greatly affect the value of products.

119

If regional companies with established brands and lower local cost bases have set the market-perceived 'going rate', the organization may not be able to command premium prices. People with free disposable incomes are needed to buy products. This is different to just looking at the average gross domestic product per person as wealth distribution can be very uneven and in some 'poor' countries there can still be an appreciable wealthy class with a demand for luxury products. Simple gross domestic product is not the whole story as in many countries, the availability of credit is a major issue as well. In 2004, the total borrowing of UK consumers topped £1000 billion for the first time.

Costs

All items of the marketing mix can need adaptation (e.g. product labelling to be changed, advertising to be adapted etc.) and this will increase costs. Physical distribution will be more costly to distant locations for products with additional costs incurred with local distribution as well (e.g. local agents' fees). Cover of exchange risk (e.g. forward currency contract) and payments (e.g. confirmed letter of credit) will also increase costs.

Legal

Given the issues of collecting import duties and protecting local industries' exports, prices can be subject to government controls. Most important are the terms of trade and contracts. In a shop, the consumer pays money and gets the goods at the same time. In realistic terms, the transaction is instantaneous. There may be a gap of several months between the manufacture of an export order and delivery to the customer with several forms of transport used. The contract, by mutual agreement, can be completed at any point. Some examples of three of the so-called 'INCO' terms are given below:

o *EX-WORKS* – Ex-works, contract completed as soon as the goods leave the factory.
o *FOB* – Free on board, contract completed when the goods are loaded onto an agreed ship at an agreed port at an agreed time.
o *CIF* – Cost, insurance and freight are included in the price.

Given that freight rates, insurance and the like are all changing, only Ex-works costs can be given in a general price list.

Pricing and sales systems

Cover of exchange rate movements with hedging strategies and use of letters of credit and others make collection of money more complicated and expensive. Local taxation can also affect the amount of money to be made on a transaction. As stated above, only Ex-works costs are fixed. Every other export order needs an order-by-order calculation as the elements are all changing. The organizational impact is that export order administration needs expert people with good knowledge of the processes and procedures.

Ratio and variance analysis

Most of the cover so far in this section has been given in the context of exporting. Where the organization elects to manufacture in the target country, all the normal budgeting rules apply but problems occur when consolidating the cash flows for overall analysis. Floating exchange rates add complexity to this process.

Case study

'Lake View Organic Farms' – Pricing of online 'à la carte' veggie boxes

Consider the situation where the management, of 'Lake View Organic Farms', have noted some feedback, that their boxes represented poor value for money. The mix of products does not suit all customers. Some customers were finding they had too much of what they did not want and too little of what they did require. Clearly, the 'one-size-fits-all' or the old Ford statement, 'You can have any colour as long as it is black', does not work for all consumers. Management think that their internal systems and packing process are sufficiently developed to make online ordering a possibility. Using the elements of Figure 4.1 as headings, an analysis of pricing decisions might be

Customer value/affordability – Given the ability to 'cherry-pick' only what they wanted, customers should see enhanced value. Online payment would add convenience.

Costs – A framework would have been developed to cost deliveries (the most likely would be a flat-rate delivery cost built into the pricing structure for an order). There are two additional costs, the web facility and addition packing costs. There would be an 'upfront' cost of building the required pages into the website and a continuing fixed cost of maintaining the facility. Any additional cost of online payments would have to be taken into account. Costs allocated that are too high would kill online ordering. Too low an allocation and the new development would not be making a fair contribution to overheads. The costs of the raw materials (vegetables and packaging) would be the standard used in the costing of the normal veggie boxes. The cost of filling the 'to order' boxes would be a little higher than the standard box (easier to put up 100 boxes of the same mix than 100 different boxes). A few experiments could establish how much longer this would take. Calculations would already have been made of the standard cost per hour for a packer. The cost of packing a bespoke box could be established. Two approaches could be used. Management could just accept that packing a 'to order' box costs a flat £#.## more than a standard box (this would make small boxes appear expensive and large boxes cheap). A slightly more sophisticated formula might say that to just put up a box and label would cost £a.aa and that each item added to the box would cost an extra £0.bb. Cost of packing a box would then be

$$£a.aa + £0.bb \times \text{(number of items ordered)}$$

This would have the effect of making small orders less expensive and larger orders more expensive. Both methods have logic. The key point to note is that methods of cost allocation are not neutral to a customer's perception of value and affordability. Cost allocation decisions should be made in the context of the overall situation, not seen as an isolated, academic accountancy exercise.

Legal conformance – No major problems. This is not an area of price regulation. It will be necessary to ensure that products are properly priced in a clear way (e.g. are cabbages to be priced by weight or just per cabbage). Not a problem as long as the customer is clearly informed.

Contracts – There has been a problem in this area with the 'online' services of the supermarkets. There has been some controversy about the value and pricing of substitute products when an item is out of stock. Care needs to be taken to make certain about the policy and careful monitoring will be needed during the launch to see that customers are happy with any substitutions that are made to cover out of stock products.

Pricing and sales systems – An Internet computer system is perfect. Given that it is properly set up with back-up and so on. Online entry would save time over telephone orders and customers have the responsibility to get their order right.

Sales analysis – The database, which would be created from these orders, would be most useful to track what was popular and what was not much liked. There might even be a spin-off. Analysis of orders might provide information to better balance the mix of products in the standard veggie box.

The setting of price is more than just plugging a few numbers into a standard equation. The numbers need management estimates where overall business insight is needed to gain appropriate figures. Different approaches are possible and the right equation should be used for the conditions of the business (e.g. the flat-rate or variable-cost approach to the cost of filling the online veggie box). Pricing is more than just spreadsheets. Good understanding of finance is clearly required. However, good decisions also need depth of marketing insight and management.

Question 4.2

What price is a cup of coffee?

Examine the issues to be considered in setting the price of coffee in a restaurant or café.

Summary

In this unit, we have explored

- The strategic pricing gap. The band within which the organization can set its prices to meet its objectives.
- The maximum price that is acceptable to consumers. This depends on their perception of value and ability to pay.
- The minimum price possible for the organization. Costs set to the lowest level at which it is feasible to price a product or service.
- The various types of costs (fixed, variable, historical, future etc.).
- The concept of profit contribution (revenue per unit less the variable costs per unit).
- The dangers of using average costs in the wrong decision context.
- The legal constraints on pricing policies that need to be observed.
- Strategies for pricing such as penetration and skimming.
- The practical management operation of setting prices and collecting money.
- The need for feedback and control systems.
- The use of variance analysis to diagnose problems.
- Some facets of pricing in the international context.

We have noted again that the pricing policies and strategies must be set within the context of the integrated marketing mix.

Further study

Dibb, S., Simkin, L., Pride, W. and Ferrell, O. (2006) *Marketing Concepts and Strategies, 5th European edition*, Houghton Mifflin Chapters 20 and 21.

Hints and tips

It is essential for a marketer to have a sound grasp of costs and cost drivers. Control of costs is fundamental to long-term success; neglect of cash flow is a major cause of business failure. When looking at the marketing aspect of developing value, it is also essential to maintain control of expenses. Cash flows and breakeven calculations often feature in CIM exams and practice will develop your skills. Typical questions are December 2005 'The Urban Culture Festival' 1(a) 'Calculate the expected revenue, costs and profit from holding the celebrity Gala Evening at each of the two venues, stating any assumptions.' and June 2006 'SMS Cars Ltd' 1(a) 'Calculate the total direct cost of both venues for the launch event and fashion show. Show your calculations and state any assumptions', 1(b) 'What other costs might there be for this type of event?' and Questions 6(a) 'Copy the following table and calculate the annual income for each model of the self-drive vehicle fleet for the past 12 months and state any assumptions.', 6(b) 'Copy the following table and calculate the annual income for each model of the self-drive vehicle fleet for the next 12 months and after the 10 per cent in crease in hire prices' and 6(c) 'What conclusions can you draw from your findings?' You should refer to the full examination paper and the specimen solutions on the CIM website. It should be noted that numerical questions can be featured in both sections of the paper. Even if you do not like calculations, it is most unwise not to develop the skills necessary to perform them.

Bibliography

Drury, C. (2005) *Management Accounting for Business Decisions*, 3rd edition, Thomson Learning.

Kotler, P. (2006) *Marketing Management*, 12th edition, Prentice Hall.

the marketing mix: place

After this unit, you will

- Be able to analyse the issues of convenience from customers' perspectives.

- Understand the options available for the physical delivery of the product or service.

- Be able to adapt concepts such as 'inventory', which are developed in product distribution, for service delivery situations.

- Appreciate the legal, safety and environmental issues in distribution.

- Be able to evaluate the range of channel outlets that might be appropriate for a given product or service.

- Understand the control issues in maintaining customer satisfaction in distribution.

- Appreciate the need for the integration of distribution within the overall marketing mix.

Syllabus references

2.5 Explain the supplier interface: negotiating, collaborating, operational and contractual aspects.

2.6 Explain how the organization fits into a supply chain and works with distribution channels.

2.7 Use networking skills in the business world.

2.8 Explain the concept and application of e-relationships.

3.2 Identify alternative and innovative approaches to a variety of marketing arenas and explain criteria for meeting business objectives.

4.5 Describe the current distribution channels for an organization and evaluate new opportunities.

5.5 Make recommendations on alternative courses of action.

5.6 Examine the correlation between marketing mix decisions and results.

Key definition

JIT – Just-in-time delivery, where goods are delivered within a narrow time-window (goods not accepted if they are either too early or too late).

Study Guide

Products are useless unless they are where people want them, at the right time. In this unit, we consider these issues using illustrative examples, the constraints on product distribution and the management of this process. However, when studying this unit, consider the products and services you use in your day-to-day life and consider two issues. What is your view of convenience for the product and what distribution stages were involved in getting the product to you? As with most of marketing, the theory of physical distribution was developed with products and you need to adapt the concepts to apply them to services. The focus should be on physical distribution, availability and convenience. The word 'Place' acts to fit this element into a P framework but does not adequately describe the activities themselves.

Rather than provide a long list of possibilities, the general issues are illustrated with specific examples to illustrate 'Place' in action. You should make notes as you work through this unit and pencil in your own examples from your experience that illustrate the factors being considered.

Convenience

In Units 1 and 3, we explored the mix element Product and worked through the implications of the idea that people do not buy products, they buy benefits. In the same way, customers do not want to buy 'Place' (what would you do with a supermarket?) but want to experience convenience. Therefore, in this unit we shall explore the nature of customer convenience needs and wants. Just as with Product we need to understand the customer demands first and then work out our marketing solutions.

Who?

For the consumer market, the answer is simple: the buyer and the consumer. These issues are covered in the segmentation and positioning considerations applicable to all marketing mix elements. Any element of the marketing mix can provide a relevant segmentation variable. The question 'Who?' is posed here as, in the B2B marketing context (covered in Unit 2), the convenience needs of all the relevant members of the DMU need to be considered. The buyer will be concerned that the order process is simple and effective, with the maximum amount of management control and the minimum of administrative costs (transaction costs must be attacked at every level of the organization and every link in the supply chain). The inbound logistics group (typically warehousing) will be concerned that the delivery arrives within the time frame (JIT means just that!), in the form that is required (e.g. the right type of pallet or drum). With JIT deliveries, quality will need to be 'zero defect' as the product will go straight onto the shelf or into production. Documentation will need to be in perfect order so the goods received can be processed, cleared and payment authorized. Again, the objective is minimum administrative overheads but with total management control.

BSE and traceability

Late in 2003, the United States had a single identified case of BSE (the so-called 'mad cow disease') in a meat processing plant. It took some time to work up the supply chain (which supermarkets had received products from the diseased animal, a potential human health risk) and down the supply chain (where had the animal come from and what had it been fed during its life – contaminated feed is the suspected transmission mechanism).

The control of the supply chain must be such that a single pack of meat product must be traceable through the chain to how the animal lived on the farm, including its feeding regime. Modern supply chain management requires 100 per cent audit for 100 per cent traceability with minimum administrative overheads. A recent example of this issue has been the problem, in the United Kingdom, of a food product contaminated with an illegal red colouring. Over 500 products had to be recalled.

Consumer concern for traceability can be used as a marketing feature. Discerning customers (e.g. upmarket restaurants with demanding clients) are not only concerned with what they buy, but its total history (e.g. dolphin-friendly tuna fish). People are prepared to pay a substantial premium for wild as opposed to natural salmon. In the Westcountry of the United Kingdom, a group of fishermen still catch wild bass with the traditional line method as opposed to the more industrial methods (considered to harm dolphins) or farmed bass. They have introduced a blue tag which is attached to the fish and reads 'Line caught wild bass from Cornwall'. Customers are able to use the Internet to trace details by logging on the website and clicking on the number given on the blue tag. They can then see pictures of the given fisherman at work. Economically meeting customers' concern for traceability has been made possible here with an imaginative application of ICT.

Where?

This is a simple question, yet one which often demands a multifaceted and complex solution. This complexity can easily be seen within mobile telephone network operations. Lots of people want to make use of their phones in city centres, so the problem may be to provide sufficient channel density in order that customers can always make a connection, even at peak times of the day. On a long train journey there is not much else to do but to chat and what do we find? We cross the moors and the line drops out. We are entering the city and want to order a taxi and the line cuts off as we enter a tunnel. Mobile telephones show just how far and just how quickly people's expectations move. We not only want to be able to talk at any time and in any place in our own country, but when we are away on holiday, the first thing we do is send home a picture of us sitting round the swimming pool. Customers want things where *they* are. Where are they? They could be anywhere, but they still want the product or service. If I am not able to use my cashpoint card at the motorway service station, I will very quickly change to one that is more versatile. B2B customers are no less demanding in wanting products where it is convenient for them.

When?

The ultimate demand for 'When' is news. News channels make the claim 'see it first on XNetwork, see it live'. This news could be war, natural disasters or sports events (to name but a few). To provide this, major news organizations such as the BBC or CNN must maintain a global network (to send a team the next day is too late) and maintain people and communications equipment in difficult and dangerous situations. The same logic applies to our demands

127

for products. When do we want that takeaway meal or home delivery? Well, right now, and they had better keep to the promised delivery time. Today, we are in the here-and-now society.

What?

Customers want the product in the quantity, quality, form and state that is right for that moment. This is one of the most irritating aspects of the web. What do you want? *An itinerary for my journey from home to New York.* How many clicks do you want to make? *As few as possible* (too often, what we get is a clutter of unwanted sites that lock onto the keyword search to offer some very strange products or services). A decade ago, this type of question may have involved a journey to a travel agent and leafing through any number of brochures and data-bases with a consultant. Now customers demand the precise information in the form needed, with the ability to order without sifting through mounds of unwanted, useless data.

How?

What is the delivery mechanism that the customer will find most convenient?

Service?

In the B2B sector, service may be a key value-added factor in a contract. Major computer companies, such as IBM, do not see themselves selling computers but providing partnerships with 'business solutions'. Only part of the delivery is the hardware, the computer. Installation, maintenance, staff training and even management consultancy may be part of the purchase package for the supply of a computer system.

 Activity 5.1

Developing and printing

At the turn of the century, people used traditional cameras with photographic film. When the roll was completely exposed, the file was taken into a collection centre (lots of small shops would act as agents). The films were collected in the late afternoon. The film was processed and prints produced in a central laboratory. The prints were then delivered back to the agent for collection by the customer the next day. Customers could also post their films and receive prints back by post. Technical developments had also allowed the development of mini-laboratories where, at busier collection centres, developing and printing could be done on-site. Prints could be ready for collection in an hour or so. Only a tiny minority of enthusiasts operated darkroom labora-tories at home. In 2005, Dixons, a major UK retailer discontinued the sale of film cameras.

As we enter the second half of the first decade of the twenty-first century, the majority of mobile phones will also have camera capabilities. Within a few years, for the majority of non-profes-sional users, the 'film' camera will go the way of the typewriter and be an interesting museum curiosity. Kodak is busy re-inventing itself as an 'image realization' company, rather than a manufacturer of film.

Review the distribution type issues that will apply to the new age of digital images rather than wet processing of traditional film.

Conformance

Legal

As with pricing, it is often assumed that there are no legal constraints on distribution. For deregulated industries (e.g. gas, electricity, telephones), law, in part, governs the nature and standard of distribution. A train franchise may not wish to run any services it thinks may be unprofitable, but often there are regulatory influences, for example the need to run uneconomic services deemed to be of social importance. Telecommunications is a particularly complex area. Even shops may be limited on hours of opening.

Sometimes an organization may wish to restrict the type of outlet where its products are sold. Indeed, for some products such as prescription pharmaceutical products, this may be a legal necessity. For other products, such as fashion clothing, this is a matter of marketing policy. There are two views of this situation. The brand owner considers that they are defending their brand values by keeping the product out of unsuitable outlets. Supermarkets, who are discriminated against in this way, will argue this is a restraint of free trade.

Account needs

In the B2B sector with JIT delivery, there may be fairly detailed specifications about the delivery schedule built into the contract. This is particularly important for certain services. If you have lost electrical power at home, that is irritating. For a hospital or an air traffic control centre, uninterruptible supplies are essential.

Environmental and safety

A key concern is environmental impact. Transporting goods over long distances involves significant fuel consumption, which can involve the use of a non-renewable resource (oil), and a contribution to greenhouse gases (carbon dioxide). To a limited extent, some use has been made of bio-diesel (waste cooking oils can be cleaned to be used as a replacement for diesel oil in modified engines). The electric milk float may be disappearing but was an early example of a zero emission vehicle. City centres are a major issue with customers demanding 24/7 availability for products. However, these same people (now calling themselves 'residents') do not want commercial vehicles in their area at night (the so-called 'not in my back yard' – NIMBY effect). A most controversial area is air travel where people want to go on holiday to exotic places. They want the airport close enough to get to conveniently, but far enough away for the noise not to be a problem. Similar problems affect utilities. We all want 'drop-out-free' mobile telephone use, as long as the radio mast is not at the end of our road. Organizations are increasingly between a rock (demands for increasing standards of service on a 24/7/365 basis) and a hard place (environmental pressure groups).

Safety in distribution is an issue of increasing pressure group concern. This can be the transport of dangerous goods (e.g. petrol, nuclear fuel etc.) or more diffuse issues (e.g. concern about cancer risks for residents close to high voltage electrical transmission lines). Issues such as these should be covered in the PLC environmental impact analysis.

Hazardous materials

Modern lifestyles would not be possible without the marketing and distribution of potentially hazardous materials. Petrol is the classic example. The material is clearly explosive when mixed with air and it is also potentially toxic (even unleaded fuel). Moreover, the escape of petrol vapour (e.g. displaced from a car fuel tank) contributes to the so-called 'VOC pollution'. The distribution of petrol and other like materials requires expert understanding of the law. Regard to safety is paramount and, increasingly, companies are compelled to achieve these two objectives with minimum environmental impact.

Implementation

Physical distribution

Having reviewed the customer demands for convenience and some of the constraints, it is now possible to consider implementation. Three aspects need to be considered:

- Transport (physical delivery of the service or product)
- The standard of service/inventory required
- Geographical cover.

Transport

Delivery of physical products was transformed in the second half of the twentieth century. It is now possible and economic to source raw materials and manufactured products on a global basis. It is more economic to make consumer electronics in China than to manufacture in Europe. In the United Kingdom, deep mining of coal declined and imports of low-cost coal soared. Transport by sea was revolutionized by containerization, providing door-to-door delivery of manufactured goods to B2B customers on a global basis at economic cost. Specialized transport provides solutions for the mass transportation of particular products (e.g. cars). For some products, hybridized solutions evolved. For over 100 years, the railways provided overnight distribution of newspapers in the United Kingdom. Now papers can be transmitted digitally to regional printing centres providing a more efficient, timely service with reduced environmental impact.

Electricity

From the twentieth-century marketing view, electricity was a dull public service. In the twenty-first century with the deregulation of the generation and sale of electricity, the market is a commercial 'Wild West' where the final outcomes are far from certain.

Some selected issues

Electricity is most odd in that, for all but the smallest uses, it may not be stored. What is being used has to be generated at the instant it is needed and we have become totally dependent on 100 per cent continuity of supply for our lifestyles. In 2003 the United States, United Kingdom and Italy had massive power cuts affecting millions of consumers and, in some cases, it took days to restore the power. A distribution system that was designed in the last century to provide security of supply is now being used to ship power in bulk in the new, free, deregulated market, leaving wafer-thin safety margins, hence the catastrophic system failures.

Environmental issues are an increasing concern. Germany is phasing out nuclear power stations. Japan and France are still dependent on nuclear power at the moment. In the United Kingdom a massive programme of wind farm construction is in progress. However, they are not a simple solution. What do you do when there is no wind?

The 100 years of taking total security of electrical supply for granted may be at an end. Micro-heat and power systems in our home may become the systems of the future (in generating electricity some 60 per cent of the power is thrown away, in the heat/power system this 60 per cent is put to good use heating water, etc.).

In the effort to provide consumers with choice and deregulate the industry, prices have been reduced to customers. However, with security of supply so critical to modern life, the balance between market forces and 'utility' provision looks to be a potential issue.

Many of the nuclear power stations, built in the late twentieth century, will have to be de-commissioned over the next decade. Replacement with coal-fired power stations would cause environmental problems (carbon dioxide and sulphur dioxide). Gas-fired power stations are less attractive with declining stocks and increasing costs. Wind power is great until you get a cold, windless day. Where will the power come from? How will it be distributed? Major political issues confront all the developed countries which are caught between depleting oil and gas reserves, environmental issues (greenhouse gases and acid rain) and ever-increasing demands for electricity.

ICT and distribution

In the earlier section, it was noted that newspapers are now distributed via a mixture of traditional and digital distribution (digital transmission to the regions, then local printing and physical distribution). The general distribution problem is to find cost-effective solutions that provide the customer with maximum convenience. The 'hot potato' of the early twenty-first century is digital entertainment. More money is spent on computer games than is taken in box-office receipts at the cinema. Films, music and computer games are, in terms of distribution, one and the same thing: large computer files. With broadband access, we need never go to the record shop or hire a video or DVD. The technology is here and now (and very alive with pirate editions). The issue for the copyright owners is how to preserve their property rights, yet provide convenience to the customers. Further consideration of ICT is given in Unit 7.

Digital distribution

Wal-Mart looks at feasibility of DVD download kiosks in stores

In the competitive world of retail marketing, every metre of shelf space must earn its keep with maximum sales. DVDs have become (as with books) a relatively recent and profitable product line with relatively high value and small physical size (yielding good sales per metre of shelf space). However, there are three problems:

1. Security is an issue, DVDs are relatively small and easy to conceal and steal.
2. The physical distribution of DVDs is relatively expensive and time-consuming.
3. To push up sales still further a larger range of titles is required necessitating more shelf space.

In late 2005, Wal-Mart was in discussion with the Hollywood studios about installing kiosks in stores from which consumers could digitally download films onto disc. One technical challenge is the 'burning' of content onto a new generation of high-definition DVDs while maintaining anti-piracy protection.

Fruit machines in a digital spin

Leisure Link, a UK operator of about 45 000 AWPs (amusement with prizes) machines in late 2005 was trialling digital versions at selected venues. A key logistics problem, with traditional electro-mechanical machines, is that customers lose interest in a given game after some 12 weeks. Every four weeks Leisure Link shifts 16 000 machines around its 30 000 venues. Digital distribution technology offers a far easier distribution method. New games can be downloaded overnight. The new software can monitor customer use accurately and report back. Money can be emptied by local staff at the distributed location but with full audit capability in place. Similar developments have already taken place with digital jukeboxes.

BBC World Service – What is the future of 'broadcasting'?

In the twentieth century, the BBC World Service reached out to its global audience with a network of short-wave transmitters. Increasingly, this international audience is listening over the Internet. The BBC now holds many of its major programmes online for a week. People now do not have to sit by the radio at a given time. People can download at any time and then listen to the programme anywhere. Cable companies are now offering this service to selected mainstream television broadcasts. The application of convergent ICT is rewriting what public service broadcasting is and how its services can be delivered.

Digital cinema

Present technology involves making a print of the master film and distributing this 'hard copy' film. The process of making the copy is rather costly and the secure (to avoid falling into the hands of copyright pirates) distribution of rather bulky reels is also slow and expensive. The physical projection process also has a significant labour cost. Projection technology is at the crossover point where digital projection technology will provide good, and later better, quality than traditional film-based technology. Moreover, costs for digital distribution will be vastly less than physical distribution. Additional copies could be made available to the smallest local cinema. Global release of a film on the same day in all potential locations could become a possibility. The distribution of films is potentially on the edge of a revolution.

Footnote

Many of the above developments require high-level data security and this is not an easy technical problem to resolve. Sony had a PR disaster when its security software on American CDs affected home PCs so they became vulnerable to virus attacks. The CDs had to be withdrawn.

 Activity 5.2

In the first wave of the dot-com age, only a minority of households had Internet connections, and domestic broadband access was not generally available. Now the majority of UK households have access to the Internet and much of that access is now over high-speed broadband access. Evaluate how this capability might change methods and channels of distribution for various goods and services to the digital home.

Service and inventory

For consumer products, people are increasingly demanding 24/7 availability. However, this has not been achieved with vast stockholdings in retail outlets. The pipeline from manufacturer to customer contains days rather than weeks of inventory; JIT delivery is normal. Any failure of the systems will quickly show up as shortages on the shelves. Chilled food needs to be moved in hours rather than days to the shelves, and must stay within a very narrow temperature window throughout the distribution chain. A highly sophisticated web of specialist logistics caters for chilled food, fashion clothing (which needs specialized transport and also rapid response to turbulent sales demands) and petrol, to mention a few.

Above we have noted the problem of maintaining certain services, which, in modern life, have become not luxuries but essentials. Terms such as 'inventory' need to be re-interpreted for services. For many services, the technical/management problem is network regulation (water, gas, electricity and all forms of digital communications). Sophisticated mathematical models (e.g. linear programming) are employed to ensure that the right capacity is provided at the right time, in the right place. Most of this work is conducted by part-time marketers in departments called production, operations and logistics. However, failure to understand the issues and work with the technical staff in service provision can result in companies selling capacity that does not exist, or failing to provide promised service levels (rail travel in the United Kingdom).

Geography

This topic has been included as it is a key segmentation variable that needs explicit consideration between the technical providers and marketing. Is it profitable for the organization to be national or would a regional focus be better in which the service might be better maintained? Area of coverage is a key marketing concern, where the technical issues of distribution play a major part in the overall decision process.

People in different locations may want the same benefits but physical delivery may be different. An isolated hotel in the mountains may want gas (the fuel of choice for master chefs in the kitchen) and broadband access. Gas pipes may not be feasible and, being remote from a town, fibre-optic links may not be available. The solution may be bulk delivery of liquid gas and satellite uplink or other radio technology for Internet access.

Activity 5.3

List all the services you use at home. What are the issues in physical delivery of the service for those services you use every day? Physical distribution issues are just as relevant to services as to products.

Channels

Figure 5.1 shows some patterns of distribution for consumer goods. The blocks represent stages where stock is held. This may be short term in a distribution centre or longer term for a distributor of imported goods. The arrows represent the physical transport process: in general, taking goods from the stock area, loading the goods, transportation, unloading the goods and storage. The message is simple: each arrow, each block, represents costs and unless these costs also add customer value the strategic pricing gap we discussed in Unit 4 is being eroded. The top distribution layer represents the distribution of an imported product sold through small retail outlets. The next shows the situation typical for a supermarket: manufacturers deliver products to a logistics centre; the assorted products for a given store are loaded into a vehicle (a supermarket may have over 10 000 lines but 10 000 vehicles do not arrive each day at every branch) and are delivered to the store. The supermarket system provides a vast array of products at reduced distribution cost. The small independent retailer has a huge mountain to climb to provide sufficient increased customer value to offset their increased costs (hence the death of the village shop/post office).

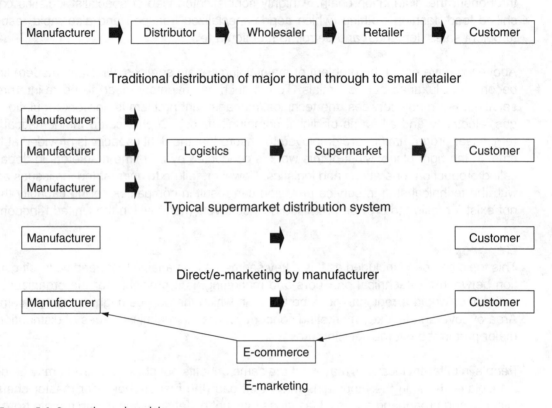

Figure 5.1 Some channel models

For appropriate goods (e.g. Dell with computers), the manufacturer can supply the goods direct. Here e-commerce can be seen as nothing totally new, it augments postal and telephone ordering. However, it is much more convenient and 'alive' for the customer (communications aspects are covered in Unit 6) and the transaction costs are much lower. The manufacturer does not need a distribution system; this can be contracted out to one of the specialist operators (e.g. DHL, UPS, etc.). However, this does not provide the customer with a wide range of products, just those made by one manufacturer. Enter the 'dot-com' company, a central 'dot-com' e-commerce company takes the order and, in an ideal world, does not play any part in the manufacture, storage or transport of the goods (e.g. an e-travel company does not own hotels or airlines). Here there is maximum customer satisfaction (armchair shopping with a wide assortment of goods) and efficient delivery with minimum transaction costs. Of course, the 'trick' is in that single arrow in the e-marketing model. Part of the problem of the 'dot-com' bubble was people were blinded by the glitz of the capabilities of the new communications channel and forgot the basics: that bargain PlayStation is no use if it arrives 3 days after the birthday and is damaged. Even if much of the distribution is conducted by part-time marketers (unlike marketing communications), it is essential to customer satisfaction and it must form an integrated element of the marketing mix.

Nature of outlets

The nature of the outlet makes a statement about the product. High fashion products do not want to be featured with discounted lines. It damages the brand image and value. The nature of the outlet is a statement about the product. Very high fashion products may only be obtainable from exclusive outlets such as Harrods, this special context exclusivity may be more important than simple convenience. Selective distribution would be through more numerous outlets that could still support the image (e.g. department store chains for fashion products) and intensive distribution where the objective is to get the product in as many locations as is reasonably practical (e.g. snack confectionery products). In this context, shops should not be regarded as merely providing products. The 'selling' part of the process should be considered as a 'service' in its own right and all the elements of the service-extended marketing mix (Unit 7) apply.

Case Study

'SMS Cars Ltd' (June 2006 CIM case study)

The SMS Cars Ltd case study featured what might be described at the traditional car dealership situation. This business model uses expensive showrooms with expensive sales staff. Ford and GM are in deep financial trouble. In China cars are being built for $5000. Is the time right for a new business model? Could there be an equivalent revolution in car sales and distribution that has been experienced in the air travel market?

The 'price savvy' car buyer will go to the main dealer for all the sales support and test drive; then cruise the Internet for the lowest price. How could a potential low cost Chinese manufacturer re-think this situation?

One possible option is to cut out the showroom entirely. Market the cars via the Internet and telephone sales. Use a national network of a car rental company to deliver vehicles for potential customers to test drive. Use a small number of distribution depots to hold cars before delivery and use the same rental network to deliver cars to clients. With regard to servicing seek partnerships with independent repair companies to provide effective servicing on a non-exclusive basis (keeping costs down but maintaining quality). An alternative strategy would be to seek a new distribution partner. TESCO and Wal-Mart sell petrol: why not cars and car servicing? The rules of marketing banking, insurance, films and music have been re-written by exploiting new technologies and new distribution strategies. Why not car sales?

Service provision

For many consumer products, no value-added service provision is needed, we do not need advice on how to use liquid soap. However, for consumer durables, service provision may be key to successful sales. For a manufacturer of kitchen appliances, installation and maintenance services may be a key element in the mix demanded by the consumer. For the B2B sector, the product may become part of a product–service continuum. Thus, an advertising agency may not be very expert in managing the essentials of the washroom and yet there is a whole market for janitorial services/products.

Activity 5.4

Consider you are away from home at an international sales conference. You have your laptop with you and you have written a report about the day's presentation and want to e-mail it back to the office. List the places where you would expect to be able to find Internet access.

Objectives

The objective process follows the model given in Figure 5.2. Having determined what the customer needs is gauged in terms of convenience (this is parallel to benefit needs analysis for product) and determined by what the constraints are, it can be decided what service levels are required and what the appropriate methods are to physically deliver the products and/or services. Distribution may be a major cost driver and marketing needs to work closely with other functions to ensure that the levels of service are physically deliverable at economic costs. This unit is shorter than others on the marketing mix since much of the delivery detail is the responsibility of part-time marketers (e.g. distribution logistics). Other elements, such as point-of-sale (Unit 6 Communications) and retail environment (Unit 7 Services), are covered in other units.

Feedback and control

Customer satisfaction needs to be monitored (e.g. customer complaints need to be tracked). However, with modern logistics systems performance measurement is built into the system (e.g. stock-outs for a supermarket, failed call attempts for a telephone network provider, etc.). However, field research is still needed in certain circumstances; for example, a laser checkout does not monitor the time the customer had to queue. One of the most complex areas is balancing customers' needs for short queuing time with the expense of operating too many channels. Too many pumps at the garage and you have too much cost, too few and customers will go on to the next, as they will not queue forever. With home services such as deliveries, a key parameter for the customer may be hitting the delivery time frame (for the consumer that lost parcel), for the B2B customer the product may be engineered on a JIT basis (late delivery = production shut down).

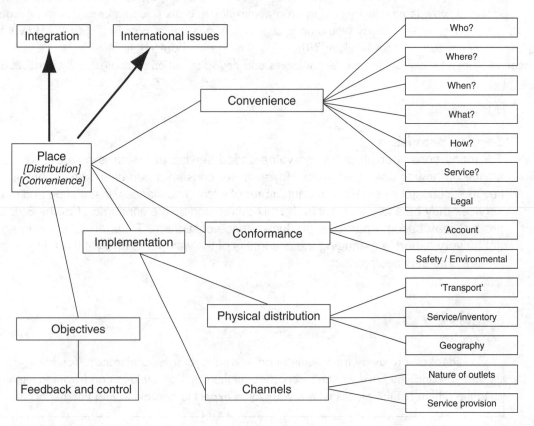

Figure 5.2 Structure of place

Case study

'Lake View Organic Farms' – Home delivery service

From the application of Figure 5.2 to the home delivery service, the following analysis can be constructed.

Who – determined from the segmentation strategy. People who are likely to be 'cash' rich but 'time' poor.

Where – location of customers' houses. Simple but the optimal call schedule (transportation) problem is one of the most complex in logistics.

When – when do customers want delivery? In the day or the evening? Fitting into specific customer time-slots would cost more than optimizing the call schedule to reduce the travel distance around the drop-off points (with much broader time-slots needed). A premium price for customers picking given time-windows over 'some time on Wednesday' might be an option.

What – in this case this is the nature of the product to be delivered? This has been considered under Unit 3. If fresh food is to remain crisp, temperature-controlled vehicles might be needed.

How – delivery to the door, nothing special. With some other products (e.g. central heating oil), how delivery is to be affected can be important.

Service – not of much significance, just the collection of packaging for reuse/recycling.

Legal – care needs to be taken with driver's hours. Poor scheduling could cause a driver to have to cut a round early or exceed statutory driving time limits.

Account – not a major issue in this B2C situation. Note the discussion in the earlier unit about agreement about action to find alternatives for 'out of stock' situations.

Safety/environmental – experienced drivers with clean driving licences. The company needs to ensure good vehicle maintenance. The possible use of 'bio-diesel' has been noted earlier in Unit 3.

Transport – temperature-controlled vehicles of appropriate size: too small and capacity will be a problem; too large and access to some properties might be difficult. The vehicle should provide easy offloading access (do not want to have to move 20 boxes to get at the next delivery).

Service/inventory – Earlier in this analysis the issue of narrow time-windows or broad blocks has been discussed. Narrow time-windows may be convenient to the client but may push up costs (non-optimal scheduling of deliveries to fit with customer needs). Inventory is a key issue. With fresh products, many having limited shelf lives, good planning is needed. Out of stock costs lost sales and damages customer relations. Over-stocking could result in write-offs when product deteriorates.

Geography – each 'round' needs to be set to ensure effective (right products delivered at right times) and efficient (cost minimization) cover. This needs to be effected within the driving hours regulations.

Channels – not an issue as direct B2C situation without the use of any channels.

International aspects

For the B2B sector, bulk tankers and the like carry the raw material of society round the world. Not many marketers will be concerned with selling iron ore to the steel industry. However, even SMEs are involved in exporting. Containerization has over the last half century revolutionized the transport of goods around the world. Infrastructure may be different in the destination market (e.g. availability of railways. In 2004 for the first time there was a cross Australia rail link) and this will impact on the selection of physical distribution methods. In addition, international logistics documentation is complex and requires specialist knowledge.

The nature of retail outlets may be different in different countries. The big five supermarkets in the United Kingdom cover over 50 per cent of the food sold in the United Kingdom. In less-developed countries, this is much more fragmented. In the United Kingdom, we buy perfume in Boots and similar large outlets; in other countries, in a specialist perfume shop.

The message again is clear: all elements of the marketing mix may need to be tailored to meet the local conditions and customer expectations.

Question 5.1

Most marketers will not be required to build a pipeline or run a transport fleet. However, most of us become involved with exhibitions from time to time. Many of the problems in exporting and export logistics apply in this situation. Consider yourself in the role of Marketing Assistant for a company making toys. The company has decided to start marketing in the United States and is to have a stand at a trade exhibition. You have been given the responsibility of sorting out the logistics. What issues might you need to consider? You may assume that the basic stand has been booked.

Summary

In this unit, we have looked at place from the customers' view as convenience. We have noted that

o There are legal and environmental considerations in the physical movement of goods and delivery of services.
o There are a range of options for the delivery of goods and services to customers (physical distribution issues).
o The concept of inventory needs modification in the context of services.
o Different channel strategies can be used to target customers.
o There is a need to measure distribution and channel performance.
o Place must be set in the overall context of the integrated marketing mix.

Further study

Dibb, S., Simkin, L., Pride, W. and Ferrell, O.C. (2006) *Marketing Concepts and Strategies*, 5th European edition, Houghton Mifflin Chapters 4, 14–16.

Hints and tips

As always in marketing, observe distribution issues as you shop and if your company has a Transport Department, go and have a chat with the people. Much of physical distribution is outside the normal management scope of the Marketing Department. In addition to reading about the topic in Marketing textbooks, more depth is given to the topic of Supply Chain Management and Logistics in textbooks on Operations Management. Aspects such as retailing are well covered in standard marketing texts.

In the CIM exams specific focus on distribution is less common but a question was featured in June 2005 'Kernow Railway micro franchise': Question 1c, subsection i 'Select FOUR elements of the extended marketing mix (7Ps) to demonstrate how you could ensure the success of this idea.' The ability to formulate an integrated marketing mix for a given situation is an important skill that is often tested in various CIM exams. Questions focusing on the service extension to the marketing mix occurred in both the December 2005 case 'The Urban Culture Festival 2006' and the June 2006 case 'SMC Cars Ltd'.

Bibliography

Burk Wood, M. (2004) *The Marketing Plan Handbook*, Prentice Hall.

Kotler, P. (2006) *Marketing Management*, 12th edition, Prentice Hall.

Waller, D. (2003) *Operations Management: A Supply Chain Approach*, 2nd edition, Thomson Learning.

unit 6 the marketing mix: promotion

By the end of this unit you will

o Understand the communications tasks required to convey appropriate messages to key stakeholders.

o Appreciate some of the restrictions imposed by self-regulation and law on communications.

o Understand the difference between the available elements of the communications mix, including advertising, publicity, public relations, person selling, point of sale, sales systems, sales promotion, direct marketing, e-communications and sponsorship.

o Appreciate the different characteristics of various media such as TV and posters.

o Be able to frame objectives for a given media/stakeholder context and consider how the achievement of these objectives might be measured.

Syllabus references

1.1 Identify sources of information internally and externally to the organization, including ICT-based sources such as Intranet and Internet.

1.2 Maintain a marketing database, information collection and usage.

1.3 Investigate customers via the database and develop bases for segmentation.

1.6 Investigate marketing and promotional opportunities using appropriate information-gathering techniques.

2.4 Represent the organization using practical PR skills, including preparing effective news releases.

2.5 Explain the supplier interface: negotiating, collaborating, operating and contractualizing aspects.

2.6 Explain how the organization fits into a supply chain and works with distribution channels.

2.8 Explain the concept and application of e-relationships.

3.2 Identify alternative and innovative approaches to a variety of marketing arenas and explain criteria for meeting business objectives.

3.3 Demonstrate an awareness of successful applications of marketing across a variety of sectors and sizes of business.

3.4 Explain how marketing makes use of planning techniques: objective setting; and coordinating, measuring and evaluating results to support the organization.

4.1 Select media to be used based on appropriate criteria for assessing media opportunities, and recommend a media schedule.

4.2 Evaluate promotional activities and opportunities including sales promotion, PR and collaborative programmes.

4.6 Describe how organizations monitor product trends.

4.7 Explain the importance of the extended marketing mix: how process, physical aspects and people affect customer choice.

4.8 Explain the importance of ICT in the new mix.

5.3 Explain how organizations assess the viability of opportunities, marketing initiatives and projects.

5.4 Prepare, present and justify a budget as the basis for a decision on a marketing promotion.

5.5 Make recommendations on alternative courses of action.

5.6 Examine the correlation between marketing mix decisions and results.

Key definitions

BOGOF – Buy one get one free, a form of sales promotion.

FMCG –Fast moving consumer goods – the day-to-day products we fill our shopping trolley with such as detergent.

SMART – this is a checklist used for planning; SMART objectives are specific, measurable, aspirational, realistic and time-bound.

Study Guide

There is a structure to this unit, which reflects the requirements of any communications system. Who are we? What do we want to communicate? Plus, who do we need to communicate with? To start considering using TV or national press before we have completed the stakeholder analysis is like starting to paint the walls of a room before they have been plastered. Successful communications are based on the foundation of well-considered objectives, sound research and good preparation. It is not an open house; marketing communications need to also comply with law and industry regulation (complex in the international context as these vary from country to country).

As with other units, the more situations you analyse the more you will gain an understanding of the processes. While reading a magazine or travelling to work, select a few advertisements and think: who are they intended for and how effective are they? When visiting an organization (e.g. a hospital) consider what their communications tasks might be. The tools are briefly outlined here; it is only practice that will give you skill and confidence.

Integration

This unit is longer than the other marketing mix units (reflecting the weighting in the syllabus). This is not because it is more important; if the product is poor and over-priced, no amount of marketing communications will overcome the problems. Rather it is an explicit recognition that part-time marketers (e.g. research department in developing new products) often conduct much of this activity. Formal marketing communications (e.g. advertising) are frequently conducted by marketing specialists. Marketing specialists will devise and implement an advertising campaign (often using an agency); thus, a greater depth of understanding implementation is relevant to the day-to-day work of the marketing practitioner in this area of the mix. This is not to overlook the contribution that part-time marketers make to building and sustaining good customer relations (e.g. a Field Service Engineer is also a company ambassador in relationship-marketing terms).

As outlined in Unit 1, the positioning and segmentation strategy needs to be set for the total mix. Although all aspects of the marketing mix can and do communicate, the promotion element is, of course, paramount in this process. As with other elements of the mix, we will consider what the task is and the constraints on the process. We will then be in a position to consider the implementation strategies and finally the planning, control and feedback systems. The overall process is given in Figure 6.1.

The communications task

The segmentation process identifies the target segments, and this profile gives an insight into how the mix proposition should be formulated (i.e. the offer that is designed for that segment). The corporate and brand values are an important foundation in reducing risk and building value. Therefore, many organizations will have a powerful and ongoing communications programme to sustain this; alongside the programme are an integrated set of sub-communications plans to support a given project (see Figure 6.1). This is key for the front-line marketer since checking conformance to house style is an important aspect of their day-to-day activities and responsibilities. There is nothing worse than finding you have 10 000 brochures with last year's logo in the wrong Pantone colour!

In Introduction to Relationship Marketing (Unit 2), we noted that it is not just customers we have to communicate with, but all relevant stakeholders. Therefore for a consumer product, the best advertising campaign (pull element of the strategy) is a waste of time if the B2B marketing to the channels has not succeeded in getting the product onto the shelf (the push element of the strategy). Sometimes in the literature on communications, stakeholders may be referred to as publics or audiences. We need to define what the corporate and brand values are before we get to the details. These set the tone and atmosphere of all policies and activities. It will then be possible to set the messages and propositions.

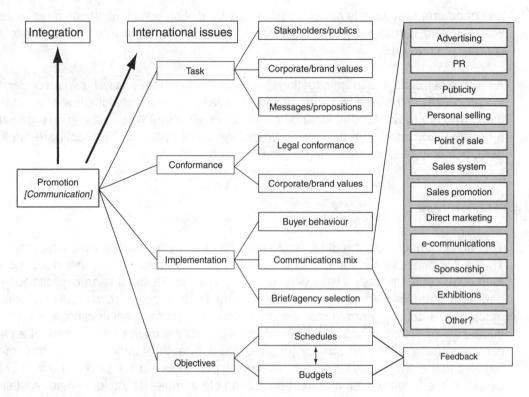

Figure 6.1 The marketing communication system

Stakeholders

Stakeholder analysis was covered in Unit 1. The first stage of communications activities is to verify the stakeholder analysis to ensure that it is complete and does not need revising or updating. The profiling process should not be reserved for the customers alone, but for all the stakeholders, so that we can understand their agendas (in American terms 'where they are coming from'). It is suggested that this should be done in either spreadsheet or database format. Later, we will see how important it is that communications intended for one audience (stakeholder group) may be received by another with a different agenda, who will put a completely different 'spin' on the message. A spreadsheet will enable the effect the communication has to be checked against all who will receive it (not just the intended target).

Question 6.1

Complete an outline stakeholder analysis for 'The Urban Culture Festival 2006' (December 2005 case study).

 ## Activity 6.1

Most major cities have a local history museum. Complete a stakeholder analysis for such a regional museum including a small bookshop specializing in publications of regional interest.

Corporate and brand values

Major companies such as Unilever and the Co-operative Society have distinctive corporate values, which are articulated in their marketing (e.g. Cooperative movement with 'fair trade' products); just as an individual makes a personal statement with their appearance, so do corporations. Virgin airlines have a very distinctive personality that is different to British Airways (BA) and this applies to all the organization's communications. As discussed in Unit 3, product, the organization and the brand may have the same identity (e.g. International Red Cross), or a firm may have a whole clutch of brands with their distinctive values (e.g. EMI's range of record labels and stable of groups and stars are each a brand in their own right). An organization must decide what it is and what its values are. Then, just as with an individual's appearance, this becomes a signal to the world at large. This is particularly important for organizations undergoing change (e.g. the difficulties encountered in moving the Royal Mail from a state monopoly to a commercial organization). Marketers need to take care not to become shallow makeover specialists. The transformation has become a favourite TV format; however, redecorating or 'mutating' the house does not make its boring owners into 'A' list celebrities invited to late-night chat shows. Putting speed stripes on a tortoise does not make it go faster! The marketing message is that all communications (including the communications aspects of the other six elements of the marketing mix) need to be consistent with the overall corporate/brand values. The marketing practitioner needs to internalize these values, as they need to be taken into account constantly, from writing press releases to appearing on a live interview where the corporate manual will not be there to refer to. Values come before message, message before media.

Messages and propositions

These will be considered in more detail under objects towards the end of the unit. However, before we can define the objective for a given advertisement, we need to know the broad aims. It may be some sweeping strategic task such as repositioning the brand (e.g. the greening of BP) or something more tactical (e.g. the launch of an individual product). The marketer should consider the organization's objective and then ascertain the state of awareness and attitudes for all the relevant stakeholders at the present time. The marketer can evaluate what is the desired state and attitude required by the organization for each stakeholder segment. This then provides the framework for formulating the communication aims.

Conformance

Legal

As with all company activities the law must be observed. Even within Europe, there are very significant differences as to what methods of communication may be appropriate for given products in specific areas. Highly sensitive areas include communications to children or promotion of sensitive products, such as alcohol, tobacco or contraceptives. This does apply not only to advertisements placed by the marketing department but also to the activities of all people associated with the product and any aspect of the extended mix. Data protection legislation must be observed in the use of address lists for direct mail and so on.

Often developments outstrip legislation (ground rules for e-communications) or move into areas where issues, for example public perceptions, of good taste are involved. Here industry tends to practice self-regulation with bodies such as the Advertising Standards Authority (United Kingdom) to arbitrate. This is desirable, as the law tends to control historical issues whereas technology and society's values are rapidly changing. A sensitive responsive system is required rather than the dead hand of bureaucrats.

Corporate and brand values

This heading has not been included twice in error. The first stage, as discussed above, is to determine and agree upon corporate values. A major task for the central marketing function is to then interpret these into visual imagery, which has to work for example for an airline, on a jumbo jet down to a ticket (this covers a fair range of objects and situations!). This is coded into a document, the 'house style' manual. The ticket printed in Hong Kong had a better look as if it came from the same company when it is put next to the magazine advertisement printed in the United States. Drawing up both this guideline and its interpretation are demanding jobs. Ensuring consistency of logo for a cruise line can start with a 50 000-ton ship and yet it will still need to look good and recognizable on a web page. It is vital that all marketers, including part-time marketers, conform to the house style or otherwise that sharp vision becomes blurred and indistinct.

Activity 6.2

Consider a shop (e.g. ASDA) that sells its own brand and leading brand products. List the types of situations where the corporate logo might be used and hence what would need to be covered in the communications manual.

Implementation

Having considered the issues in establishing the aims for and constraints upon communications, it is now possible to consider the implementation issues. To understand the unique values of the various elements of the communications mix, some aspects of consumer behaviour and communication will be reviewed. In an integrative text, it is not possible to provide full treatment of this key topic, further reading references are given at the end of the unit. The elements of the communications mix will then be reviewed. Most marketing practitioners will be involved in presenting aspects of a brief to agencies and participate in the selection process; some of these key issues will then be highlighted.

Consumer behaviour

The first and most vital fact to understand is that even when the purchase decision appears to be instantaneous (e.g. selecting a packet of crisps), marketing communications have started long before with the establishment of the brand values and product attributes. The communications activities need to take the customer along a pathway. The simplest model is AIDA: awareness, interest, desire and action. For our treatment, here we will use the adoption model (Figure 6.2), as this is most useful for B2B marketing, whereas the AIDA model is better restricted to consumer products. Physicists are exploring the 'general theory of everything', in marketing we have yet to find our Newton or our law of gravity, so care should be taken in selecting a model that fits the immediate need; we have no general theory of marketing yet.

People may decide that they have a problem (e.g. the car fails its MOT and needs £500 of repairs) or 'I need a better job.' However, for new products people may have to learn that they have a problem: for example, vacuum cleaners have been around for decades; why should people pay several times as much for a Dyson? People had to be educated by Dyson that they had a suction problem. Information searches may be formal (motoring press for a car, college prospectuses for new qualifications) or informal (chats with friends). Internet searches can be formal or informal depending on the attitude of the person to the potential purchase decision. Evaluating alternatives may be highly objective (e.g. car fuel consumption or staff/student ratios in a college) or informal (style for a car or quality of nightlife for a university city). Often the closing of the sale for a major purchase may involve elements of personal selling (test drive for a car or open day for a college). Then comes the difficult bit for the individual making a major purchase ('Should I have bought that Japanese car rather than the American one?' or 'Would I have been better at Oxford rather than Cambridge?'). The marketer needs to manage all the stages. Post-purchase issues are important as, with relationship marketing in mind, we are not only concerned with this car but the one the customer will purchase in 3 years' time. With the college degree, the institution is already planning the student's MBA and PhD.

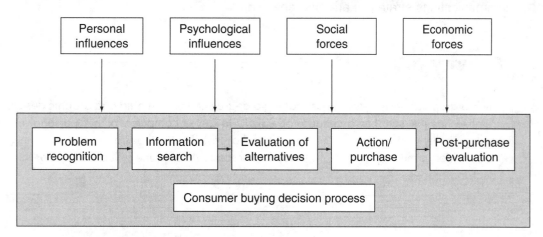

Figure 6.2 The process of adoption
Source: Adapted from Dibb, Simkin, Pride and Ferrell (2001)

Personal influences

Personal influences relate to the individual's characteristics; in the marketing context, these are potential segmentation variables. These include age (mature students are different to people entering college direct from school), situational (e.g. grade achieved or not achieved in entry exams) and level of involvement (a 1-day course in time management is a different issue to 3 years of PhD research).

Psychological influences

This is a complex area where one is concerned with issues such as an individual's self-image and relationship with the product. People's relationship with chocolate may be far from simple; it can be self-indulgent, a reward or comfort. Purchase motivations and relationships to brands for even apparently simple products can involve deep feelings and attitudes. This is why quantitative information is rarely enough. Qualitative information is needed as to *why*? Research can use relatively simple methods such as focus groups, to more sophisticated investigations conducted by psychologists.

Social forces

There is no simple dividing line between nature (personality) and nurture (e.g. culture). However, what a person is and how they feel are not just a matter of genetic programming but family, friends and role model reference groups are all important in shaping people's attitudes. The rapid penetration of mobile telephones was as much due to them becoming the 'must have fashion accessory' as reductions in price. The bottom line is the key problem that economists have yet to solve: what is value? Value has no logic; it is largely subject to whatever rationalization we put on it. What is the value of an old bit of faded paper with a simple sketch on it? Well, millions of pounds if it is by Leonardo Da Vinci. A first edition of Kotler may have curiosity value but a first edition of Newton's work on planetary motion is worth a fortune. In the units on Product (Unit 3) and Price (Unit 4), we noted the issues of intangible benefits (product) and perceived value (price). The bedrock of marketing is how the customer values the product offered and their relationship with it.

Economic forces

The second half of the pricing model for the consumer is affordability and the relative valuation placed on elements of the purchase basket. Technology can change things so rapidly. Postal services appear very expensive and slow compared with the near instantaneous capability of an e-mail that costs nothing once the account is set up. The costs and availability of various communications strategies are ever changing.

Activity 6.3

Jill is a graphics design student just starting a degree course in media and graphic design. A rich relative has just sent her a cheque for £3000 to buy a computer for her personal use in her college halls, where her room has broadband access. List the types of issues that Jill might need to consider in moving through the adoption process. Also list the influences on her through the decision process.

Communications mix

The tools available are shown in Figure 6.1. The precise balance to be used depends on a number of aspects including the nature and context (e.g. B2B or consumer) of the communications task(s), the size of the target audience(s) and not least of all the size of the budget. In the following sections a focused overview of each of the tools is given. Each topic area is worthy of a book in itself, and selected references for further reading are given at the end of the unit.

Advertising

Possibly the most visible aspect of marketing is advertising. Advertising is part of our daily life, and every working day we are exposed to hundreds of messages from the time the radio alarm wakes us up to the end of the late-night film. Advertising FMCGs is an exciting area with big budgets and lots of scope for creativity. It is not the intention here to debate issues of creative impact. Using the earlier analogy of the marketer as the grand architect, if we have a bit of blank space in the Sistine Chapel, we do not grab a paint roller and say *we will have it sorted in a week (who is that artist person in any case?)*. Just the fact that we have a word-processing package does not give us the capability to write the next Booker Prize-winning novel. We can and do need to write simple copy, so simple advertisements are fine. For major projects, commission the experts (at the end of this section, how to brief and select an agency is outlined).

Advertising is the paid-for exposure of a message to selected target group(s). The precise mix of 'inter' (e.g. TV, Press) and 'intra' (e.g. having selected Press, the precise titles: *Sunday Times*, *News of the World*, etc.) depends on certain simple basic principles. The first and most basic of these is, '*Nothing will work if the target audience does not receive the message.*' Some key issues relating to coverage are shown in Figure 6.3. The media cover and the target groups are represented by the shaded areas. With Media 1, we gain a number of hits (hits of the target group are called 'cover' and are expressed as a percentage of the hits on target).

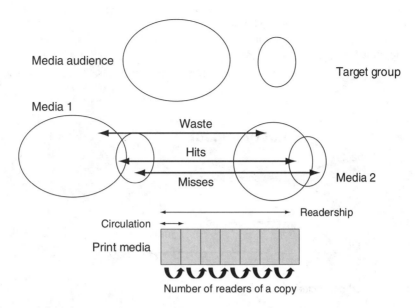

Figure 6.3 Efficiency of media

Media 2 is more efficient and gains more coverage with less wastage. Media will often give figures of 'cost-per-thousand [people reached]' but this needs to be adjusted for cover, so if the efficiency is 50 per cent, the actual cost per thousand is twice that given by the media owners.

Care needs to be taken with the difference between circulation (e.g. ABC figure), which is the number of copies of a publication distributed ('distributed' is used here as some trade publications have both free and paid-for circulation), and readership, the number of people who read the publication. Two or three people in a household may read a single copy of the Sunday newspaper. The figures of interest for most marketing decisions are the readership cover and the cost per 1000 readers. This implies we need to know the number of readers per copy for our target group (this may need some research).

Related to this is the next issue: the number of times that a given individual in the target audience will see the message. Clearly, for a TV advertisement, that is one for each transmission (this has to be adjusted by the probability that the target will be watching TV at the time). For a poster in the entrance to a railway station, it could be seen every journey.

Different media have different characteristics, which make them better for some tasks and more limited for others. Figure 6.4 gives selected characteristics of the various media. A TV or radio spot lasts a few seconds and is, therefore, not able to convey much information. If needed, the Press can carry many thousands of words (e.g. technical-financial advertisement for a limited company with a new bond issue in the *Financial Times*). If the lack of information conveyed is a limitation of TV, the increased visual impact makes it much more powerful in the right circumstances. With surround sound, a monster screen and no ability to use the remote to 'zap' the advertisements, the cinema possibly represents the ultimate in media capability for creative impact. The TV advertisement is there and in seconds it is lost forever. Trade directories may last for years. One can cut out a Press advertisement, whereas with the TV, it's not so easy! These are just a few of the considerations when comparing the various merits of the advertising media available.

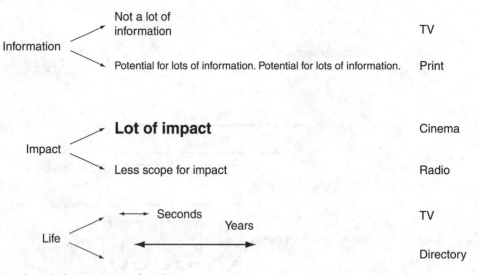

Figure 6.4 Selected characteristics of media

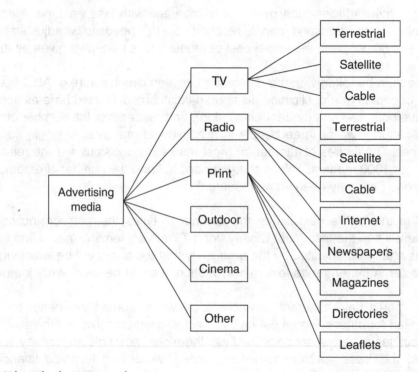

Figure 6.5 Selected advertising media

Practical tip

A problem in the past was using 'personal' company e-mail addresses in long-lived media (e.g. brochures). If the person leaves, who is going to take the messages? Either use a postbox address (e.g. enquiries@organization.com) or a fictitious personal address (e.g. John@organization.com).

As we discuss each of the media, their advantages and limitations will be covered. Some suggested further reading is given at the end of the unit. However, considerable caution is advised in reading publications more than 1 or 2 years old. Not since the introduction of commercial television, half a century ago, has there been so much change in progress with the media, this comes down to one word 'digital'. Given that terrestrial analogue signals are to be turned off in a few years' time and that digital has achieved 50 per cent penetration into households in the United Kingdom, only digital technologies will be considered.

TV

TV audience ratings range from many millions for big events (e.g. World Cup) to highly focused with ethnic, special interest and regional channels. Traditionally, the enormous audience has made it a favourite medium for mass awareness of consumer products and for corporate branding campaigns (e.g. IBM). As with most mass media, the wastage can be high. In terms of viewing figures, this is not as easy to check, as some authorities would say. If the TV is on, how many are watching? The ability to zap between channels or have a quick look at teletext can lower the actual viewing figures during advertisements. Advertisements can be welcome comfort breaks in long programmes. Although their impact is now getting close to cinema, with wide screen, digital quality and surround sound systems, advertisements still only typically last 30 seconds. Choosing this medium can come with a heavy price tag; major TV campaigns run into millions of pounds. Local coverage with limited creative content can be achieved on more modest budgets.

Radio

Radio does not tend to have the largest audiences, but overall its total daytime audience is surprisingly high, with people tending to dip in and out. The year 2004 saw the first mass introduction of lower cost, truly portable, digital receivers. However, with its more restricted bandwidth, radio has two features not enjoyed by TV, both relating to the Internet. Sound files are much smaller than visual files so programs can be made available on demand via the Internet. This also gives radio a global reach via the Internet at low cost. The BBC World Service needed to maintain a complex network of 'short-wave' transmitters to achieve its global reach. These are still required in less-developed countries where the Internet has not achieved high penetration but, increasingly, in developed countries, listeners prefer Internet radio to short wave. As with TV, targeting can be variable and high wastage. Radio with only sound is possibly the most limited in terms of ability to convey information and has only modest freedom for creative impact and again, once the 20 seconds burst is over, it has gone. However, production costs are dramatically lower. With both a national and a regional capability, it is a highly flexible medium. It is also a far more intimate medium. Popular high listening locations are in people's own space bubble, the car, or when working around the house. Here, the radio not only entertains but also conveys traffic information.

Print

Here, there is a vast range of possibilities from the national daily press with its TV-sized readerships to local and specialist publications with a circulation of hundreds rather than thousands. The cost of advertising varies from tens of thousands of pounds for a colour spread in a paper or major magazine to free for personal or charity diary event listings in local papers. The cost to the reader can range from relatively high (well over £100 for some directories) to free (e.g. free distribution weeklies).

The potential in the press is to have vast amounts of information if needed (see Financial Press for examples). The range of impact can be almost zero for a small black-and-white text advertisement to relatively high for a full-colour, double-page spread in the glossy magazines with the highest quality printing standards. Longevity again varies dramatically from a day for *The Sun* to years for a trade directory.

Newspapers

A wide range of options is open, from national to regional and daily to weekly. With regional editions and regional printing of national titles, some regional capability is available from the national press. In the United Kingdom, the press is more important than in most other countries with more national titles and higher daily readerships.

Magazines

Yet again, the dynamic range is vast from circulations of millions for global titles (e.g. *Time*) to just a few hundreds for a club newsletter. Quality is equally widely varied from the highest quality colour printing seen in a fashion magazine to 'design on a budget' in a student union magazine. Targeting can be problematical; from difficult to gauge (e.g. Sunday colour supplement magazine) to laser accuracy for special interest groups (e.g. *Mixmag* – the must-have magazine for clubbers and dancers). A key area for the B2B marketer is the vast range of national and international trade magazines such as *The Bookseller* used by many buyers in bookshops who use it to make stocking decisions. Although these may have a circulation of just a few thousand, they reach key decision makers in the DMU and are often circulated with high readerships per copy (they are often augmented with annual directories and websites).

Directories

These are given a special, if brief, reference as they can be highly targeted if necessary, as with trade magazines. 'Yellow Pages' is still the local standby for many people. We have not yet reached the stage where all such publications are Internet-based, although many people will now use the Internet rather than resorting to a chunky and cumbersome volume. The key thing is their exceptional life, they find their way into reference libraries and have lives measured in years.

Leaflets and brochures

For some organizations such as holiday companies and universities, the brochure is a major cost and consumes a major slice of the advertising budget. A website has the potential ability to convey all the information in a brochure and may indeed mirror its contents. However, you can put a brochure or leaflet in your pocket and read it on the train. With good impact and high convenience, it is still an important medium. Most practising marketers will be involved in the production of a brochure or leaflet. Skills in copy writing and an eye for layout are necessary. The set-up costs for traditional colour printing are high but almost any computer system can produce low volumes of fair quality, colour leaflets for even the smallest organization.

Some rules for brochures include the following:

1. Who is it for? – Define users to ascertain what information they will need to make buying decisions (pack sizes, VAT, minimum order, deals on bulk).
2. What should it include? – Whole range or part (Thomson Italy/Thomson Med./Thomson Europe).
3. Consistent – same format used throughout so that it is easy to use.
4. Clear index – the customer will need to be able to find what they want easily, otherwise they may not use it.
5. Clear and easy to complete response form with obvious prices.

Outdoor and posters

A slight liberty has been taken with the term 'outdoor' and a fair range of posters are not truly outdoors but are used in areas such as airports and railway stations that are covered. Posters can be part of a mass campaign with billboards on main roads or highly targeted (time, place and audience) in and around exhibitions (e.g. the Boat Show). The general comment is that they must not convey too much information as people have limited time to view. However, in certain places, for example posters around station platforms, people do not have much else to do so they can contain more information. Electronic versions can rival the cinema for impact. If we take a slightly liberal view of posters to include neon signage, what would Las Vegas be without them? Their lifespan can vary from just a few days for an exhibition, to years for a major neon sign. Unlike directories, the lifespan of the sign is under the control of the advertiser.

The term 'outdoor' can include a wide range of other options from the sandwich-board person used for the launch of a city centre restaurant to the transport fleet (each vehicle should be regarded as a potential moving poster display, even if it is only conveying the company logo). Airships can be effective around sporting events where they may get media coverage.

Cinema
Although it is a relatively mass medium, it may be quite reasonable to select the audience by the type of film. The impact is the ultimate available; here, the same time limitations are not there as with TV, and a mini epic can result. Again, however, once out of the cinema it is just a memory. For a mini epic, the budget is likely to be anything other than mini. At this creative level, we will see the most expensive medium available. However, it is often the case that the costs can be spread over more than one country (culture can be a restriction) and/or TV. It is also an interesting medium for small local organizations, for example restaurants, targeting selected audiences (cinema goers are also likely to be people who eat out).

Other
If you can put a message on it, someone will sell you the space. Even the back of a bus ticket or a supermarket receipt can be yours for a price.

Question 6.2

What are the advantages and disadvantages of radio over newspapers as an advertising medium?

Question 6.3

You are marketing a product to a local market. The area has both a local morning paper and an evening paper. The morning paper has a circulation of 50 000 and 40 per cent of the readers are in your target segment. The cost of a given advertisement would be £1000. The evening paper has a lower circulation of 30 000 and the cost of the same advertisement would be lower at £750, and 30 per cent of the readers are in the target segment. The advertisement asks for readers to respond by telephoning or e-mailing. Past experience has shown that targets are twice as likely to respond from an advertisement in the evening paper. Analyse this situation and make recommendations.

Public relations
Some of the communications needed by an organization are not best conducted by mass media. Therefore, for the management of political publics (e.g. planning application for a supermarket) it may be appropriate to have briefing sessions for local key decision makers (e.g. local politicians).

Many organizations may not have a formal marketing department but will have a communications and public relations function (e.g. the Police). In this context, a key responsibility will be agreeing, maintaining (here internal marketing may be key) and enforcing the corporate-communications manual. Often event management will be the responsibility of PR specialists. The opening of new facilities or a product launch are activities that most marketers will get involved with sometime in their careers.

A key aspect is developing and maintaining good relations with the media publics/stakeholders. This is not achieved by sending out a press release commenting on the annual report, but is a continual process of developing and maintaining contacts. Here personal professional integrity is vital. One definition of PR is, 'the truth told well'. This is the very opposite of 'spin'. Your job is to get over the organization's message; the media's responsibility is to get news. Taking airlines as an example, their press communications may one day be good news about the launch of a new route, the next, the worst of news, an accident or safety scare. PR contingency plans are, therefore, vital. The long-term relationship built up with the media is key to this. If the experience is that the organization has been 'economical with the truth' then it should be no surprise that trust will be lacking.

Cost of borrowing

A senior high-street bank executive was giving evidence to a Parliamentary Committee and made the statement that he would not advise his children to use credit cards for borrowing as the interest rates were too high and there were less expensive sources of money.

The facts were of course true and the issues well understood by the educated financial press and did not excite comment there, but the 'spin' headline that could be put on this statement by a tabloid paper was an editor's gift from heaven. One of the golden rules of PR: there is no such thing as an 'off the record' comment when the press are around!

The value of good strategic PR is often underestimated. You pay for the message and the media in advertising. A favourable mention in editorial carries more conviction. For many organizations, such as charities with modest communications budgets, good PR can make all the difference.

Publicity

Publicity is where the organization gets media coverage without payment yet it is not free. The PR activities and back-up do not come cost-free. The advantage of publicity is that when it is good it has high credibility. The downside is that, as there is no direct control of the copy, inaccuracies or unfavourable comments can be made. However, for modest budgets, it can be most powerful. The Eden Project established a world-recognized brand without advertising but with the most expert use of strategic PR to generate vast amounts of publicity; this media space would have cost many millions of pounds to buy.

Question 6.4

What are the advantages and disadvantages of publicity compared to advertising?

Personal selling

This is often not included in the marketing budget, but if all the costs of personal selling were added up the spend would far exceed the spend on advertising. For major consumer purchases (cars, mortgages, etc.), this element of the mix is vital. In B2B, the sales role is usually one of the more important elements of the communications mix.

The job interview

The personal selling system is a good model for job hunting. The prospective employer is your target and you are the product. The CV is an element in your marketing communications to gain that interview.

This seven-stage model provides a framework for the process:

1. Prospecting and evaluation
2. Preparing
3. Approach
4. Presentation
5. Overcoming objections
6. Closing the sale
7. Follow-up.

Prospecting and evaluation

Remember the 80:20 rule. Eighty per cent of the business tends to come from 20 per cent of the customers. Do not overwork this 'rule of thumb' but the message is clear: be selective. There is a critical mass of effort needed to win an account; if you do not achieve this critical mass, there is no result. Effort spread too thinly over too many accounts results in dismal sales. The key skill is in determining which are the attractive accounts (not always the large ones, it could be a small account if we expected it might grow) and having a sense of which ones are winnable. In real life, much time can be spent chasing dead accounts that are happy with their supplier but need some other quotations to satisfy their internal purchasing system. In short, devote the sales effort to where it is likely to be profitable.

Preparing

Cold calling (arriving at an unprepared client) is usually a waste of time as much of the effort is spent catching up on the ground that careful preparation would have covered. Preparation of the client can be generic (e.g. advertising in the trade press) or specific (e.g. tailored mailshot).

Apart from preparing the client, the sales person should also prepare. If the client has been visited before then details of the client DMU should be on file (sales reports are a key element of the MkIS, covered in Unit 8). A cuttings file should be kept with copies of press reports and so on regarding the company. For both old and new accounts a check on the website for any relevant news (e.g. expansion plans and other announcements) is useful.

Approach

Care should be taken over housekeeping issues such as parking, facilities for presentations and demonstrations (many of the best sales people take their own laptop and portable projector – this way you do not get software problems!). Using network contacts to break the ice or following up from an exhibition can all be useful. This element is most important to get right, as the wrong foundation here will not support the rest of the efforts. This is very much relationship marketing in action; trust and a working relationship need to be built up. There is no 'one-size-fits-all' approach. Individuals are different and culture provides an additional layer (the working breakfast may work in the USA but not in some other cultures).

Tip – the best sales people are the best listeners. Customers want their needs and wants satisfied in the purchase. How do you know what they are? Listen and then make the sales approach.

Presentation

This is the 'show and tell' part of the process. Having identified the prospect's needs and wants and evaluated the appropriate company products, this is the presentation of the tailored offering.

Often supporting materials such as samples and documentation will be required by the client. Making certain that all needs are identified is vital in the preparation and approach process.

Overcoming objections

This is where the sales person must know their product and full marketing mix, and have a deep understanding of the client needs. This is negotiation written large. A typical objection in a B2B sale might be 'we do not have the capital budget for this at the moment'. Earlier, in pricing, we noted that affordability was a key aspect of pricing strategy. A smart company may, therefore, come up with a scheme like a leasing option (convert capital expense into a revenue expense).

Closing the sale

This is the term used in the model given in the texts – life is not always like that. Several visits may be needed to land a big contract. However, the key issue is to end with an agreed milestone (e.g. 'We will meet in one month, after you have completed the trials on the samples I brought today'). Do not leave with 'We will meet sometime' (next month, next year, next decade?) – it is best to note in a diary here and now.

Follow-up

Getting the first sale is not the end. In relationship-marketing terms, it is another milestone in building and maintaining an ever-ongoing partnership to the mutual benefit of both parties. Again, a good MkIS is vital. If there is to be a delay in delivery, best the account manager talks to the client immediately before they set up a production run needing a product the supplier knew was going to miss the deadline. It is essential to build relationships that can endure even when there are difficulties.

Question 6.5

You are a sales representative for an international company. You are to meet some potential clients from overseas, from a different culture, for a business meeting. What issues would you need to consider?

Point of sale

If personal selling tends to be more important for B2B situations, point of sale (POS) is often key for the FMCG sector. This is, in effect, the opportunity to close the sale. The product must be displayed in as attractive a-way as possible with as much convenience for both the buyer and the retailer (e.g. the confectionery display next to the pay point in the convenience store). Care must be taken with not only the style but also the location of display in the store. Proper grouping of products will increase overall sales. Attractive POS material may be offered free of charge for a minimum order value.

Sales system

This links with Unit 4, Price. However, sales systems are no longer just slot machines. The laser checkout can collect lots of information to target direct marketing communications. The system can itself be a part of the communications activity with rewards such as Nectar points or offers printed on receipts. ATMs are not passive. The screen content can also be an advertising medium. When e-banking to pay a bill, the screens are also a mechanism for communication, pushing other services offered by the bank such as insurance or loans. In relationship-marketing terms, the sale is not just when we grab the money (either literally or electronically) but also a chance to build and maintain relationships.

Sales promotion

The key issue with promotion is that it is an invitation and incentive to act now, *everyday low prices* is not a promotion. This is a pricing strategy and should be considered as an element of the pricing aspect of the marketing mix. However, a *two for one* (BOGOF) promotion for a post-holiday, slow sales period is a promotional activity. There are a whole range of options including competitions and gifts. Sales promotion efforts are key in inducing trial of a new product for example using various forms of sampling to consumers.

In the B2B sector, promotion still has its part to play. Competitions can be used to motivate sales staff as distributors. When introducing a new computer product, free training could be offered.

Direct marketing

Even in the e-commerce age direct mail is still a major tool. The first and most important issue is to obtain 'clean' contact address lists. These can come from an organization's data retrieval form, an effective in-house MkIS (e.g. profiles constructed from purchases using a loyalty card) or from purchased lists (e.g. lists can be purchased from learned societies for professionals interested in specific areas such as analytical instruments). In this area, there are significant conformance issues, and the legal issues regarding data protection are quite restrictive (the interpretation of data protection legislation is an evolving area and the law is different in different countries); if in doubt, the legal authorities should be consulted.

Care must be taken to get copyright and determine what will be an attractive proposition to the target. Given the limitations, the work and the costs, one might ask, 'Is it all worth it?' A key issue is that with a good list you can be highly targeted with minimum waste. Thus, though the costs per thousand are very high, when compared to many other options, the targeting and the quality of the presentation may make all the effort rewarding.

ICT and e-communications

You do not become Bill Gates because you have a computer. Many companies, however, think in this way when they create a website; using the basis that everyone has a website so they must too. e-Communications have not changed the laws of marketing. It does not matter whether the order comes by e-mail or snail mail if you get the product to the customer late and damaged.

E-commerce is a very powerful addition to the integrated communications mix and just as jet travel made long-haul holidays affordable in price and feasible in travel time, it has created entirely new business opportunities. The key is to understand what is different about e-communications and how the differences can be exploited by an organization and importantly by other stakeholders (pressure groups have been quick on the uptake).

Some key differences are noted in Table 6.1

Table 6.1 E-communications: selected differences

Issue	E-commerce	Traditional
Cost per hit	Near zero. Site costs fixed rather than variable	Cost of postage and brochure printing for traditional direct mail very high
Time	Quick and 24/7/365	Slow and needs people so not 24/7/365
Ability to update	With good organization can be near real-time	Brochures once printed are pretty much fixed for the season without vast additional cost
Amount of content	With care, almost unlimited	If we take a directory still limited and selectivity not possible, client has to select and supplier has the cost of providing 99.999 of useless information
Selectivity	With good navigation and key words, excellent	Hard work as often only indexed one way
Feedback and control	Sophisticated tracking tools can be built into the system using cookies and so on.	Mail shots can be tracked but the process is slower and more labour-intensive and expensive
Security	Probably high but customers are still concerned, a major issue for financial transactions	With registered post can be high but so are the costs of insurance
Two-way communications	Good but need care to manage responses	'Clunky' with snail mail but can be minimized with fax-back forms

There are clearly many major advantages to e-commerce but a number of issues that need to be kept in mind. The best website is of no value if people do not find their way there. Building 'hooks' into the site so a site appears early in searches is vital for sites where 'cold' discovery is important (e.g. a customer requiring a maintenance service for emergencies is not going to look through 20 screens). In an integrated mix, traditional communications methods can be used to point people to the website. In addition, many sites have paid search engines like Google, Yahoo or AltaVista to pull their address up in the first 10 or 20 responses to a general search. Product information on a pack should point to the appropriate part of the website as well as the helpline. Calls are expensive; the more the customers can do for themselves, the better it keeps transaction costs down.

It is not too difficult to get an agency to build you a website (briefing and working with an agency is covered in the next section). A key management issue is to ensure accuracy, not only when the site is set up but keeping it maintained too. The potential for liability (this covers e-mail communications also) is considerable and complex (it has still yet to be fully resolved which law applies: where the site was set up, where it is hosted or even where the information was downloaded). Pricing can be dangerous. When has a legal contract been made? If your website has automatic order confirmation built into the system and someone mis-prices a product (e.g. leaves out a zero so £100 becomes £10), have you built in an automated system to legal disaster? Maintenance is not only about keeping the site fresh but also making certain that no gremlins get added by accident.

Security is a major issue. Clients are clearly concerned about the security of fund transfers and other confidential information. Sites can be open to 'raids' by irritating hackers or more sinisterly by organized cyber-criminals from less well policed parts of the world (the age of the electronic safe-breaker located on the other side of the world).

In relationship-marketing terms, e-communications have very attractive targeting features. With restricted access either via a company Intranet or a passworded-only section of a website, customers, distributors and staff can be well informed. Badly written notices in cold corridors should be a thing of the past. However, this all-pervasive availability of often commercially sensitive information is in itself a security issue. The average company would not keep their money under the Managing Director's bed but the level of e-security for many organizations is about as sophisticated.

Sponsorship

This may be useful for small companies as well as the major fashion houses. The marketing press will, each week, report several sponsorship deals. With merchandising, the big money in sport is in sponsorship. Success builds the brand (the star quality) and then the sponsors move in. However, a small local company may find opportunities, such as local arts events, round-abouts and flowerbeds that work in the same way but on a reduced scale. There is risk attached. The team sponsorship that looked good before the season started is not so hot when the team get eliminated in the first round. The prevalence of sponsorship demonstrates its value in brand building. Some forms (e.g. the Performing Arts) are especially useful in corporate image building (raised profile and company represent a good corporate citizen).

Exhibitions

These can have value for some consumer markets and if a wider view is taken, these are key for some selected small businesses (e.g. local artist needs exhibition space to sell paintings). However, a major arena is the B2B event. The word 'event' is used here, as very often the exhibition will have some parallel activities such as a technical conference. This generates interest for people attending and gives exhibitors sponsorship and PR opportunities. There is more consideration of exhibitions in Unit 9.

Other

A wide range of other opportunities exist; for example, messages can be printed on bus tickets.

Case study

'Downtown Arts Cinema'

The December 2005 case study 'The Urban Culture Festival 2006' featured a film festival. 'Downtown Arts Cinema' is a small cinema which can hold 100 people. It has an adjacent art gallery. The marketing communications for such a venture must be conducted on a rather limited budget. Important stakeholders would include customers, potential customers, sponsors, local arts groups and media. A key issue is maintaining a large core of loyal customers who visit the cinema and art gallery frequently. Marketing activities might include the following:

o A monthly review of films and arts events mailed out to customers. Loyal customers could join the 'Friends of Downtown Arts Cinema Club' and receive special privileges (e.g. priority booking).
o The monthly review could also be distributed to libraries and other arts centres and groups. Posters could be displayed at such locations as well.

- ○ Personal selling would be required to local sponsors to support special events (e.g. themed art exhibitions).
- ○ The theatre would conduct PR activity with the local media to get cover of the various programme events (e.g. interviews with local prominent artists when their work was being featured in the art gallery).
- ○ Full information on events could he held on the website. This should have links to other various local arts websites.

The above are some basic suggestions, you may think of some other creative options.

 ## Activity 6.4

Many people using this text will be attending a college. Keep a diary of the communications activities that are going on; comment on which publics they will reach and how effective you think they were. Try not to miss ongoing aspects when you start entering in your diary (e.g. corporate communications such as direction signs) and note events as well (e.g. press releases). Visit the website once a week. If you are not attending and do not have access to a college then substitute any other organization (e.g. the one you work for) as the subject of your diary.

Question 6.6

Consider that you are the Marketing Manager for a college that is to introduce the CIM qualifications for the first time in the next academic year. What would your proposed communications mix be for this situation?

Agency selection and briefing

As with the personal selling process, part of the secret of this is in the preparation. If you do not know what you want from the agency, then you are unlikely to select the right one or draw up a good brief. The first stage is to ensure that you have a full definition of the project. Points to consider include the following:

- ○ What are the objectives?
- ○ Who will be involved in your organization (e.g. providing information)?
- ○ How does the activity to be briefed integrate with other elements of the communications and overall marketing mixes as well as other company activities (e.g. staff training for a new product launch)?
- ○ What is the budget?
- ○ What is the projected schedule?
- ○ Responsibilities (e.g. Who has the ultimate authority/responsibility to clear copy?).

The briefing process costs money for both sides, and agencies are beginning to resent the pitch for a brief being used as free consultancy. It is not only considerate, but also a commercial necessity to conduct the briefing and selection process fairly and professionally. Some selected criteria for agency selection are as follows:

- Size fit (a large agency may not be appropriate for a modest account).
- Has their past work been successful (awards are great but we also want communications that work cost-effectively)?
- Have they got experience of integration (e.g. linking in with e-communications)?
- Can they cover the scope of the brief?
- Do they have the right people (qualifications, skills and track record of success)?
- Can they work with your organization's team?

Selected issues which should be covered in the briefing documentation and process are as follows:

- A focused situational analysis including competition
- The promotional objectives
- Identification of the targets
- View of the offer and the communications proposition
- Integration with the other elements of the communications mix and company activities
- Must haves (for example if the company demands that its logo should be included)
- Must not haves, for example pictures of students clubbing and drinking for international students with differing views on alcohol consumption
- Budget
- Schedule
- Points of contact and authorities (e.g. clearance of copy)
- Ground rules for the pitch
- Debriefing arrangements.

 ## Activity 6.5

After you have kept your diary for a couple of weeks, consider how the college (or your other selected organization) may make appropriate use of agencies. For one of these (e.g. the website) draw up a brief.

Communications objectives, schedules and budgets

It may be helpful to consider the customer/sales communications objectives first and then to consider the range of communications objectives with other key stakeholder groups (e.g. financial publics). For the purchaser we have to then move through stages (the impulse purchase can be considered in the same way, except the process takes place very quickly). Consider the situation of a major brand launching a new product into the consumer sector. Their objectives might be for the target segment(s):

- Maintain general brand-awareness and positive attitudes during planning period.
- Create # per cent awareness of the new product, within # period.

○ Convert awareness of the product into trial at # per cent conversion rate, within # period.

○ Achieve # per cent of conversion into repurchase and long-term adoption, within # period.

To make the objectives fully SMART the figures inserted in the '#' spaces must be realistic and be based on research. In Porter's Value Chain there are primary activities and support activities. General support of the brand for a whole range of products can, therefore, be seen as a long-term support activity and the tactical launch plan for the specific product seen as the primary communications activity.

Having set our target for awareness, we can then move on to sub-objectives. We will need to mirror the consumer awareness in the distribution channels with B2B marketing. We may wish to gain favourable publicity (for perfumes this would be in the fashion press) and again we will need to mirror consumer awareness in the fashion press using the publicity to influence our ultimate audiences. In setting and achieving the core objective, we need to set and achieve objectives for key publics.

For other stakeholder groups (e.g. local community for a supermarket building a new outlet), objectives may be formed in more qualitative terms such as the move from

○ hostility to sympathy

○ ignorance to knowledge

○ resistance to support.

For an organization's overall communications plan, all the activities should be listed with their schedules and associated budgets. A spreadsheet of marketing communications activities can act as a checklist; when tackling a communication directed at one audience the impact on another can be considered (e.g. an announcement to reassure financial publics about cutting costs by moving call centres to India will clearly have an impact on the internal publics as well).

As is often the case in marketing, the ability to be creative (that great new advertisement) needs to be supported with meticulous attention to detail (no good if an incorrect web address is included) and rigorous project management (that innovative poster is of no value if it was delivered a week late to the invoice address and not to the exhibition stand in Australia).

Feedback and control

In some ways not much has to be said here. All the hard work starts with the objectives. There is no point in setting objectives (they are not SMART) if how they are to be achieved has not been considered, that is, administrative follow-up to track the responses from the exhibition and evaluate their value (e.g. 'should we use this event again?' is a key question that needs an evidence-based decision). Feedback and control costs both money and effort, the analysis should be built into the action plan chart and the budget. In general, both quantitative (is brand awareness holding up?) and qualitative aspects (are feelings more supportive to the brand or is hostility developing?) should be tracked.

One should not fully commit the total budget. Some contingency should be built in for cost overruns (watch agency spends!) and reaction to market events (e.g. an adverse press release from a pressure group needing to be addressed).

ICT, Internet and convergent technologies

In the United Kingdom, over 50 per cent of TV audiences are receiving their pictures through a digital media (digital 'free to view' terrestrial, satellite or cable). More than 50 per cent of the population have access to the Internet, increasingly via broadband rather than 'dial-up'. TVs are becoming communications centres. Computers can become TVs, integrating computer games, TV and communication capabilities within the same system. The view in this book is that 'E' issues are not something separate but something to be taken into account in all aspects of developing marketing plans. Thus, there are references to these issues throughout the units. However, it is appropriate to summarize the issues since exam questions can have a specific focus on ICT and related issues.

Spreadsheets

Spreadsheets can do lots more than the 'four functions' of a cheap pocket calculator (addition, subtraction, multiplication and division). They have a wide range of mathematical and statistical functions providing the ability to do fairly sophisticated work without resorting to specialist software packages (e.g. specialist statistics packages). Moreover, they can provide simple database capabilities (e.g. select and search) and interface with mail-merge software aspects of standard packages, such as 'Word'.

Databases and data capture

Once the preserve of the computer specialist and expensive to run, database applications are now available to the smallest operations with packages such as 'Access'. Data can be held on customers and extracted with relevant selection criteria and data sorted. This provides an immense range of flexibility. Increasingly, data can be captured by automated processes, magnetic strips (credit cards), smart chips (credit cards), smart tags (electronic chips that can not only identify a product but can identify down to the specific item – not just a shirt but the 234 678th made and shipped) and various optical methods (e.g. bar codes). This data can be moved around company and industry systems (e.g. EDI – Electronic Data Interchange) in real time. This not only feeds stock-control systems (MRP – Materials Requirements Planning systems) but also allows almost real-time analysis for marketing (e.g. evaluating a new promotional pricing initiative for a product).

Increasingly, the information contained in these systems forms a significant proportion of the company's value. For more than a century accountants have been able to value physical assets. It is more difficult to value the information in a customer database but it is critical for effective marketing (e.g. loyalty schemes within an overall Relationship-marketing strategy). These together with brand rights, copyright and so on form the intellectual property of a company. Just as with physical assets, successful companies lever the advantage from their intellectual assets to increase their profitability.

The Internet

This is a robust communication system originally devised for military applications. Once people have subscribed to broadband, it provides access to almost unlimited information and international communications. Access in this context has zero marginal cost to the user.

Websites

Provide a way for organizations (and even individuals) to showcase all aspects of their activities. Good website design is highly technical and should be left to the professionals (e.g. security issues). However, just as with advertising copy, marketing staff should collaborate to ensure that electronic media messages integrate with all the other media being used. Electronic communications should also conform to company house rules (e.g. use of company logo). It is possible to construct a basic website on a limited budget of a few thousand pounds. Massive websites (e.g. government information, BBC news) cost large sums of money to construct and maintain.

The ability to link databases provides even greater insight. Thus, a firm's customer data can be combined with a geo-demographic database (e.g. in the UK by linking across on the postcode). Linked with e-mail and other technologies (e.g. mobile telephones) sophisticated targeted communications can be aimed, with laser accuracy. Even with this new technology, however, direct mail still has a lot of use. Analysis of patterns of spending for an individual may allow targeted special offers to be sent, these offers can be included with the invoice sent to customers each month. There is no additional postal cost if overall weight and size of mailing is kept to appropriate limits.

Electronic mail

Once companies and individuals are linked to broadband, the marginal costs of communications (including large attachments) is zero. Business e-mails are covered in Unit 9.

Intranet

This is a restricted Internet that can only be accessed by nominated people. It is used by companies to disseminate information on a secure basis. Many companies make their marketing research information (e.g. on competitors) available on an Intranet so staff can use it, as needed (e.g. a PR manager writing a press release).

Extranet

An Extranet allows nominated external users to access pages with a measure of security. A typical use would be to distribute information to agents and suppliers. This is a powerful tool in relationship marketing.

Electronic Data Interchange (EDI)

Data once captured at an EPOS or other systems can be exchanged with other sites (e.g. EDI). A typical use is supermarket stock control, where the supply chain is driven in real time by sales recorded from EPOS.

E-business

E-bay and other business such as online gambling have been made possible by convergent technologies. E-bay is not just an electronic car boot sale. It provides a mechanism for new small business to operate internationally. Larger companies can also use it as a non-traditional channel to sell products (a typical use would be to offload obsolete stock without disrupting conventional channels).

Increasingly, airlines are 'E' ticketing. This speeds up the process and reduces costs (e.g. self-check-in at airports). 'E-banking' has not only provided additional convenience and attractive costs to customers but also greatly reduced the costs to banks as well. However, note the security issues (see later in this section). Additional consideration of ICT is given in Unit 5 focusing on distribution issues (e.g. distribution of music).

E-mail marketing

The penetration is there. However, just as people do not like junk mail and unsolicited telephone calls, they hate 'Spam'. E-communications should only be sent to people who want the information – most organizations have 'Spam' filters. However, on a sign-up basis within a loyalty scheme, it can be most useful. The same comments apply to text/images to mobile telephones.

Internet research

Google is going to make some of the world's largest academic libraries available online and searchable. The wealth of world knowledge is only a click away. Reaching a company before a job interview has never been easier. News websites (e.g. BBC online) keep you informed in real time if you desire.

However, take care regarding the standing of the site. Any strange organization can put up a website. Just because it is on the web does not make it true. Always maintain your critical judgement. Guidance on how to refer a website is given in Unit 9.

Land telecommunications

BT is converting its whole network to digital operation. Data, sound and images will move around networks with increasing capability, truly creating the joined-up world.

Mobile telecommunications

Just as with e-mail they provide a good mechanism of communication (text, audio and increasingly images). However, junk communications are resented. Note the use of 'hot spots' and wireless connections to enable people to use their laptops to access the net in public places (e.g. airports).

Total convergence – the wired-up environment – with no wires

TV, computers and games consoles are tending to converge into home networks. Watch one TV programme; record another onto a hard drive. Hold your music collection there. Buy your films and music over the Internet. Take your music anywhere on your MP3. The digital 'e' revolution has a lot further to go.

Legal and security issues

Freedom of information and data protection legislation is increasingly making the construction and use of databases and so on more complicated. What you may hold, how you may hold it and when and how you may have to disclose it are becoming increasingly regulated.

165

All this connectivity is great, however, without appropriate firewalls, and so on companies are leaving their intellectual property wide open with an invitation to intellectual thieves and vandals to steal (e.g. personal detail cloning for credit card fraud) or destroy information (computer viruses).

Even small organizations and individuals must take care to conform to the law and take steps to protect themselves. What is the point of locking the front door if you leave your computer open to every hacker?

Exam questions are often asked regarding the usage of ICT: June 2006 'SMS Cars Ltd' case study Question 7: 'Produce a short report to be circulated to Departmental Managers which explains how ICT can enhance the marketing mix (product, price, place and promotion) to generate sales and encourage customer loyalty to all departments of SMS Cars Ltd'.

Case study

'Lake View Organic Farms' – Communications analysis

The application of Figure 6.1 to the 'Lake View Organic Farms' situation gives the following outline analysis:

Stakeholders and aims

Internal publics (staff, owners of the co-operative, etc.) – keep informed with internal marketing.

Customers and potential customers – gaining awareness and developing favourable attitudes. Note both for B2C and B2B customers.

Supplier publics – keep produce suppliers informed. Marketing suppliers also need to be kept informed (e.g. the website might be maintained under contract by a marketing consultancy company).

Media publics – local press, radio and TV, to gain favourable coverage and lever a very limited communications budget.

Corporate/brand values – (message is discussed below). To be consistently integrated in all media – farm signage, the delivery vans, packaging, letter heads and so on, website and marketing communications (e.g. advertisements).

Message/proposition – good honest food from the land, with nothing taken out and nothing added. Prices you can afford. Convenience of delivery to the door. Honest food from honest people.

Legal issues – care must be taken with copy not to make false claims. This is a particular problem with 'health foods' and food supplements. Scientific evidence is often rather sketchy and controversial. Often direct statements are not possible; for example, 'Eat this and you will suffer less illnesses' is not likely to be acceptable copy. More like 'Nutritionists advise a balanced diet with a mix of vegetables. Our vegetables not only taste great, they are also a rich source of vitamins and minerals.'

Brand values – a house style needs to be developed to ensure consistency of the messages.

Buyer behaviour – a mix of communications to take potential customers though the AIDA process. Advertising to make aware, good website to provide information and make trial easy.

Communications mix (see Figure 6.5)

Advertising – TV and radio: none. Limited advertising around food features in local press. Outdoor/posters. Use farm signage and vehicles (moving billboards) to maximum effect. Limited posters in wholefood outlets. Cinema: none. Word of mouth: support this by including a leaflet 'Pass onto a friend' with each 'Veggie' box.

PR and publicity – good relations with local journalists by PR. Press releases when there is a good story, for example local follow-up where there is a good story (e.g. national story 'GM foods not good for you' – onto TV to give the local Organic Food Growers focus). Tactical activities undertaken to support the strategic objectives.

Personal selling – to B2B customers only.

Point of sale – for home delivery not an issue.

Sales systems – cash or credit/debit cards. 'E' transactions accepted. Orders by telephone, e-mail or website.

Direct marketing – It is unlikely that a business of this size could afford a good quality database. What would be required would focus on being able to pick out suitable local 'wholefood' customers. It is possible this might be available from a local wholefood shop's customer lists.

e-Communications – good website and e-mail facilities. Intranet to provide framework for communications to internal publics. Extranet to provide communications to suppliers of produce and other goods and services.

Sponsorship – possibly not effective for this type of operation.

Exhibitions – presence in farmers' markets and food exhibitions.

Other – make the farm itself an attraction with a visitor/education centre.

Budget – a limited budget. Make selective use of an agency for website and PR. Monitor activities and evaluate impact on business (e.g. does the farm get more web hits after a local TV interview?).

Scheduling: the above discussion has been in the context of normal trading. The situation during the launch of a new product is considered in Unit 10.

Activity 6.6

Many colleges produce a prospectus and also maintain a website. Have a look at both for a selected college and consider how, if you were the marketing assistant looking after these, you would track their effectiveness.

International aspects

All elements of the communications mix can be affected, including the segmentation and positioning of the product. Fishermen's Friend is a product to use when you have a cold in the United Kingdom and a confectionery product in Germany. When considering a communications programme in an overseas market all the other elements of the marketing mix together with segmentation, targeting and positioning should be reviewed. The message and objectives can then be evaluated to decide if they need to be adapted. Communication and imagery is very culturally sensitive and an advertisement acceptable in one culture might give deep offence in another. Moreover, the availability, reach and characteristics of the media may be different in the overseas market. For example, in the United Kingdom, the number of morning daily papers is high as is the proportion of the population who read a daily paper when compared with many other countries. If that was not enough, detailed laws may affect what you can promote and the way that promotions may be effected. Considerable re-balancing of the media mix may be required.

Question 6.7

'Fair Trade Coffee'

Outline the B2B marketing communications activities that might be appropriate for a company selling 'fair trade' coffee through supermarkets and to B2B customers. Before considering your communications complete a market segmentation review.

Summary

In this unit, we have considered who the organization needs to communicate with and the range of messages that are needed. The legal and other constraints have been presented. In implementation a vast array of potential tools are available for the marketer. The elements of the marketing communications mix have been presented with some debate about the inter and intra media mix decisions that also have to be made.

An integrated view of the communications mix was adopted. Communications activities need objectives and control processes as do every other element of the marketing mix. The need to frame objectives in the context of the various communications stakeholders has been explored.

Questions on communications mix often feature in the CIM exams, for example December 2005 'The Urban Culture Festival 2006' Question 3 'Describe the advantages and disadvantages of advertising using the following media specifically in the context of the Urban Culture festival 2006: television, radio, cinema, magazines and other alternative media (please specify)', and June 2006 'SMS Cars Ltd' Question 5b 'Make recommendations as to how the promotional mix could be used to increase demand for the Vehicle Servicing Department.'

Further study

Dibb, S., Simkin, L., Pride, W. and Ferrell, O. (2006) *Marketing Concepts and Strategies*, 5th European edition, Houghton Mifflin, Chapters 4, 17–19.

As an integrative module, you should also review the other coursebooks at this level

Cheeseman, A., and Jones, M. (2007) *CIM Coursebook – Customer Communications in Marketing*, Butterworth-Heinemann.

Lancaster, G., and Withey, F. (2007) *CIM Coursebook – Marketing Fundamentals*, Butterworth-Heinemann.

Oldroyd, M. (2007) *CIM Coursebook – Marketing Environment*, Butterworth-Heinemann.

Hints and tips

Throughout this study text, link your study and reading to real-life experience. Pick some products and services of interest to you and review the communications activities that are used to promote them. It is essential to read the marketing press to keep up with current developments and campaigns. Remember, evidence of reading around the subject and the use of good topical examples will gain you more marks.

Bibliography

Shimp, T., and Delozier, M.W. (2003) *Advertising, Promotion and Supplemental Aspects of Integrated Marketing Communications*, 6th edition, Thomson Learning.

Smith, P., and Taylor, J. (2004) *Marketing Communications: An Integrated Approach*, 2nd edition, Kogan Page.

unit 7

the integrated marketing mix: service extension (people, physical evidence and process)

Learning objectives

By the end of this unit you will

- Understand how the service model can be adapted to provide insight into the detailed structure of service.

- Appreciate the difficulty of measuring service quality.

- Understand the map of the people mix at the organization and individual level.

- Comprehend the role of physical evidence in signalling service quality.

- Appreciate the nature of process in service delivery and how this must be tailored for different segments.

Syllabus references

2.1 Describe the structure and roles of the marketing function within the organization.

2.2 Build and develop relationships within the marketing department, working effectively with others.

2.6 Explain how the organization fits into a supply chain and works with distribution channels.

2.8 Explain the concept and application of e-relationships.

3.2 Identify alternative and innovative approaches to a variety of marketing arenas and explain criteria for meeting business objectives.

171

4.5   Describe the current distribution channels for an organization and evaluate new opportunities.

4.7   Explain the importance of the extended marketing mix: how process, physical aspects and people affect customer choice.

4.8   Explain the importance of ICT in the new mix.

5.8   Examine the correlation between marketing mix decisions and results.

Key definition

SERVQUAL – A model for the evaluation of service quality.

Study Guide

As with the previous elements of the marketing mix, applying the concepts and listing examples from your own experience will develop your skills and knowledge. In particular, consider the product–service continuum. Many products have services associated with them. Most services have some product element involved in the service process.

The people element of the mix is of particular importance as this is at the heart of relationship marketing. Therefore, in working through this section, think not only of your experiences in the marketplace but also your experiences with internal stakeholders. In RM terms, other departments can be considered as internal customers.

The architecture of service

In Unit 3, the detailed structure of product was considered. The model (Figure 3.4) needs adaptation in only two ways to complete the analysis of services, and earlier in Unit 2 we explored some of the differences between service and product marketing. As a service is by its very nature intangible, it may not have signal attributes. To make the intangible tangible, we have the service-extended marketing mix elements: people, physical evidence and process. For products, we considered the extension issues of the required services (e.g. for a car, maintenance services), and for services, we just have to switch labels and consider that the products are an integral part of the service (e.g. in a hair salon, the nature and quality of shampoo, conditioner, hair colourants, etc.). This merely reflects that we are in a product–service continuum, with many packages purchased being bundles of both product and service. All the other elements in the model remain the same (e.g. we do not buy services, we want benefits: I do not want to sit in the hair salon for two hours, I want to look and feel good).

Activity 7.1

Apply the Plymouth product model to the installation of a replacement gas water heater.

Service quality

In the Plymouth product model, product quality and product performance were discussed. With a physical product, it is relatively simple to measure weight or look for damage. It is more difficult to evaluate some of the performance characteristics such as the quality of chilled chicken tikka meal. However, we have pointers such as colour and, with trained panels of tasters, some approach to consistent quality assessment can be achieved. How do I measure and convey to a customer the quality of a mortgage or an insurance policy? Certainly, some aspects of service can be measured objectively: for example, how long it takes to play Chopin's Waltz No. 6 in D flat Op No.1 (the so-called 'Minute Waltz')? My recording is actually 1 minute 40 seconds. Should I return the CD? We may use seconds to measure the performance length and decibels to measure the noise level of the orchestra, but would a music critic consider these in their newspaper report the next day? Quality expectations must be managed. Therefore, if we announce that there will be a train at 12.32, the train needs be there then, not at 13.12. However, note that appropriate quality is required, not absolute quality in the service. Thus, if the train is 22 seconds late, not many people will notice. However, if the BBC 'pips' for midnight were 22 seconds late it would be an issue.

What time is midnight?

The 'pip' issue has become a problem. If I am standing on the bridge over the river Thames next to 'Big Ben', I can hear the chimes a fraction of a second after the bell is struck. With a portable radio, a person 100 miles away will hear the sound around the same time, to a small fraction of second. A person listening via a satellite link is a few seconds behind. They get to see midnight a little later. When setting your watch this is a slight irritation (do I care if I am 4 seconds slow?); for an airline navigation system travelling at many hundreds of miles an hour, however, those few seconds could be really significant!

Therefore, the issue for the marketer is to manage customer expectations and deliver service in customer terms. It is suggested that customers perceive five vectors of quality:

1. *Reliability* – consistent delivery of the appropriate performance.
2. *Responsiveness* – the intelligent flexibility to provide a tailored response.
3. *Assurance* – the degree of trust in the system, hope the crew knows what they are doing on an aircraft when we are 38 000 feet above the sea.
4. *Empathy* – people are not machines so we have different needs and wants. To what extent do the service providers understand this and provide a caring service?
5. *Tangibles* – things to make the intangible service tangible.

The same researchers identified five gaps in service quality:

1. *Gap between consumer expectations and management perception* – often a problem in international marketing, where benefit needs and expectations in one country and culture are very different from another.
2. *Gap between management perception and service quality specification* – a controversial issue in education regarding league tables and disputes as to whether they really measure quality of educational experience or not. There is a real danger here that people will measure what can be measured. We need to make certain that what we do measure truly links to customer satisfaction. An evidence-based approach is appropriate.

173

3. *Gap between service quality specifications and service delivery* – is the system built and staff trained and motivated to actually deliver. For example, in the mis-selling of financial service products, the regulatory requirements and senior management policies were in place but collapsed at the implementation point with the clients.

4. *Gap between service delivery and external communications* – expectations must be met. Do not incite expectations that may not be sustained. You might irritate the advertising standards authority (that is bad) but you will also lose customers (that is a disaster). For example, a mail order company achieved 90 per cent delivery within 2 days. To avoid the gap 4 problem they advertised 3-day delivery. The 10 per cent of people who got their goods in 3 days were happy (expectations were met). People who got their goods in 2 days were delighted, their expectations had been exceeded.

5. *Gap between perceived service and expected service* – this is where the quality of the service may be good, but the consumer does not see it as such, for example one of the problems of service provision is variability. A very fast service in a restaurant may be seen as a bonus by a businessperson at lunchtime, but may be seen as intrusive for that romantic evening meal. Same place, same food, same staff but the satisfaction outcome can be different. This is an illustration of one of the great skills in marketing: *empathy* – it is essential to see the product or service (in fact the entire integrated mix) from each individual consumer's view. The marketer is the full-time ambassador of the customer in the organization.

Relationships and service quality

A company was contracted to provide crop-spraying services to farmers. On one occasion, a complete strip in a large field had not been treated, resulting in a loss of yield of several hundreds of pounds.

The farmer called in the sales representative with whom he had a good relationship to discuss compensation. He took the representative to the field to inspect the damage. The sales representative said, 'You have always disputed the quality of this service and its cost. Well now you can see it for yourself!' The farmer replied, 'OK, but lunch is on you!'

Service quality in relationship-marketing terms is as much about managing the quality of the relationships as the management of the quality of the service.

 ## Activity 7.2

Some authors talk about 'moments of truth' in the delivery of a service. In the face-to-face encounter between the customer and the organization (in RM terms, with a part-time marketer), the customer experiences a moment of truth. Either the expectation is met or exceeded (customer satisfaction) or it is not (customer dissatisfaction). Consider your experiences the last time you took an airline flight. List the positive and negative aspects of the service experience.

People

Relationship marketing is founded on the bedrock that people buy the service that is provided by other people. The effectiveness and efficiency of this process depends on relationships. Companies do not have relationships, people in companies do business and have relationships with other people in other companies. For effective service delivery, relationships must be good not only between the front-line staff and the customer, but also with all the internal stakeholders in the organization supporting the front-line contact for all the part-time marketers. Many companies often state, 'People are our most valuable asset.' Back to gap 4 of the SERVQUAL model! If management states one thing in the mission statement and does not deliver to its own internal stakeholders, it should be no surprise that the organization fails. A structure for analysing the people element of the marketing mix is given in Figure 7.1.

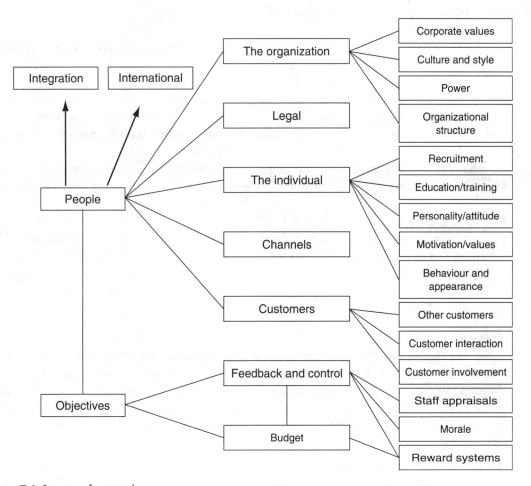

Figure 7.1 Structure for people

The organization

Corporate values

Organizations in the same marketplace do not hold the same values. The Co-Operative Society is one of the top ten retail organizations in the United Kingdom but has considerable concern for 'fair trade' policies that are not so high on the agenda with other retail organizations such as Wal-Mart. We talk about corporate culture, but what is intended by this is the inner core of stakeholders who set the mission (usually the owners, board and top management). Corporate governance is a mechanism that society is imposing on organizations to ensure that values such as honesty (e.g. attitudes to 'insider dealing') are maintained to acceptable standards. This is more than merely observing the letter of the law.

Culture and style

Organizations are not machines. They are social organizations. In international marketing, we recognize that the culture of Japan is different to that of France. It is the same with organizations. The culture of commercial organizations (e.g. retail shop) can be very different to a not-for-profit organization (e.g. a warship in a combat zone). Even in the same industry sector, companies evolve their own personalities from their history with rituals (e.g. the office party or lack of it) and traditions. A culture can be very autocratic and centralized or much devolved.

Could you manage a hospital?

A major problem is culture clash. This is often aggravated when change is imposed on the organization.

In the present health service, a value-for-money context has been evolving. Thus, to simplify a complex issue, a hospital Chief Executive has a finite set of resources and budget. Given this, a very legitimate view is that this should be used to the greatest good for the greatest number.

An individual doctor (very rightly) is concerned about the individual patient, and, if that implies some very expensive treatment, that is what they should receive. 'I want the very best for my patient.'

Both these people are highly motivated and intend to do good. However, when it gets down to the difficult issues of finite resources, they have differing cultures and professional contexts. It is not surprising that culture clashes will occur.

Power

Who has the power to make things happen? A major issue for traditional managers has been the loss of power to a devolved front-line workforce that needs to make quick decisions whilst in front of the customer. Resources and power must be given in the right measure to people who have been given the responsibility. A mismatch of responsibility and power not only means the job does not get done but that the internal stakeholders become de-motivated.

Organizational structure

In large organizations, people need to be organized to achieve objectives. Taking a value chain approach (Unit 1), people have front-line jobs (e.g. sales) and others provide support (e.g. purchasing). Therefore, this would imply a simple functional organizational structure. Life is not so easy. If we are to launch a new product then people from all functions will need to be involved. Thus, a project team may be convened to see the project through to completion. Just as we have full- and part-time marketers, you may have full-time team members (e.g. Design Engineers) and part-time team members. This is not a specialist text on human resource management so we cast the discussion in relationship-marketing terms. The need is to ensure that power, information and the like flow appropriately. The extent to which this happens depends on appropriate people relationships. This implies that, as usual, the 'one-size-fits-all' approach does not work. Different cultures may have different organizational structures to support the healthy development of the network relationships.

Legal

The employment of people and the interaction of organizations with people are highly regulated. As a working professional, the marketer must observe not only the letter, but also the spirit of the law. In the selection of staff, equal opportunity issues must be properly handled. Staff working practices should not only be legal but fair and reasonable to ensure the right relationships are developed and maintained. The needs of all segments may need to be considered (e.g. ease of wheelchair access to buildings). As with product liability, the skilled marketer will refer to appropriate legal and other specialists.

The individual in the extended marketing team

Recruitment

If a good meal depends on the purchase of good ingredients, the future of a company depends on recruiting good people. Too often, this is seen as a simple selection process. In taking an RM view, we can see that potential job applicants are a key stakeholder group. We want the best applicants. Increasingly in the post-industrial society, there are not enough people with key skills. Therefore, selection starts with having an organization that able people will want to work in. If we take a marketing view of employment, it is a free exchange process of mutual benefit to both parties (the RM principle that only win–win relationships work in the long run). A clear specification for the role and person needs to be drawn up not only in hard terms (e.g. qualifications, professional memberships), but also in softer areas such as personality (one view is 'hire for attitude, train for performance'). Customer service is as much about values as skills.

Relationship marketing applies to the internal stakeholders. Retention is critical; poor management will only encourage good staff to move. Replacement and subsequent training of the new staff are expensive. In knowledge-based industries, such as an advertising agency, the greatest asset the organization really has is the creative talents and professionalism of its staff.

Education and training

People need to be recruited with the right education, training and experience. However, change in all aspects of work is a fact of life and both the individual and the organization must understand that education is a lifelong process; continual tracking of development is vital with continuous enhancement of skills (e.g. CIM framework of continuing professional development).

In the post-industrial society, knowledge needs to be levered around the complete organization. Organizational learning (ensuring that hard-won insights and skills are rapidly diffused through the complete organization) as well as individual learning and development is necessary for continued success. In the past, much has been written about depreciation and the effective management of physical resources. In many organizations, the key asset is knowledge and the ability to innovate. The management of innovation and knowledge at both the organization and the individual level is vital.

Personality

People not only have different skills but also differ in their personality. Some people may be introverted and others extroverted. In building a team, we need to take account of team types and personalities to ensure the effective running of the team. This is not only a process of observing others, but also a process of self-awareness and understanding ourselves and how others perceive us. There are two ends to relationships such as sales–client and the company needs to understand how the relationship is perceived at the client's end.

177

Behaviour and appearance

In discussing customer perception of service quality, a significant issue is empathy. People in the front line, delivering the 'moments of truth' to the customer, must demonstrate caring yet professional behaviour. The perception of a person's likely behaviour is signalled by body language and appearance. Supermarkets need to take as much care over how people appear and act as they do about the shops' appearance. In a hospital, there are a variety of uniforms not only for practical reasons but they also act as visual signals.

Channels

This should, in this context, be taken to be both the supply channel to the company and the distribution channel down to the ultimate consumer. All the points mentioned above apply to channel members and, as far as possible, channel members should be selected as having a good fit. This is not always possible (e.g. if you want a PC you have to work with Microsoft). That wonderful relationship you have built with the customer is worth nothing if your contract carrier turns up late with an aggressive driver. From the operational view, you may have outsourced the work but, from the customer's view, you should not have outsourced your concern for the relationship.

Customers

Other customers

Often, other customers are an important aspect of perceived service quality. It is a special reflection of segmentation issues. Train companies have 'business carriages' for the laptop addicts and 'family carriages' for people with children. This reflects not only that some people do not mix well but that, in segmenting, you can also provide a better-targeted mix (e.g. games packs for children in the family carriage).

Customer interaction

In some circumstances, customer interaction may be key (e.g. partners needed in a tennis club), but in others, customer interaction may need to be kept to a minimum (e.g. reading bays in a research library).

Customer involvement

Sometimes customer involvement with the service is important. A university education is not just about knowledge. Student societies are an important element of the total experience. The university can provide facilities (e.g. good student union buildings), but the involvement of students in running their own societies is key. The university may then use its vigorous and dynamic student societies in its marketing communications to potential students.

A related area is where the customer is a vital part of the service. This can be the use of an automated access (e.g. automatic credit card ticketing). One key area is health care. If diabetics do not track their glucose levels then they are putting themselves at risk. Health care is possibly more about patients' participation in changing lifestyles than in just undergoing surgery. This issue is covered further in the section on process.

Objectives

As always with any element of the marketing mix, effective planning requires the setting of SMART objectives. These can relate both to the organization (number of staff to be recruited) and to the individual (personal development plans). This is much the same as for marketing communications: you have a global corporate image plan and individual communications plans for each new product launch. The objectives may be quantitative (e.g. 90 per cent of staff will attend the customer care course over the next year) or qualitative (e.g. staff attitude research).

Budget

Much of this is predetermined as the overall payroll is not normally under the marketing department's control. However, some elements should be actively scrutinized by marketing. Incentives that impact upon customer care (e.g. sales incentives) need to be properly designed to achieve their desired objectives. The implication is that there must be a feedback system to evaluate actual performance.

Sales-based commission trap

Many organizations motivate their front-line staff with sales-related commission payments. There are a number of problems with this attractive, simple approach. Sales are paid for a given period. In relationship terms, you are concerned with the lifetime value of the company. With part-time staff and frequent staff turnover, often individuals are concerned with this month's bonus – not what it might be in 18 months' time. The drive may be to gain sales and not maximize profits (e.g. it may encourage sales representatives to 'give away' discounts too easily). Who achieves the sale? Was it the sales representative or the marketing person who put together the PowerPoint presentation? Just giving the sales staff a commission can be seen as divisive within a team. Broad performance bonuses do not link exceptional efforts directly to a diffuse reward given to all much later. This is not only an issue within the company but also for reward systems applied to agents and distributors.

Training for staff will also need to be built into budgets (e.g. field training for maintenance staff for a new product).

Feedback and control

If care has been taken with the formulation of SMART objectives, then measurement should not be too difficult. Control is a different issue. Identifying underperformance by an individual is relatively straightforward, but what to do about it can be a problem (e.g. with complex employment law, dismissal is not always easy, it may not be easy to terminate a distributor's contract).

Staff appraisals

Staff appraisals are used by many organizations as part of their staff development programmes. Apart from responsibility for their own staff, Marketing Managers should discuss how marketing and customer care objectives should be written into job descriptions and appraisal schemes for part-time marketers.

Morale

Morale and staff attitudes are key to developing and maintaining a corporate culture. Organizations do not have culture: this is the manifestation of the collective culture of the staff and the quality of leadership of management. A manager asking a member of staff how they feel about their job just before reviewing their bonus for the next year is not likely to get a realistic view of the situation. This is one place where anonymous research by an outside agency may be appropriate.

Reward systems

Some of the difficulties in this area were covered in the section on objectives. Here we note that appropriate figures need to be collected to feed into the system. This needs some care, as, just as with costs and pricing, the figures used for the company accounts may not be right in this specific context.

Why are sales high in December?

A researcher was investigating potential seasonality of sales in a B2B context. Statistical analysis showed a significant upturn in sales in December and a drop in January. Investigation revealed that sales staff were paid their commission on sales booked in the calendar year. If their sales were a little below target for the year they would book a fictitious order just before the Christmas shutdown and bank their bonus. In January, by the time they had received their bonus, they would cancel the order.

 Activity 7.3

Discuss with your CIM group how the people element of the service-extended mix applies to the delivery of a CIM module at a college.

Case study

'Lake View Organic Farms' – People

Using the structure from Figure 7.1 and the following analysis of 'people', issues can be constructed for 'Lake View Organic Farms':

Corporate values – Green marketing companies develop and express their green values. The classic example of this is the 'Body Shop', not just another cosmetic store.

Culture and style – Organizations with a strong set of ethical values are likely to have an inclusive management style – more than a job, moving into a mission.

Power – The structure of a co-operative involves a broader decision-making process than which occurs in some other organizations. Members of a co-operative tend to be more actively involved in the management of their organizations than shareholders (as long as shareholders get share value growth and dividends, they tend to be happy and keep out of executive management issues).

Organizational structure – This is not a massive organization but there would be a need for definition of roles. The warehouse operation would be preparing and packing the produce. Distribution would be by the co-operative's own vehicles or by the franchisees. The management issues of finance, purchasing, human resource management, marketing and sales (including the website) would need a small flexible team.

Legal – Employment law is complex and expert advice should be sought for drawing up contracts of employment. The employment of drivers involves special issues, for example the recording of working hours. Farms sometimes employ part-time staff for peak-level seasonal work. Legislation has been tightened around this practice after some serious safety lapses. As with all operations, health and safety is a key management responsibility.

Recruitment – Different areas would require different skills, and a clear identification of these would be needed. Care needs to be taken with the recruitment of delivery staff as they do most of their work outside direct management supervision. Moreover, as part-time marketers (in relationship-marketing terms), they are the 'face' of the company to the customers.

Education and training – Some jobs may need relatively little training (e.g. packing). Management staff may need continuing professional development to track emerging needs (e.g. new software developments). All staff must be trained and informed about green issues. This will be particularly important for front-line staff.

Personality/attitude – Some organizations take the view 'Hire for attitude and train for performance.' There is some logic in this. It is easier to give people new skills than change core values. Given the culture, staff must be committed to green values.

Motivation – This is a tricky issue where people are working in such diverse roles. The packing group is likely to have a fair measure of team values. This is more difficult with drivers who have a more solitary role. Company events such as 'open days' can provide a way to give all employees a sense of belonging.

Behaviour and appearance – Particularly important for the people in front-line contact with customers. Earlier we noted that customers want reliability, responsiveness and assurance. Front-line staff (part-time marketers) have a key role in delivering this. They have the face-to-face 'moments of truth' with the clients. This is where company reputation is built or lost.

Other customers – This is not like a club, where customer–customer interactions are key. However, the knowledge that a top restaurant purchases its produce from 'Lake View Organic Farms' can be useful. It can indicate the high quality of the products to potential new customers (any mention of this should always be with the client's permission).

Customer interaction – Ordering produce does not constitute a strong involvement in the organization (unlike the situation with a school where the parents may have strong interactions and involvement).

Staff appraisals – Staff and management need to be involved in a continual development of the team's skills. Appraisals if well conducted can help with this.

Morale – Not the context for the hiring of a consultant to conduct a massive attitude survey. However, the management need to get around (sometimes called 'management by walking around'), so they can gauge the atmosphere in departments and gain feedback.

Reward systems – This is not just the money in the pay packet but issues such as holidays and pension provision. Even for small organizations, these are substantial issues. Without some reasonable provision, key professional staff (e.g. marketing) may be reluctant to join the organization. Complex laws (e.g. maternity leave provision) may surround these issues. Expert advice is needed in this area.

Remember business models are more like checklists than mathematical equations, so sensible interpretation is often necessary to apply the model. However, models do prompt us to ask the range of relevant questions, whereas without a model it is easy to leave gaps in the analysis and thus in the resulting plan.

Physical evidence

Services are intangible; physical evidence provides something tangible enabling people to 'feel' the quality of the service (Figure 7.2).

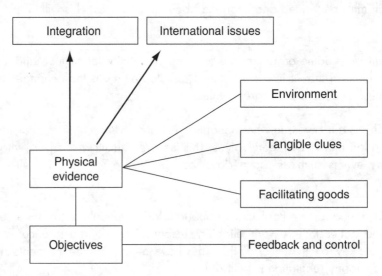

Figure 7.2 Structure for physical evidence

Environment

How many people come into a shop? How long do they spend in the shop? What they buy is affected by the ambience and physical layout of the store. Lighting, heating, sound, colour and even smell (remember your last trip to the bakery) all contribute. This can be large-scale, such as the construction of a shopping mall, to the physical display of goods (there is no sharp dividing line between environment and point of sale for a shop). Airlines, theatres and museums all take care with their physical environment. Appropriate environments and even music can speed up recovery rates in hospitals.

Tangible clues

Many services have small 'products' associated with them. The classic example is a ticket (e.g. travel, theatre, car park, etc.). The design and quality all make a communications statement. An invoice is not only a request for money but, in relationship-marketing terms, also an opportunity to communicate. An area where there has been much consumer dissatisfaction has been insurance policies and guarantees (the 'small-print syndrome'). These were (and still are by some poor companies) simply seen as legal documents. Of course they are, but they are also customer communications; if they are written in a language the customer does not understand, they have failed (every time you insure your car you do not want to consult your solicitor for a translation of the policy document).

In many contexts, products may be a substantial element in service provision. The quality of training manuals in a distance learning course or the food in a restaurant are all key to actual and perceived quality.

Facilitating goods

This links up with the change of 'service' to 'product' in the extension part of the Plymouth product model given in Figure 3.4. Tangible clues are an essential part of the service: you do not get onto the aircraft without your boarding pass. Facilitating goods are products that are associated with the service, which may or may not be supplied by the service provider. A golfer may have their own clubs or hire a set for the day. An opera-goer may purchase a copy of the opera libretto to add to their enjoyment or they may bring their own copy. Again, this should be viewed like a spectrum. A Manchester United shirt may be worn to the game as part of the ceremony surrounding the event. The coffee mug is a brand extension in Ansoff mode (Unit 11). Fine distinctions as to where you classify the product in the model are not too important. What is important is that such products are often major sources of income. The National Trust and museums exploit their 'service' brand image with a wide variety of goods, a major additional income stream to grants and subsidies.

Objectives, feedback and control

Physical checks can be made on the standard of facilities (e.g. in a hotel washroom you may see a sign along the lines 'These toilets were inspected by #### at ####, any problems contact #####'). Plans can be made to refurbish to an agreed timetable. New styles (e.g. concept stores) can be test-marketed at just a few locations to see if they achieve the desired objectives. Tangible clues and facilitating goods are products, so they can be checked by normal product means. Budgets should be set for the sales of facilitating goods and variances investigated in the ways outlined in Unit 4.

Case study

'Lake View Organic Farms' – Physical evidence

Using the structure from Figure 7.2, the following analysis of 'Physical evidence' issues can be constructed for 'Lake View Organic Farms'.

Environment – for home delivery possibly not a major issue. However, for farm-based purchases the sales area has to give the right appearance. A farm not a supermarket, a different, more 'back to nature', buying experience.

Tangible clues – as a green organization, care must be taken with items such as packaging (re-usable and/or recyclable) and documentation such as invoices (printed on re-cycled paper).

Facilitating goods – with the green values of the firm, customers should be encouraged to compost their waste, where possible. Compost bins might be an option. Certain ways of cooking food can destroy the vitamin content or produce harmful products (e.g. frying at too high a temperature). Cooking equipment that preserves the nutritional value (e.g. steamers and woks) might be another option. Facilitating goods help the customer to better enjoy the service and also generate additional revenue for the organization.

Activity 7.4

Banking is becoming more automated and less personal. Personal visits to the bank have started to be replaced by telephone banking and online banking offers the potential prize to banks of lower transaction costs and potentially a more responsive service to customers (24/7 banking). However, this comes at a cost: the service is becoming more impersonal and less tangible (no bank building, no cashiers). Make a list of the aspects of your bank account that demonstrate the concept of physical evidence.

Process

This has been an area of dramatic change. Shortly after the advent of the mobile phones, telephones achieved majority cover in the developed world and telephone insurance became a reality, not just a possibility. It took a century for telephones to achieve this level of penetration. Domestic Internet broadband is set to do this within a decade. The advantages of the Internet were outlined in Table 6.1. Here we shall concentrate on the nature of the service delivery, the procedures and policies that underpin the service, the level of involvement of people outside the organization in service delivery and, finally, issues of control and feedback.

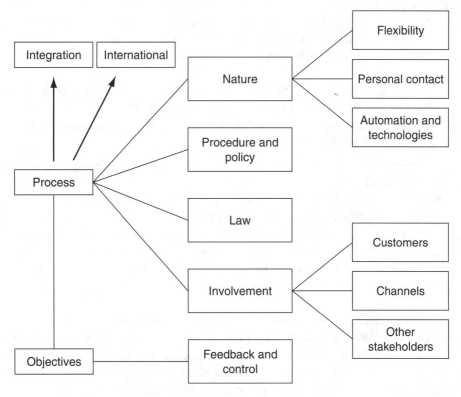

Figure 7.3 Structure for process

Case study

UR R@ is in the trap

The use of ICT is providing some novel and unexpected improvements to services. Rentokil is a company providing a number of services to industry including pest control. In large computer installations, rats and mice can cause havoc by nibbling their way through cables. Frequent inspection of the humane traps is wasteful, time-consuming and expensive (most of the time the traps are empty). To improve the service and cut costs, the cyber mousetrap has been developed. The trap is selective. A pressure sensor measures the weight of the animal's paw. If it is a mouse or rat the trap is activated. Squirrels and rabbits do not activate the system. When the trap is triggered, a cell-phone unit (minus a microphone) sends a text to the nearest pest controller.

Nature

Flexibility

There is both strength and weakness with people in service delivery and that is flexibility. Flexibility can be a problem as it implies, to some extent, variability of service quality. However, people can be very adaptive and machines are not very empathetic. Sometimes we do not require great flexibility. When we turn on the tap we just want water, not apple juice or a milk shake. However, in many instances, the reverse is true and people may put considerable value on flexibility. If I need to be able to travel to the airport at any time by any train, a full 'open ticket' will cost many times that of a 'super APEX' that has to be bought many days before with specific, unchangeable journey times. This is the key problem of mass transit systems that take people from a relatively few fixed points to relatively few points at relatively infrequent and inconvenient times. The car or taxi can take us from any location in a large city to virtually any address, at our convenience. The flexible delivery of a service can often command a premium price (e.g. the cost of a taxi is more than the cost of a bus).

In the post-industrial society, the aim of the marketer is for mass production (keep transaction costs down) of individually tailored offerings (totally tailored marketing mix for the individual). The Internet search engine goes a long way to do this, finding just the information you want from an almost unlimited information bank.

Personal contact

At times, the customer may not be concerned with personal contact. At midnight in the city centre, we are happy to get our money from an ATM. At other times, personal contact is vital. That cup of coffee at 02.00 in the early morning at the airport from a machine is fine. However, after paying £50 for that romantic meal for two, we do not expect to be told 'fifty pence from the machine over there' when we ask for our coffee. A music fan will buy the DVD and then pay £50 to go to the concert for the 'personal', live atmosphere.

The marketer needs to be sensitive regarding the extent that personal service is required. Many operations-orientated people running call centres enthuse about the efficiency of touch key 'flexibility' at the front end. Most customers appear to be irritated by having to go through a series of not very helpful recorded messages that are costing them money when they want to talk to a responsive, flexible and empathetic human being.

Procedure and policy

This aspect of the mix should not be seen in isolation from the 'people' element. One of the key decisions in organizations is the degree of flexibility and authority to interpret policy by front-line service providers. Procedures and policies are clearly necessary. Safety in gas repair should not come as an optional extra from just a few installation staff. However, sensible interpretation of policy is required, the obverse of this is the 'job's worth' approach you can see in any local paper – 'Traffic warden gives ticket to ambulance on emergency call' and so on. As often in business life, what is required is a balance. There is a need for efficiency and, sometimes for other good reasons (consistent delivery of service quality); there need to be fixed and firm procedures and policies. However, inflexible mechanical application of rules and procedures can result in an outcome a million miles away from customer care.

More than my job's worth

The actual legal situation was unclear at the time of this event in 2003 but this case does starkly highlight the problems of rigid application of rules. A gas company disconnected the supply to a house for non-payment of bills. The people concerned were very old and frail. Some months later, in the winter, they were found dead. The company said they were not allowed to inform the social services because this was not a legitimate legal use of their data under the terms of the UK Data Protection Act.

This account is not to be taken as a criticism of the action of the company. On the best legal advice, the management had to observe the law. Clearly, when the laws and rules for interpretation were put in place by well-meaning people, it was to protect people's individual freedom and civil rights. It was not intended at the same time to allow people to freeze to death. Yet, the apparent inflexibility permitted by the law resulted in just that.

Legal

The above example demonstrates not only the need for flexibility in interpretation and implementation but the impact of law on how services are provided. In our information-rich age the issue of civil liberties has needed laws to evolve. Therefore, just what a security company can and cannot do in its operations, such as the storage and use of CCTV footage, are subject to legal constraints.

Financial services are another area where legislation has an impact on service provision processes. Not only must financial consultants be appropriately trained and qualified, but also the process of discussion with clients must cover specific issues. Safety in service provision is also not only covered by general liability, but also sometimes by industry-specific legislation of processes (e.g. processes and procedures in maintenance for a certificate of airworthiness).

Involvement

Customers

This part of the process mix is a vital aspect of the 'people' element. This reminds the practising marketer that, very often, to make our processes work, winning, customer-involvement in the service delivery situation is important. Whereas several years ago, we would have expected that when purchasing fuel at a filling station, the attendant would not only fill up the car but also clean your windscreen, take your payment and return with your change. Nowadays, we are more concerned with paying as little as possible and spending as short a time as possible at the fuel station. The customer could well perceive these extras as driving up transaction costs and therefore they are no longer expected to be there. The same fuel station protocols are, however, still current in some very rural areas or in other cultures, since within these marketing environments the customers expect these services to come as standard and are prepared to pay for them.

Many processes depend on customer consent. Take cyber-fraud, which is on the increase. One form is 'card cloning'. Here the information on a victim's credit card is copied (e.g. when out of the owner's sight in a restaurant). In the United Kingdom, there is a move to PIN terminals widely used in other countries. In this process, the restaurateur enters the amount into a battery-operated portable terminal, the customer inserts their card and keys in their PIN. This makes cloning more difficult but not impossible (all your data is still recorded in the terminal). The need is for identifying that the person is the legitimate cardholder, so some cards bear a picture of the owner. With passports, there is a move to increase the bio-information they hold (e.g. fingerprints and experiments with iris recognition). The common thread is that many processes depend on customer consent and participation in the process of service provision.

Medical consultations in a multi-cultural environment

In a multicultural, multilingual environment, communications between people of different cultures may be difficult. This can be a major problem when the communication is between a patient and a medical practitioner. Willing disclosure and accurate communication of symptoms are essential. In these circumstances, the process of diagnosis is impaired because of the difficulty the customer (the patient) has in being able to fully and effectively participate in the process. Clearly, the balance between providing medical care to a budget (time available for doctor/patient consultation and the likelihood of multilingual staff) and ensuring absolute clarity for patients/clients is key.

Channels

Many companies do not deliver their service but rely on channel intermediaries to perform the service on their behalf. Many of the companies that *sell* you electricity do not *supply* electricity. There is only one cable into your house. When you change supplier they do not dig up the road and lay a new cable. All the alternative sellers are relying on that one contractor for physically connecting to the consumer. If the distribution system fails, you do not have a customer. In setting quality standards, the practising marketer needs to involve all the channel members who impact on the quality of the service delivery.

Other stakeholders

Other stakeholders may be important to the quality of service provision. A marketing-orientated proactive view needs to be taken or unfavourable outcomes damaging service quality can result.

Standards, legacy and customer expectation

The law may regulate some aspects, such as mains frequency for electricity distribution, or times for delivery in city centres. However, many aspects of our post-industrial society require cooperation and coordination. EPOS terminals will only work if computer and packaging manufacturers agree on a standardized bar code system. The codes would be meaningless without the agreement of all involved in assigning the numbers (Article Numbering Association). Currently, there are efforts to replace bar codes with a new standard method of tracking goods with radio frequency identification (RFID) chips. Such chips would allow better tracking of goods, yet some consumers also see them as an invasion of privacy.

Communications systems rely on various agreements on issues such as who owns which radio bandwidth (TV, radio, mobile phones, emergency services, taxis, military, etc. are just some of the users, and radio space is international as well) and on communications protocols. The ability to provide an effective and efficient service often depends on obtaining and maintaining appropriate standards. The bodies that set and enforce these are key stakeholders influencing service provision.

A century ago, when the first mechanical typewriters were invented, a skilled operator could type so fast that all the keys would jam up. To slow operators down, the keys were placed in an inconvenient layout. In the twenty-first century, people around the world still have to live with the QWERTY keyboard and it is the standard. However inconvenient it is, we are content to continue using it despite its inconvenience and the necessity for it in the first place no longer exists due to computerization.

Why is this the case in a modern world full of short cuts and time-saving ideas? Think about two other similar issues.

Why do some countries drive on the left, whereas the majority drive on the right?

Why is there more than one mobile phone system worldwide?

Case study

'Lake View Organic Farms' – Physical evidence

Using the structure from Figure 7.3 the following analysis of 'Process' issues can be constructed for 'Lake View Organic Farms':

Flexibility – Earlier we noted that people wanted responsiveness in a service. Flexibility in the options and systems we provide gives the customer options. There is a trade-off between flexibility and costs. It costs less to pack a standard 'veggie box' than a custom-ordered one. With Internet ordering and a modest premium the customer should be able to have the flexibility they want, with the profitability of the firm maintained.

Personal contact – People tend to like some personality in their service. The ordering may be automated and impersonal but with the careful selection of delivery staff (earlier section 'People') a personal link with relationships can be built up (relationship marketing).

Automation and technologies – Standing order, telephone, e-mails and website ordering provides a range of technologies to suit both the 'techno-phobe' and the 'techie'. This helps us satisfy one of the other criteria for customer service satisfaction 'empathy'. Not everyone wants to order online.

Procedure and policy – A key problem for online ordering systems, for a basket of products, is the procedure for stock-outs. Should the firm substitute nearest equivalent of equal value without further reference to the customer? Clear procedure and policy needs to be in place to satisfy both the firm's needs and the customers' needs.

Law – When orders are taken, a contract is being entered into: nothing too complex here. This is not the same situation as selling financial services where there is a whole range of 'do's and don'ts' set in law for the selling process.

Customer involvement – People can place their orders online. Others can elect to talk to a real person on the telephone. There is a range of levels and types of involvement provided to accommodate a range of customer preferences.

Channels – Not an issue for direct delivery, there are none.

Other stakeholders – A key group is the franchisees. Care must be taken in their recruitment and selection, not only for business and financial skills, but they will also be the 'face' of the organization to customers. We need the franchisees to give as good a service as our own staff.

 Activity 7.5

This CIM module can be taken by either continuous assessment or by examination. Consider the differences between the processes for the two routes from the point of view of a candidate and the Chartered Institute of Marketing.

Question 7.1

Consider a regional newspaper with a city centre shop where people can place advertisements and order pictures and others (many newspapers make additional income by selling pictures that have appeared in the paper). Consider how the concepts of the service-extended marketing mix can be applied to this situation.

International aspects

The service extension is most sensitive to cultural issues. As we reviewed in Unit 1, culture influences education, motivation, appearance and behaviour. Thus, all aspects of the people element of the service extension may be impacted by cultural issues. Behaviour and appearance that might be acceptable in one culture are less acceptable in another. Physical evidence has a cultural dimension, good style depends upon cultural aesthetics. The style of process and the degree of automation will vary from country to country. When a supermarket decides to go global, its international buying power and logistics may be levered but the actual shopping experience in the store needs to be tailored to the local market needs and culture.

Case study

'SMS Cars Ltd.' – International aspects

International aspects featured in the 'SMS Cars Ltd' case study, June 2006, with Question 2c 'What factors must be considered when important guests from other countries are coming to such an event?' Below are some of the issues that might be considered for the elements of the service-extended marketing mix for an international event (e.g. a conference or an exhibition):

People – in selecting people for such activity, language skills would be one of the elements to be considered. People with a multicultural outlook sensitive to the needs of different cultures would be required. Care should be taken that dress style do not cause cultural difficulties.

Physical evidence – appropriate consideration of cultural needs such as translation of key documentation and provision of appropriate food and drink for religious conformance.

Process – should be flexible to allow for different needs: 100per cent online booking may be appropriate for delegates from a developed country but may be more problematical for delegates from a less developed country. Most of the developed world is online with broadband access but still limited in some parts of the world.

 ## Activity 7.6

Think back to when you were on holiday. When you went shopping for food, how was the experience different from your home country?

Summary

In this unit, we have further explored the nature of service with a focus on service quality perception. To achieve this, all four elements of the product mix still need to be considered. To augment these, the additional three Ps of People, Process and Physical Evidence have also been explored. In each section, ways to set objectives and measure performance were explored. It is especially important in this area; some of the issues are more diffuse (e.g. customer service culture) but still need to be managed well for organizational success. The service extension provides the marketer with some tools to achieve the objectives indicated by the application of relationship-marketing principles. Questions on the service-extended marketing mix feature appeared in the CIM exams: for example, Question 4 in the December 2005 examination, 'Compare how the THREE elements of the service marketing mix (people, Process and physical evidence) might differ in application between the Urban Culture Festival and a financial services provider.' Another question on the service extended marketing mix occurred in June 2006, Question 5a 'Produce a briefing paper to be forwarded to the Manager of the Vehicle Servicing Department which describes how THREE elements of the extended marketing mix (people, process and physical evidence) can be used by the Vehicle Servicing Department to improve customer service.'

Question 7.2

Apply the concepts of the service extension of the marketing mix to an international airline.

Further study

Dibb, S., Simkin, L., Pride, W. and Ferrell, O. (2006) *Marketing Concepts and Strategies*, 5th European edition, Houghton Mifflin, Chapters 13 and 22.

As an integrative module, you should also review the other coursebooks at this level

Cheeseman, A., and Jones, M. (2007) *CIM Coursebook – Customer Communications in Marketing*, Butterworth-Heinemann.

Lancaster, G., and Withey, F. (2007) *CIM Coursebook – Marketing Fundamentals*, Butterworth-Heinemann.

Oldroyd, M. (2007) *CIM Coursebook – Marketing Environment*, Butterworth-Heinemann.

Hints and tips

As with other sections, use the models to evaluate your experience of services. Consider what, if the experience was not as good as it should be, you might do as a marketing manager to make the experience better. Given the wide range of marketing contexts, simple models need to be adapted and interpreted to provide the appropriate insight. Marketing models do not work like spreadsheets, where numbers are simply plugged in. Marketing cannot be reduced to a simple equation; skill in interpretation is required and this needs practice.

In the CIM examination, case studies are often set in a service marketing context: for example The 'Urban Culture Festival 2006'.

Bibliography

Douglas Hoffman (2005) *Essentials of Services Marketing*, The Dryden Press.

Gummesson, E. (2002) *Total Relationship Marketing – Rethinking Marketing Management: From 4Ps to 30Rs*, Butterworth-Heinemann.

Hollensen, S. (2004) *Marketing Management – A Relationship Approach*, 1st edition, Prentice Hall.

Jeannet, J. (2005) *Global Marketing Strategies*, 6th edition, Houghton Mifflin.

Kotler, P. (2006) *Marketing Management*, 12th edition, Prentice Hall.

Kotler, P., and Scheff, J. (1997) *Standing Room Only – Strategies for Marketing the Performing Arts*, Harvard Business School Press.

unit 8
the management of marketing information

When you have completed this unit, you will

- Appreciate the areas from which data needs to be collected.

- Appreciate the need to check the validity of data for specific applications.

- Understand the difference between data and information.

- Appreciate the different types of data such as quantitative and qualitative.

- Understand the more important approaches to market research.

- Appreciate the role of market intelligence in formulating marketing plans.

- Appreciate the value of internal data and how this can be integrated with other sources to provide valuable information.

- Understand how to use database systems to manage raw data.

- Understand how computers and other systems are used to convert raw data into useful information.

- Understand the role information plays in the business decisions an organization makes.

Syllabus references

1.1 Identify sources of information internally and externally to the organization, including ICT-based sources such as Intranet and Internet.

1.2 Maintain a marketing database, information collection and usage.

1.3 Investigate customers via the database and develop bases for segmentation.

1.4 Explain information-gathering techniques available.

193

1.5 Source and present information on competitor activities across the marketing mix.

1.6 Investigate marketing and promotional opportunities using appropriate information-gathering techniques.

1.7 Gather information across borders.

3.4 Explain how marketing makes use of planning techniques: objective setting; and coordinating, measuring and evaluating results to support the organization.

4.6 Describe how organizations monitor product trends.

4.8 Explain the importance of ICT in the new mix.

5.6 Examine the correlation between marketing mix decisions and results.

Key definitions

Quantitative data – Information that is easy to convey in numbers, for example how many people buy a product and how much they use.

Qualitative data – Key for developing deep plans as it involves more difficult but key questions such as 'why and how do people view my brand?'

Study Guide

Research is an activity in itself. When you are working through this unit, consider the information you use in your daily work and where you get the information. Keep asking yourself 'Is this information perfect for the decisions I have to make, or is this all that can be found, therefore am I just making the best of what can be obtained?'

Remember, when working out what research you need to do, start at the end. The first question is, *what is the information going to be used for*? It will then be possible to consider the areas where the various types of raw data will have to be collected. Data collected by market research, market intelligence and internal data need to be integrated within appropriate computer systems. Appropriate ordering, patterning and transformation of the data in analytical systems will provide the decision-making information specified in the first part of the process.

The information system

It is inappropriate to consider how to do market research until you know what information you need and what use you are going to make of it. This is especially important now, since certain types of data will fall under data protection legislation. If its potential uses have not been specified in the past then it may not be legal to use the data for other purposes later. To start collecting information without knowing what the uses will be is rather like a drunk person holding onto a lamp post: the effect is more for support than illumination. In Figure 8.1, the data system is shown. We need to collect information on the environment, the marketplace and our own performance. This process enables us to make appropriate management decisions. Only selected examples are shown in Figure 8.1. Different types of data require special methods of collection (e.g. focus groups for some types of qualitative data). Having decided what the information will be used for and what data will be required, it is then appropriate to devise ongoing systems or special research projects to gather the data. Data often needs sorting and analysing to yield information. Often some mathematical process may be required. To look at how sales are progressing a business analyst will want to compare like with like, removing the effects of seasonality and price changes. In comparing retail sales two Christmas sales periods may be compared and price rises adjusted to give a measure of true volume growth.

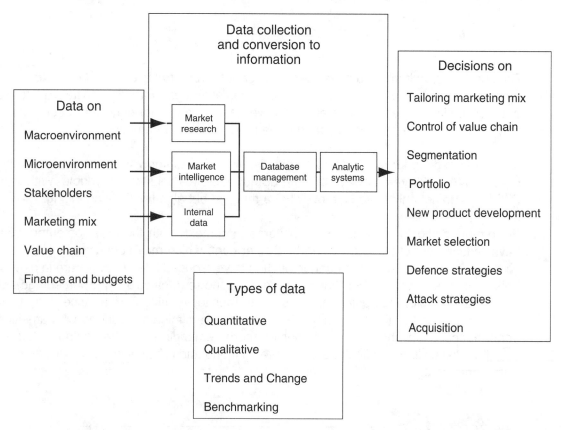

Figure 8.1 The Marketing information system

What data?

General trends in the macroenvironment and microenvironment need to be tracked. It is all too easy to miss a trend until serious damage to the business is already happening (e.g. impact of new technology introducing new competitors). All the key stakeholders need to be tracked including consumers, customers, distributors, suppliers, competitors and even internal stakeholders. In a dangerous business environment, you need to understand your competitors as well as understanding your own business. This can be the difference between being a victim and being a winner. In this context it is not only the performance of your own marketing mix that needs to be tracked but also that of your competitors.

When you run a car, you check tyre pressure, oil levels and so on from time to time. As you drive you will note that temperatures are within limits and warning lights will inform you if something is wrong (e.g. a door not securely closed). The company value chain does not run itself. Just as with the car, performance and operations need to be checked continuously (e.g. are we invoicing and receiving payment promptly?). Money is the lifeblood of organizations.

195

A charity will go bankrupt if it does not keep within its budgets. There is no point in setting budgets unless cash flows are monitored and discrepancies investigated.

Activity 8.1

List the information that a business school might need for developing new courses in marketing.

Types of data

Data can be quantitative, such as *how many people came to the concert last night*? In addition, it can be qualitative: *how do they feel about medieval organ music*? Qualitative information is often vital, since to tailor a marketing mix we need to know not only what people do but also why they do it. 'Why?' questions tend to be more difficult to frame.

It is not enough to know where something is. We need to know where things are going. That bullet may be 100 yards away but if we do not duck, we could be in trouble. With shortening PLCs, we do not only have to know what a thing is, but also how it is changing.

Performance should be constantly monitored in context. With the new computer system, we have reduced our costs of invoicing by 20 per cent, which may sound good. However, if our costs are £2.00 per order and our competition have reduced it to £0.25 we are in deep trouble. This is often a relative rather than an absolute issue (e.g. calculating a percentage). Suitable benchmarking reference points are needed to monitor relative performance. Fifty years ago, the world celebrated the first person to run a mile in 4 minutes. Just as with athletics, good performance is not absolute. Life is getting more demanding and the goalposts keep moving (e.g. that dial-up line was fine until you visited a friend and found how much quicker things were with broadband).

Activity 8.2

A company intends to launch a new variety of chocolate bar. List the types of information they would need to collect.

Information for management decisions

The list of management issues given in Figure 8.1 shows some of the more important decisions facing most organizations. Marketers are always fine-tuning and balancing the marketing mix as the marketing environment changes. The performance of the company (the value chain performance) needs to be monitored so adjustments can be made (e.g. excessive overtime working could result in stress and may indicate that additional staff should be recruited). As markets change, so segments may grow or die. Segmentation strategies need to evolve. It is not possible to complete a portfolio analysis without defining your market segments (e.g. in a BCG analysis, Unit 11, you need to define the market segment and then measure the rate of growth). If a company does not keep a balanced portfolio it can be storing up major problems, when those cash cows slide into scruffy dead dogs (we need some stars to take over).

Ansoff strategies may demand we develop new products and/or establish new markets (Unit 11). To achieve these successfully and minimize risk good quality, timely information is required. This is not done in some nice isolated business laboratory but in a rough playing field where the competition will do all they can to steal our business. Attack and defence strategies again need good quality information. One particular type of growth strategy is 'acquisition'. All too often, this disappoints investors, since the homework has not been done and the acquisition process is not well handled. Business decisions are like decorating a room. The final result can be no better than the quality of the preparation allows. Good business decisions have, at their foundation, good quality information.

Activity 8.3

Outline the various decisions that have to be made when a successful, high-fashion, London hair and beauty salon is considering expansion?

Data collection and conversion into information

Marketing research activity can be divided into two types: primary research and secondary research.

1. Primary research is where you go out into the field to collect new data using appropriate research methods (e.g. questionnaire).
2. Secondary research is where you actively research existing data, which is available from a rich variety of sources (e.g. government statistics).

Confusingly, secondary research should be completed before primary research, since primary marketing research is expensive in both time and physical resources. Having defined the issue(s) and information needed in the outline, the first stage is to see what information may already exist. This may, in part, answer the problem (if you are lucky, possibly completely). If not, it will give you a better understanding of the issues and enable you to be more focused and pursue the primary research more effectively and efficiently. There is no replacement for market sense. Secondary research and informal investigations provide the foundation for primary research. The most difficult issue in marketing research is developing sufficient understanding of the relevant issues so as to be able to ask the *right* questions.

To maintain its position, Coca-Cola has an extensive programme of marketing research. Much research was conducted by 'blind' tasting of the 'standard' products and new 'improved' formulas and it was believed that a new version of Coca-Cola was needed to cater for changes in consumer tastes. A modified product came out top in these preference tests. However, in the event, people wanted the original version and 'Classic' Coke re-entered the market. The wrong question had been asked. Many years on Diet Coke has slowly increased its share of the market as people have become more calorie aware.

Having captured information, it is important to store and retrieve the information in a relevant way. To make sense of it the researcher is often looking for order and patterns in data. Here, database management and graphical analysis can be most helpful and should be included in any research process. These processes can then be taken further by using statistical and other analytical techniques. For much work, basic systems based on normal MS Office software might be sufficient (e.g. Access for database work and Excel for statistical work). For a more major investigation, there are more powerful packages such as SPSS. It takes 3 years to get a degree in statistics so, again, talk to experts; you do not get on a jumbo jet and say 'Hi! OK if I take the controls today?' It is easy to realize that if you get a landing wrong, the plane crashes. Similarly, if you get the design and analysis of a research programme wrong, going bankrupt can be just as terminal for the organization. In this discussion of methods for obtaining data some specific focus is given to the pitfalls.

Market research

Secondary market research

Secondary research is usually much less expensive and enables primary research to be more successfully completed. Thus, it is the appropriate place to start. Increasingly much of this is now available online. Below are some selected issues to consider when using secondary sources:

- o Date of the research. When was the data collected? In fast-moving market situations, research can quickly become outdated. If you pull a piece of fresh chicken out of the fridge, the first thing you do is check the use-by date. The danger is that secondary data does not come with warning signs and use-by dates. Government statistics are often interesting as they are collected regularly on a more or less consistent basis and so give information about trends.
- o How was the data collected? If possible, check on where the sample was taken and how the research was conducted. It may have been sufficient for the original researcher's needs, but is it right for your new context? International market research can be difficult as criteria can be defined differently in various countries (e.g. the age at which you may drive a car differs in some countries).
- o 'Political' research: this is where the researchers have deliberately, or simply through ignorance, framed the research in such a way that they get the 'right' result. The newspaper survey is a typical situation: *Look at the pretty pictures of Arctic seals, send in this coupon if you think these nasty big people should not kill them.* Not surprising the next day you get the headlines '99 per cent of our readers support the ban' – who was that one person who does not like cute seal pictures?

Primary research

Questionnaires

The questionnaire is an effective research tool when used well in the correct circumstances. At the end of this unit, there are some references to sources that cover the issues in questionnaire design and use in more detail. Here we note some of the more obvious errors to avoid.

1. Frame the question in such a way that you are not 'leading' the respondent to an answer. The newspaper survey-type questions are clearly outrageous and represent an unethical approach but it is very easy to draw up a leading question simply in error.

2. Frame the question so that the meaning is clear. An American researcher who had investigated motor cycle apparel in the United States, decided, while on a visit to the United Kingdom, to find out if there were any differences in purchase patterns to the United States. Fortunately, the questionnaire was piloted before the full survey. Asking UK male bikers if they wore 'suspenders' was not a good idea (where the survey was originally run, this term was used for braces)! This type of issue is a major consideration in international market research where much care is needed to get the right words and language.

3. A variant of this issue is the question for which you will not get an honest or correct answer (e.g. ask the question 'Do you have a police record?' and you are unlikely to get many positive answers. Around 25 per cent of UK males have a police record).

4. Always check for bias in the sample used. In postal surveys, you may have a good address list to mail out your sample. However, your respondents may skew your results, for example typically those with strong feelings about an issue are more likely to reply than the apathetic who may be the silent majority.

Demographics of college students

Consider that you have been asked to research the demographics of students at your college and for this case study situation you may not have access to the student records. Therefore, you will have to estimate the demographics by using primary research. Here we will consider just one aspect. What is the gender distribution? Consider that it has been decided to observe students leaving lectures and sample the ratio.

Bias in the sample – Stand outside an Engineering lecture and your result will be over 90 per cent male. Always ask yourself *'Is the sample subject too subtle? Possibly hidden bias?'*

Sample size – You have decided that if you observe students paying fees that this bias should not exist. For this simple discussion, we shall assume that the real population is balanced (50 per cent male and 50 per cent female). If you observe one student, you clearly have an absurdly small sample size and your answer for the total population will be either 100 per cent male or 100 per cent female. Therefore, you have an equal chance of obtaining either of the (wrong) estimates. If you observe two people in succession, you have four possible results (girl/girl, girl/boy, boy/girl and boy/boy). You have a one in four chance of estimating the college is 100 per cent female, a one in four chance that it is 100 per cent male and an even chance that it is 50 per cent girls and 50 per cent boys. Mathematicians call this type of distribution a binomial distribution. Let them do the calculations, just worry about the results. To make any reasonable estimate in this type of situation you need a sample size of at least 50 people. As we noted above, we need also to know that the sample is not biased as well. In forecasting the results of an election, sample sizes of the order of 1000 are needed. Again, care is needed to ensure that the sample is representative and not biased.

 Activity 8.4

Discuss with your group the sources of unintentional bias that can introduce errors in marketing research.

Market intelligence

Specific research is needed to support a unique project such as a product launch. However, knowing how the market is moving (e.g. whether a new product launch is required) needs a continuous flow of data and information. A key activity is not only monitoring changes with customers, but also competitors' activities. New launches and new advertising campaigns will impact on our business, and if the organization were to wait 6 months to see what happens, it will be too late to act. Specialist trade magazines may be expensive but they do contain the industry 'hot' gossip. Who has moved from one company to another (watching competitor recruitment gives you an idea of what skills they are strengthening for future projects) and other key news such as product launches and capital plans. For new products in technology-rich areas, patent abstracts are useful. Company websites, annual reports, advertisements and other publications are all useful sources of information. One of the key reasons for attending a trade conference is to gain competitor and market intelligence. Every visit to a customer is a chance to gain intelligence. For example, an organization uses a given company to provide photocopiers; the organization becomes unsatisfied with the existing supplier and decides to trial a competitor company. The technician from the original supplier arrives to repair the existing photocopiers and notices the competitor's machine. He then informs his boss, and a representative arrives the next day to see if there are any problems.

A major technical activity for many organizations is retro-engineering products. A company produces a new DVD drive or a new washing powder. The first thing for the competitor is to obtain samples, get them into the laboratory and strip them down to see how they have been built. This is, in part, to check the strength of the competition (market leaders) and to (where legal) copy with a counter-type (a typical activity for a supermarket's own brand). This can also be applied to services, with researchers acting as 'mystery' travellers on an airline for example.

Insight

If you are collecting intelligence about the competitor, is the competitor collecting information about you and your organization? Therefore, when you publish or take action, remember your competitors are listening (e.g. if you intend to move into a new area and need to recruit staff, consider using a head-hunting agency rather than advertise for staff in the trade press, thus, the secret is kept for longer). In the Second World War, the slogan *'careless talk cost lives'* was used in a poster campaign. The same rules apply in business: never discuss confidential information in a public place (one of your competitor's staff may be in that seat behind you!).

 ## Activity 8.5

When you go to a trade exhibition, what market intelligence data will you seek out on the competition?

Internal data

For the company value chain to operate normally, lots of information needs to be collected (e.g. production figures for accounts and raw materials ordering). These are a vital input into the system. The warning has already been given that it is necessary to check (on the basis of collection and calculation) to ensure that the figures are appropriate for the marketing decision in hand. For example, historical costs will not necessarily be appropriate for that export order to be delivered in 3 months' time. Apart from the obvious sources such as data from EPOS and so on, care should be taken to collect more informal data which may be of considerable value; for example, customer complaints can be a resource for new product developments.

Database management

Information is a vital asset for a company. To manage the future you need to be able to effectively and efficiently manage information. The company's core information will most often be under the control of IT specialists who will take care of security (both against loss and 'hacking') and legal aspects (data protection legislation) on core databases such as payroll and so on. However, with each person controlling a PC on their desk and having wide Internet access, all staff need to be alert and professional. That handy personal database you have set up without any password may fall within the jurisdiction of data protection legislation and may be vulnerable to unauthorized access. For smaller organizations with no formal IT function, there is still the need for virus protection and the like. Take specialist advice when appropriate; a Marketer may not always be a computer consultant.

What is of concern to a manager is the management of information. If the Systems Engineers ensure security, it is up to managers to make certain that the staff enter accurate data or that appropriate equipment (e.g. scanners) is available. This is particularly important in e-commerce, where Marketing, Logistics and IT must ensure a fusion of product that looks good on the screen, works fast on customers' systems, is secure and has a back-up system that ensures customers get their products.

With clean information safely stored, the next issue is to be able to go back and ask new questions. One of the meteorological office's major activities is not in predicting future weather but in analysing the patterns of impact of past weather. Modern computing and data collection allow weather to be observed at a more micro level than was possible in the past. What is happening in the city? This could be more important than the weather for the whole 100-mile radius. The microclimate may modify conditions at a local level very significantly. As an example, an historical analysis could be made of petrol sales against hours of sunshine in the day (sunny day = let's go out for the day?). The key point is that two records collected for different independent reasons may suddenly give a Marketer new insight into a new problem. In devising systems, potential future use of the information needs to be considered (for data protection reasons as well). A special database of particular importance is the mailing list. This has a high data protection profile and is difficult to keep clean and updated. Further consideration of the use of databases and ICT is given in Unit 9.

A professional society noted that some 20 per cent of its membership were retired. A regional branch decided to hold a few special events for retired members in the year. However, the mail-out was a little unfortunate. The list used by the branch was compiled a year earlier. Retired members are clearly rather old and the mail-out produced a significant number of sad letters 'My partner would have loved to come but they died # months ago.' Database marketing is brilliant for relationship marketing (e.g. targeted invitations to match interests), but only if almost fanatical dedication is devoted to keeping the database clean and up to date. This is not just a question of simple economics but of good relations. The communication that was just right last year may be counter-productive in changed circumstances.

Key management issue – it is relatively simple to set up a website or a database. The problem is to ensure it is still relevant, clean, accurate and up to date 4 years later.

Activity 8.6

List the types of useful internal information that should exist in a normal supermarket situation.

Analytical systems

Clean up the data

Data can be affected by the way in which it was collected and it may be necessary to adjust, not fiddle (and there must be a valid reason for the adjustment), or transform it in some way.

Issues of date – One problem in the United Kingdom is looking at trends in sales such as travel, hotel bookings or visitor attractions, where the Marketer is concerned with how things are on a year-on-year basis. It may be OK to compare the second week of February with the second week of February last year. But take care in springtime as the date of the Easter Bank Holiday moves and this year's week may not include a bank holiday where last year's did. Clearly, what needs to be compared is the Easter performance not the calendar weeks in this situation.

Issues of number – Consider the situation where a company runs an annual staff attitude survey. The analyst reports to the Board that there is a big problem, since twice as many people are dissatisfied with their job as there were last year. Well is there? If there had been a fourfold increase of staff over the last year, this actually might be good news. What is required is a percentage figure. 'Good news – work dissatisfaction down by 50 per cent!'

Analyse the data

There are many ways to extract further information. At the end of the unit some selected further reading references are given. To illustrate some of the general issues we shall consider only one selected tool which is widely used (and misused!) – regression analysis. A key problem facing the Marketer is predicting next month's sales. If the product is seasonal (e.g. ice cream sales), then next month's figures may be affected by the time of year (summer/winter) and any long-term trend (up or down) in people's consumption of ice cream. For simplicity, we will just consider long-term trends and ignore seasonal effects (the references at the end cover these techniques). If we observe that there is a 2 per cent increase in sales each month for the last 12 months then we might expect that sales next month might also be up 2 per cent. The estimate might be a bit fuzzy as some random effects (e.g. weather) may affect the estimates, and statisticians will use a technique called 'regression' to ensure that the 'best' estimate is made. However, there are some health warnings:

- o It may not be too unreasonable to say that next month's ice cream sales are likely to be up 2 per cent but people still have a regrettable temptation to extend the estimate too far into the future. Consider the situation around the year 2000, where there were increases in sales of mobile telephones equal to a few per cent per month. Therefore 'UK sales of mobile telephones will be tens of millions a year by 2005 – well no!' Mobile telephones differ from ice cream. I buy an ice cream today and I may buy one tomorrow. I buy a mobile telephone today but I do not buy another for some considerable time. Even then, I may just change the handset and will not need a new contract. The market will become saturated. All too often, people overestimate demand by projecting a trend past this saturation point. Remember also from Unit 3 that PLC effects may come into play and modify the longer-term trends.

- o 'Lost' figures – Deep inside the mathematics that keep statisticians happy is an assumption that any variation of the figures from the expected are random and uncorrelated (i.e. not linked to other observations). For sales figures, this may not be the case. The classic example is a batch of 'lost' figures. A batch of sales figures is entered into the system late and misses the cut-off for the month so that the sales figures are lower. However, early in the next month the 'lost' figures are included. If care is not taken, these figures may be taken onto the new month. In this situation, the assumption built into the mathematics is not observed as the low figures are linked to next period's high figures (the solution is to take the lost figures back into last month and re-run the calculations). A problem for the Marketer is this: how do you know if there were lost figures if they are collected in, for example, another country?

- o Cause and effect – One problem for Marketers in the clothing business is sizing and size distribution. Consider that a researcher takes figures from research on the weight of healthy young men (say the data was collected by the army on successful recruitment). 'Great, all we have to say is that if a person is 100 kg they will be 2.00 metres tall.' Well no! The sample was not even right for young men as the selection process eliminated unhealthy, overweight candidates. Moreover, should this figure hold for people with 'middle-age spread'? People do have different shapes, so people with a 107-cm waist need not have arms the length of a giant – they could be chocoholics!

Case study

'SMS Cars Ltd.' – Information

The 'SMS Cars Ltd' case study, June 2006, featured a car dealership for a region. An outline is given below of some of the information activities that such a car dealership might engage in:

- o *Market research* – key national research will have been conducted by Ford so the need is for specific local information to implement the strategies locally. Secondary research would be needed to examine local demographics (e.g. in a rural farming area there may be a need for more practical off-road vehicles). National advertising would be orchestrated by Ford but locally media research would be needed to find the best methods for local implementation of the national strategy (e.g. in a rural farming area, is there a farming supplement published in the local evening paper; if so what is the readership?). One special element in this type of situation is researching local 'placement' opportunities. If there is a big local golf competition, arranging with the golf club to display new cars and have promotional material available. When the new

'Bond' film is released, 'SMS Cars' should make arrangements to have the 'Bond' car on display in the cinema car park and so on.

o   *Market intelligence* – what are the competing dealerships doing? What launches and promotions are they conducting. 'SMS Cars' would need to track local competitive advertising and check out competing local websites. A little informal 'mystery' shopping and visits to local competing dealerships might not be out of place.

o   *Internal data* – a vital element in relationship marketing. A good database of existing customers is needed. This will allow selective mail-outs (e.g. when launching a new off-road vehicle the mailing need only go to the right targets, profiled from the data base information). Service records and past purchase should be recorded (e.g. after three years from the purchase of a new car, SMS Cars might mail out customers with information on special trade in deals to encourage a new purchase).

o   *Analytic systems* – a key element is to track how sales are progressing. This needs to be more than tracking month-on-month sales. Many products have seasonality in their sales patterns so care must be taken to adjust for this in looking for trends. Supermarkets tend to report 'like for like sales' comparing this year's June sales with last year's June sales. If they are increasing their number of sales outlets they will also take account of this in their comparison.

Take care with all statistical analysis and always try to talk with an experienced person. In scientific work, statistical analysis is subject to careful review by editors before being accepted for publication. Even so, there is considerable concern about the validity of some work. Any fool can (and they do!) enter a set of numbers into a spreadsheet and hit the regression function and get a prediction. This is like purchasing a second-hand car. It may be either a bargain or a rust bucket that is going to fall apart in 6 months. The paint may look good just as the regression might look good. Do not buy information, any more than you would buy a used car, unless you have some real understanding of the situation.

Are people driving more safely?

If annual road deaths are down 20 per cent over a 10-year period, does it mean people are driving more safely? Not a simple question as we have not defined what 'safe' is.

An injury that might have killed you 10 years ago may now be survivable due to advances in medical technology. We could have the same number of accidents resulting in serious injuries and still record an overall reduction in road accident deaths.

Let us think again. If people who are injured are more likely to survive then the mortality figure is not going to help us. What we should do is re-run the analysis using the figure for road accident injuries. Sorted!

Well, no! Over this period, it is likely that new models of car will have new safety features built into them (e.g. in the past, air bags and advanced breaking systems). Now an accident from a similar dangerous situation may result in less damage to the vehicle and the improved feature may lessen or even eliminate passenger/driver injury.

Other factors that make this question more difficult are the number of drivers, driver demographics (e.g. young men have more accidents), distances people drive a year, type of journey (motorway driving safer than town driving) and demographics of cars (some types more dangerous than others, e.g. older cars). Even things like weather conditions can affect insurance claims for accidents (exceptionally wet weather or freezing fog: climate change can even affect accidents).

The business health warning is as follows:

Do not accept figures without reservation.

Always try to get the best possible understanding of how the data was collected. Also, note that a tight and specific definition is needed. One person may imply the number of road injuries measures safe driving, another could imply the same from the number of accidents. Sloppy definitions are a major problem in market research. Make certain that what has been measured or will be measured is right for your specific question.

Activity 8.7

Above we have considered the problem of accidents. Another difficult area is in appraising the effectiveness of Police anti-crime activities. List some of the problems that face a Communications Officer for a major city's police department in analysing crime figures.

International issues

Secondary data may be less accurate or unobtainable in developing countries. The basis of collecting figures may be different. It is often stated that in the United Kingdom unemployment is low. However, many people are now drawing incapacity benefit and so do not appear in the statistics. Other countries do not have the same system. Care must be taken when looking at statistics from different countries where the systems of collection and classification may be significantly different. Changes in classifications over time may also cause problems in looking at long-term trends (e.g. change in customs classifications on import and export statistics).

Primary research needs local knowledge. Sampling may be difficult, and questionnaires need to be tested for language (a native speaker is needed) and for relevance to local conditions. Cultural sensitivity is required; questions that would not cause offence in one culture may be an issue in another. If this is an issue with questionnaires, it is even more of an issue with qualitative research such as focus groups. A market research agency with local knowledge is helpful. One factor to take into account when selecting a domestic agency is could they provide local support in your overseas markets as well if needed?

Case study

'Lake View Organic Farms' – Preliminary information needs for a new round

Within this context, we shall examine the situation facing 'Lake View Organic Farms' when they consider moving into new territory. With a population of some 100 000, New Town might be an ideal opportunity for a geographic expansion. The questions posed are, 'Will there be enough potential customers to make the business extension profitable? If there are enough potential customers, how can the company reach them?' This is a significant expansion with some risk and substantial sums of money involved. However, a full market survey, which might cost many thousands of pounds, is not likely to be a realistic option. The firm must find a way to lever its present information and project it into the new context.

Secondary research can provide a geo-demographic profile of the new target area. Analysis of existing sales areas with the same geo-demographic tool should allow the firm to make a realistic projection of the potential in the new area. Adopting the STEEPLE model, we can highlight issues that might be considered for the new target area (general issues were considered in Units 1 and 2).

Social/cultural – The geo-demographic analysis should give a sound overview of the ethnic and social demographics.

Technological innovation – Is broadband access available in the target area? If so, what is the level of penetration?

Economic issues – The nature of the wealth (disposable incomes) in the target area should come from the geo-demographic analysis.

Education/training – Probably nothing new to be considered here.

Political – Food delivery is not likely to feature on any local political agenda (not the same as a supermarket constructing a road across the local cricket pitch).

Legal – Are there any special local issues regarding access (e.g. congestion charging)?

Environmental protection – Some areas (e.g. London) have limitations on access for commercial vehicles for certain times of the day. The existence and nature of any restrictions would need to be investigated. A link-up with any local recycling initiatives might be appropriate.

A brief competition analysis is essential. Using the Porter competition model from Unit 1, the issues would be as follows:

Direct competition – Is there any other operator offering direct delivery of organic produce?

Substitute products – Wholefood shops and other outlets stocking organic produce. Directories and local guides would be useful here.

Buyer power – Patterns can be extrapolated from existing areas using the geo-demographic information.

New entrants – Scan local newspapers and others for any news on potential start-ups.

Supplier power – We are the suppliers so not an issue.

The general stakeholder issues have been considered in Units 1, 2 and 6. Research would be needed to identify potential B2B customers (restaurants, hotels, etc.). Yellow Pages, trade directories and the local papers can help here.

A review of the marketing mix would be appropriate.

Product – The likely uptake of various ranges (product mix issues) can again be estimated from performance in other areas with the use of geo-demographic data (extrapolation).

Price – As with product, estimates of price/purchase can be made from extrapolation from past experience. Local competition might have an impact here if there is a strong local supplier with a low-cost base.

Place – A key issue. Effective route planning is vital to effect the maximum number of calls with the minimum of dead time (e.g. held up in local traffic jams). Some research is needed to find out local road and traffic conditions to plan the new sales routes.

Promotion – TV coverage is unlikely to be valuable. Radio may not be expensive but would the audience of local commercial radio match the footprint of our target area and demographics of our intended market segments? Local papers and free news-sheets might be suitable. Readership and targeting can be investigated. Selected leafleting would be a viable option. B2B segment would require personal selling, possibly after a direct mailing of the general brochure. Research would be needed to identify contacts and DMUs in the selected B2B targets. Some additional points on communication are made in Units 6 and 10. Obtaining advertising rates and so on would then allow the construction of a tentative communications budget.

Service extension mix issues have been considered in Unit 7. The key issue would be 'Who to appoint to the new area? Should the firm move an experienced member of staff into the new area?' The firm could then appoint a new member of staff to one of the existing routes. Here the challenge might not be so great and training easier. Another option might be to appoint the new person earlier and get them to shadow an existing person as part of an integrated training programme. The nature of the decision might affect the employee search process.

Question 8.1

Consider you are the Marketing Manager for a local evening newspaper, and management want to build up the circulation of the newspaper.

What information would be useful in this situation?

How might this information be collected?

How could this information be used to better market the paper and increase its profitability?

Summary

Questions on information needs occur in the CIM exams: for example, June 2006 Question 4 'Produce a short report, for consideration by the Marketing Department, which: (a) identifies what information SMS Cars Ltd would want on their customer database in order to segment the marketplace effectively and assist with future marketing activity. (b) explains how this information could be gathered.'

We have reviewed the need to establish how data is to be used and which areas need to be investigated before considering what methods of data collection (e.g. research and intelligence) are appropriate for an organization. Most managers consider they have too much data and not enough good information. We have considered the ways in which data can be stored, sorted and analysed to provide information that enables managers to base their decisions on firm foundations.

Further study

Dibb, S., Simkin, L., Pride, W. and Ferrell, O. (2006) *Marketing Concepts and Strategies*, 5th European edition, Houghton Mifflin, Chapter 9.

As an integrative module you should also review the other coursebooks at this level

Cheeseman, A. and Jones, M. (2007) *CIM Coursebook – Customer Communications in Marketing*, Butterworth-Heinemann.

Lancaster, G. and Withey, F. (2007) *CIM Coursebook – Marketing Fundamentals*, Butterworth-Heinemann.

Oldroyd, M. (2007) *CIM Coursebook – Marketing Environment*, Butterworth-Heinemann.

Hints and tips

As always, relate the theory to your own marketing experience. Do not begin to decide what research you will do until you have considered what the information is required for. Without a sense of direction it is easy to waste effort on researching factors that will have little impact on the organization. It is also easy to miss key aspects. Good research starts by knowing what the right questions are. Typical questions for the CIM exams are as follows:

- What information is required?
- How might the information be obtained?
- How can the information be used to develop marketing plans?

The question will be presented in the context of a specific case study and for good marks the answer should not be a list but should discuss the issues with context-specific development (e.g. the 'SMS Cars Ltd.' Case study in June 2006).

Bibliography

Kotler, P. (2006) *Marketing Management*, 12th edition, Prentice Hall.

Wilson, A. (2006) *Marketing Research: An Integrated Approach*, 2nd edition, Prentice Hall.

unit 9
skills for the marketer

By the end of this unit, you will be able to

- ○ Formulate copy for written communications and understand housekeeping conventions for business communications.

- ○ Write press release copy that is appropriate for journalists and understand how to support the copy with images.

- ○ Appraise the contribution of an event within a communications plan and appreciate the key issues in planning and running successful events. Understand the additional needs when planning international events.

- ○ Appreciate from the management view (not the 'bits & bytes') key issues of database management.

- ○ Understand the basis of person-to-person communication, the building blocks of networks – the heart of relationship marketing.

- ○ Prepare presentations that appear professional and achieve their objectives.

- ○ List strategies for time management and 'manage your manager'.

- ○ Know how to network successfully in the e-commerce age.

- ○ Understand the key stages in planning and running successful projects.

Syllabus references

- 2.2 Build and develop relationships within the marketing department, working effectively with others.

- 2.3 Explain the 'front-line' role: receiving and assisting visitors, internal and external enquiries.

- 2.5 Explain the supplier interface: negotiating, collaborating, operational and contractual aspects.

- 2.6 Explain how the organization fits into a supply chain and works with distribution channels.

- 2.7 Use networking skills in the business world.

2.8   Explain the concept and application of e-relationships.

2.9   Describe techniques available to assist in managing your manager.

3.1   Describe the scope of the individual's roles in marketing: meetings, conferences, exhibitions, outdoor shows, outlet launches and press conferences.

3.2   Identify alternative and innovative approaches to a variety of marketing arenas and explain criteria for meeting business objectives.

3.4   Explain how marketing makes use of planning techniques: objective setting; and coordinating, measuring and evaluating results to support the organization.

3.6   Explain how an organization should host visitors from other cultures and organize across national boundaries.

4.1   Select media to be used based on appropriate criteria for assessing media opportunities, and recommend a media schedule.

4.2   Evaluate promotional activities and opportunities including sales promotion, PR and collaborative programmes.

4.3   Explain the process for designing, developing and producing printed matter, including leaflets, brochures and catalogues.

5.3   Explain how organizations assess the viability of opportunities, marketing initiatives and projects.

5.5   Make recommendations on alternative courses of action.

Key definitions

SERVQUAL – A model for evaluating customer perceptions of service quality.

ASFAB – A framework for evaluating a potential venue for a marketing event.

Study Guide

As with each of the earlier units, reading the coursebook is not enough. This unit is about practical skills needed by a professional marketer. Apart from the activities and case studies, if you are undertaking a project that requires some of the skills outlined in this unit, keep a diary of your practical experience to add to the necessarily brief guidelines in this unit. For those areas in which you are not currently involved (e.g. briefing an advertising agency), talk to people in your organization or your fellow students and again augment these guidance notes. Some of these skills are very much practical, so if your job does not involve you in presentations, carry out a few mock ones and get colleagues and friends to feed back. Do not wait until you have that make or break presentation to learn the skills. In the Olympic games, the 100 metres may be over in a few seconds but years of training and devotion go into those seconds. Remember business is tougher than the Olympic games: if you come second in a race, you get a silver medal, but if you come second in a job interview, you get nothing.

Practical communications process for the marketer

The day-to-day communications of the marketer should not be viewed as something entirely separated to the formal marketing communications of the organization. In an integrated view of communications, advertisements and others have their place. However, in the buying process, some stages may need other communications, for example responding by e-mail to a query on goods damaged in transit at a 'dot-com company'. Even the communications within the organization can be viewed not as something separate, but as internal marketing (within the overall integrating context of Relationship Marketing covered in Unit 2). Your internal markets (stakeholders) are key. A detailed cover of formats (types of letters, etc.) is given in Customer Communications in Marketing (Cheeseman and Wood) and the treatment here is tailored to the integrative nature of this CIM module, alongside the need to demonstrate an integrated understanding of all the syllabus elements in your project reports or exam questions.

It is suggested for today's marketers that the standard model of communication (left-hand side of Figure 9.1) needs amplification. All the elements (encoding, sending, noise in transmission, receiving, decoding and feedback) apply. However, in this integrated view of marketing, some amplification of the 'sender' context and process is required.

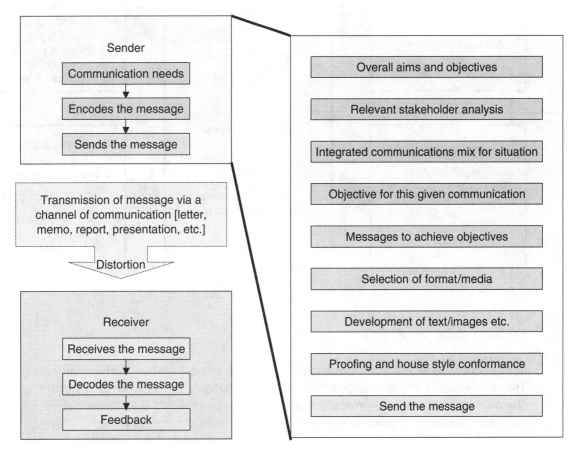

Figure 9.1 Amplification of standard communications model for practical implementation in marketers' communications

Overall marketing aims and objectives of the organization

Communications do not take place in a vacuum. For effective communication, the individual's activity must be viewed in the context of an organization's internal mission aims and business objectives. How these objectives are pursued is in turn affected by the macroenvironment and the microenvironment (e.g. requirements of data protection legislation). How the earlier units of this coursebook integrate in this process is shown in Figure 9.2. Units 1 and 2 provide an introduction to the context and Units 3–7 give the overview of the integrated marketing mix within which these specific communications take place. In the exam situation, it is important to review the context of the case study with a preliminary analysis to structure the format(s) and content of your answers. This also applies to assignments where it is essential that the submission reflects the relevant flavour of the selected organization's context. Remember from Unit 2 that an organization may have more than one aspect to its context (e.g. 'small and service', 'international, green and product').

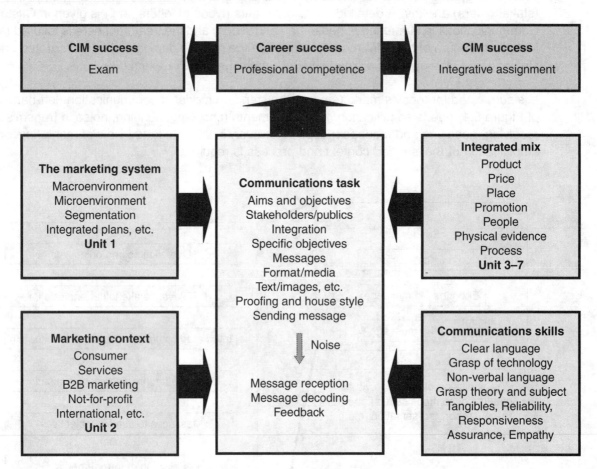

Figure 9.2 Marketing knowledge and communications skills for communications tasks

Stakeholder analysis

In this coursebook, the term 'stakeholder' has been used, as it is a useful overarching concept. The concepts of market segmentation and DMU can be viewed as different aspects of stakeholder analysis (customers are one of an organization's key stakeholders). Writers on communications sometimes use other words such as audiences or publics. They are of course stakeholders, so do not be confused. The term 'stakeholder', it is suggested, is more useful as communications do not only reach the intended targets (e.g. a company's annual report key objective is to inform the shareholders and potential shareholders but is most avidly analysed by the business analysts in competitor organizations). In any communications situation, a brief review of the key stakeholders is important (e.g. if a customer enquiry is not properly managed, your management may become involved in reviewing how well your communication conformed to the organization's aims, objectives and culture). A general overview of stakeholders is given in Unit 1. The list of key stakeholders should be developed with an analysis of the organization's aims and objectives for the stakeholder segment; an outline is provided in Table 9.1. In the day-to-day work of a marketer, it is not possible to sit down and do a complete environmental/stakeholder analysis every time a letter is written. A politician being interviewed live on TV is also not able to do this. Part of the professional skill is to take on the brief, internalize all the factors, and then be able to respond naturally and quickly. That is why, even when moving to the same job in a different organization, induction is still important to gain this peripheral vision and cast communications in the right context.

Case study

'Marketing': 'We'll Call You.' There is no such thing as a private communication in business

At first sight, you might not consider that a telephone call would have anything to do with media stakeholders. However, the magazine *Marketing* runs a back-page feature ('We'll Call You'). This is where a reporter (acting as a mystery shopper) rings up a company. The outline of the call is given and at the end the verdict is given. You do not want your conversation to be the one that gets 2/10. Media consumer features (TV, radio and press) live off unfortunate communications. That unguarded e-mail may feature on prime-time TV, with your director having to defend the company. This is not the best way to advance a career!

Table 9.1 Outline of stakeholders for a typical organization

Stakeholder	Stakeholder agenda	Organization's objectives	Comments
Customers	Good marketing mix offering	Promotion of mix, building relationship (RM)	Full analysis needed here for each key customer segment
Consumers	Good marketing mix offering	Promotion of mix, building relationship (RM)	The buyer need not be the consumer (e.g. gifts)
Owners	Development of stakeholder value	Reassurance on how value is being built	Note: not always shareholders. Private companies and charities with trustees and so on. Note: not-for-profit 'value' as well
Employees	Stakeholder value (pay, prospects, pension, etc.)	Development of commitment, attraction and retention of key staff	Note: segmentation issues (e.g. management, front line, etc.) may be taken to include potential employees
Suppliers	Stakeholder value (continued profitable business)	Relationship marketing: building and maintaining supply chain partnerships	Not only raw materials but all goods and services. May segment (e.g. small and international)

Stakeholder	Stakeholder agenda	Organization's objectives	Comments
Political	Balancing competing pressures (e.g. job and green issues)	Understanding pressures and providing reassurance about corporate objectives	May segment (e.g. for supermarket such as TESCO: national politics about consumer credit and local politics about problems with car parking at a new super-centre)
Pressure groups	Often focused agenda (e.g. green issues) with not-for-profit elements	Understanding agenda and providing reassurance and conflict resolution where possible	Need proactive rather than reactive management. Note: may also segment (e.g. national – over-packaging; local – back to that car park and location of bottle bank (see above))
Media	Want a story to build circulation. Some publications are significant not-for-profit issues	Develop long-term positive relationships to give out good news and manage bad news	Segments (e.g. TV, radio, press; international, national and regional, etc.)
Partners	Stakeholder value (continued profitable partnership)	Often full mix delivery requires partners (e.g. hotel and an airline collaborating on packages)	Often occurs in B2B (e.g. several companies may work collaboratively with a computer company developing an integrated range of hardware/software components)

Integrated communications mix for given situation

In Units 1 and 6, the concept of integrated marketing communication was introduced. A company letter or report is not normally written in isolation. A customer complaint may have arisen from extravagant expectations given in advertising and poor instructions on the packaging. A letter (or e-mail) attempting to resolve the issue may also draw on additional information on the company website. Additionally, the letter (or e-mail) will conform to organizational house rules (e.g. font used as well as headed paper or e-mail format – more about this is covered under 'Proofing and house–style'). The communication needs to be seen as part of two sets of integrated communications:

1. The full range of communications sent out by the organization
2. The full range of communications received by the stakeholder.

The specific communication under consideration must be consistent with all the other messages from the organization. It must also fit into all the other communications received by the stakeholders who will/might receive the communication.

Specific communications objectives

Having determined the context of the communication it is now possible to consider the specific objective(s) it has. This can range from simple – a letter confirming the receipt of an order (likely only to be considered by just one stakeholder or possibly a small DMU group) – to a somewhat more complicated communication, a press release (wide range of stakeholders and an indirect means of communication through publicity). For simple communications, this decision-making process is implicit in our understanding of the situation. However, for complex communications such as exam answers (e.g. write a letter) or an assignment on communications, explicit consideration of the specific stakeholder objectives is recommended, even if this is restricted to rough working and question planning.

Messages to achieve objective

Again, there is a wide range of possibilities. Not much explicit planning is needed for: 'We have received your order.' However, a report to a client on a mix of advertising media to be used will need planning, as there may well be a basket of issues needing to be addressed to get the overall desired effect: 'Place your account with us.' It is important to understand both ends of the equation. The message must not only be appropriate to our needs but also meet the stakeholder needs and expectations. The message 'Buy our product as it is cheap' may not be right for a wealthy client more interested in green issues. In constructing the message, some anticipation of stakeholder reaction is needed.

Format and media

Increasingly, communications at the one-to-one level are moving into electronic media. E-mails provide audit trails (you can tell if an e-mail has been received but not an ordinary letter); they are quick, cheap and, with attachments, can carry vast amounts of data (reports, images, etc., can be attached as files). It is important to provide the communication in a medium that is convenient for the receiver. Poor quality format and construction detracts from the quality of the message. See the later section on 'Communications viewed as a service activity'.

Insight

Special communication needs

Society and governments have rightly taken the view that all members of society should be treated with consideration. Therefore, a large organization will need to ensure that communications can be provided for people with impaired hearing (e.g. sound loops at bank counters) or sight. In our stakeholder analysis, they represent a segment with some very specific communication needs that must be addressed by an organization that wants to be perceived as a 'good corporate citizen'.

Composition of the communication: text, images and other communication forms

Text should be written in clear language that is appropriate for the target audience.

- Keep your sentences short.
- Use active verbs.
- Use 'you' and 'we'.
- Choose words appropriate for the reader.
- Don't be afraid to give instructions.

- ○ Avoid nominalizations.
- ○ Use positive language.
- ○ Use lists where appropriate.

These are the points given by the 'Plain English Campaign'.

This is available from www.plainenglish.co.uk/guides.html. There are many other guides that are also available from the same site: How to write in plain English, The A–Z of alternative words, CVs, Design and Layout, Forms, Letters, Medical Information, Proofreading, Reports, Websites, Wills, Financial, Legal and Pensions.

The consumer electronics instruction book that expects you to have a PhD in electronics and 4 years of practical experience of programming in C++ is not appreciated or welcomed. Electronic media now enables easy attachment of colour images that can greatly help in communication (e.g. a map is the easy way to communicate a company's location).

In the exam setting, tables, diagrams, models and flow charts and the like are all welcome, provided they are made context specific; if an Ansoff matrix appears appropriate to the answer, make it context specific with examples of market penetration activity and so on. In assignment reports, extravagant graphics are no substitute for context-specific content. An example of a 'dog' product in a BCG matrix will gain you more credit than finding the right 'dog' image from your clip art files.

Proofing and house style

Proofing your own work is never easy. Here you need a good friend or colleague who has that special skill to know when a ';' rather than ',' is required and to spot the spelling error. A significant number of papers/projects come headed 'Marketing in Practise' rather than 'Marketing in Practice'. Spell check does not pick up all errors! A spelling error on the front page of a report will give a bad impression to the client.

Insight

Proofing errors are not only irritating but also a product liability issue

Product labelling is a nightmare. Each country has its own specific requirements as to what must be given on the label, language and descriptions to be used (e.g. use of 'E' numbers in the EU). Even when all appears correct, a simple machine error on 'expiry date' can cause a liability problem (e.g. with an expensive total product recall).

In a well-run, marketing-orientated company, all communications should conform to the 'style manual'. Much of this will be set at a relatively senior level (e.g. company logo). However, it is up to all marketing staff to see that communications disciplines are maintained. A particular problem arises when agents and distributors want to use images in their own communications. Letters and other communications about the use of corporate images should strictly state how they should be printed (e.g. specific colour instructions) and the context in which they can be used.

Sending the message

The method of sending the communication needs a little thought. Two security issues need to be considered. How important is non-authorized, third-party access to the message (e.g. a major issue in the UK drive for computerized patient records, and communication is the potential for unauthorized medical information being accessed for illegitimate purposes) and how certain do we need to be of delivery? Encryption technology is starting to make electronic communication more secure and this has advantages in terms of cost and speed. On the other hand, certain communications can still only be delivered by the 'physical' secure delivery of a document (e.g. your CIM diploma). Consideration of how the message is to be received is also important and needs to be considered before transmission (e.g. that wonderful logo and graphic in your e-mail template are just fine with colleagues with broadband and large-capacity mailboxes. Possibly this would not be so popular with friends with slow dial-up access and small-capacity mailboxes).

Noise and distortion

In this context, we confine ourselves to transmission problems. Clearly, the signal as sent should be the signal received and that signal should be received in good order. For a business presentation, everyone should be able to hear the speaker and see the visual aids. In electronic transmission, general noise and distortion can clearly be a problem (now reducing with the penetration of broadband). However, clashing communication protocols/software anywhere along the 'sending – transmission – receiving' process can cause problems (e.g. with formatting in a complex document sent for commercial printing).

Message reception

The issues here can be divided into hard (associated with hardware and software covered in earlier sections) and soft (language, culture, etc.) problems with reception. Issues of culture and language are considered in the next section. In this section, we consider the more practical issues of individuals receiving a message. Where (at home, in the office, whilst travelling) will the message be received? What mood will the person be in when the communication is received (e.g. that bright 'good morning' call may not get the expected reception if the person is halfway round the world and you have woken them up)? What attention will the message receive? How quickly do you empty your mailbox of spam? This is why, despite the high cost, corporate travel and PR hospitality have their place. You have the ambiance (you have selected the meeting place and atmosphere) and the right concentration and focus on your messages.

Message decoding

General issues of culture have been considered in Unit 2. Key issues include the following:

o *Words do not translate* – even between 'American' English and 'British' English. The 'Insight' below gives two examples of brand names and messages that have not survived the translation gap.
o *Humour* – that great joke which broke the ice in the home sales conference may cause profound offence in a presentation to export customers.
o *Message or context* – different cultures put different weights on the simple content of the text and the emotional and non-verbal communications used in the delivery.
o *Not feeling free to express true feelings* – in some cultures a direct 'no' might be considered offensive and coded language may be used.
o *Technical jargon* – the pre-knowledge of the group is important. There is a communications 'window'. Go in and 'baby talk' to a technical audience and they will not be impressed, even if they understand. Use lots of technical jargon on a general audience and they simply will not understand (even if they stay awake during the presentation!).

217

Insight

Brand names and messages do not always travel well

The sweet called 'Skum' and the confectionary called 'Schmuck' are not too appealing in the UK context.

Feedback

The great advantage of face-to-face communications is that you can get some feedback, often non-verbal as to how the message is being received. With an advertising campaign, it is possible to do some research to see how perceptions are moved by a campaign. It is much more difficult to find out if your e-mails have the right tone, style and technical content. Only by talking with friends, colleagues or attending courses on communication can this be improved. Networking and personal selling/communications are major subjects; some suggested reading is given at the end of the unit.

Communications viewed within the context of the service-extended marketing mix

Parasuraman, when researching the SERVQUAL model for consumer perceptions of service quality, focused on five dimensions (given below). These concepts can be extended to communications activities.

Tangibles – Physical facilities, equipment and appearance of personnel. Poor format, poor proofing and poor-quality printing and so on in communications damage credibility. The signal given out is if you do not take care of the appearance of the communication, you have not taken care of the content. This is not to say appearance is all. Customers expect both content and appearance (this also applies to exam answers and assignment reports).

Reliability – Ability to perform the promised service dependably and accurately; prompt responsive replies (e.g. returning telephone calls) with content that does not make promises which are subsequently broken.

Responsiveness – Willingness to help customers and provide prompt service. One of the magic ingredients of communications is to show that you care about the addressee's agenda and want to be helpful.

Assurance – Knowledge and courtesy of employees and their ability to inspire trust and confidence. Tone of communication must respect the addressee's concerns and not be dismissive. The content must reflect real command of the issues. In a CIM assessment, this implies a demonstration of the relevant theory applied in the specific context.

Empathy – The caring, individualized attention the organization provides its customer. A most important skill for a sales person is 'listening'. Our problem (e.g. lost luggage on an airline) is real to us and we want a real response from a real person. This is an issue of debate in the provision of financial services. Automated banking is fine until something goes wrong and then people want a personal response, not 'press # for . . .'.

Communications is a service, so we may selectively apply the concepts of the service-extended marketing mix.

People: Who is the person behind this communication? What are their qualifications, what is their experience? This aspect is especially important in face-to-face situations such as formal presentations. Here you are selling yourself as much as the message. *Facilitating goods*: This reflects the Parasuraman 'Tangibles' element in the SERVQUAL model above. The implication of poor presentation is that you do not care about the content or the audience. *Process*: Increasingly, communications are moving to electronic processes (speed, cost, flexibility, etc.) but the process must be acceptable to the recipient (we all love that 'hold' music for minutes at a time that you are paying for). Communications is not about technology but about people. No matter how good you are with PowerPoint, remember the presentation is the media and you are the messenger. Technology should not replace human understanding but allow you to project your empathy and support for the client.

There is a vast range of potential communication formats that a marketer might be involved in developing or delivering. In Unit 2, we noted that there are over 1000 contexts which could apply to a case study. Within this, any of the communications below might be relevant; the total number of possibilities is enormous. Some selected examples are given in this unit. Further examples and activities are given within the other units, reflecting the integrative nature of this CIM module. You are unlikely to get the question 'What are the various forms of a business letter?' You are much more likely to get a question along the lines of 'Write a letter to current and potential customers inviting them to attend the launch event. Include a method of reply to confirm their attendance' 'SMS Cars Ltd' case study, June 2006. This answer format also featured in 'The Urban Culture Festival', December 2005; Question 1(d) 'Draft a letter to potential sponsors selling the benefits of involvement with Urban Culture Festival 2006.'. Communications formats that have been used or referred to in recent CIM exams are indicated with '*'. More examples of letters, memos and so on can be found in the CIM coursebook 'Customer Communications in Marketing'. Other useful sources are given at the end of the unit. The basic issues of the communication process apply (with appropriate interpretation) to all communications formats, so issues such as the need to use clear and appropriate language are not repeated again in each section. Having reviewed the fundamentals, the implication in selected formats/media is given in the following sections. Table 9.2 provides a summary.

Table 9.2 Communications formats that may be required by a marketer

Communication	Selected comments
Articles*	
Brief	For example, advertising agency brief
Briefing Notes*	
Budgets*	Spreadsheets may need exploration of issues (e.g. basis of sales figures)
Certificates	For example, certificate of origin for an export order
Chart	For example, GANTT
Contracts	
Copy	Advertisements, leaflets, brochures, catalogues, prospectuses and so on*
CV or Resume	Not only job-hunting, but also in support of bids/tenders (e.g. research grants)
E-mails	
Face to Face	
Instructions	Product instructions and so on
Interviews	Press, Radio and TV
Letter* or Fax	Letter often sent by Fax instead of post
Management documentation	Job descriptions and so on
Manuals and Guidelines*	Corporate house-style manual and so on
Meetings	Including agenda preparation and minutes
Memos	
Negotiations	
Notices	

Communication	Selected comments
Packaging	Copy, design and branding issues
Plan	Marketing, communication, launch*, media and so on, including schedules*
Presentation	
Press advertisements	With and without graphics
Press release	
Press Conference	
Quotations and Estimates	
Questionnaire*	
Radio and TV advertisements	
Reports*	
Research documentation	For example, questionnaires*
Specifications	
Talk*	Talk may be regarded as a version of a presentation
Tenders	
Telephone	
Video conference	
Website*	

The business letter

Figure 9.3 provides a general outline structure for the typical business letter. The address block will contain the full contact information for the organization (address with postcode, telephone and Fax). This block may include website information or this may be printed as a 'footer' on the bottom of the company-headed paper. The printed heading may be customized a little with the personal contact information of the sender (e.g. direct telephone line and e-mail address). The reference section gives reference information to identify the document. In past days this might have been the typist and author. This is often now the location address for the letter's word-processing file. The date should be in the specific organization's house style (e.g. US companies use a different format). Standard options are given in Word and other packages. The address block should contain the recipient's correct title (Dr., Rev., etc.), name and address (including postcode or zip). Word allows this block to be highlighted and then used to address an envelope or a label so full postal information is required. The salutation is the formal address line (e.g. Dear Dr. Smith). The salutation and recipient's address block are almost invariably left justified. The heading block can be centred, left or right justified according to the organization's house style. The reference and date blocks will usually be left or right justified, according to house style. The heading (if used) will often be in bold and may be left aligned or centred according to the house style.

The body of the letter will generally contain a line or two of introduction and conclusion. The main body of the letter contains the substance. In the exam setting, this is where you will demonstrate your understanding and context-specific application of marketing knowledge. The signature block will contain an ending salutation (e.g. Yours sincerely,) followed by a space for the sender's signature. Often handwritten signatures are illegible, so the name and qualifications (where relevant, e.g. FCIM, Chartered Marketer) need to be added below the signature, with the position (normally one line below), and if only general Internet information is given in the heading the personal direct e-mail contact information should be given below that. If the letter has supporting documentation (e.g. reports, specifications, etc.) this may be listed at the foot of the page. If other people have been sent copies of the letter, the circulation list may also be given. Some examples of common business letter variants are given in the CIM Coursebook 'Customer Communications in Marketing'.

Insight

Beware of 'cut and paste' and 'templates'

In developing letters and mailings on a word processor, 'cut and paste' sections and 'template' answers can be useful but take care to ensure that all the content is strictly relevant to the issue you are writing about. People need to know that care has been taken with the communications. An 'urban myth' marketing story is told of a customer who complained about a cockroach in her hotel bedroom. She was very pleased with the full letter of apology until she noted a 'Post It' slip left on the letter with a note 'John, just send her the standard bug letter'.

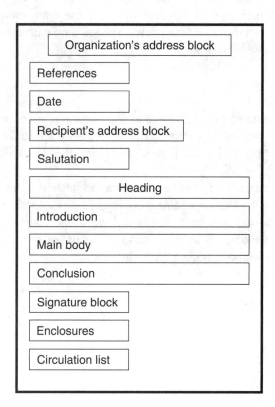

Figure 9.3 General outline of a simple business letter

Case study

Lake View Organic Farms

Presentation to potential franchisees

In Unit 1 the 'Lake View Organic Farms' case study was introduced. The following memo has been received:

MEMO

To: CIM Candidate

From: MD Lake View Organic Farms

Date: Exam date

Possible new location for next franchisee meeting

From my network contacts, I have received good reports for the 'Star' hotel. In 8 weeks we wish to have a meeting with our new franchisees (8–10 people) to update them on our new products and website development. We will want to have a tasting session of some new products. Can you check out the 'Star' and see if it can meet our requirements?

Managing Director

Below is an outline of a letter that might be written in response to an exam question 'Write a letter to the Conference Manager of the "Star" enquiring as to if they have the facilities for the franchisee meeting.' We assume that a website study has confirmed normal facilities (e.g. disabled access, etc.) are fine.

The general context of the case study has been considered in Units 1 and 2. The two key stakeholders in this role-play situation are the Conference Manager (and relevant staff at the 'Star') and the Managing Director (one key way to manage your manager is to show you are on top of the job). The other examination issue is to demonstrate understanding of the needs of selecting a venue for a meeting or conference. Some comments have been inserted in *italics*.

Lake View Organic Farms

Lake View Farm

Exam date

Conference Manager

Star Hotel

Dear M# ##### [in real life a check on the website would give the name]

Franchisee meeting

I have visited your website, and your facilities look impressive. We are considering the 'Star' as the location for our next franchisee meeting on ######.

I would be grateful for some further information on the following points:

Accessibility – We shall require normal facilities for parking for delegates and presenters but will also need access for our stands and other presentation equipment. Also, do you have arrangements for the collection of delegates travelling by rail or air?

Suitability – This is going to be an informal meeting but participants will need to make notes. Can you confirm you can accommodate a horseshoe arrangement with table seating?

Facilities – We wish to demonstrate our website; do you have broadband access in your conference suite? We also wish to have a tasting session on our new products and will need collaboration from your chef in the preparation of this. Will this be possible?

Budget – Can you please confirm your daily delegate rate for a group of this size (see enclosed schedule)? Will additional charges be made for broadband access and preparation of the food samples?

I look forward to meeting you soon and making a preliminary visit to your conference centre.

Yours sincerely,

CIM Candidate

Enclosure: full schedule of conference needs

Copy: MD, Lake View Organic Farms

In the exam setting, more information would be provided and the letter could be developed further. However, the above illustrates the use of the general structure given in Figure 9.3. In the exam, to gain high marks, the context-specific development of the relevant marketing issues is essential in the body of the letter.

 Activity 9.1

We all have to apply for jobs from time to time. Write a brief cover letter to be included with your CV to a potential employer for a job as a Marketing Executive. The position, as a Marketing Assistant to the Marketing Manager of a local theatre, specifies a person following the CIM qualifications. The role will have specific responsibility for the development and management of the loyalty programme 'Friends of the Theatre'. The reply is to go to Ann Smith, Marketing Manager, New Theatre, South Street, New Town, Home County, XY23 ZA19, and the advertisement has a reference AS/23/2006.

Business e-mails

Figure 9.4 gives the general outline structure of a business e-mail. Contrary to many people's expectations, e-mails are much more permanent than a paper letter. Once the hard copy (copies) of a letter are shredded, it is destroyed. E-mails go through systems with back-up security (in the sending organization, in transmission and in the receiving organization). There can be 'stray' copies around that you have no knowledge of and no control over. For this reason, and with the implications of data protection legislation, every care should be taken over e-mails just as you would with letters. That clever suggestion or lively joke could take on a different implication when examined in the cold light of day. Remember there is no such thing as a private communication in business (leaks and data protection legislation ensure this).

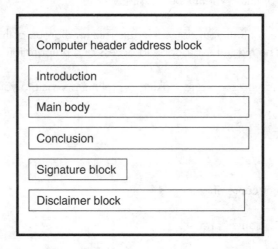

Figure 9.4 General outline structure of a business e-mail

Computer header address block: Gives all your addresses, your name and e-mail contact information. The 'To' block is for the target stakeholders (public/audience). The 'Cc' block is for people who may need to be kept informed. The 'Bcc' block allows you to circulate the e-mail to other people without the other recipients ('To' or 'Cc') knowing. The subject [title] block should give a one-line overview of the content. With busy inboxes, people often only display the 'From', 'Date' and 'Subject' fields. A meaningless subject (e.g. Re: as default from the software setting) might only get you a quick click into the delete box. The date and time is automatically picked up. In most software, the heading block will also give the file names and type (e.g. PowerPoint, word, etc.) of any attached files. Remember people with dial-up access and small-capacity inboxes do not appreciate large picture files.

The body of an e-mail follows the rules of introduction, main body and conclusion. The introduction and conclusion may be very brief or completely missed for a simple e-mail.

The signature block is best set up by customizing your software. This is much the same as for the signature block of a letter, but may also contain other contact information such as direct dial telephone number, website reference and so on.

Disclaimer block: Normally this will be set up by the organization and will be written by the Legal Department. It may cover such issues as to the non-disclosure of content if received in error, declaration of non-liability for virus damage, statement of organization's communications policy (offensive content) and in some organizations (e.g. journalists working for TV, radio or press) that the individual's views are the individual's and do not necessarily represent the policy of the organization.

Business e-mails

For all their ease and speed, e-mails are part of the permanent record. The implications of data protection legislation are that only a fool will commit to an e-mail something that they would not like to defend in the media or in court. Some software allows tracking options that allows the sender to know when you have received the message, when you have read it and when you have deleted it. More like an instant 'recorded delivery' than an informal method of communication! Some organizations (sending, transmitting or receiving) may be monitoring content for offensive words. An e-mail is not an electronic Post-It!

Insight

A good time to bury bad news? A PR 'own goal'!

A government PR executive sent out an e-mail, after a major disaster, that it was 'a good day to bury bad news' (if there is a lot of other major news, small issues will not gain any attention and they can in effect be swept under the carpet). The e-mail leaked into the public domain and was picked up by the media. A PR 'own goal'.

Activity 9.2

You are the Marketing Manager for a college that offers the CIM programme, but no specialist programmes in PR. You have received an e-mail from a Jill Jones (j.jones@anyprovider.com) with a key question: 'I am interested in PR and Marketing but not certain what the difference is between these for a career. Can you give me some advice?' Draft out an e-mail for this situation.

Memorandum (Memo)

Figure 9.5 shows the general outline of a memo. The case study context for the section on letters shows a very simple example of a memo. The e-mail format above can be considered as an electronic format for a memo to be transmitted directly, rather than printed and sent by 'snail mail'. The heading is almost identical (clearly you cannot list 'blind' copies at the top of a memo!). The body follows the same rules. The signature block is usually simple and allows space for the handwritten signature, the sender's name and management position. Most memos are now composed within a word-processing package, and for convenience a note of the file name is often useful. In some organizations, individuals may not file a hard copy of memos but maintain the file in a structured archive folder; attachments can be listed here too in this block. This way, duplicate copies of a document need not be held (in e-mails, attachments consume disk space, this way the memo block points to the original document file and this can save disk storage). Computer files take up no floor space and can be backed up systematically. Hard copy can get lost or destroyed (it only takes one coffee!).

MEMO
To:
From:
Copy to:
Date
Title
Introduction
Main body
Conclusion
Signature block
Reference

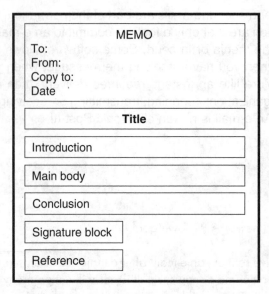

Figure 9.5 General outline structure of a memo

Rather like the Fax, the use of the memo in business is decreasing (decline phase of PLC) and being replaced with the quicker, cheaper, more environmentally friendly (no paper, no toner), more permanent, more secure (you can put an electronic track on an e-mail, you can never tell when a memo has been received or lost) and instant e-mail. The memo format is frequently part of the CIM exams (either as part of a case study file or as a required exam question format).

Business and academic reports

The single most important format for a CIM candidate is report format. Unless otherwise stated, all exam answers and assignment projects should be submitted in report format. Given the importance of the academic project report, the focus will be on this and differences in exam reports and business reports will be noted. Different contexts demand different house styles and the general framework (Figure 9.6) given below should be adapted as required.

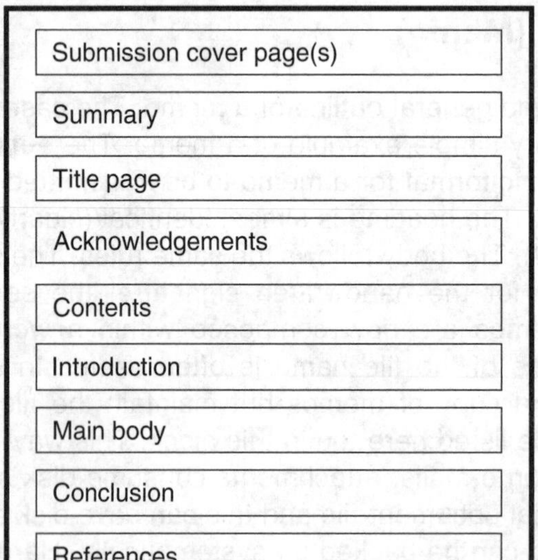

Submission cover page(s)
Summary
Title page
Acknowledgements
Contents
Introduction
Main body
Conclusion
References
Bibliography
Appendices

Figure 9.6 General outline of a report for an academic project

1. Submission cover sheet(s) – contains all the necessary information for submission of the assignment. As cover documentation it is not part of the formal report. For the CIM, full instructions are given on the CIM website.

2. Title page – including title of project and date. For CIM integrative assignments, the question number should be included. Lavish colour graphics are not required; presentation is no substitute for content. A good, clear, professional presentation is required.

3. Summary – focused and brief (150–300 words), should include key words for computer indexing of the project for more formal academic reports, and is important for longer formal reports in the business context. Provides senior management with an overview and directs further selective reading.

4. Acknowledgments – assistance may have been given with resources (e.g. assistance with running focus groups) or other support. It is good manners to acknowledge support.

5. Contents – helps people find their way around a longer project. Longer academic projects might include page numbers of main topic headings, appendices and lists of diagrams, figures, tables and illustrations. Reports should be page-numbered.

6. Brief introduction – a clear definition of the hypothesis, issue(s) or problems covered in the report. For CIM company-based assignments, a brief overview of the company context is helpful. Lengthy descriptive sections do not earn high grades and eat into the word count.

7. Body of the report – with full use of headings and subheadings. In academic reports, the more formal style should be used (e.g. 'the view is advanced' rather than 'I suggest'). For business reports, the organization's house style should be followed (e.g. in less formal companies the view might be that you take ownership of your recommendations and write, 'I recommend'). Figure 9.7 shows a possible structure for headings for advertising within an overall report on the communications mix. Typical frameworks for marketing and communications plans are given in the CIM specimen answers to case studies. For a typical academic project, the major section headings might be 'Literature review', 'Primary research' and 'Conclusions & recommendations'. Cut and paste submissions are in danger of a marginal fail. What is required is some critical understanding of the relevant theory with application to the question set and integrated into the context of the selected organization. Two pages of précis of textbook theory, with a few pages of unrelated description of what the selected organization does, are not sufficient.

8. Conclusion – this section should summarize the findings and, if appropriate, give recommended courses of action (e.g. in a CIM assignment how the selected organization might improve its operations in the area covered in the report).

9. References – these are particularly important in academic work. Failure to properly reference work quoted can leave a suspicion of plagiarism. The CIM framework expects candidates to read around the subject and keep up with developments. References provide evidence that you have done this. Tables 9.3 (books), 9.4 (journals) and 9.5 (websites) give the accepted referencing system used professionally and in academic institutions. The 'Harvard' system for referencing in the body of the report is the most widely used in business and academic work. There are many good websites from various universities that give good comprehensive guidance on referencing. The address for The Open University's guidance site is http://library.open.ac.uk/help/helpsheets/cite.html#eg1.

10. In business, full referencing is generally not required, but indication where information has been obtained from is usually good practice (e.g. source of statistical data in a table). In the exam setting, full referencing can be too time-consuming, but where you use a theory, you may wish to briefly acknowledge the source, for example Value Chain (Porter). References are the sources that you used directly in writing your report.

11. Bibliography – the same conventions in referencing the source apply, but this is the more general material that you consulted in your overall research but have not used directly and quoted in the body of your report.

12. Appendices – should be restricted to essential support material. Complete copies of annual reports and others are generally not required. If some primary research was conducted with a questionnaire, then an example copy of a completed questionnaire might be appropriate. If in doubt, consult your tutor.

Usually word count is taken to include the introduction, body and conclusion of a report. Greatly exceeding the word count can result in failure in academic work. You are strongly advised to consult the precise regulations covering your submission. Length is not the test of quality (1 kilo of cold, soggy chips is not a good eating experience; quality and quantity are different issues). What is required is a focused delivery of knowledge, understanding and application of relevant theory in the light of the given question/task and in the context of the selected organization.

Table 9.3 Outline of how to reference a book

Field	Example
Author(s) or editor's surname followed by initials	Kopperl, D.
Year of publication in brackets	(1965)
Book title in italics	*Manual of Document Microphotography*
City where published	Boston
Publisher name	Focal Press

(*Source*: Elsevier author guidelines with adaptation)
Kopperl, D. (1965) *Manual of Document Microphotography*, Boston, Focal Press

Table 9.4 Outline of how to reference a journal

Field	Example
Author(s) surname and initials	Kopperl, D.
Year of publication of journal in brackets	(1965)
Paper title in inverted commas	'Techniques of Photography'
Journal title in italics (abbreviations or acronyms are acceptable here)	*J. Appl. Photogr. Engn.*
Volume	2
Issue number	2
Part/section (if applicable)	1
Page numbers plus date article written if available	117–120

(*Source*: Elsevier author guidelines with adaptation)
Kopperl, D. (1965) 'Techniques of Photography', *J. Appl. Photogr. Engng.*, 2, 2, 1, 117–120

Table 9.5 Outline of how to reference an Internet source

Field	Example
Author(s) surname and initial	Kopperl, D.
Year the website was constructed in brackets	(1965)
Title of the document (in italics) followed by [online]	*Techniques of photography [online]*
Website title plus complete URL	www.marketingonline.co.uk
Date you accessed the site in round brackets	(03/07/04)

(*Source*: Elsevier author guidelines with adaptation)
Kopperl, D. (1965) Techniques of photography [online], *The Online Journal of Applied Photographic Engineering*, www.JAPE.co.uk/Kopp/TechPhot.html (03/07/04)

Exam reports – In general, only the briefest of headings should be given, with introductions and conclusion short and focused. It is the quality of the content of the body of your report that will score high marks. As noted above, there may not be time for full references. The CIM website provides good examples of specimen reports in a range of exam contexts.

Company reports – Most organizations have their own house styles and conventions. This may be contained in a company style manual. If not, when you come to write your first report, talk to your manager and ask for the report that is considered to have been the best in recent past. This will give you an indication of the company style. The submission cover page will normally be replaced with a front page giving the title, author(s), date of submission, edition (if taken though various drafts), executive summary and the distribution list. The summary and title pages are not necessary in this context, as all the information will be contained on one page. Figure 9.7 shows how a report format for marketing communications plan might be structured.

Font style – You should follow house style for company reports. For CIM reports, 12-point proportional type is recommended. Times New Roman and Arial are good, popular type styles. Some obsolete university instructions refer to Courier – this is an obsolete non-proportional type used in times past when work was not word processed (conventional typewriters could not use proportional type which is easier to read). If proportional type is used, single line spacing is acceptable. Justification provides a neater report, but is not essential. Pages should be numbered.

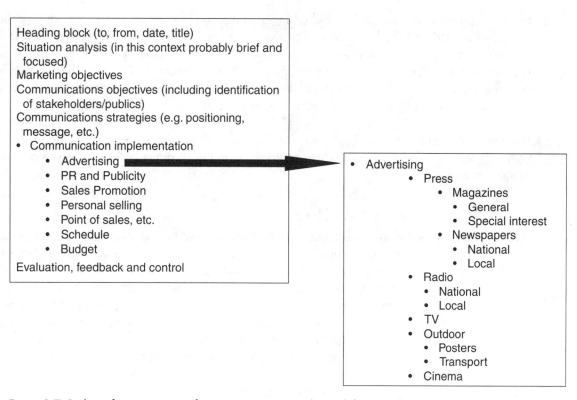

Figure 9.7 Outline of report structure for a communications plan with focus on the element 'advertising'; headings and sub-headings

Press releases that get published

In marketing communications terms, a press release is the same as a typical 'push and pull' strategy. You have to write copy that will attract the attention of the editor and then lead on to an article, TV or radio feature that will also appeal to your ultimate audience. Again, the secret is to understand what the two target audiences need. Many (possibly most!) fail at the first test:

are they 'newsy'? Being 'newsy' is rather like beauty or an elephant. It is easy to recognize but not easy to define. 'Newsy' articles get printed; the ultimate target audience also reads them.

Activity 9.3

Buy a copy of your local newspaper. Look at and evaluate the business news stories.

Fifteen minutes of fame

A postgraduate programme had, as one of its modules, a module on leadership with a residential weekend. An opportunity presented itself to take the group to a Navy training establishment for the group to undertake some 'Practical Leadership Exercises'. One of these was adapted for the group from a damage control simulator; this placed the group in a full cross-section of a 'damaged' ship. This would then fill with water pumped in at high pressure unless the damage control party made effective temporary repairs. There is nothing remarkable about this exercise. The unit is in use every day and no one is allowed to go to sea without successfully completing this exercise.

However, an alert PR manager found the 'angle' that made this 'newsy'. This was not a group of dedicated service people, but a normal group of business students who never expected to find themselves in this type of situation! The extra dimension was that the film 'Titanic' had just been released and was a box-office hit. The headline was, 'You have seen the film; these business students lived the experience!' This resulted in two television crews: one standard and one equipped with wetsuits and an underwater camera, which went into the simulator with the group.

The communications objective for the Business School in this context was, 'You can go and learn from stale lecturers and dry books or you can get out and learn at the cutting edge with a sense of excitement and adventure.'

The skill in successful press releases is to remain focused on the longer-term communications objectives and not just get carried away. Yet, at the same time, news is by its very nature transient and when the opportunity presents itself it has to be grasped. The above story would not have worked if the film had not been released, thus giving the story the 'hook' for the editor. Having found a framework that will carry the desired message and be newsy, how do we get it written up as a press release that gets printed? Think of the editor's agenda. Give them a good story and make it simple for them to use it. Many organizations now send out their press releases by e-mail as an attached file. The editor can then simply download the file and edit – no need to waste time in re-keying with reduced possibility of errors. Many journalists use the WHAT model and it is a good framework for your press release:

- **W**: Who? What? Why? Where? When?
- **H**: How did it happen? What are the implications?
- **A**: Additional information?
- **T**: Tie up loose ends.

Figure 9.8 gives an outline of a suitable structure for an 'electronic' press release. This allows all the points in this model to be covered.

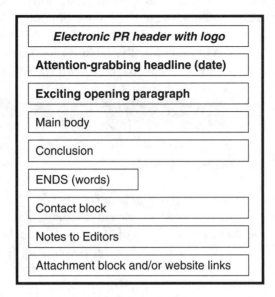

Electronic PR header with logo

Attention-grabbing headline (date)

Exciting opening paragraph

Main body

Conclusion

ENDS (words)

Contact block

Notes to Editors

Attachment block and/or website links

Figure 9.8 An outline for press releases sent as e-mail attachment

Electronic PR header with logo – Press releases are a front-line communication to key people in the media and so should look both attractive and professional. The press release template can convey the organization's logo and others just as with a paper letterhead.

Attention-grabbing headline – This can be repeated in the title block of the e-mail. An editor is faced with a very busy e-mail inbox and letter tray, so it is essential to have something to grab attention from the screen full of e-mails and from the overflowing in-tray on the desk. In the attachment, the heading is usually in bold and in a larger font size than the body.

Exciting opening paragraph – The secret is in a fairly short paragraph to make the key points and to provide the editor (and later the ultimate reader/listener/viewer) with a reason to stay with the story. Often this will be in bold but in the same font size as the body.

Main body – Contains the detail of the story but, for most press releases, needs to be fairly short: 200–400 words would be typical.

Conclusion – The 'wrap-up' paragraph to the story. A good punchy quotation from a key person is one way to do this.

ENDS – It is a common practice to indicate the ending of the story and it can be useful for editors to know the word count.

Contact block – Information for contacting the PR person who is going to manage the story. This should typically include office telephone number, 'office' mobile (in the 24/7/365 world, a major organization will have a PR rota so that the press can get information at any time, for example when a story goes international and followed up through various time zones) and, of course, e-mail contact. In the instant communication age, this is important as news editors may be scanning their screens for stories, so the first call can come in seconds.

Notes to editors – Editors may wish to expand upon the story so more background information can be given here, without cluttering up the main focused story.

Attachment block and/or website links – Most often now images will be held in high-quality digital format. These can be attached to the e-mail, but not all recipients may have facilities for very large files. Often the image files will be held on the PR area of the organization's website; these can be downloaded as needed by the editor or journalist. Past press releases may also be archived here, so that they are accessible to journalists doing follow-up features.

Insight

Internal stakeholder expectations

A common problem for the marketer is to manage unrealistic expectations of some internal stakeholders. The managing director might expect the PR department to issue a press release every week. This is not realistic. There can be a few weeks when nothing of news value happens and another week when there is more than one story. The critical element is being newsworthy. A dean might consider that a press release should be issued for one of his staff who has just published a paper on '5th order partial differential equations n dimensional space'. The newspapers are not likely to print; it has no news value and has no visual impact. In 2006, an academic with a passion for fireworks entered the 'Guinness Book of Records' with the most rockets set off at one time. The record was attempted at the 2006 National Firework Competition. This was news and some excellent pictures. It gained full cover in national and regional cover in the press and TV (not such a good story on the radio!). The University message is, 'This person is fun and if he does this just to pass the time, just think what his research is like!'

Case study

CIM Student Award

Case study scenario

Consider yourself in the role of PR Manager for New Town College. You have just been informed that a CIM student (Ann Smith*) on your CIM Professional Postgraduate Diploma in Marketing has gained the highest marks in the 'case study' exam in your region and will be presented with a certificate at the local Branch's AGM at the College (date ##/##/##) by the Chairman (Jennifer Jones*). On checking the records, you note that the student is the Communications Manager for a local company building racing boats. On receiving the news, the company arranged for a photograph of her launching one of their new range of boats. An outline analysis of the situation and a brief draft of a press release that might fit the situation are given below.

Outline stakeholder analysis, objectives/messages

Students – Existing (we are learning in a good place) and potential (this is the place to come and succeed).

College staff – (we work with our students to get success), CIM (best Marketing learning centre in the region).

Local employers – (the place to develop your professional staff).

Winning student – (Ann herself, family, fellow class members, colleagues and management of 'Silver Arrow', celebration of success).

Tutors on the course – (celebration of success).

Silver Arrow's stakeholders – (e.g. trade press – industry success story).

Media – (good news story with images, local person/company/college celebrating success). 'Woman presents student with certificate' is not an exciting headline, nor an eye-catching image. One possible strategy might be to issue the press release about 1 week before the presentation so that local TV and radio as well as the local press could get in on the act . Given below is a possible skeleton press release with comments given in italics.

Launched to Success!

Silver Arrow's Communications Manager Ann Smith has been launched to success as best CIM student in the region in the June 200# exams. Ann will receive her prize at the CIM Branch AGM at New Town College on #### day from Jennifer Jones.

Silver Arrow is one of our most successful local companies [paragraph on marketing in context, marketing is not just sitting in an office. Good for New Town College's stakeholders but also links in with Silver Arrow's stakeholders]

New Town College centre of regional marketing excellence [*paragraph on the course to address New Town College's publics*]

Ann Smith said, 'I have had such a good time with my fellow students gaining skills that I use every day in the successful marketing of our products' [*Concluding quotation on a strong note*]

ENDS (### words)

Contact block might include contact information for you as New Town PR contact, Silver Arrow (they might well want to issue to their trade magazine, etc.) and the CIM (potential follow-up on regional activities). Facilities for attending the event or arranging interviews might also be given here.

Notes to editors might include few paragraphs on the CIM course at New Town College, Silver Arrow and the local CIM Branch. Full details of the event (e.g. time, room number, etc.) might also be included here or in the earlier section.

The image of Ann launching the boat could be attached (note file size issues) or posted on the website for downloading on demand. Links could be given to other pages/sites of potential interest to editors/journalists covering the story.

The aim of this press release would be to (hopefully) gain regional press cover just before the event, with the potential to follow up after the presentation. Releasing slightly early might allow local TV and radio to do a brief feature on the local news (e.g. Ann being interviewed on one of the boats).

* Fictitious names for case study use only.

In the 'Fifteen minutes of fame' case study above, there was the opportunity for some good action pictures, not just somebody talking into a microphone in front of a computer (contain your excitement!). Know when your story will have that additional dimension – not just being 'newsy' but visually exciting (important for both the press and TV).

Activity 9.4

Earlier in this unit, a short case study was given on a practical leadership event. Imagine that you were to run this event and had been asked to write a press release. Draft this press release. If you have recently been on a field trip in your studies, substitute this. If you are studying with other CIM students, write independently and compare your copy. If you have access to the Communications Department, ask for some selected PR copy along with cuttings of the resulting media coverage. Debate in your group and/or with friends just what makes a good news story.

Managing marketing projects

Projects vary from simple (e.g. arrange a meeting) to complex (e.g. launch a new product). There are a number of stages to the planning process (Figure 9.9):

○ *Pre-initiation* – Pre-planning and feasibility. What do we need to do? What are the costs and time issues? Will the proposed project deliver the required benefits? What resources will be required (e.g. staff time)? How will it integrate with other activities? Some writers refer to just four stages (given below) but some consideration of the pre-initiation context is valuable. A major plan consists of a series of projects. How these integrate to achieve the organization's overall aims and objectives is important.

○ *Initiation* – Project definition including the objectives, scope, what is to be delivered/achieved, any constraints, any assumptions (e.g. delivery dates promised by suppliers), resources, outline schedule and project team (including responsibilities). Team selection should ensure that all skills are covered and that, apart from functional contributions (e.g. computer knowledge), team roles are covered (e.g. Belbin team roles: chairperson, shaper, plant, company worker, team worker, monitor-evaluator, resource evaluator and completer-finisher). Some writers call this project definition the project 'charter'.

○ *Planning* – Detailed preparation of the plan including assignment of responsibilities, scheduling of activities, with appropriate costing(s) and budget(s). Some consideration of contingencies should be made.

○ *Implementation* – Continual tracking of the activities against plan with action. Where key activities are slipping (e.g. late delivery of copy), corrective action is needed. Monitoring of costs (both invoiced and committed) against the budget agreed. Good communication within the project team and with key stakeholders is essential.

○ *Close-out* – Close down, check all expenses have been paid and close down budgets. Appraisal and review. Every project is a learning experience. What went well? What did not go so well? How can we do it better next time?

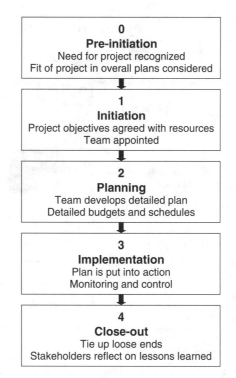

Figure 9.9 Flow chart for phases of project

We will consider a simple project to produce a promotional 'fact sheet' for the CIM programme at a college. In this case, there may not be large formal meetings but the project manager would still have, in effect, a virtual team contributing to ultimate success.

The targets are prospective students and sponsoring employers. Other stakeholders include tutorial staff, college management (e.g. conformance to house rules on style), existing students, general public, media, CIM (use of CIM logo), authors and printers.

Pre-initiation – Simple project – collect information and material and convert into a stylish, persuasive document (conforming to college and CIM style rules). Cost (in this case) should probably be easy to estimate, as many such documents will have been produced in the past. Potentially more of a problem could be information and copy, with academics tending to disappear to conferences and field trips. Activity must link with other initiatives (e.g. CIM open day at the college).

Initiation – Formal definition will confirm the above and agree to the details such as names for the team (could mostly be a virtual team with no lengthy formal project meetings).

Planning – Detailed consideration of major issues and scheduling constraints (e.g. the printers may not typeset until they have the final copy). It is often useful to chart this, and an outline chart is given in Figure 9.10. To prepare the chart, start with the end and work backwards. Time estimates are needed for each of the activities and these must be placed in the correct logical sequence, as shown in the specimen chart. Experience shows that care needs to be taken of loose ends (e.g. just because images are held on file does not necessarily mean that the college has full copyright for all purposes). Such issues can take time to resolve. Deadlines should clearly be indicated and agreed with members of the team (e.g. deadline for information to be provided). Progress can be updated on the chart and/or checklists kept. The checklist should indicate the activity, status, deadline and the person responsible, possibly with a comments field. For ease of updating and communication, a simple spreadsheet can be used (then if needed this can be distributed as an e-mail attachment to the team members). Additional reading references to project management are given at the end of the unit.

Activity	W1	W2	W3	W4	W5	W6	W7	W8	W9	W10	W11	W12
Agree general content	■											
Get information		■	■									
Write copy			■	■								
Agree deadlines with printer	■											
Agree images to be used		■	■									
Clear copyright file images				■	■							
Clear images and copy with authorities												
Final sign-off of total copy							■					
Dispatch files to printers							■					
Printer typesets								■				
Receive proofs and proof									■			
Get final sign-offs of copy										■		
Amendments sent to printer										■		
Leaflets printed											■	
Delivery from printer											■	
Distribution of leaflets to departments												■

Figure 9.10 Outline time plan for printing a leaflet

Implementation – Once the plan is put into effect, zero monitoring of adherence to deadlines and clear communications are necessary. Corrective action may be necessary to bring the project in line (e.g. if an information provider is away or ill, then a replacement source for the information must be found). In this situation, progress should be tracked (do not wait until a week after you need the information to check on things). A critical area is proofing and signing off copy. Errors in the final leaflet reflect badly on the team and college. Late corrections can be expensive and could take the project over budget (printers may charge extra for corrections required from the original agreed copy).

Close-out – Appraisal of team members' performance (e.g. who did or did not provide accurate information on time), were there any problems (e.g. communications with the printers)? Make certain all bills have been paid and close the budget down. How well was the final product received by the key stakeholders?

The typical type of question that you might expect is illustrated with the December 2005 case study 'The Urban Culture Festival 206' with Question 7 'Produce an event plan for the 2007 Urban Cuktyre festival using a suitable event planning model.' To answer this type of questions well, it is important to have a sound appreciation of tailoring the mix as required (Unit 6) and an appreciation of the scheduling issues (i.e. pre-launch, launch and immediate post-launch). The specimen approaches to these questions are available on the CIM website.

Event management

Events can range from the simple (e.g. sales meeting for a few sales executives), to the enormous (e.g. Olympic Games). The framework adopted here is that the management of events is a special type of project. Events management is of particular importance to marketers. In the NPD process, the marketer is not likely to be responsible for the development of the product (e.g. new computer), but will be involved in such activities as planning a PR launch event. The adaptation of the general project management flow chart for events is given in Figure 9.11. Most events are about communications (e.g. exhibitions), although this may be internal marketing communications (e.g. sales conference). Some generic aspects of the skills needed for event management have been covered in earlier units. Stakeholder analysis has been covered in Unit 1, communications issues reviewed in Unit 6.

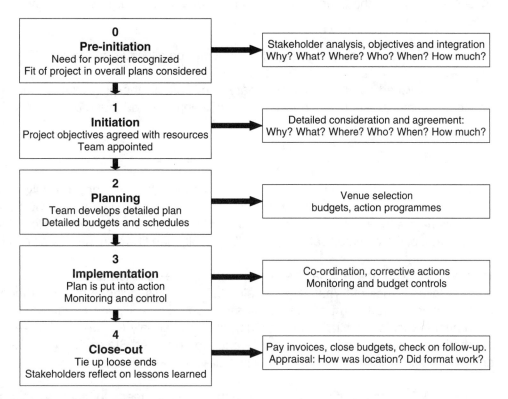

Figure 9.11 Flow chart for phases of an event project

Pre-initiation

Stakeholder analysis, objectives and integration

Below, the question 'Why?' is considered. To answer this, the starting point should be the overall communications aims, activities and objectives of the organization. Most events are not 'stand alone', they are part of an integrated plan and media schedule. A typical event that involves marketers is the press conference. In the launch of a product (e.g. opening of a new theatre, nightclub, etc.), part of the overall communications plan might well include a press conference (the type of activity we are considering here). Within this 'event' activity, there will be sub-activities (i.e. sub-projects) such as 'prepare the press pack' (the type of project considered in the earlier section).

Why? – Why have an event? How does this fit in with our stakeholder analysis and stakeholder objectives? How does this fit in with the rest of the communications plan, which in itself fits within the overall marketing plan?

What? – What type of event? For example, a 'sales launch'. Do we want a separate event? Would it be beneficial to link it to an exhibition?

Where? – Where is the geographic location, and other details? This can be very important for international conferences, where travel connections and visa requirements may be a significant issue.

Who? – Who among the general stakeholders will be involved? Do we need/want additional stakeholders for this particular event?

When? – Timing of the event may be vital, for example, to fit in with the overall plans for a product launch.

How much? – How much of the overall budget can be allocated to the event?

Having established some general boundary conditions in the pre-initiation phase, the actual project initiation can start. The above questions can be asked in a more detailed fashion.

Initiation

Why? – The answer to 'Why have an event?' shapes the aims and objectives of the event which should now be defined in detail (where possible, objectives should be SMART). 'How does this fit in with our stakeholder analysis and stakeholder objectives?' 'How does this fit in with the rest of the communications plan?' 'Does this then fit within the overall marketing plan?'

What? – The type of event has been defined from pre-initiation and we can now move on to more detailed issues of 'What' is physically required. This includes a whole range of detailed issues which will form part of the venue selection criteria. Issues can include food (e.g. for international clients', special dietary needs), electrical supply (do we need three phase, i.e. in international contexts supply may be different, e.g. in United States 120 volts 60 Hz), Internet access, computer projection systems, water, drainage and so on.

Where? – A detailed set of criteria for the venue selection needs to be drawn up (this aspect is considered in more detail in the next section). Some of the technical issues for facilities have been covered above. Other issues include access, size, appropriateness and costs.

Who? – General stakeholder analysis has been completed in the provisional phase but should be refined here. In particular, the project team needs to be appointed and consideration of issues such as speakers, VIP guests and others should commence.

When? – More in-depth consideration of schedule(s) to provide a framework for detailed planning in the next phase.

How much? – Confirmation to the planning team of the overall budget allocation. Costs feed into the equation in venue selection.

In some books, the output of this phase is called the project 'charter'. It provides direction and purpose for the planning team to develop the details for successful implementation.

Planning

Venue selection
One of the key tasks in the planning phase and one of the early actions is to select and book the event location. Issues surrounding event locations have been featured in recent CIM exam questions (e.g. June 2006 'SMS Cars Ltd.' Question 1(c) 'Produce a report for your Managing Director (MD) that recommends which venue [Durley Hall or National Motor Museum] to select.

Justify your recommendation, explaining what criteria you used to come to your decision.' In the December 2005 case study 'The Urban Culture Festival 2006' there was a similar question; 1(c) 'Considering financial and non-financial factors, what venue [City Hall or The Warehouse] would you recommend for the Gala? Justify your decision.' The ASFAB (Access, Size, Facilities, Appropriateness and Budget) model can be used. Remember this process needs to be adapted to the context of the specific case study and actual question asked. Table 9.6 lists some of the criteria to be considered. Facilities have been split into three for convenience (conference, accommodation and technical). Special care must be taken with a technical and a non-technical marketer; there can be problems if the appropriate checks are not made. In the international context, electrical power supplies can be different, and different versions of software may be used. For product launches where equipment is to be demonstrated, special services may be needed (e.g. three-phase electrical supply). Where technical products are to be involved, there must be an appropriate level of technical knowledge and expertise in the project team. Access for heavy items (e.g. boats, cars, etc.) may require specialist venues with this type of access.

Table 9.6 ASFAB criteria for venue selection: Access, Size, Facilities, Appropriateness and Budget

Issue	Comments
Access	Is the venue in the right regional location? Is the venue going to be available at the time required (popular venues may be booked years in advance)? Is the venue easily accessible for delegates using various forms of transport (e.g. roads, rail links and airports)? Is the venue suitable/ accessible for disabled delegates? Remember exhibition stands may need heavy vehicle access. What are the conditions for set-up/take-down access before and after the event, and the like? How long will it take to set up and dismantle the stand?
Size	Is there enough room for the event? Are delegates going to be comfortable? Health and Safety issues need to be addressed. What is the official capacity of the venue? Will that be exceeded with delegates and service staff within the venue? Are there enough rooms of the right type and quality?
Facilities: conference	What facilities do you need for your event? Seating – how many delegates? Can the venue provide the required seating plan? Is presentation equipment readily available (e.g. projection screens)?
Facilities: security	Valuable samples and products may be at risk, appropriate provision required
Facilities: accommodation	What accommodation is needed? Are delegates bringing partners who need to be accommodated? Is the accommodation comfortable, suitable with required facilities for delegates' needs (e.g. Internet access, disabled access)?
Facilities: technical	Broadband/communications facilities, power supply, special services (e.g. extraction, water, drainage, etc.), and is computer software/hardware compatible? Many laptops do not have floppy drives, so if your speaker comes with a presentation on a floppy disk it could be problematic. Also, back-up systems in case of system failure.
Appropriateness	Right ambience (exciting and original for new perfume launch or just professional for a routine sales meeting). Types of venue include hotel, conference/exhibition centre, other (theatre, concert hall, museum, art gallery, etc.), unusual (e.g. sail training ship). Is the venue going to attract the right audience? Does it have appropriate entertainment facilities?
Budget	More consideration below, but should include all the organization's direct and indirect (staff time) costs. An appreciation of delegate cost is important. That exciting low-cost venue may be difficult to get to and expensive in fares for international delegates. Table 9.7 gives typical budget headings for an event

Budget

Table 9.7 Typical budget headings for an event

Cost	Comments
Venue costs	Delegate rate (*x* number of delegates), stand/room hire, extras (telephone, cleaning, maintenance services), services, flowers and so on. If quotation is in the form of a day delegate rate, care must be taken to ensure what is included and what will require extra payments
Staging costs and production costs	Design, transportation and erection of stand. Preparation of presentations, printing of brochures, purchase of special materials (e.g. giveaways) and so on
Pre-event communications	Advertising, costs of invitations and so on
Team's costs of travel and accommodation	Care must be taken to ensure that individual members of the team do not go over budget with extravagant claims (e.g. international telephone calls from a hotel can be very expensive)
Internal costs	Allocation of internal costs such as support staff time and so on.
Contingency	Some allocation for unexpected additional costs

Pre-event checklist and action programme

An outline checklist is given of things that need to be considered before an event and controlled during the event.

Checklist prior to exhibition:

o   Have all the issues in ASFAB process been considered?
o   Has the budget been agreed and authorized?
o   Have the aims and objectives been agreed and approved?
o   Have all the relevant contracts been obtained and checked (including subcontractors, e.g. catering, photography, etc.). Contracts must be in detail and cover all the relevant issues (e.g. water supply, power, communications, cleaning, security, insurance and refuse disposal, etc.).
o   Have payment terms been agreed?
o   Has stand design been finalized and agreed? Has all stand fabrication been completed and transport and erection at the venue been arranged? Are all components in order (including fittings such as display stands, lighting, signage, etc.)?
o   Have the safety arrangements been checked and any necessary permits obtained?
o   Has all the promotional material been designed, copy cleared and material printed (and checked!)? Do not forget press releases and briefings.
o   Have guest lists been approved and invitations dispatched? Do not forget other stake-holders such as the media.
o   Have all the staff been briefed?
o   Have all accommodation and travel arrangements been made for staff and guest presenters?
o   Have all transport arrangements been made for stand, fittings, promotional material, demonstration equipment and promotional literature?
o   Have all the arrangements for erecting and dismantling of the stand been agreed and checked?
o   Has a rota for manning of the stand been agreed and all relevant staff briefed? This should include all guest speakers and others.

o   Have events been arranged and guest presenters briefed (e.g. press conference)?
o   Have all the integration aspects been agreed and checked (e.g. links with general advertising)?

A Gantt chart can then be used to schedule all the activities (more cover of schedules is given in Unit 10.

Implementation (Execution)

In the planning process, all the team members and key participants (e.g. speakers) should know their roles, responsibilities and deadlines. Good communications are essential alongside good relationships with the locations event management staff. The basics are simple, make certain everything is running to plan and adjust programme if unexpected issues arise (e.g. sickness of a speaker). In reality, event managers can expect a busy and eventful day. Good planning, along with a motivated team, communicating well, should ensure a successful event. It is important to maintain discipline, or that sudden idea for an addition to the venues requirements may take you over budget with an unplanned expense.

Close-out

All invoices and expense claims should be checked to ensure only what has been agreed is being paid. Once all expenses have been cleared, then the relevant budget can be closed. One of the last actions of the event team leader is to ensure that follow-up is completed. This can be administrative (e.g. courtesy letter of thanks to speakers) or more marketing management (e.g. checking sales have got all the new contact information and are progressing with the new leads, issuing of conference proceedings, etc.). An outline checklist of points for appraising an event is given below.

Venue – Were access, parking, catering, support (e.g. direction signs) acceptable? Were the rooms large enough? Were the rooms well-serviced and not too hot/cold? Did all the equipment work properly? Were all the required services and equipment available? Did delegates and speakers feel the ambience was appropriate? Were there any complaints about the facilities? Were rooms arranged (e.g. horseshoe) as required? Was there enough time and support for setting up – taking down?

Speakers – How was their contribution received? Were they well prepared? Did they arrive on time?

Administration – How effective was pre-event publicity? Was all event material delivered on time? Were there errors or gaps in the documentation (e.g. missing name badges)? How did registration proceed?

Costs – Were there any cost overruns on the budget?

PR – Were arrangements for the media satisfactory? Was the eventual media cover satisfactory in tone and quantity?

Specific objectives – Were these attained, for example, for a training event; did people come away with new skills they could apply in the workplace?

Additionally for exhibitions:

Stand – How did it compare in quality and impact with the competition? Was it erected and taken down on schedule? Did it and all the services function satisfactorily?

Objectives – How many new contacts were made? What was the cost per new contact made? Did we gain any useful knowledge about the competition? Was overall attendance satisfactory in numbers and quality?

International events

The general issues of international marketing have been covered in Unit 1. Some issues to consider for international events are given below.

Language – Will translation of proceedings be needed? Not all venues have the facilities for simultaneous interpreting to participants.

Religion and culture – Does the date clash with religious or national holidays with key delegates or speakers? Does the venue cater for the range of dietary needs that may be required? Different cultures have different attitudes to dress (e.g. in the United States, a conference dress code is likely to be 'business casual' in daytime sessions, but in the United Kingdom, 'formal business attire', i.e. business suit, may be expected). Indicative comments on dress codes may be appreciated to avoid embarrassment. For a major international event, it may be appropriate to appoint an official travel agent who will provide general support (e.g. arranging transport for long-haul delegates from the international airport). Alcohol consumption is not universally appreciated, so a suitable range of non-alcoholic options should be available. Remember the reverse: a hard-drinking sales team may not appreciate the 'location' within a culture where alcohol is not readily available.

Political/Legal – Visa requirements have become much stricter post 9/11. Visas may take some time to obtain (sometimes months), so early planning is needed. Visas may need supporting documentation from the organizers (e.g. formal letter of invitation). Event documentation should make visa issues clear. In general, it is the delegate's responsibility to ensure compliance with passport/visa requirements.

Payment – If there is a payment for the event, how will payment be accepted (e.g. what currency, what form of payment, etc.)?

Costs – International delegates may have substantial travel costs (even visas may not be a trivial expense). With the high value of pound (£), the United Kingdom can appear a very expensive location for an event for some international participants.

Access – International air travel can be disrupted and schedules may involve arrivals in the middle of the night. Can delegates check in 24/7? Flight patterns may dictate that international delegates may have to arrive at an earlier and/or depart at a later date. Are the costs of additional days reasonable and are the rooms available?

Insurance – Travel, health and other insurance are normally the delegate's responsibility and this should be made clear in the event documentation.

Health – Many overseas locations have health requirements (e.g. inoculations and anti-malaria medication). Note the need for health insurance above.

Accompanying persons – International delegates may wish to take advantage of the trip for a holiday stopover and may bring partners. A social programme for such accompanying persons might be appropriate for a major event. Note there may be visa problems with accompanying persons. In some circumstances, the accompanying person will not be considered to be a delegate (conference visa) and may need a 'holiday' visa.

Other types of events

Meetings: These are arranged for face-to-face communication. Typical meetings include sales, planning, briefing and negotiations. Many of the earlier issues apply but on a reduced scale (e.g. agreeing venue, date, time, agenda, etc.).

Conference: From the organization's view, conferences are very much like exhibitions. Often conferences are arranged linking it with an exhibition. Issues such as travel arrangements are identical. The design of the exhibition stand is replaced with detailed arrangements for seating for the delegates and arrangements for the speakers (e.g. microphone and projection facilities, etc.). Pre-event publicity is much the same as for an exhibition, except that different mailing lists will be required. It is good practice to get 'PowerPoint' files delivered early (check with authors and get them sent by e-mail if not too large) and check they project as intended. A minor 'PowerPoint' gremlin is that when you change from system to system, the same file may reverse an imbedded image in a slide (i.e. left of the image may become the right or the top become the bottom). It is only a couple of mouse clicks to use the 'flip function' to correct this. It is best to do this the evening before and not halfway through the presentation. If the proceedings are to be published, ask the presenters to deliver their 'Word' files at the same time as their PowerPoint files. Any final text should be cleared with the authors before the proceedings are finally published.

Telephone and video conference: Telephone conferences are sound only. Video conferences add images so body language is visible and the exchange is more lifelike. These are fine for short meetings with dispersed team members. Note the problems with time zones with international video conferences.

Press conferences: General arrangements are much the same as for a conference. However, timescales may be compressed (e.g. disaster PR – press conference after a major fire or other incident). Journalists and technical support staff (camera operators, etc.) appreciate appropriate provision of refreshments (they may have travelled long distances at short notice). A key issue is to ensure adequate provision of services, power, sound feeds, communications links, and parking space for transmission vehicles or mobile studios. Good coordination is necessary to ensure the availability of key people for follow-up with one-to-one interviews for the various channels. Where it is possible press briefing packs should be available. These can be supplied as hard copy and/or as downloadable files from the organization's website. Many organizations hold their past press releases on their website for a few months to provide journalists with background.

Launch events: The general issues are the same as for an exhibition. In fact, many products are launched at exhibitions where the footfall may be higher than for a special single 'one-off' event. The first key issue is to double-check that all the services that may be required at the venue exist. For industrial products, these might be quite specialized (e.g. three-phase electricity supply). The second key issue is to check that the equipment has been fully field-tested. Things are usually fine in the laboratory and workshop but field conditions are different. As an example, in less-developed countries the electricity supply may have 'spikes' (short periods of very high voltage for a fraction of a second) and/or 'brown outs' (drop to low voltage for some seconds). Such conditions may damage standard computer equipment. In such conditions, an un-interruptible power unit may be essential. Always get expert technical advice. Wherever possible have technical staff on hand to assist.

Activity 9.5

In some major towns, careers convention happens each year, where major employers and learned institutions talk to students and people seeking a career change, education and job search. Consider that you have been elected by a CIM Group as 'Student Member Representative'. You have been given the responsibility of preparing and running an exhibition stand in the local town hall in 6 months' time. What would you do?

The marketing presentation

All the rules of stakeholder analysis apply here. One way to view the process is to regard it not so much as a mass communication, but a whole series of 'one-to-one' communications that happen to be going on simultaneously. Thus, as with personal selling, start with the audience. In one-to-one contact, you have a single agenda and personality. In a sales presentation, you will be talking to a group of different people with different roles in the client DMU. Therefore, the task is a little more complex, as it takes place in a rather short space of time and needs careful presentation. Some simple rules are provided below:

o   As with one-to-one interactions, know your agenda and the probable agendas of the target audience.
o   Decide on the media: most often it will be computer based, but check; older media such as slide projectors are not always available unless requested beforehand. Check that your software is compatible. At a conference in China, there was considerable confusion with several different versions of the same presentation software in circulation. Not all worked on the hotel's computers and there were some late-night file conversions! Check what facilities will be at the venue before you prepare your material.
o   Prepare the material (including any supporting documentation and samples, etc.) and get another person to proof (do not just rely on the spell checker. More than one PR manager has got up to talk about 'pubic' rather than 'public' relations!).
o   If possible, carry out a run-through to make sure that it works and to check timings.
o   At the venue, try to arrive early and check all the last-minute details (e.g. will you have a radio microphone, a fixed microphone or can you choose?).
o   Remember that in the actual presentation, you are building many one-to-one relationships. Try not to look at your script too much (prompt cards treasury tagged together so they stay in order is a popular option), sweep the audience with your eyes. Then people in the back row will feel that they have not been forgotten.
o   Remember housekeeping points. Is the presentation informal (so you are happy to take questions at any time) or, is it more formal so questions will only be taken at the end? Make certain you have agreed to these points with the chairperson if it is a formal meeting.
o   Prepare your 'deliverable' handouts, brochures and the like well in advance. Make certain they are sent by secure means if you are not taking them yourself. In international meetings, take special care; there can be problems with, for example, customs clearance.
o   As always in marketing, reflect on the process. This is not your last presentation so think of it as a continual learning experience where you gain more and more skills; this is an important area for the practising marketer.
o   Remember the X factor – positive energy and enthusiasm. If you are not excited about the subject how are the audience to stop falling asleep?

Activity 9.6

If you are not scheduled to give a presentation, arrange to give one to your CIM class or to friends. If that is not possible, sit in on a presentation and take notes on what was effective and what was not effective. What is the difference between a lecture and a presentation? What makes a lecture good for you?

Negotiations

One of the important relationship contexts is that of engaging in negotiations. This may be with external stakeholders such as customers and suppliers or internal with colleagues or your manager. The issues might be major (the price for next year's contract) or minor (Where shall we have the team away for the day?). Figure 9.12 provides an overview of the process for negotiation.

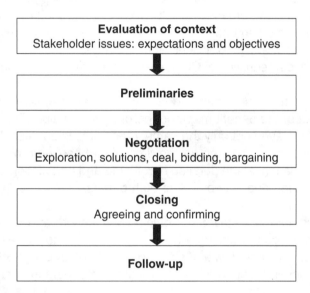

Figure 9.12 Process for negotiation
Source: Adapted from Hatton and Worsam (1998)

Evaluation of context

For major customer negotiations, this may involve a thorough review of the macroenvironment/microenvironment. For an internal negotiation, it may involve consideration of the office politics, pressures on the individuals and their personalities (e.g. leadership style of a manager). The need is to evaluate the negotiations on stakeholder expectations, objectives and agenda. This includes an objective analysis of your own situation and agenda.

Preliminaries

For a major programme of negotiation, this may involve fact-finding sessions and agreement of the negotiation process (e.g. scheduling negotiation meetings). For internal negotiations, the process may be much less formal such as a brief e-mail: 'Smith is away for a month with a broken leg, we need to re-negotiate workload allocations. Can we meet tomorrow?' The need is that there should be a shared, agreed understanding of ground rules and roles by all relevant stakeholders.

Negotiation

Exploration – The objective of this phase is not to negotiate. This phase is for the stakeholders to state their position and agenda. This stage is not about countering or bidding but parties seeking utmost clarity of the full range of relevant stakeholder issues. For a contract for foodstuffs to a supermarket, the supermarket might start by outlining the competitive pressures making a price reduction necessary. The supplier may outline that higher energy costs make a price increase necessary.

Solutions – Here the RM issues are most important. If the stakeholders do not have trust, there will be a barrier to free exchange of ideas. One side may go for a killer win strategy (this normally results, in the long run, in a lose–lose situation). Good relationships came from building long-term relationships. Continuing the supermarket–supplier discussion, the need is to reduce costs in some way. This way, both sides could gain their objective (maintain profitability). Creative problem-solving is needed. In one case, a supermarket was re-negotiating for a product delivered to a central supply depot from a regional factory. The creative solution: the supplier's transport picked up the mix of goods, from the supermarket's depot, for delivery to the supermarket's outlets near the regional factory. Between the two organizations, two empty vehicle journeys had been saved. This overall cost reduction could be shared, satisfying the need for the supermarket to contain costs and the supplier to maintain margins – relationship marketing and supply chain management in action. The net effect was also a reduction of CO_2 emissions; therefore, the solution was also greener.

Deal – Failure to maintain focus and clarity on detail is an area where negotiations may fail. In the above case, the benefit might not be of uniform value. The supplier saved one journey. The supermarket saved not only the same journey miles but also the costs of the local travel to a few outlets and the time taken for the drop-offs (these were picked up by the supplier now). Clearly in this situation, some detailed bargaining and negotiation is needed to finally come to a solution which is fair and acceptable to both parties.

Bidding – This is the detailed bargaining discussed at the end of the above section. The supplier might go in claiming a high percentage of the overall cost reductions. The super-market could take a 'high' view and start bidding at 50 per cent each split of the cost reductions. There may be several rounds of give-and-take in reaching the final settlement area.

Bargaining – Striking the bargain: the stage at which the final agreement is reached. The bidding exploration might have taken place with a small working party. However, more senior executives may need to be involved in the final stages.

Closing

Once the final framework is agreed, the outcome should be clearly stated and summarized. Both parties must clearly understand what is being agreed. In simple cases, the agreement may be confirmed in writing or a formal agreement signed for major contracts.

Follow-up

As always in business, evaluation and control must be exercised. In the case we have been discussing, the supplier may be concerned that excessive time is not spent loading goods at the supermarket's depot or in unloading at the branches. In their turn, the supermarket will be concerned that delivery schedule 'windows' to the branches are maintained.

Good negotiation requires good interpersonal skills, good command of the facts and rapid logical thinking.

Managing your manager

Develop your competences

A good place to develop is 'yourself'. Lack of professional and management skills is not the best calling card in developing good working relationships with senior staff.

Lifelong learning

Your study for the CIM qualifications is only a starting point. After gaining all your CIM qualifications, you will undertake continuing professional development to maintain and develop your professional skills (e.g. developments in e-marketing) and managerial and interpersonal skills (e.g. team leadership). To gain the most from both formal learning (e.g. CIM course) and informal learning (reflecting on practical work experiences) you should understand a little about your learning style.

o Activist learning is the 'here and now' attitude. Activists will do anything once and love lots of activity! Nothing boring here!
o Reflective learning takes a multifaceted view of the issues. In this approach, different avenues are explored and the learning is set in the 'bigger picture'.
o The theorist's learning style attempts to see how things fit in some generalized pattern. Basic assumptions, principles, theories and models are integrated into a 'systems' way of thinking.
o Pragmatic learning styles resemble the 'innovators' in the adoption curve behaviour. Early practical experimentation and application of the learning is the order of the day.
o Experience-based learning in the workplace proceeds through stages. We do something and this is a learning experience (e.g. your first meeting as Chair). We observe and then reflect on the experience (how did the meeting go? What went well? What could you have done better?). The reviewing process results in some conclusions. This in turn leads on to planning, testing and evaluating (e.g. how about the next meeting as a video conference?).

In the context of managing your manager, remember your learning style and your manager's learning style may differ, learning style is in part a facet of our inbuilt personality. Personalities differ; understanding self and our interactions with others is an important component in developing networking skills. Cameron (2001) provides a good overview of learning styles in the context of management learning. Parker provides a good overview of self-image and personality in the context of the workplace.

Assertion skills

In approaching a potential conflict situation with your manager, there are three strategies. You could avoid the problem or just pretend it does not exist: 'If I keep out of the way the problem will disappear.' You could become aggressive: 'I know my rights, I will go in and stand up for them!' Assertion is the third, middle way, between submission and aggression. This framework of thinking declares that we have basic rights such as

o The right to ask for what we want and don't want
o The right to be listened to and respected
o The right not to know something and not to understand
o The right to make mistakes
o The right to change our minds
o The right to judge our own behaviour and take responsibility for the results
o A responsibility to respect the assertion rights of others.

Good assertion skills can be seen as part of the make-up of the skilled negotiator. Parker (2003) provides a good review of assertion skills in the management context.

Time management

One classic conflict issue between an individual and their manager is workload. The individual may consider themselves overworked with management not understanding the full amount of time needed to complete a task (e.g. write a good press release). The manager might well think that the individual is just not up to it and just wastes their time. A classic comment would be, *you just need to learn how to manage priorities*! There is one management resource that a CIM student has as much of – as Bill Gates or the president of the United States – time! Complex personal organizers or software packages are available for this. They are not necessary; paper and pencil can be fine. Use a framework that works for you. Set aside a few minutes each working day to time-plan. Learn to develop good time management skills and avoid time-wasters. Table 9.8 shows a simple framework for an interactive 'to-do' list to run on any spreadsheet package such as Excel. Setting one up only takes a few minutes and updating is quick and simple. The sort function allows the list to be re-ordered to reflect changing priorities and others.

Table 9.8 Framework for a simple 'to-do' list to run on a spreadsheet package

Priority	Project	Deadline	Delegated	Comments
1	Complete CIM assignment	30/05/0#	–	Research completed
3	New college leaflet	22/06/0#		Waiting images and copy
1	Copy for new college leaflet	12/05/0#	Jill	Problems with information on planning module
2	Images for new college leaflet and so on	12/05/0#	John	Images collected, selection needed

Some selected practical tips for good time management are given below. Cameron (2001) provides a good overview of managing time at work, when also studying part-time.

Delegate – You do not have to do everything. Pass work on. If the staff do not have the skills, arrange for training.

Say no – A key assertion skill is to learn how to say 'no' when your work 'in tray' is full. Learn how to close interruptions and appointments.

Stop doing things – Why have a monthly meeting if it is not effective?

Meeting to attend – Prepare, read agenda and minutes beforehand. Don't contribute to time wasting, if you have nothing to say that is fine. Delegate attendance if you can and it is appropriate.

Meeting to hold – Rule one don't! Much can be achieved by e-networking and virtual conferencing. Only hold a meeting for a defined purpose. Fix start and end times. Do not wait for late arrivals. End at 17.35 means just that! Circulate minutes/action plans immediately after meeting. Get a person at the meeting to draft the minutes for you, directly onto a laptop during the meeting. Then you only have to edit and e-mail it off. If you have lots of contributions to make to the meeting possibly get someone else to chair.

Don't panic – Check with people what deadlines are fixed and may not be changed and those which may be flexible and can be adjusted.

Learn to work effectively – Develop good IT skills. Learn to speed read. Keep communications short and focused. Control the electronic 'inbox' and snail mail in-tray. Handle item once – action – delegate – file – dispose of – try to keep pending file small (empty is good). Maintain good filing disciplines for physical and computer files (back up these regularly onto DVD or flash memory).

Organize work space – Keep desktop clear (there should be nothing on it when you leave at night).

Control time – Control appointments: 'we will meet at 15.20 for 15 minutes'.

Know your good and bad times – Know when you are good, are you a morning person? You should schedule complex work into the time when you work well.

Focus – Work on one thing at a time and allocate enough time to make an impact.

Control interruptions – There is no such thing as a 1-minute interruption, concentration is destroyed and takes many minutes to be recovered. Control your telephones when you are working on something complex – that is what voicemail is for. Control your e-mail, set aside a part of the day for electronic and physical 'snail mail' correspondence.

Diary and 'to-do' list – To-do list has been discussed above. Electronic diaries are fine but group disciplines need to be observed, for example 'meeting' clear times, times of the day when meetings may not be booked so people can focus on project activities (some colleges do not schedule lectures on Wednesday afternoons to allow time for sporting and other group activities).

Steal time – For longer business journeys, take the train rather than drive. Good time to catch up with CIM background reading and many long-distance trains now have laptop power points (book ahead and reserve a table seat).

Managing your manager

A range of key skills to help you do this have been outlined earlier in the coursebook including clear office communication, project management, negotiation, time management and assertion. Using your learning style to your advantage and general self-awareness will develop your professional capacity and personal self-confidence. Managing your manager can be considered as a particular context of negotiation, where the discussions should be conducted within the ground rules of assertive behaviour. Developing the skills outlined in this unit will strengthen your hand in these negotiations.

Feeding into your 'to-do' list should be a clear interpretation of your manager's workload allocation. Together with your properly documented project management plans, you have prepared the ground for discussions and negotiation about issues. These can form the objective basis for negotiation. Avoid the trap of 'I have too much to do!' and 'You are ineffective!' when the manager has little total understanding of real workload (i.e. not been kept informed by you). You will start your negotiations with some sense of confidence through good preparation. Earlier the issue about 'knowing self' was introduced. In addition to this, you should have developed an understanding of your manager's personality and style. It is unlikely to be the same as yours. As with selling to customers an empathetic understanding of the other person's frame of reference and outlook helps greatly. This with clear communications (e.g. well-focused e-mails, etc.) and assertive behaviour should help avoid confrontational meetings. A final tip is the power of positive thinking. Thinking 'This is going to be a bad meeting and I feel stressed' can become self-fulfilling. With good preparation and a positive attitude you should go into this situation feeling that the outcome will be win–win.

Activity 9.7

Earlier in this unit, you were invited to write a press release on a student activity. Consider that you are the Marketing Manager of the college and your press release made the front page of the local advertising paper, with a circulation of 150 000. This was included as local news item by BBC News Online with a link to the BBC's main news page. The Dean's PA has just telephoned you to say that the Dean was unhappy as he considered the *Financial Times* and the *Times Higher* to be his target media. You have been asked to see the Dean in an hour. What would you do? How would you want to handle the discussion?

Networking: relationship marketing in action

What network?

It is easy to collect vast numbers of cards at exhibitions and conferences. This is not successful networking. The first stage of successful networking is to understand your own objectives and use the concepts of segmentation and stakeholder analysis. It is important to understand that networking involves more than an exchange of addresses – computers can do this. There needs to be a relationship and that implies you must be sensitive to the other person's agenda and make the relationship work in both directions (win–win relationships). Table 9.1 provides an outline of stakeholders for a typical organization. An analysis of the networks that a young marketer working in a communications department might wish to build might include the following:

Social – Meeting new people and making new friends including social networks, such as boat clubs and so on.

Internal – Develop good relationships with colleagues. Good relationships with key people in support functions (e.g. security, etc.) are also invaluable. This is, in RM terms, internal marketing.

Media – Develop and maintain good relationships with media (editors and journalists – key asset for the PR professional). This can be vital when bad news breaks, and confidence in you from the journalists and editors is vital.

Customers – Use events such as exhibitions to strengthen network links with existing customers and develop new links with potential customers.

Suppliers – Good relationships with suppliers (e.g. printers, marketing agencies, etc.) should be developed, treating them as extended members of the team and working partners.

Competitors – The marketer should remain on good professional terms with their organization's competitors. You may be competing in the marketplace but in other areas you may collaborate (e.g. two high-street fashion retailers may be competing but if there is a problem with city centre crime, such as shoplifting, they will collaborate).

Local business community – Managers should network to develop a range of contacts through the various types of associations that exist at local (e.g. local Chamber of Commerce) or national level (e.g. CBI) as appropriate.

Professional – Good network relationships with other professionals are vital to the marketer. Do not restrict yourself to marketing and PR contacts. Topics such as 'project management' and 'time management' are of interest to many professionals and interesting local events are often hosted by other professional groups such as the Institution of Electrical Engineers (who publish the excellent *Journal of Engineering Management*), The Chartered Management Institute, Chartered Institute of Personnel and Development. Many institutes post their local diaries on their website. Most institutes are very welcoming to guests from other institutes (the diversity of perspective allows both sides to develop new insights). E-mail contacts are usually given on the website to check that a meeting is open (guests welcome) or closed (strictly for members only). This part of networking is helping you build your skills and contacts for moving to more senior positions. You need to have a flexible career plan as how you wish to progress your professional life.

Practical networking

Where to network

Day-to-day events such as internal meetings provide a rich variety of networking opportunities. These opportunities should be exploited. However, your network plan above will imply the need to create new networking opportunities to extend your range and level of network contacts. Seek out new networking opportunities, the professional equivalent of speed dating. Events can include seminars, conferences, exhibitions, professional meetings, training courses (internal and external to the organization) and business school–based professional qualifications (you can learn as much from your fellow students as from the tutor on an MBA).

How to network

Applying the concepts of the service extension to the marketing mix, behaviour and appearance (People element) is important. If in doubt, check on the dress code for the event. Often professional meetings may have an informal dress code (e.g. factory visits, etc.). Behaviour should be professional and lightly assertive. Be selective and, where a contact is not likely to be relevant to your networking objectives, politely close the discussion and move on. If you are in a working situation, you may have a company business card (Physical evidence, tangible clue). However, for personal professional networking you may wish to have a personal professional business card. Good stationers or computer stores provide easy-to-use kits to print out on a colour printer. Most word-processing packages have this option (look in Tools). If you work in a consultancy or educational institution, the organization may maintain a web page profile of you. For personal professional networking, you may wish to maintain a personal web page and e-mail address; you may not wish your current employer to be aware of your job-hunting activities. Internal e-mails are not being considered private or secure in this context.

In Unit 6, 'The marketing mix: promotion', the personal selling process was outlined. Networking can be viewed as personal selling of the product to you and the outcome is a successful network relationship. Prospecting and evaluating: as stated above, you are concerned with building up relevant contacts not filling up a card index system. The 80–20 rule: only a minority of people at the event are likely to be valuable networking contacts. Be selective and, as stated above, politely close and move on if it is clear this person is not likely to be a relevant member of your network. Prepare: many conferences will post the list of delegates on the conference website. This can help you identify key prospects before you arrive. Most conference organizers will ask participants to wear their name badges. If you do not spot a prime contact, remember many events will have a participant's message board where you can post a message requesting a meeting. Networking is a lot less formal than a sales presentation, so the 'approach and presentation' is not so tightly structured. However, you should introduce yourself briefly. The objective of the conversation is to explore if a network relationship is appropriate for both parties and then to start to establish this. Active listening is

251

as important as talking in a productive conversation. Your CPD activities and reading around the subject will ensure you are able to maintain a lively and topical professional conversation. Table 9.9 lists some of the barriers to communication. Table 9.10 identifies some issues surrounding effective person-to-person communications. Good networkers develop the skills of remembering faces and names, people like to be treated as people. Closing the sale is establishing the next step to establish the network relationship. This may be a simple exchange of business cards (note for some national cultures this is a serious matter to be done with due style) or a diary appointment for a meeting and so on. Notes for follow-up can be made on the back of the card. Follow-up is important. Network relationships require maintenance; increasingly this may be electronic. The objective is not to see how big a collection of business cards you can develop. You want quality network relationships. Part of the follow-up should be filing and indexing. Physical systems are on sale for this and can be seen on many executive desks. However, your contacts are too valuable to leave in the office; you want them with you 24/7/365. Good e-mail software systems (e.g. Outlook) will include an electronic diary; card information should be added to this as part of the networking event follow-up.

Table 9.9 Barriers to good communication

Barrier	Comments
Premature judgement	People can jump to conclusions without hearing the full story
Poor listening skills	If a message conflicts with what the hearer is expecting then selective listening may occur. After the discussion of a product with a customer only the good comments may be remembered
Culture	Different cultures have different emphasis on forms of verbal and non-verbal communication
Filtering in transmission	It can appear to be an easy option to only communicate positive messages to avoid friction. Thus, a customer may comment on the positive aspects of a presentation. However, the customer may have sufficient reservations that they do not intend to buy but do not communicate these to avoid an embarrassing situation

Table 9.10 Issues for clear interpersonal communication

Issue	Comments
Nature of language	Take care to use appropriate language. If the person is not an expert do not use technical words
Be complete	Try to give the context and the complete information or the recipient may only get half the picture
Take possession	In person-to-person contacts, take possession of your opinions. Say 'I think' rather than 'It is thought that'
Use all the channels of communication	Remember that your non-verbal communications will also help. Gestures and facial expressions are all part of person-to-person communication
Be congruent	Ensure that your actions reflect your statements; for example, if you say you will follow up with an e-mail, ensure that is it is sent. Failure may damage credibility

ICT in networking

The business e-mail was discussed earlier in this unit. E-mails are possibly the favourite means of maintaining professional contacts. Costs are low (marginal cost can be zero, unlike a telephone call). Communication is normally quick. Delivery can be tracked. Large amounts of information can be delivered in attachments. However, good 'e' etiquette demands that you only send relevant e-mails. Mass e-mailing after a conference can be viewed as personal 'spamming'.

Many organizations (professional institutions, universities, colleges and research institutions) hold searchable web pages for staff interests (e.g. to find that special person for a PhD viva in a specialist subject). Company web pages can provide information on potential contacts. Trade directories are increasingly appearing in electronic format, thus they can be quickly searched for potential contacts. Professional institutions (e.g. Institution of Electrical Engineers [IEE]) are setting up virtual special interest groups (e.g. IEE with consultants), so people can network without geographical constraints. Video conferencing can vary from a simple webcam to a sophisticated video conference suite. For small, virtual meetings, a simple telephone conference call may be appropriate. The open electronic diary is very useful if people keep to house rules (e.g. certain times of the day maintained free of meetings). This maintained in software such as 'Outlook', links up with your electronic contact list (built from the processes given above). The diary can be downloaded onto your laptop or PDA so it is with you anytime, or simply accessed from the other side of the world via the Internet. There is much to commend the maintenance of one master personal electronic diary and contact list. Updating is easy. It is globally accessible. If hard copy is wanted, it can be printed. Normal good computer discipline will ensure that back-up files are held. When your company car is stolen, the loss of your laptop and 'Filofax' diary can cause as much trouble as the loss of the car.

Activity 9.8

You have been approached by a younger colleague who is attending a conference for the first time. Write notes on what preparation the person should do for effective networking at this event.

Database management

The 'bits and bytes' of database management should be left to the computer experts. Key issues to be assured of are data security (both unauthorized access and loss/corruption) and ease of access. With ever-increasing data protection regulation, managers must ensure that both the database and the specific application are legal (e.g. it may not be possible, in certain circumstances, to use a database constructed for one purpose for another).

A typical database on customers might contain the following:

- o *Name* – note issues such as formal names and 'known' name: a person christened Robert may be known in the working context as Bob. On an airline ticket the passport name will be required; in other cases it may be more appropriate to use Bob.
- o *Contact Information* – addresses, these may be segmented so they can be searched (e.g. keeping city as a specific field, telephone(s), fax, e-mail).
- o Role/occupation
- o *Profile information* – as appropriate (e.g. age, etc., for a consumer database, role for a B2B database).
- o *Purchase records* – (e.g. value of purchases, type of purchases – from sales records).
- o *Media profile* – plus past responses to promotions.

253

There are two key aspects of database management (from the marketer's specific point of view) and they are related to the issue of whether we get the message to all the right people (high percentage of cover) with minimum wastage. First, this implies that the database is clean (e.g. dead addresses eliminated) and has the selection criteria we may need to build into the structure (e.g. make the address searchable not just a character 'string'). The second is that when we present the information to the person, the communication is relevant and persuasive. This profile of interests and past purchases allows us to tailor the message.

As with most systems, when you use consultants and everyone is enthusiastic about a new project, constructing a new database can seem hard work but, with care, is usually done well. The problem is one of continual maintenance and tracking of address changes and the like. People change address and jobs every few years and it is typical to find that 20–50 per cent of entries will need amending each year. A 'dirty' database is a waste of money and damages the reputation of the organization.

Activity 9.9

In an earlier activity, we considered a careers fair exhibition. If you were the marketing manager for a university manning a stand aimed at sixth-form students just starting their studies, what database might you consider for follow-up? This is a relationship-marketing situation. The university wants to start to build a relationship so that when these students come to make their university selection, they feel that there is only one university that cares for them.

Question 9.1

What is the range of communications that a marketer may use in the management of a conference? What are the strengths and weakness of each form of communication?

Summary

In this unit we have

o Reviewed the general communications model for marketing communication and extended the framework to cover day-to-day written communications of the professional marketer.
o Explored ways in which communications integrate content from various directions (marketing theory, macroenvironment/microenvironment, company objectives) must be integrated to provide the substance within the communications. As the Americans might say, 'Where is the beef?' A format without content is like a bun without content, it is not a burger meal.
o Considered some of the main written communications formats used by a professional marketer, including letters, e-mails, memos, reports, plans and press releases.
o Noted the special needs for academic project reports (e.g. CIM project assignments).
o Discussed the phases of project planning and management and the use of charts.
o Explored how the general framework of project management can be adapted to the planning and execution of successful marketing events.
o Discussed the phases of the negotiation process.

o   Considered the need to manage yourself before being able to manage your manager.
o   Considered strategies for managing your manager.
o   Reviewed networking and the role ICT may play in successful networking.
o   Considered how to manage a typical marketing database.

The December 2005 exam 'The Urban Culture Festival 2006' required the following formats and styles: report, event plan and letter. The June 2006 exam 'SMS Cars Ltd.' required formats including briefing paper, press release, letter and report. The content of a good answer integrates appropriate elements from all earlier units into the required answer format.

Specimen answers are outlined on the CIM website (www.cim.co.uk).

Further study

Cameron, S. (2004) The MBA Handbook – Study Skills for Postgraduate Management Study, 5th edition, FT Prentice Hall.

Martin, P., and Tate, K. (2001) *Getting Started in Project Management*, John Wiley.

Parker, C., and Stone, B. (2002) *Developing Management Skills for Leadership*, Prentice Hall.

Tayeb, M.H. (1996) *The Management of a Multicultural Workforce*, Wiley.

As an integrative module, you should also review the other coursebooks at this level

Cheeseman, A., and Jones, M. (2007) *CIM Coursebook – Customer Communications in Marketing*, Butterworth-Heinemann.

Lancaster, G., and Withey, F. (2007) *CIM Coursebook – Marketing Fundamentals*, Butterworth-Heinemann.

Oldroyd, M. (2007) *CIM Coursebook – Marketing Environment*, Butterworth-Heinemann.

Hints and tips

In particular, this unit requires you to move from reading to developing skills. You do this in part by not only practising yourself but also observing how others work; learn from best practice.

A significant number of the CIM exam papers pose questions for you to either demonstrate that you understand these skills issues (e.g. in December 2005, Question 5(b) 'Explain how you could use networking and personal selling skills to attract and retain sponsors for this and future Urban Culture Festivals.') or use them (e.g. in June 2006, Question 2(a) 'Write a letter to current and potential customers inviting them to attend the launch event. Include a method of reply to confirm their attendance.').

Bibliography

Belbin, R. (2003) *Management Teams: Why They Succeed or Fail*, Butterworth-Heinemann.

Hollensen, R. (2002) *Marketing Management – A Relationship Approach*, Prentice Hall.

Schneider, S.C., and Barsoux, J.-L. (2002) *Managing Across Cultures*, 2nd edition, FT Prentice Hall.

Tayeb, M.H. (1996) *The Management of a Multicultural Workforce*, Wiley.

budgets and schedules

By the end of this unit, you will be able to

o Prepare a schedule for a marketing activity.

o Prepare a budget.

o Complete a breakeven analysis.

o Understand the difference between fixed and variable costs.

o Understand the role of budgeting in the evaluation of marketing opportunities and activities.

Syllabus references

2.6 Explain how the organization fits into a supply chain and works with distribution channels.

3.2 Identify alternative and innovative approaches to a variety of marketing arenas and explain criteria for meeting business objectives.

3.4 Explain how marketing makes use of planning techniques: objective setting; and coordinating, measuring and evaluating results to support the organization.

4.1 Select media to be used based on appropriate criteria for assessing media opportunities, and recommend a media schedule.

4.2 Evaluate promotional activities and opportunities including sales promotion, PR and collaborative programmes.

4.4 Analyse the impact of pricing decisions and the role of price within the marketing mix.

4.5 Describe the current distribution channels for an organization and evaluate new opportunities.

4.6 Describe how organizations monitor product trends.

5.1 Demonstrate an ability to manipulate numbers in a marketing context.

5.2 Explain the process used for setting a budget and apportioning fixed and overhead costs.

5.3 Explain how organizations assess the viability of opportunities, marketing initiatives and projects.

5.4 Prepare, present and justify a budget as the basis for a decision on a marketing promotion.

5.5 Make recommendations on alternative courses of action.

5.6 Examine the correlation between marketing mix decisions and results.

5.7 Evaluate the cost-effectiveness of a marketing budget, including a review of suppliers and activities.

Key definitions

Balanced scorecard – A framework proposed by Kaplin and Norton that long-term business success requires a balance between financial perspectives, internal business perspectives, innovation and learning perspectives and customer perspective.

Breakeven chart – A chart where fixed costs, variable costs, total costs and sales income are plotted against sales volume. The point at which there is no loss/profit (zero loss/profit) is the breakeven point. The figure can also be calculated directly from the information contained in an appropriate spreadsheet.

Contribution – The amount of cash generated from sales when variable costs have been taken into account (Sales price per unit-Direct variable costs per unit).

Contribution chart – An alternative presentation of the breakeven chart where variable costs, total costs and sales income are plotted against sales volume. The point at which there is no loss/profit (zero loss/profit) is the breakeven point. The figure can also be calculated directly from the information contained in an appropriate spreadsheet.

Cost/volume chart – An alternative presentation of the breakeven information where profit is plotted against sales volume. The point at which there is no loss/profit (zero loss/profit) is the breakeven point. The figure can also be calculated directly from the information contained in an appropriate spreadsheet.

Fixed costs – Costs that do not vary with the sales volume (e.g. rent on a shop).

Sales revenue – The total cash income from sales (price per unit × selling price per unit).

Variable costs – The direct costs to produce one additional unit of product/service.

Study Guide

Budgets and schedules are normally prepared on computers. When working through this unit check out how you can perform these activities with the particular software that is available to you. High marks are possible with numerical questions so practise these with the specimen examination papers.

Schedules

In looking at project management in Unit 9, we looked at a Gantt chart, which scheduled all the activities for a project. This gives an order of actions to be taken. A typical project is the launch of a product. In such a situation, marketing communications are key, and mechanical scheduling does not give you the media mix or schedule to use. This involves a set of marketing communications decisions. Consider the situation facing a company launching a new food or drink product (e.g. an organic premium ice cream, to be sold to the consumer market and upmarket restaurants and hotels). A typical communications launch strategy might look as shown in Figure 10.1.

A typical outline stakeholder list in this situation might include internal, customers (segmented, including as appropriate B2B and B2C), suppliers (both for product and for marketing, e.g. printing, advertising agency), channels, media, pressure groups (organic lobby) and regulatory (trading standards for labelling, Advertising Standards Authority for claims).

Activity	Pre-launch			Launch		Normal trading			★	Normal trading		
B2B Marketing 'on trade'												
Personal selling												
Trade press												
Push strategy consumer market												
Personal selling												
Advertising in trade magazines												
Promotional price to outlets*												
Pull strategy consumer market												
Advertising												
TV												
Radio												
Press												
Posters and so on												
Point of sale												
Sales promotion*												
PR and Publicity												
Website												

Figure 10.1 Communications schedule for a typical launch

B2B market segment

Many restaurants and hotels are members of large chains and do not make purchase decisions for menus at a local level. For example, the management of the local branch of McDonalds do not run to the supermarket each morning to get the day's supply of burgers. Purchase decisions are made centrally and the major communications effort would be personal selling. There is also a market segment for local independent restaurants and hotels. They buy their supplies from local 'cash & carry' wholesalers who form part of the supply chain to this market segment.

To attack this market a push-and-pull strategy would be needed: personal selling to push the product into the 'cash & carry' outlets and advertising in the trade press as the pull element. Personal selling will often precede the actual launch. The trade press advertising might continue into the launch period for small independent outlets.

B2C market segment

In general, for FMCG products, brand manufacturers will use a concurrent push-and-pull strategy. The push strategy would parallel that for the B2B sector, in this case with personal selling to the supermarkets. The small local independent convenience store (corner shop) may well buy its supplies from the same 'cash & carry' outlets as used by the local hotels and restaurants, so the activity above will also cover this aspect of the plan. However, there are different trade magazines for retail outlets, and advertising in these might be beneficial. As above, the activity will take place prior and during the launch. Often there may be a trade promotion to get outlets to take up the product.

During the launch period the pull strategy would involve advertising through selected media, a generalized selection is given in Figure 10.1. Most of these actions involve costs that do not vary with the level of sales. The advertising will be booked and contracts agreed before any product is actually sold. Sales promotion is marked with a '*' to remind us that some sales promotion costs can vary with sales volume (e.g. money-off coupon). The website pages would continue to provide a constant stream of information to customers and other stakeholders (e.g. pressure groups who might want details on just how organic the product is). The website might be segmented with special pages for the B2B segment or there might be a separate site for B2B customers. We note the special situation for PR. There will often be a burst of PR activity prior to and during the launch. There always needs to be a watching PR brief for the product (e.g. the potential for a disaster, such as a general product recall). From time to time, there may be a flurry of communications activity, indicated in Figure 10.1 by the period headed by a star; for this product, it might be special times of the year; for example, in Europe, Christmas and the early summer start of the barbecue season might be appropriate times for a burst of communications activity. Every product and marketing segment will have special needs and operate in particular conditions. Therefore, the generalized outline given here needs to be tailored to fit every individual product and market circumstance. More consideration of communications mix issues is given in Unit 6.

Insight

Many FMCG products for the B2C market may also have the potential to have a B2B segment as well. We have considered the situation for food and drink products above. For example, with hair care products, the salon market is a profitable sector. Apart from being a profitable sector in its 'own right', this sector can be integrated into the overall strategy. Upmarket hair salons are used by people who influence trends (they may be regarded in this context as the innovators and early adopters). 'As used by stars and salons' can be a positioning lever for the B2C market.

Case study

'Lake View Organic Farms' expansion into 'New Town'

'Lake View Organic Farms' have decided to add 'New Town' to their direct delivery area. They will recruit a new member of staff and hire an additional delivery vehicle. They intend to deliver to domestic customers, restaurants and hotels. A communications schedule for this situation might look as in Figure 10.2.

Activity	Pre-launch			Launch			Normal trading		
B2B Marketing 'on trade'									
Personal selling									
Pull strategy consumer market									
Advertising									
Leaflet distribution									
Press									
Posters									
PR and Publicity									
Website									

Figure 10.2 Communications schedule for Lake View Organic Farms new delivery area

The stakeholder list in this situation would include internal (including the new member of staff), customers (B2B: restaurants and hotels and B2C: possibly segmented on a geo-demographic basis), suppliers (growers and marketing), media and local pressure groups. We are selling direct, so there is no channel involvement. We are selling an existing product range, so there should be no new regulatory issues.

B2B: personal selling during the pre-launch period.

B2C: burst of advertising in the 2 weeks before the launch and in the 4 weeks of the launch. Leaflet distribution to homes in target segment (pre-launch), press advertising in food page of local weekly newspaper, limited posters in selected organic food shops. Two press releases in the first of the two weeks before the launch, the second during the first week of the launch, holding brief for problems (potential problem issues can come at any time, e.g. press story about maggot in organic apples). Website: new page for the new route (e.g. 'introducing Jill who will be your delivery person'), internal pages to inform suppliers and internal staff of continued growth.

Aspects of marketing communications and media plans regularly feature in the CIM exams. In December 2005, the 'The Urban Culture Festival' case study: Question 3 'Describe the advantages and disadvantages of advertising using the following media specifically in the context of the Urban Culture Festival 2006: television, radio, cinema, magazines and other alternative media (please specify).' Additional cover of media issues is given in Unit 6.

Budgets

In the schedule given in Figure 10.2 and in the analysis of projects (with Gantt charts), many activities have costs. If, instead of just blocking out the activities, we insert the projected cost of the activity for the period, we can construct a budget. Budgets are useful to marketers as they aid planning, help coordinate activity (as with Gantt charts), communicate management decisions, motivate staff and managers, help evaluate the performance of staff and, with analysis of deviations from budget, provide a mechanism to aid control (control of marketing plans is also covered in Unit 11.

Budgets are now developed in spreadsheet packages such as Excel. The schematic structure of a typical product launch budget is given in Figure 10.3. In the time-line, there are three activities/expense phases: pre-launch, launch and steady state. In the pre-launch phase, there are the costs of developing the product (e.g. R&D, market research, etc.) and other elements of the mix (e.g. promotion/marketing communication – creative work for advertising; and people – training of field sales staff). There will also be a need to build up the launch stock and fill the supply chain for the launch (in this simple model actual costs of manufacture are taken into the body of the table, but in real life some of these costs may have to be paid a little earlier). During this period there may be a burst of 'launch' marketing communication, and activities such as training continues (this is indicated in the figure by the block 'launch costs').

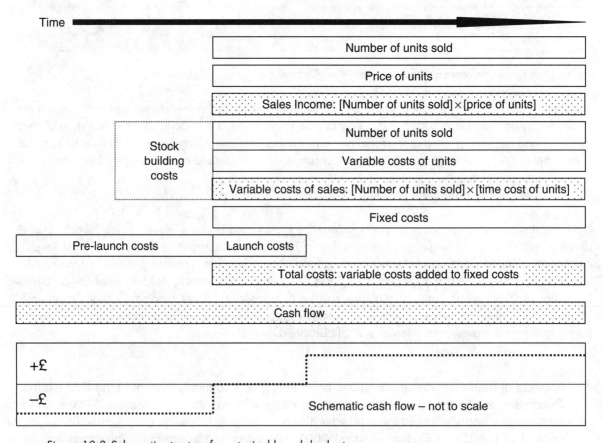

Figure 10.3 Schematic structure for a typical launch budget

In the main body, the normal trading conditions are established after a (hopefully!) successful launch. The sales revenue is calculated from estimates of the number of units to be sold and estimates of the price to be paid by the customer for these units. The same unit volume estimate multiplied by the variable costs estimated for each unit (e.g. raw materials and manufacturing costs) provides the variable costs of sales. Fixed/non-variable costs are costs that do not vary with the volume of units manufactured and sold (e.g. advertising costs are fixed by the media plan/budget and do not change if we sell more or less than planned). The fixed costs added to the variable costs give us the final estimate of all costs. Subtracting the total costs from the sales revenue gives us the final estimate of cash flow. In the pre-launch phase, we have no sales and expenses. The cash flow is negative; we are investing money in the product. During the launch, the launch costs (e.g. initial burst of advertising) depress the profits in this period and the cash flow may even be negative. We are still investing in the product. After the initial launch period the product enters normal trading where typical profits should be earned and the cash flow is positive.

Figure 10.4 gives a simple spreadsheet for the calculations for this straightforward launch situation. The figures indicated '#####' are estimates to be made by the management team constructing the budget. The figures indicated '^^^^^^' are figures calculated from these estimates. The spreadsheet formulae to do these calculations are shown in the comment column.

	Cash flow element	Pre launch Week 1	....	Launch	....	Steady state	....	Comment
	Sales income							
1	Sales volume in units			#####	#####	#####	#####	
2	Selling price			#####	#####	#####	#####	
3	**Sales income**			^^^^^	^^^^^	^^^^^	^^^^^	(line 1 × line 2)
	Variable costs							
4	Sales volume in units			#####	#####	#####	#####	Same as line 1
5	Variable cost of unit			#####	#####	#####	#####	
6	**Variable costs**			^^^^^	^^^^^	^^^^^	^^^^^	(line 4 × line 5)
	Fixed/non-variable costs							
7	Stock building		#####					
8	Pre-launch costs	#####	#####					
9	Launch costs			#####	#####			
10	Fixed costs			#####	#####	#####	#####	
11	**Non-variable expenses**	^^^^^	^^^^^	^^^^^	^^^^^	^^^^^	^^^^^	Lines from 7 to 10 added together
12	**Total costs**	^^^^^	^^^^^	^^^^^	^^^^^	^^^^^	^^^^^	Line 6 added to line 11
13	**Cash flow**	^^^^^	^^^^^	^^^^^	^^^^^	^^^^^	^^^^^	Line 12 − line 3 (income − total expenses)

#####	Estimated figure
^^^^^	Calculated figure

Figure 10.4 Schematic summary spreadsheet for a typical launch budget

Life is a little more complicated than indicated in Figures 10.3 and 10.4. These represent the type of summary consolidated budget that you might see for a launch. However, each estimate may have a supporting spreadsheet to calculate the estimate. Figure 10.5 shows this cascade of supporting spreadsheets getting deeper and deeper into the detailed costs.

Level 1 detail – non-variable/fixed costs – might include Rent, staff, insurance and communications.

Level 1 detail – communications – might include PR, publicity, sponsorship, exhibitions and advertising. Note a little care is needed here, as some communications are variable to the number of units sold (e.g. money-off offer on a pack for a given period). Unit 6 Promotion gives a starting point for options.

Level 2 detail – advertising – might include TV, radio, website, posters and press. Unit 6 gives some options as a starting point.

Level 3 detail – press advertising – might include – newspapers and magazines. Unit 6 gives some options as a starting point.

Level 4 detail – magazines – specific magazine titles.

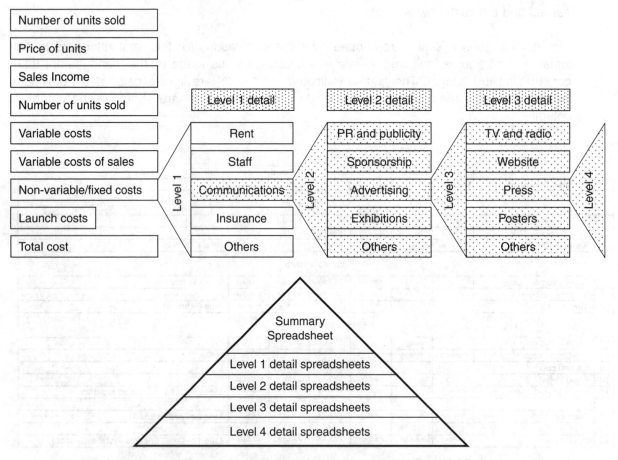

Figure 10.5 Cascade of more detailed budgets with focus on communications costs

The stages of the budgeting process include the following:

- ○ Communication details of budget policy and procedures (e.g. agreed frameworks for fixed cost allocation).
- ○ Assigning responsibility for preparing the individual budgets, the cascade of more detailed budgets given in Figure 10.5. Responsibility also has to be assigned for coordination of activities (e.g. provision of information) and consolidation of detailed budgets to give the overall budget.
- ○ A process of negotiation (e.g. to reduce costs) to achieve budgets, consistent with the organization's overall business objectives.
- ○ Final coordination and review.
- ○ Senior management approval of budgets.
- ○ Continual review of budgets to reflect significant changes in the conditions (e.g. during 2005 the increases in fuel costs had a major impact on many organizations' budgets).
- ○ Monitoring and control. Evaluation of actual performance against budget with analysis of reasons for any deviations from budget (e.g. lower sales, as a result of competitor activity, might indicate more marketing communications, such as sales promotion, might be needed). Part of the 'feedback and control' system of the marketing plan (Unit 11).

Case study

'Lake View Organic Farms' expansion into 'New Town'

The management have estimated that they will gain 80 business accounts and 1300 domestic accounts. For simplicity, it is assumed that the range is simple: catering boxes (cost £30 and sales value £50) and consumer boxes (cost £3 and sales value £5). The pre-launch costs are estimated to cover preparation of advertisements, printing of leaflets, modification of web pages and recruitment and training of new members of staff and so on. Estimates are given in the spreadsheet. Wages, transport costs (hire and fuel) and allocated overheads are estimated to be £1500. The press advertisement each week will cost £500 at first then drop to £250 and zero once the round is established. The leaflets will cost £1500 to print and distribute over the 2 weeks, the posters will cost £100 for the few sites selected. Each press release will cost £300 to produce, send out and follow up. The allocated expense for the PR holding brief is £50. Additional work to the website is estimated to cost £500 to update and an allocation of £100 after. It is assumed that there will be a build of sales over the launch to 100 per cent over the 4 weeks (estimates in spreadsheet). The budget might look as given in Figure 10.6.

| Cash flow element | Pre launch | | | | Launch | | | | | | Comment |
	W1	W2	W3	W4	W5	W6	W7	W8	W9		
Sales										3	
B2B sales										4	
Sales volume boxes					50	60	70	75	80	5	*Management estimates*
Selling price a B2B box					50	50	50	50	50	6	*Management estimates*
Sales income	0	0	0	0	2500	3000	3500	3750	4000	7	*Line 5 × line 6*
B2C sales										8	
Sales volume in units					1000	1100	1200	1250	1300	9	*Management estimates*
Selling price a B2C box					5	5	5	5	5	10	*Management estimates*
Sales income	0	0	0	0	5000	5500	6000	6250	6500	11	*Line 9 × line 10*
Total sales income	0	0	0	0	7500	8500	9500	10000	10500	12	*Line 7 + line 11*
										13	
Variable cost of sales										14	
B2B sales costs										15	
Sales volume in boxes					50	60	70	75	80	16	*Same as line 5*
Cost price a B2B box					30	30	30	30	30	17	*Management estimates*
Costs	0	0	0	0	1500	1800	2100	2250	2400	18	*Line 16 × line 17*
B2C sales costs										19	
Sales volume in units					1000	1100	1200	1250	1300	20	*Same as line 9*
Cost price a B2C box					3	3	3	3	3	21	*Management estimates*
Costs	0	0	0	0	3000	3300	3600	3750	3900	22	*Line 20 × line 21*
Total variable costs	0	0	0	0	4500	5100	5700	6000	6300	23	*Line 18 + line 22*
										24	
Non variable expenses										25	
B2B personal selling	500	500	500	500	250	250	0	0	0	26	*Management estimates*
B2C Advertising										27	
Leaflet	750	750								28	*Management estimates*
Press			500	500	500	250	250			29	*Management estimates*
Posters			100	100	100	100	100	100	100	30	*Management estimates*
PR and Publicity			300	300	300	50	50	50	50	31	*Management estimates*
Website	500	100	100	100	100	100	100	100	100	32	*Management estimates*
Other non variable costs	250	250	750	750	1500	1500	1500	1500	1500	33	*Management estimates*
										34	
Total non variable costs	2000	1600	2250	2250	2750	2250	2000	1750	1750	35	*Sum line 26 + lines 28 to 33*
										36	
Total Costs	2000	1600	2250	2250	7250	7350	7700	7750	8050	37	*Line 35 + line 23*
										38	
Cash flow	−2000	−1600	−2250	−2250	250	1150	1800	2250	2450	39	*Line 12 − line 37*

Figure 10.6 Outline spreadsheet for start-up situation for Lake View Organic Farms new delivery area

Activity 10.1

Prepare an outline communications schedule and budget for the 'Film Festival' ('The Urban Culture Festival 2006', December 2005).

Breakeven analysis

For many marketing situations, breakeven analysis is useful. Typical situations include sales volumes for products, attendance at a theatre and sales volumes from an Internet site. Here we will consider the simple situation of a product with fixed and variable costs. Figure 10.7 gives the cash flows for fixed (non-variable) costs, variable costs, total costs and sales income. The lower triangle indicates the zone of loss and the upper triangle indicates the zone of profit. The calculations needed for the breakeven analysis are indicated in Figure 10.7. The number of units where the operation makes neither a loss nor a profit is called the 'breakeven' point. If the breakeven point is close to the production capacity for a product (seat capacity for a theatre), this may be a cause for concern as any modest drop from target capacity may take the organization into a loss-making situation.

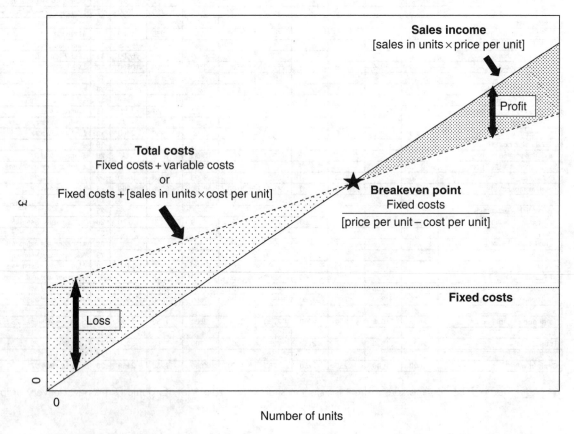

Figure 10.7 Schematic breakeven analysis

Alternative presentations of this data are possible. Figure 10.8 shows a contribution chart. The lower line is now the variable costs. To this is added the fixed expenses. This gives a higher parallel line (identical to Figure 10.7 of total costs. This again gives us the breakeven point. A third type of presentation of the data is shown in Figure 10.9. A slightly more complicated equation shows how the loss/profit changes with volume. This is the profit–volume presentation. Where there is neither a profit nor a loss (zero profit/loss), this is again the breakeven point. All these calculations are easy to set up on a spreadsheet such as Excel. Practise some examples as calculations of this nature can occur in the exam situation.

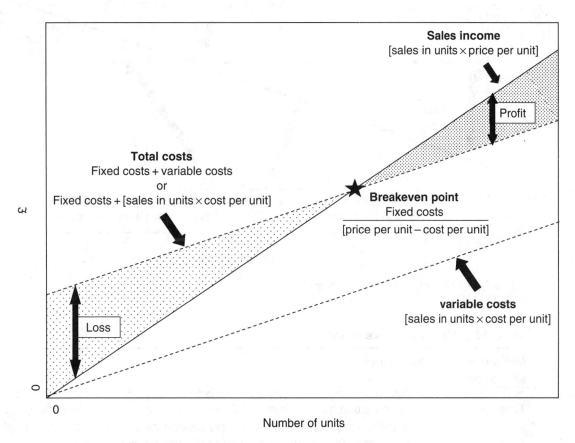

Figure 10.8 Schematic contribution chart

Fixed (non-variable) costs

As discussed in earlier parts of this unit, some costs do not vary with the number of units sold. The rent on a shop does not change with sales volumes. In drawing up a budget for a given product, it may be necessary to allocate fixed costs. The product may be manufactured along with a range of other products in a single factory with only one rent bill. In marketing communications, a whole product range may be supported by a single company website. The greatest possible care must be taken in deciding the model used to allocate fixed costs. They feed into the pricing marketing decision. Feeding the wrong type of estimate will give the wrong price (more consideration of this impact on pricing decisions is given in Unit 4. In a shop situation, it may be reasonable to allocate the fixed costs for a product group as a percentage of the total cost of the shop, based on the percentage area occupied by the product group. For an advertising agency, the fixed costs might be allocated to a given department on a similar percentage basis but in this case based on staff numbers. Some possibilities are given in the Table 10.1.

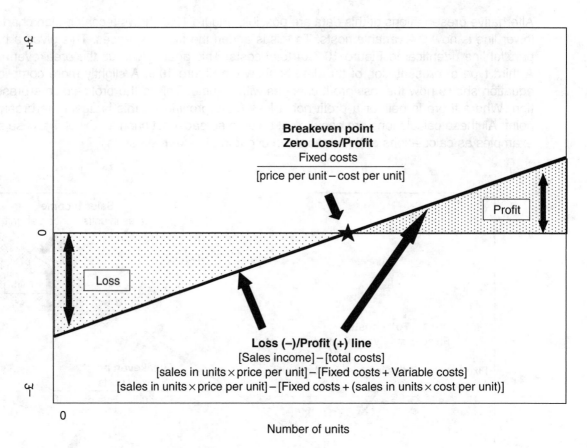

Breakeven point
Zero Loss/Profit
Fixed costs
[price per unit − cost per unit]

Profit

Loss

Loss (−)/Profit (+) line
[Sales income] − [total costs]
[sales in units × price per unit] − [Fixed costs + Variable costs]
[sales in units × price per unit] − [Fixed costs + (sales in units × cost per unit)]

Number of units

Figure 10.9 Schematic profit–volume graph

Table 10.1 Allocation of fixed costs

Method of allocation	Comments
Time	Machine time in manufacture, R&D hours for development, PR activity in hours committed to project. Person's costs divided by the hours available to give an hourly rate. Then hours used charged to the project
Space	Exhibition stand space, shop sales by department. Total costs divided by available space gives the cost for unit of space in the given period. Space occupied multiplied by the this unit area cost gives the cost allocation for the period
Ratio	Staff overheads (e.g. personal administration) might be split according to the number of staff in the various departments

Budgets in decision-making

Budgets are widely used in management and marketing decision-making. The spreadsheet provides a financial model for the situation under consideration. If the budget indicates that the project will run at a loss, the decision may be not to run with the new product or service. The decision may be that some alternative framework of approaching the situation may be required. A typical situation facing UK retailers is finding UK manufacturing costs too high and therefore changing suppliers. So, they move to suppliers that operate in a part of the world where manufacturing costs are much lower (e.g. China). The budget allows the analysis of cost drivers and highlights where to look for cost reductions. The budget also indicates the profit sources and may direct marketing actions. For UK supermarkets, the higher margins on non-food products (e.g. personal care and fashion) have driven an expansion into these product areas and added others (e.g. books and DVDs). Budgets can help a company decide on the right product range and depth to have in the marketplace (product issues are covered in more depth in Unit 4. Alternative frameworks of distribution can be explored. Should the company employ its own staff or sell through agents? Two parallel budgets can be constructed for the two scenarios and the financial issues considered. However, life is not that simple. Broader issues such as impact on brand value need to be considered. Budgets are an important facet of marketing decision-making (make a loss too often and you are out of business), but a balanced view of issues needs to be taken in tailoring the mix (covered in Units 3–7). Moreover, a balanced view has to be taken about the present and the future. Spend too much on staff development this year and you may have financial problems this year. Spend too little on staff development and you may have operational problems next year. Product portfolio analysis gives us the same message. Have too many question marks and rising stars and you will have financial problems now. Have none to replace your cash cows as they become dead dogs and you will have problems next year (Unit 1). Table 10.2 gives some typical issues facing a marketer.

Table 10.2 Selected example marketing mix budgeting decisions

Decision	Examples and Comments
Product	New product development. Will sales generate enough profit to justify the development costs or would the money be better spent on advertising? See Unit 3 for more on Product issues
Price	Payment framework. Would the costs of arranging finance for customers be recovered? See Unit 4 for more on price issues
Place	Channels. Would a new outlet generate enough revenue to cover the additional costs? See Unit 5 for more on place issues
Promotion–communication mix	Decisions about distribution around the mix. Would a change from personal selling to Internet trading be appropriate for an insurance company?
Promotion–advertising–media mix	How should spending be directed? Would a move from TV to direct database marketing for financial services be appropriate?
Promotion–advertising–media mix–titles	For a given media just what spending pattern would we adopt? Costs per 1000 are not the whole story. The quality of the hits is also important? For an investment product, the higher cost per 1000 of the *Financial Times* might be well justified over a more mass circulation paper. See Unit 6 for more on promotion issues
People, physical evidence and process	Staff appearance. Would a new uniform for front-line staff be a justified cost?
Logistics	Would a new distribution contractor be better than one that costs more but appears to offer better service?

Kaplan and Norton suggested an approach to maintaining a balance called the 'Balanced scorecard'. The four areas to balance are as follows:

o *Financial perspective* – Return on capital, cash flow, profit growth and so on.
o *Internal business perspective* – Manufacturing process and costs, quality, time to market and so on.
o *Innovation and learning perspective* – New product development (maintenance of balanced portfolio), continuous improvement (e.g. staff development) and so on.
o *Customer perspective* – Service/product performance, complaints, perceived brand value and so on.

Setting the marketing budget

Table 10.3 gives a summary of methods used by organizations to set marketing budgets. The objective and task method has much to commend it on the basis that this takes account of changing marketing environments (e.g. new competition) and changing objectives (e.g. move into a new market sector). However, all the methods listed are used, despite their potential limitations. The reality of marketing life is to stretch an inadequate budget as far as possible.

Table 10.3 Some common approaches to setting marketing budgets

Method	Comments
Historical	Spend the same as last year. Advantage: simple. Disadvantage: takes no account of changed conditions
Percentage of sales	Spend some fixed percentage on sales volume projected (can use an existing percentage or a changed one). Advantage: simple. Disadvantage: takes limited account of changed conditions
As much/little as possible	Power struggle between finance and marketing. Advantage: none. Disadvantage: complex, time-consuming and takes no account of market conditions
What the competition spends	Match the competition. Can be percentage-based (same percentage as the competition) or actual sums of money spent. Advantage: does take account of competition. Disadvantage: the competing organizations may have very differing marketing contexts

Question 10.1

'Urban Culture Festival' charity concert

The organizing committee for 'Urban Culture Festival 2006' have decided to stage a classical concert to raise some money for local charities. The cost of marketing communications, hire of the theatre and payment to the performers is estimated to be £15 000. The theatre's capacity is 850 people. It is proposed to charge £22 a ticket. What is the breakeven number of tickets to be sold? One of the committee members considers that the price should be set on the basis of a 50 per cent breakeven number. What price would this require?

Question 10.2

'Urban Culture Festival 2006' (December 2005)

'Sprit of the Dance' silver model

To celebrate the dance festival the committee has commissioned an original sculpture 'Spirit of the Dance'. As an additional source of funds to support the events the committee has decided to have miniature replicas of the sculpture made in silver as a limited edition. The preliminary estimates are selling price £250, cost of packaging, insurance and postage £24, labour cost of manufacture £25, cost of silver per model £170 (at current silver prices) and a set-up cost of £3950 (fee to the artist and manufacturer of the mould).

o   Calculate the number of models that have to be sold to breakeven.
o   If it was decided that a breakeven number of 100 models was appropriate, what would the price have to be?

Some of the committee think that the breakeven number of 100 is about right but the projected price is too high. One solution to be investigated is a reduction in costs. Sometimes when costs rise it may force the price over a critical psychological break such as 'over £1.00' – '£0.99' is perceived to be a 'lot cheaper' – less than a pound). One option in this case is to reduce the price by reducing the size of the product (e.g. a bar of chocolate) or reducing the number of units in a pack (e.g. cigarettes reduce from 20 a pack to 17 a pack). One solution would be to make the model of the 'Spirit of the Dance' slightly smaller and thus use less silver.

o   If the price was to be held at £250 and the breakeven number was to be 100, how much smaller would the model have to be in percentage terms?

Use a calculator not a computer spreadsheet programme for the calculations (you will not have a computer in the exam).

Activity 10.2

In Question 2, you used a calculator. This is important, as in the exam you will not have a laptop with spreadsheets to help you. In real life, you would set up a spreadsheet on your computer. In a review meeting, you can open up your spreadsheet model. As people make suggestions, you can instantly enter the 'What-if?' numbers (e.g. price increase) and the impact on the project can immediately be fed back into the group discussion. Set up a spreadsheet model and evaluate a set of 'What if?' questions. As an example, the price of gold (2006) is at a high and still rising. Metals such as silver, gold and platinum have somewhat volatile commodity prices. What would the impact be of a price increase of +10 per cent and –10 per cent of silver?

Presenting numbers

Many people do not 'see' numbers. A spreadsheet is just a jumble of numbers with no meaning. For presentations and reports, a graphical representation is useful. Table 10.4 gives some sales figures for 'Lake View Organic Farms'. Three typical types of representation are shown in Figure 10.10a–c. The sales figures are shown as a bar chart and graph. The final split of sales is shown as a pie chart. The graphical presentations can be generated automatically from normal spreadsheet packages such as Excel.

Table 10.4 Sales for Lake View Organic Farms

Period	Large box £	Medium box £	Small box £	Total £
1	20 000	30 500	15 000	65 500
2	21 000	29 500	15 500	66 000
3	20 500	32 000	16 000	68 500
4	22 000	31 500	17 000	70 500
5	21 500	30 500	16 500	68 500
6	23 000	29 500	17 500	70 000
Total	128 000	183 500	97 500	

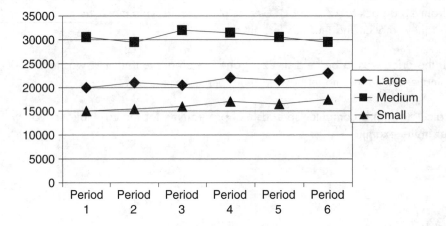

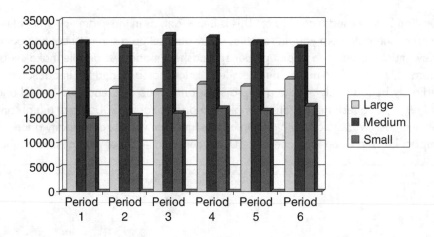

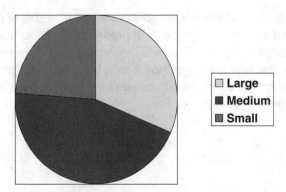

Figure 10.10 (a) Sales as a graph. (b) Sales as a bar chart. (c) Total sales as a pie chart

Question 10.3

In December 2005, 'The Urban Culture Festival 2006' Question 3 was 'Describe the advantages of advertising using the following media specifically in the context of the Urban Culture Festival 2006: television, radio, cinema, magazines, other alternative media [please specify].' An alternative question might have been 'Prepare a media plan for the 'Urban Culture Festival 2006' within its immediate geographical area, within a budget of £20 000. Justify your decisions regarding your media choice.'.

Summary

In this unit we have

o Considered the scheduling process.
o Reviewed the budgeting process.
o Considered the issues in breakeven analysis.
o Discussed the allocation of fixed costs and the difference between fixed and variable costs.
o Considered the role of budgeting in the evaluation of marketing opportunities.
o Reviewed the presentation of numerical information.

Further study

Drury, C. (2006) *Management Accounting for Business Decisions*, 3rd edition, Thomson Learning.

Hints and tips

Budgeting and breakeven calculations need practice. So, review the numerical questions in the specimen papers and check that you understand the necessary calculation approaches.

Bibliography

Dibb, S., Simkin, L., Pride, W. and Ferrell, O. (2006) *Marketing Concepts and Strategies*, 5th European edition, Houghton Mifflin.

unit 11

bringing it all together: the marketing plan

Learning objectives

After your study of this unit, you will be able to

o Appreciate that plans are not written in one go, but are developed from basic outlines with continual refinement. Further research provides the required information to fill in the gaps and working assumptions.

o Understand that organizations do not have just one grand plan, but a whole family of interlocking plans which increase in detail the closer they get to the implementation of all the various objectives and development of the various operations.

o Appreciate the difference between missions, aims and objectives and the role they play in shaping marketing plans.

o Understand the process of evaluating the marketing environment and situation analysis: where is the organization?

o Understand that segmentation variables and strategies need to be continually reappraised.

o Appreciate the need for formulating strategic alternatives and the selection of appropriate options.

o Appreciate that, after formulating the overall SMART objectives, it is necessary to formulate more detailed operational objectives, for example for all the individual elements of the marketing mix.

o Understand that to formulate outline plans, working assumptions need to be made. These highlight to the Marketer the information gaps that need to be researched.

o Appreciate the need for control and feedback systems for the management of marketing plans.

o Understand the need for some contingency reserves and strategies to be built into plans that will have to operate in an uncertain trading environment.

275

Syllabus references

2.1 Describe the structure and roles of the marketing function within the organization.

3.2 Identify alternative and innovative approaches to a variety of marketing arenas and explain criteria for meeting business objectives.

3.4 Explain how marketing makes use of planning techniques: objective setting; and co-ordinating, measuring and evaluating results to support the organization.

4.7 Explain the importance of the extended marketing mix: how process, physical aspects and people affect customer choice.

5.3 Explain how organizations assess the viability of opportunities, marketing initiatives and projects.

5.5 Make recommendations on alternative courses of action.

5.6 Examine the correlation between marketing mix decisions and results.

Key definitions

Nine-cell matrix – A flexible model for portfolio analysis focusing on two issues, market attraction and competitive advantage.

SMART – Framework for objectives: they should be Specific, Measurable, Aspirational, Realistic and Time bound.

Study Guide

As we have said throughout this text, marketing is like music; it is not a passive subject. If you wish to play the violin and write music you have to study, you will also need to practise and analyse great artists' performances. Talk to colleagues and fellow students as well as examine other people's marketing plans. Consider to what extent they have used the concepts outlined in this integrative unit. If they did, then how did the concepts apply? If the plans appeared to be under-structured and not to use many of the elements given in this unit, consider whether the application of the frameworks and concepts would have increased the depth of insight contained in the plan or not. Good planning and implementation of marketing plans comes from reflection on past efforts and using this in a continuous loop-learning process. Lessons learned from previous activities make the next ones more successful.

Not one plan but a family of plans

A large multinational will have a global plan. Unilever will have a grand strategic design of market sectors it wishes to enter and countries in which it wants to develop business. Fine fragrances are one sector and plans will be developed both globally and nationally. When a new fragrance is launched, there will be within this global initiative, a detailed plan for each country in which the product is to be launched. For a given country, each major store will have its own local plan of events and marketing activities. Most Marketers are not devising global plans for multinational companies but are involved in the day-to-day implementation of various projects developed at the local level. These plans must, when taken with all the other multitude of sub-plans, add up to an overall successful integrated plan for the company. However, each sub-plan must be well-framed and self-consistent. The best global plans will not work if the basic implementation plans are not well enough conceived to match local conditions or are not professionally executed.

A common misconception is that planners start with a blank page (well the electronic equivalent), start to write the plan and 3 months later, the complete, perfect plan emerges. This is just not so. First a rough skeleton plan is drafted. This is important – as you progress though the CIM qualifications you will find a frequently asked examination question is to draft out an outline plan of some type (e.g. marketing communication plan). In order to draft the plan, certain assumptions will need to be made. The Marketer will then consult the appropriate research to fill the gaps and update the plan. This often highlights more issues that require further research. The Marketer updates, researches and updates for as long as is needed to produce a workable plan. Sometimes it becomes obvious that the plan will not work (e.g. if costs are too high for the selected market). However, the process is still valid, as not implementing a plan that was doomed to failure can save a lot of money. This is why companies test-market products to check out the full plan and marketing mix. The first stage of this process can be regarded as a plan for a plan. This stage is needed because some idea of what is required has to be decided in order to direct the research work. Earlier, in Unit 8, we noted that the key question in research is probably 'knowing the right questions to ask'. This outline structure and pre-plan allows you to do just this. Going out into the street with a clipboard and asking 'which products do you think will make us a lot of money?' will not. The best market research builds on past experience and understanding of the market. Groundbreaking marketing is like groundbreaking science; we reach further as we stand on the shoulders of the work and concepts that have gone before. The outline of the planning process is given in Figure 11.1.

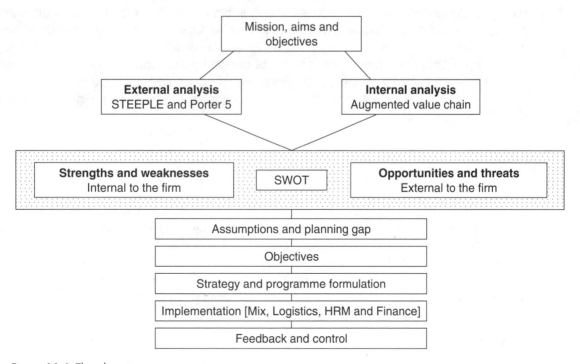

Figure 11.1 The planning process

Figure 11.2 shows the generic plan which cascades down, level by level, in increasing detail. For a major international company, the corporate plans have to be developed in detail for each of the functional divisions (e.g. international product groups). These in their turn have to be developed into the plans for each operating unit (e.g. product groups within a given country). The cascade then progresses downwards to the detail of all the individual projects (e.g. re-launch of a given product, within a given brand, within a given country, within a given division). Not only do these plans have to integrate in the vertical sense (corporate to individual product projects) but must also integrate across functions. When a pyramid is constructed, the stones must link both vertically and horizontally; so must a marketing/business plan.

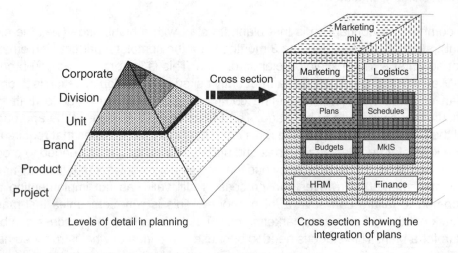

Levels of detail in planning

Cross section showing the integration of plans

Figure 11.2 Levels of detail in planning and integration of plans

The cement that holds the functional elements together consists of the integrated plans, schedules and budgets. To construct these and the individual plan elements, information is needed and this is provided from the MkIS activities within the organization. Within each of the major sections there are the individual building blocks constructing the function detail (e.g. marketing: integrated mix elements (7 Ps) of the service extended marketing mix, etc.). Each of these, in their turn, is amplified in detail (e.g. see the development of the detailed communications plan in Figure 10.5). Integration is not only important for the co-ordination of the operations but also for economies of scale. Thus the explosion of detail into individual advertising bookings must be co-ordinated. A company such as P&G will have many advertising activities for its range of products and brands. If every media booking were considered an individual element the media buying power of the whole group would be wasted. Integration not only provides co-ordination but allows the exploitation of consolidated buying power. The detail should be considered as part of the whole.

Mission, aims and objectives

How do you know you have arrived successfully if you do not know where you are going? Plans without a sense of direction just have the organization going round in circles while the competition race to the winning line. It is odd, but you have to consider both the beginning and end of the plan at the same time. The last section in a typical marketing plan is the control and feedback section. There is no point in writing objectives unless you can see ways to measure performance and attainment against these objectives.

Mission

This is the broad direction and policy of the organization. It defines the organization and the values of the key stakeholders. The mission only changes slowly with time. As the grand international plan cascades down to the ground implementation level, the objectives help frame the mission at lower levels. The international plan sets objectives for each country, which then adopt this in setting their regional mission, aims and objectives.

Activity 11.1

Select a few different types of major organizations (e.g. companies, hospitals, government departments) and log onto their 'corporate' website. Many of these will contain their mission statement. Select two or three of these and debate with your fellow students or friends. For example, do they give a sense of direction and value to the key stakeholders associated with the organization?

Aims

These set the general direction of the company. A supermarket may decide that it intends to move into fashion clothing since this represents a higher margin sector where the brand image could be levered successfully. Aims do not give sufficient detail for a plan to be written. To do this the aims need to be developed still further into objectives.

Objectives

Just as in the earlier section there is a cascade of objectives for each level of the plan. A way of remembering what objectives should be is to use the acronym SMART.

- ○ *Specific* – should be focused on the key actions that need to be achieved.
- ○ *Measurable* – where possible should be numeric but can be a standard when a single number will not suffice (e.g. achieve ISO 9000).
- ○ *Aspirational* – objectives should be motivating.
- ○ *Realistic* – objectives that are not framed realistically are not motivating and are irrelevant.
- ○ *Time bound* – the time limits for achievement should be defined (e.g. achieve ISO 9000 by the end of next year).

Activity 11.2

You can set objectives for your personal life. Set out your aims and objectives for the next year.

Marketing environment and situation analysis

Plans are not written in a vacuum and so it is necessary to define the context. The elements have been covered in Unit 1. The macro-environment (STEEPLE environment), micro-environment (segmentation, competition and marketing mix context) and internal environment (value chain analysis) should be considered. You do not need a shopping list but you should focus on the key issues that will impact specifically on the plans in hand.

Marketing tools such as Ansoff and portfolio analysis can provide frameworks both for diagnosing the problems (no new rising stars) and direct attention to potential solution strategies (e.g. Ansoff strategies of market penetration, product development, market development and diversification).

Overall, this process can be rather diffuse with a large number of potential pressures to be evaluated. To refocus, a SWOT analysis can be completed, which distils the broad analysis down to the core factors to be addressed in the implementation plan. The SWOT analysis should, in effect, lead onto an action focus, the management and marketing imperatives that face the organization.

Microsoft 2010

In the late twentieth century Microsoft become one of the most profitable companies in the world with its original PC operating system and later with 'Windows'. In the 1980s IBM was one of the most profitable companies with a business that was largely based around 'computers'. In the early 1990s IBM crashed and recorded record losses. It then had to reinvent itself. Now in middle of the first decade in the twenty-first century, it makes more money out of services than computers and has sold its PC computer business into China. Another established name, Rover (an icon of car manufacture in the mid-twentieth century), went bankrupt. Discussions in the financial press (late 2006) speculate on the level of risk that Ford and GM could follow Rover to disaster in the next 10 years. To stand still is not an option. Microsoft could follow Rover if it remained a single product company, focusing on past successes.

Threats to Microsoft include the following:

A move to open systems might challenge Microsoft's operating system (e.g. Linux is under consideration by some organizations).

Since value in computers moved from hardware to software in the 1990s, could the value move still further on into communications, searching and content in the twentieth century? Could Google do what TESCO did to Sainsbury and overtake Microsoft?

Could games become even more important to 'computer' sales, an area where Sony (e.g. PS2) and Nintendo have been a match for Microsoft (sales of 100 million for Sony PS2 against 22 million for Microsoft Xbox)?

Microsoft clearly appears to be alert to the environmental challenges and, as a learning and creative organization, is responding. In the launch period, Microsoft shipped 3 million Xbox 360s. Learning from the lesson of the 'Incredible Hulk' (gamers' description of the large black industrial boxlike appearance of the original Xbox) and the stylistic success of the twenty-first century design icon the iPod, the Xbox 360 is white and sleek. The product is now not designed for the techno-geek's bedroom but for the living room and the whole family. It provides facilities for digital downloads and viewing of digital pictures. Xbox Live allows free access to simpler arcade-style games and multi-player games that involve participants from across the globe. Microsoft is responding to the challenges of the external macro and microenvironment with a multi-functional product for the twenty-first century lifestyle and design excellence to signal the product's positioning.

Great companies only remain great if they read the environment and respond. If Microsoft stood still, Google and Apple (to name only two) are ready to move on and take over.

Segmentation

Having completed the environmental analysis, the segmentation structure of the market should be re-examined. Has it changed? Are some sectors growing while others are declining? As discussed in Unit 1, the Marketer uses the data from the audit to develop segmentation profiles and can identify target segments using portfolio analysis. In Unit 1, the Boston matrix approach was presented with some of its limitations. In the next section the nine-cell GE matrix is presented which is a more flexible model.

Strategy alternatives and selection

Figure 11.3 Shows the Ansoff matrix. This model presents us with four strategy alternatives.

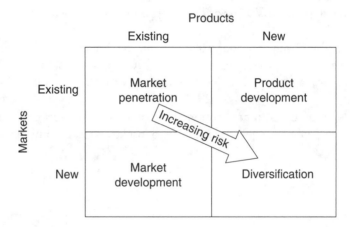

Figure 11.3 Ansoff matrix

Existing products	Existing markets	Market penetration	Least risk
New products	Existing products	Product development	Some risk
Existing products	New markets	Market development	Some risk
New products	New markets	Diversification	Most risk

With market penetration the organization seeks to grow market share. As both the customers and products are known, risk is modest. However, it is not possible to pursue this strategy indefinitely; for example, once you have a Tesco supermarket in every major town, you start to reach saturation level. At this stage, the organization can change one of the Ansoff variables; either by offering new products to existing customers (e.g. supermarkets moving into financial services) or by moving the product mix into new markets (e.g. Tesco in Poland, Wal-Mart in the United Kingdom as Asda). Launching new products or entering new markets carries risk; this strategy is more uncertain and risky when compared with a market penetration strategy. The final alternative is to change both variables and go into diversification. This has two risky variables and so has the maximum level of potential risk. To reduce risk and uncertainty, good market intelligence is needed, as outlined in Unit 8.

Although the concepts of the Ansoff matrix are straightforward, it is often poorly used. To make effective use of the model, an 'X' factor is needed: imagination. Analysis will not always tell you what new products your existing customers may want. New product development needs imagination and invention. Likewise, market segmentation is not a mechanical process and imaginative segmentation can create new, valuable market opportunities.

Insight

Ansoff for a supermarket

Many supermarkets such as Tesco have growth as part of their corporate objectives. Below are four examples of Ansoff strategies:

Penetration – Aggressive marketing communications to gain more market share in existing Tesco product lines such as food.

Product development – The development of new products and services to sell to existing customers. Supermarkets now sell books, DVDs, sports clothing and even financial services.

Market development – Given the near saturation in the home market, Tesco has now moved into international markets. Tesco will have more than 50 per cent of its activities outside the United Kingdom. Much the same strategy is being followed by Wal-Mart from its original US base.

Diversification – New products to new customers. Tesco collects a vast amount of market data from its EPOS systems. Tesco can market this as a service to market research organizations.

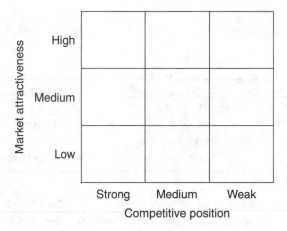

Figure 11.4 Adapted GE matrix

Figure 11.4 shows the adapted version of the GE nine-cell matrix. Having profiled the sectors, each product group to sector match is a potential business. The dilemma is that with Ansoff new strategies and existing portfolio, there will almost always be more opportunities than the organization can pursue. A selection process is required. We noted that one such approach, the Boston Matrix, had some limitations (Unit 11). The GE approach is more flexible. There is no point in entering a business that is unattractive. Therefore, it is essential to have an understanding of what is attractive to the organization and have a framework to rate this attractiveness. There is no point in entering a business sector if your marketing mix does not provide a competitive offering. If you do not have a strong competitive position, you will fail. The second task is to decide which factors give you a competitive advantage.

If we measure market attraction as market growth and competitive advantage as market share, the GE matrix gives us the same type of results as the Boston matrix. The Boston matrix is just a special, limited version of the GE matrix. The Boston version tends to work best with FMCG branded products and often not very well with B2B products where competitive advantage may come from such elements of the mix as field service and technological superiority.

Within a segment, an organization may pursue a number of potential strategies. Porter suggested three important alternatives:

1. Cost leadership strategies (everyday low prices – sustained by having the lowest cost base in the sector)
2. Differentiation strategies (a distinctive, differentiated offering)
3. Focus strategies (niche-type marketing with a specialist, targeted offering).

Other aspects, such as positioning approaches (e.g. for food, ease of preparation, degree of naturalness, etc.), have been discussed in Unit 1.

Insight

Porter in action

Wal-Mart with its vast buying power and superb supply chain management is able to operate a cost leadership strategy (every day low prices).

The Body Shop with its positioning, product range and philosophy differentiates itself from the other high street personal care retailers.

In the B2B sector there are many 'value-added resellers' of computers. They offer a 'turn key' solution to organizations with both hardware and specialist software. Such companies often operate in specialized niche markets such as systems for medical records in a health centre, accounting systems for farmers and so on. These organizations have a focused strategy on a narrow group of customers with specialized added-value products and services.

Implementation objectives and information needs

The imperatives that come from the analysis can now be developed into more detailed objectives for strategy implementation. There can be broad marketing objectives (e.g. gain # market share by?), and then specific ones for all elements of the integrated mix. The detailed formulation of the integrated marketing mix has been covered in Units 3 – Product; 4 – Price; 5 – Place; 6 – Promotion and 7 – People, Process and Physical evidence. The marketing objectives need to be complemented by financial, logistical and human resource plans. In the initial plan for a plan stage, it may not be possible to fill in the '#' marks; figures may be followed by a question mark. The next stage is to define the information needs and research that will be required (covered in Unit 8), so the '#' and '?' can be removed from the plans.

283

Control and feedback

In order to control a plan you need data. Intelligence and information are necessary for it to be effectively managed. The techniques were covered in Unit 8. A marketing information system must be specified and information provided to the management decision-makers. Part of the plan will be financial and the budget not only sets out the range of financial objectives in detail, but also provides the framework for analysis of performance compared to the plan (using diagnostic variance analysis).

Contingency plans

The one certainty in planning is that plans will not work as intended. It is not possible to predict the competition's reaction and there may be sudden changes in the marketing environment. It is not possible to prepare detailed contingency plans for every eventuality, but flexibility needs to be built into the plan (e.g. a contingency reserve in the budget). For a market launch, it might appear that sales in excess of plan would be good news. However, as stated earlier, if production cannot be increased, you may have prepared a platform for the competition to enter at your expense.

Below is an outline marketing plan for the launch of a new fragrance. In working through this, think of it as a framework. It is not a pre-constructed answer for any situation. The models given in the earlier units prompt the asking of certain questions; relevant, imaginative answers are the hallmark of a good plan. Marketing plans are not the business equivalent of 'painting by numbers'. Both analytical and imaginative skills are needed to provide innovative solutions to the novel problems to be addressed in an ever-changing marketing environment.

Fantastic fragrances UK launch of 'Be Happy'

In the earlier units we have considered various elements of the 'Lake View Organic Farms' situation. Here we consider a different type of situation where big budget advertising is relevant.

'Be Happy' is a new fragrance just being launched in the United States. You are the UK Marketer charged with the launch in the United Kingdom in 1 year's time. The fragrance is aimed at young, professional women aspiring to a 'balanced lifestyle'. Below is a provisional outline marketing plan for this situation based on a selection of the elements from the above framework and models given earlier in this coursebook. Some working assumptions have been made, as you might need to do in the exam. In real life you would confirm these through research or by checking with management. The task is a typical, major tactical implementation plan requiring action within an overarching global plan. This type of project is a typical stepping-stone to the top strategic jobs. Assumptions and commentary are given in '[...]'; clearly the commentary would not appear in the exam setting, though you might note the working assumptions.

Mission

To bring the benefits of 'Be Happy' to the UK public.

Aim

A successful launch with a concurrent push and pull strategy into the target market.

Objectives

[Assumption – Fantastic Fragrances have other successful products and the timescale has been set by the international strategy group.]

To achieve the same sales levels and market share as achieved in the last launch in 1 year [in real life these targets would be debated and confirmed with senior management].

Environmental analysis

STEEPLE

Social – Check out latest fashion trends including latest dress and lifestyle moods, also media habits and role models and opinion-formers in the target group [a key activity in such companies is to track all of these trends and much would be available in-house from the ongoing MkIS activities].

Technical – Key features in the fragrance such as novel fragrance materials. Impact of Internet selling on purchasing habits of this group [this, it could be argued, could be considered under 'social' however, it is the identification of the issue rather than its classification that is of most practical importance].

Economic – Given the international status of the company and differing economic cycles, the financial objectives need to be reviewed in the light of likely exchange rates and sector activity. [Many fragrances are created in the United States on a $ cost base. Therefore, some of the costs are not controllable and this may affect margins. The general state of the market should be taken into account. If the sector is surging ahead, ambitious targets might be appropriate; if the sector is stagnant a more conservative view might hold.]

Education – The sales force will not be aware of the features of the new fragrance with the implication that there needs to be an internal marketing aspect to the plan.

Political – Normally for this type of product not a real issue [occasionally truth in advertising and standards of acceptability can be a political issue. Opium perfume advertisements have explored the limits of acceptability in this sector].

Legal – Double-check issues such as trade marks [should have been done at the outset] and registrations for Internet names which may be used or to prevent their misuse. Labelling needs to be checked for legality especially in the light of the European Cosmetics directives [CIM candidates may not be expected to have detailed knowledge of each sector. However, in real life, expert knowledge is required to ensure compliance; the technical legality of labels should be referred to in-house experts (most major companies have a regulatory compliance department) or checked out with industry sources.] Security features should be checked so that counterfeit and 'grey' imports from the US launch can be identified. [This is a particular problem with high-value fashion goods – labels and packaging now have sophisticated security features built in.]

Environmental – Any environmental issues in the packaging and product should be checked. Key in the United Kingdom will be animal testing and animal-derived products [attitudes to these issues are different in the United States and Europe].

Competition analysis

In-sector – A complete review of the major brands, their positioning and strengths and weaknesses will be needed to formulate this plan. Market intelligence such as tracking international launches for any new competition [with over 200 launches a year this is a crowded competitive market].

New entrants – New personalities can brand products; again care should be taken with market intelligence to pick up early signals.

Buyer power – The end consumer is volatile, following the latest trends; thus brand switching is common and frequent. [This is both an opportunity (people prepared to experiment) and a threat (difficult to build up long-term brand loyalty). There may also be some collateral brand damage with people switching from another Fantastic Fragrances product: better they stay with our new one rather than a competitor's.]

Supplier power – Since the product is manufactured by us, it should not be a major problem; however, it should be checked. [Always wise to check, if a fashion launch suddenly hits the jackpot, sales can very quickly grow in excess of the plan, this is only an opportunity if you can get the additional production capacity.]

Substitute products – No real direct substitute product but expenditure on other fashion products [this element should have been picked up in the social and economic aspects of the STEEPLE analysis].

Internal analysis

Given this is just an addition to the range, the internal value chain issues should all be in place and no extensive changes would be needed. [*Note*: if the product involved totally new technology, for example Kodak moving into digital imaging, this would become important.]

SWOT analysis

Strengths – exciting new product

Weaknesses – unknown sub-brand at the moment

Opportunity – to gain new customers

Threats – competition

Implementation strategy

Focused as with other products in our range.

Marketing mix

Product – Ensure appropriate modifications to package and labels. Ensure stock build for launch [you might include this in distribution].

Price – Check final price structure and issue price lists to sales force and distributors.

Place – Ensure delivery of new POS materials. Ensure stock build.

Promotion – The key issue – only in outline here, as this is the question at the end of this unit.

Push – Personal selling into the sales channels.

Pull – PR and publicity for launch and advertising. Plan to take target market through the AIDA process [key issue is to induce trial when we hope the quality of the product will prompt re-purchase].

People – Training of the front-line sales consultants in the shops.

Physical evidence – Nothing new except for the new POS materials.

Process – Nothing new.

Action plan

Not given here, but a chart of activities.

Budget

Not given here, but in real life, a budget would be agreed.

Control and feedback.

Sales against plan.

Consumer awareness of the launch.

Number of people re-purchasing.

Attitudes to the product.

Tracking of the media cover from the PR and Publicity in the fashion press.

Note: Fantastic Fragrances and 'Be Happy' are fictitious names for assessment purposes. These are general situations that will confront Marketers working with major brands such as Chanel.

Question 11.1

A frequent question in the CIM exams is to tailor the communications mix and/or the media mix (advertising media) for a given situation. In December 2005, 'The Urban Culture Festival 2006' Question 3 was 'Describe the advantages and disadvantages of advertising using the following media specifically in the context of the Urban Culture Festival: television, radio, cinema, magazines, others (please specify).' To gain high marks, you need to demonstrate that you have knowledge of the available communications options, understand the communications tasks and can formulate specific tailored actions to the specific case study context with justification.

Taking the above example of a fragrance launch, produce an outline communications plan for the fragrance launch covering the period before the launch, the launch itself and after the launch follow-up.

Your plan should cover all the key stakeholders involved. [This question is longer than you are likely to get in the exam where some more specific focus on part of the plan may be given. However in working through this complete programme you will practise and develop your skills.] You should also compare your approaches with the specimen answers available on the CIM website (www.cim.co.uk).

Question 11.2

'Urban Culture Festival 2006 – Film Festival'

In the 'Urban Culture Festival 2006' the two weeks of film shows only gained an audience of 647 people with revenue of £3 235. This represents only 46 per cent of the available capacity. Some additional information is given below.

Fact File

A local restaurant has agreed to collaborate with a joint promotion with a joint meal and cinema ticket deal. The meal will be themed on the country featuring in that evening's film. As part of the arrangements for this deal two screenings of the film will operate. Audiences for the earlier screening will have a late evening meal; audiences for the late screening will have an early evening meal.

Outline a marketing plan for the 'Urban Culture Film Festival 2006'. This should take account of the need to significantly increase the audience numbers. Make use of the information in the case study and the above additional information. Where there are gaps in the information provided, make realistic assumptions. In this case make a note of the research approach you would need to check your assumptions.

Summary

In this unit we have seen that the overall planning process of an organization involves a whole web of interlocking plans with ever-increasing detail. We considered that success does not only depend on the grand vision and big picture, but on the meticulous planning and implementation of the details. In the formulation of plans, missions, aims and objectives give Marketers 'hooks' to hang ideas on and develop elements of strategy. In this unit, we noted that it was necessary to evaluate the organization's situation and environment and reappraise strategies, formulate new approaches and determine the best way forward. In developing our understanding of how plans are evolved, we have seen that outline plans need to be drafted using working assumptions. These assumptions and gaps then provide the direction for the marketing research to move the plan onto a revised and improved draft. The process is then repeated as many times as necessary. Only briefly noted in this unit is the need to fully tailor the extended marketing mix. The framework of how to do this was given in the earlier units.

Building a marketing plan with no control is rather like building an aircraft without a cockpit. The aircraft would then become a mere projectile, a bullet, which can travel quickly but then comes to a permanent end. Controls must be planned in at the start, not added on as an afterthought. To allow for environmental turbulence, some contingency should also be built in. To follow the aircraft analogy, a little extra fuel would be a good idea, just in case we get a bit of a headwind.

Further study

Dibb, S., Simkin, L., Pride, W. and Ferrell, O. (2006) *Marketing Concepts and Strategies*, 5th European edition, Houghton Mifflin, Chapter 23.

As an integrative module you should also review the other course books at this level

Cheeseman, A., and Jones, M. (2007) *CIM Coursebook – Customer Communications in Marketing*, Butterworth-Heinemann.

Lancaster, G., and Withey, F. (2007) *CIM Coursebook – Marketing Fundamentals*, Butterworth-Heinemann.

Oldroyd, M. (2007) *CIM Coursebook – Marketing Environment*, Butterworth-Heinemann.

Hints and tips

As with every section of this unit, the more you practise on case studies the better your skills will become. Spend as much time working on case studies as reading. A quick read-through of the notes before the exam will not give you the level of skills to do well in these professional examinations. Employers do not just want people with qualifications; they want people who can perform. Performance needs skills – skills come from practice. You are not doing this for the CIM or your tutor. You are doing this to advance your career.

Bibliography

Burk Wood, M. (2003) *The Marketing Plan Handbook*, Prentice Hall.

Gummesson, E. (2002) *Total Relationship Marketing – Rethinking Marketing Management: From 4Ps to 30Rs*, Butterworth-Heinemann.

Hollensen, S. (2002) *Marketing Management – A Relationship Approach*, Prentice Hall.

Kotler, P. (2006) *Marketing Management*, 12th edition, Prentice Hall.

appendix 1

guidance on examination preparation

Preparing for your examination

You are now nearing the final phase of your studies and it is time to start the hard work of exam preparation.

During your period of study you will have become used to absorbing large amounts of information. You will have tried to understand and apply aspects of knowledge that may have been very new to you, while some of the information provided may have been more familiar. You may even have undertaken many of the activities that are positioned frequently throughout your coursebook, which will have enabled you to apply your learning in practical situations. But whatever the state of your knowledge and understanding, do not allow yourself to fall into the trap of thinking that you know enough, that you understand enough, or even worse, that you can just take it as it comes on the day.

Never underestimate the pressure of the CIM examination.

The whole point of preparing this coursebook for you is to ensure that you never take the examination for granted, and that you do not go into the exam unprepared for what might come your way for 3 hours at a time.

One thing is for sure: there is no quick fix, no easy route, no waving a magic wand and finding you know it all.

Whether you have studied alone, in a CIM study centre, or through distance learning, you now need to ensure that this final phase of your learning process is tightly managed, highly structured and objective.

As a candidate in the examination, your role will be to convince the Senior Examiner, for this subject, that you have credibility. You need to demonstrate that you can be trusted to undertake a range of challenges in the context of marketing and that you are able to capitalize on opportunities and manage your way through threats.

You should prove to the Senior Examiner that you are able to apply knowledge, make decisions, respond to situations and solve problems.

Very shortly we are going to look at a range of revision and exam preparation techniques, and at time management issues, and encourage you towards developing and implementing your own revision plan, but before that, let us look at the role of the Senior Examiner.

A bit about the Senior Examiners!

You might be quite shocked to read this, but while it might appear that the examiners are 'relentless question masters', they actually want you to be able to answer the questions and pass the exams! In fact, they would derive no satisfaction or benefits from failing candidates; quite the contrary, they develop the syllabus and exam papers in order that you can learn and then apply that learning effectively so as to pass your examinations. Many of the examiners have said in the past that it is indeed psychologically more difficult to fail students than pass them.

Many of the hints and tips you find within this appendix have been suggested by the Senior Examiners and authors of the coursebook series. Therefore, you should consider them carefully and resolve to implement as many of the elements suggested as possible.

The Chartered Institute of Marketing has a range of processes and systems in place within the Examinations Division to ensure that fairness and consistency prevail across the team of examiners, and that the academic and vocational standards that are set and defined are indeed maintained. In doing this, CIM ensures that those who gain the CIM Certificate, Professional Diploma and Postgraduate Diploma are worthy of the qualification and perceived as such in the view of employers, actual and potential.

Part of what you will need to do within the examination is be 'examiner friendly' – that means you have to make sure they get what they ask for. This will make life easier for you and for them.

Hints and tips for 'examiner friendly' actions are as follows:

- o Show them that you understand the basis of the question, by answering *precisely* to the question asked, and not including just about everything you can remember about the subject area.
- o Read their needs; for example, how many points is the question asking you to address?
- o Respond to the question appropriately. Is the question asking you to take on a role? If so, take on the role and answer the question in respect of the role. For example, you could be positioned as follows:

  – 'You are working as a Marketing Assistant at Nike UK' or 'You are a Marketing Manager for an Engineering Company' or 'As Marketing Manager write a report to the Managing Partner.'

These examples of role-playing requirements are taken from questions in past papers.

- o Deliver the answer in the format requested. If the examiner asks for a memo, then provide a memo; likewise, if the examiner asks for a report, then write a report. If you do not do this, in some instances, you will fail to gain the necessary marks required to pass.
- o Take a business-like approach to your answers. This enhances your credibility. Badly ordered work, untidy work, lack of structure, headings and subheadings can be off-putting. This would be unacceptable in the work situation, likewise it will be unacceptable in the eyes of the Senior Examiners and their marking teams.
- o Ensure the examiner has something to mark: give them substance, relevance, definitions, illustration and demonstration of your knowledge and understanding of the subject area.
- o See the examiner as your potential employer or ultimate consumer/customer. The whole purpose and culture of marketing is about meeting customers' needs. Try this approach – it works wonders.

- Provide a strong sense of enthusiasm and professionalism in your answers; support it with relevant up-to-date examples and apply them where appropriate.
- Try to do something that will make your exam paper a little bit different – make it stand out in the crowd.

All of these points might seem quite logical to you, but often in the panic of the examination they 'go out of the window'. Therefore, it is beneficial to remind ourselves of the importance of the examiner. He or she is the 'ultimate customer' – and we all know customers hate to be disappointed.

As we move on, some of these points will be revisited and developed further.

About the examination

In all examinations, with the exception of Marketing in Practice at Certificate level and Analysis and Decision at Postgraduate Diploma level, the paper is divided into two parts.

- Part A – Mini-case study = 40 per cent of the marks
- Part B – Option choice questions (choice of three questions from seven) = 60 per cent of the marks.

Let us look at the basis of each element.

Part A: The mini-case study

This is based on a mini-case or scenario with one question, possibly subdivided into between two and four parts, but totalling 40 per cent of marks overall.

In essence, you, the candidate, are placed in a problem-solving role through the medium of a short scenario. On occasions, the scenario may consist of an article from a journal in relation to a well-known organization; for example, in the past, Interflora, EasyJet and Philips, among others, have been used as the basis of the mini-case.

Alternatively, it will be based upon a fictional company, and the examiner will have prepared it in order that the right balance of knowledge, understanding, application and skills is used.

Approaches to the mini-case study

When undertaking the mini-case study there are a number of key areas you should consider.

Structure/content

The mini-case that you will be presented with will vary slightly from paper to paper and, of course, from one examination to the other. Normally, the scenario presented will be 250–400 words long and will centre on a particular organization and its problems or may even relate to a specific industry.

The length of the mini-case study means that usually only a brief outline is provided of the situation, the organization and its marketing problems, and you must therefore learn to cope with analysing information and preparing your answer on the basis of a very limited amount of detail.

Time management

There are many differing views on time management and the approaches you can take to manage your time within the examination. You must find an approach to suit your way of working, but always remember, whatever you do, you must ensure that you allow enough time to complete the examination. Unfinished exams mean lost marks. A typical example of managing time is as follows:

Your paper is designed to assess you over a 3-hour period. With 40 per cent of the marks being allocated to the mini-case, it means that you should dedicate somewhere around 75 minutes of your time to both read and write up the answer on this mini-case. Some students, however, will prefer to allocate nearly half of their time (90 minutes) on the mini-case, so that they can read and fully absorb the case and answer the questions in the context of it. This is also acceptable as long as you ensure that you work extremely 'SMART' for the remaining time in order to finish the examination.

Do not forget that while there is only one question within the mini-case, it can have a number of components. You must answer all the components in that question, which is where the balance of time comes into play.

Knowledge/skills tested

Throughout all the CIM papers, your knowledge, skills and ability to apply those skills will be tested. However, the mini-cases are used particularly to test application, that is your ability to take your knowledge and apply it in a structured way to a given scenario. The examiners will be looking at your decision-making ability, your analytical and communication skills and, depending on the level, your ability as a manager to solve particular marketing problems.

When the examiner is marking your paper, he or she will be looking to see how you differentiate yourself, looking at your own individual 'unique selling points'. The examiner will also want to see if you can personally apply the knowledge or whether you are only able to repeat the textbook materials.

Format of answers

On many occasions, and within all examinations, you will most likely be given a particular communication method to use. If this is the case, you must ensure that you adhere to the requirements of the examiner. This is all part of meeting customer needs.

The likely communication tools you will be expected to use are as follows:

- o Memorandum
- o Memorandum/report
- o Report
- o Briefing notes
- o Presentation
- o Press release
- o Advertisement
- o Plan.

Make sure that you familiarize yourself with these particular communication tools and practise using them to ensure that, on the day, you will be able to respond confidently to the communication requests of the examiner.

By the same token, while communication methods are important, so is meeting the specific requirements of the question. This means you must understand what is meant by the precise instruction given. *Note the following terms carefully*:

o *Identify* – select key issues, point out key learning points, establish clearly what the examiner expects you to identify.
o *Illustrate* – the examiner expects you to provide examples, scenarios and key concepts that illustrate your learning.
o *Compare and contrast* – look at the range of similarities between the two situations, contexts or even organizations. Then compare them, that is ascertain and list how activities, features and so on, agree or disagree. Contrasting means highlighting the differences between the two.
o *Discuss* – questions that have 'discuss' in them offer a tremendous opportunity for you to debate, argue, justify your approach or understanding of the subject area – caution, it is not an opportunity to waffle.
o *Briefly explain* – this means being succinct, structured and concise in your explanation, within the answer. Make your points clear, transparent and relevant.
o *State* – present in a clear, brief format.
o *Interpret* – expound the meaning of, make clear and explicit what it is you see and understand within the data provided.
o *Outline* – provide the examiner with the main concepts and features being asked for and avoid minor technical details. Structure will be critical here, or else you could find it difficult to contain your answer.
o *Relate* – show how different aspects of the syllabus connect together.
o *Evaluate* – review and reflect upon an area of the syllabus, a particular practice, an article and so on, and consider its overall worth in respect of its use as a tool or a model and its overall effectiveness in the role it plays.

Source: Worsam, Mike, *How to Pass Marketing*, Croner, 1989.

Your approach to mini-cases

There is no one right way to approach and tackle a mini-case study; indeed, it will be up to each individual to use their own creativity in tackling the tasks presented. You will have to use your initiative and discretion about how best to approach the mini-case. Having said this, however, there are some basic steps you can take.

o Ensure that you read through the case study at least twice before making any judgements, starting to analyse the information provided, or indeed, writing the answers.
o On the third occasion, read through the mini-case and, using a highlighter, start marking the essential and relevant information critical to the content and context. Then, turn your attention to the question again, this time reading slowly and carefully to assess what it is you are expected to do. Note any instructions that the examiner gives you, and then start to plan how you might answer the question. Whatever the question, ensure the answer has a structure: a beginning, a structured central part of the answer and, finally, always a conclusion.
o Keep the context of the question continually in mind: that is, the specifics of the case and the role which you might be performing.
o Because there is limited material available, you will sometimes need to make assumptions. Do not be afraid to do this, it will show initiative on your part. Assumptions are an important part of dealing with case studies and can help you to be quite creative with your answer. However, do explain the basis of your assumptions within your answer so that the examiner understands the nature of them, and why you have arrived at your particular outcome. *Always ensure that your assumptions are realistic.*

    ○ Only now are you approaching the stage where it is time to start writing your answer to the question, tackling the problems, making decisions and recommendations on the case scenario set before you. As mentioned previously, your points will often be best set out in a report- or memo-type format, particularly if the examiner does not specify a communication method.

    ○ Ensure that your writing is succinct, avoids waffle and responds directly to the questions asked.

Part B: Option choice questions

Part B at the certificate level is comprised of six or seven more traditional questions, each worth 20 per cent. You will be expected to choose three of those questions, to make up the remaining 60 per cent of available marks.

Realistically, the same principles apply for these questions as in the case study. Communication formats, reading through the questions, structure, role-play, context and so on – everything is the same.

Part B will cover a number of broader issues from within the syllabus and will be taken from any element of it. The examiner makes the choice, and no prior direction is given to students or tutors on what that might be.

As regards time management in this area, if you used about 75 minutes for the mini-case, you should have around 105 minutes left. This provides you with around 30 minutes to plan and answer a question and 5 minutes per question to review and revise your answers. Keep practising – use a cooker timer, alarm clock or mobile phone alarm as your timer and work hard at answering questions within the time frame given.

Specimen examination papers and answers

To help you prepare and understand the nature of the paper, go to www.cim.co.uk/learning-zone to access Specimen Answers and Senior Examiner's advice for these exam questions. During your study, the author of your coursebook may have, on occasions, asked you to refer to these papers and answer the questions. You should undertake these exercises and utilize every opportunity to practise meeting examination requirements.

The specimen answers are vital learning tools. They are not always perfect, as they are answers written by students and annotated by the Senior Examiners, but they will give you a good indication of the approaches you could take, and the examiners' annotations suggest how these answers might be improved. Please use them.

Other sources of information are available at www.cim.co.uk/learningzone. The CIM Learning Zone website provides you with links to many useful case studies which will help you to put your learning into context when you are revising.

Key elements of preparation

There are three important elements to think about when preparing for your examination:

1. Learning
2. Memory
3. Revision.

Let us look at each point in turn.

Learning

Quite often students find it difficult to learn properly. You can passively read books, look at some of the materials, perhaps revise a little, and regurgitate it all in the examination. In the main, however, this is rather an unsatisfactory method of learning. It is meaningless, shallow and ultimately of little use in practice.

For learning to be truly effective it must be active and applied. You must involve yourself in the learning process by thinking about what you have read, testing it against your experience by reflecting on how you use particular aspects of marketing, and how you could perhaps improve your own performance by implementing particular aspects of your learning into your everyday life. You should adopt the old adage of 'learning by doing'. If you do, you will find that passive learning has no place in your study life.

Below are some suggestions that have been prepared to assist you with the learning pathway throughout your revision.

- o Always make your own notes, in words you understand, and ensure that you combine all the sources of information and activities within them.
- o Always try to relate your learning back to your own organization.
- o Make sure you define key terms concisely, wherever possible.
- o Do not try to memorize your ideas, but work on the basis of understanding and, most important, applying them.
- o Think about the relevant and topical questions that might be set – use the questions and answers in your coursebooks to identify typical questions that might be asked in the future.
- o Attempt all of the questions within each of your coursebooks since these are vital tests of your active learning and understanding.

Memory

If you are prepared to undertake an active learning programme, then your knowledge will be considerably enhanced, as understanding and application of knowledge does tend to stay in your 'long-term' memory. It is likely that passive learning will only stay in your 'short-term' memory.

Do not try to memorize in parrot fashion; it is not helpful and, even more important, examiners are experienced in identifying various memorizing techniques and therefore will spot them as such.

297

Having said this, it is quite useful to memorize various acronyms such as SWOT, PEST, PESTLE, STEEPLE, or indeed various models such as Ansoff, GE Matrix, Shell Directional and so on, as in some of the questions you may be required to use illustrations of these to assist your answer.

Revision

The third and final stage to consider is 'revision', which is what we will concentrate on in detail below. Here just a few key tips are offered.

Revision should be an ongoing process rather than a panic measure that you decide to undertake just before the examination. You should be preparing notes throughout your course, with the view to using them as part of your revision process. Therefore, ensure that your notes are sufficiently comprehensive that you can reuse them successfully.

For each concept you learn about, you should identify, through your reading and your own personal experience, at least two or three examples that you could use; this then gives you some scope to broaden your perspective during the examination. It will, of course, help you gain some marks for initiative with the examiners.

Knowledge is not something you will gain overnight – as we saw earlier, it is not a quick fix; it involves a process of learning that enables you to lay solid foundations upon which to build your long-term understanding and application. This will benefit you significantly in the future, not just in the examination.

In essence, you should ensure that you do the following in the period before the real intensive revision process begins.

- Keep your study file well organized, updated and full of newspaper and journal cuttings that may help you formulate examples in your mind for use during the examination.
- Practise defining key terms and acronyms from memory.
- Prepare topic outlines and essay answer plans.
- When you start your intensive revision, ensure it is planned and structured in the way described below. And then finally, read your concentrated notes the night before the examination.

Revision planning

You are now on a critical path – although hopefully not too critical at this time – with somewhere in the region of between 4 and 6 weeks left to go to the examination. The following hints and tips will help you plan out your revision study.

- You will, as already explained, need to be very organized. Therefore, before doing anything else, put your files, examples, reading material and so on in good order, so that you are able to work with them in the future and, of course, make sense of them.
- Ensure that you have a quiet area within which to work. It is very easy to get distracted when preparing for an examination.
- Take out your file along with your syllabus and make a list of key topic areas that you have studied and which you now need to revise. You could use the basis of this book to do that, by taking each unit a step at a time.
- Plan the use of your time carefully. Ideally, you should start your revision at least 6 weeks prior to the exam. Therefore, work out how many spare hours you could give

to the revision process and then start to allocate time in your diary, and do not double-book with anything else.

o Give up your social life for a short period of time. As the saying goes 'no pain – no gain'.

o Looking at each of the subject areas in turn, identify which are your strengths and which are your weaknesses. Which areas have you grasped and understood, and which are the areas that you have really struggled with? Split your page in two and make a list on each side. For example:

Planning and control	
Strengths	**Weaknesses**
Audit – PEST, SWOT, models Portfolio analysis	Ratio analysis Market sensing Productivity analysis Trend extrapolation Forecasting

o Break down your list again and divide the points of weakness, giving priority in the first instance to your weakest areas and even prioritizing them by giving them a number. This will enable you to master the more difficult areas. Up to 60 per cent of your remaining revision time should be given over to that, as you may find you have to undertake a range of additional reading and also perhaps seeking tutor support, if you are studying at a CIM Accredited Study Centre.

o The rest of the time should be spent reinforcing your knowledge and understanding of the stronger areas, spending time testing yourself on how much you really know.

o Should you be taking two examinations or more at any one time, then the breakdown and managing of your time will be critical.

o Taking a subject at a time, work through your notes and start breaking them down into subsections of learning, and ultimately into key learning points, items that you can refer to time and time again, that are meaningful and that your mind will absorb. You yourself will know how best you remember the key points. Some people try to develop acronyms, flowcharts or matrices, mind maps, fishbone diagrams and so on, or various connection diagrams that help them recall certain aspects of models. You could also develop processes that enable you to remember approaches to various options. (But do remember what we said earlier about regurgitating stuff, parrot fashion.)

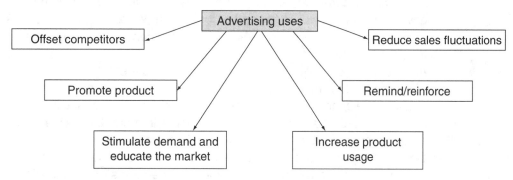

Figure A1.1 Use of a diagram to summarize key components of a concept
Source: Adapted from Dibb, Simkin, Pride and Ferrell, *Marketing Concepts and Strategies*, 4th edition, Houghton Mifflin, 2001

Figure A1.1 is just a brief example of how you could use a 'bomb-burst' diagram (which, in this case, highlights the uses of advertising) as a very helpful approach to memorizing key elements of learning.

○ Eventually you should reduce your key learning to bullet points. For example: imagine you were looking at the concept of time management – you could eventually reduce your key learning to a bullet list containing the following points in relation to 'effective prioritization':

- Organize
- Take time
- Delegate
- Review.

○ Each of these headings would then remind you of the elements you need to discuss associated with the subject area.
○ Avoid getting involved in reading too many textbooks at this stage, as you may start to find that you are getting confused overall.
○ Look at examination questions in previous papers, and start to observe closely the various roles and tasks they expect you to undertake, and importantly, the context in which they are set.
○ Use the specimen exam papers and specimen answers to support your learning and see how you could actually improve upon them.
○ Without exception, find an associated examination question for the areas that you have studied and revised, and undertake it (more than once, if necessary).
○ Without referring to notes or books, try to draft an answer plan with the key concepts, knowledge, models and information that are needed to successfully complete the answer. Then refer to the specimen answer to see how close you are to the actual outline presented. Planning your answer, and ensuring that key components are included, and that the question has a meaningful structure, is one of the most beneficial activities that you can undertake.
○ Now write the answer out in full, time constrained and written by hand, not with the use of IT. (At this stage, you are still expected to be the scribe for the examination and present handwritten work. Many of us find this increasingly difficult as we spend more and more time using our computers to present information. Do your best to be neat. Difficult-to-read handwriting is often off-putting to the examiner.)
○ When writing answers as part of your revision process, also be sure to practise the following essential examination techniques:

- Identify and use the communication method requested by the examiner.
- *Always have three key parts to the answer.* An introduction, a middle section that develops your answer in full and a conclusion. Where appropriate, ensure that you have an introduction, main section, summary/conclusion and, if requested or helpful, recommendations.
- Always answer the question in the context or role set.
- Always comply with the nature and terms of the question.
- *Leave white space.* Do not overcrowd your page; leave space between paragraphs, and make sure your sentences do not merge into one blur. (Do not worry – there is always plenty of paper available to use in the examination.)
- *Count* how many actions the question asks you to undertake and double-check at the end that you have met the full range of demands of the question.
- *Use examples* to demonstrate your knowledge and understanding of the particular syllabus area. These can be from journals, the Internet, the press, or your own experience.

- *Display your vigour and enthusiasm for marketing.* Remember to think of the Senior Examiner as your customer, or future employer, and do your best to deliver what is wanted to satisfy their needs. Impress them and show them how you are a 'cut above the rest'.

o Review all your practice answers critically with the above points in mind.

Practical actions

The critical path is becoming even more critical now as the examination looms. The following are vital points.

o Have you registered with CIM?
o Do you know where you are taking your examination? CIM should let you know approximately 1 month in advance.
o Do you know where your examination centre is? If not, find out, take a drive, time it – whatever you do don't be late!
o Make sure you have all the tools of the examination ready. A dictionary, calculator, pens, pencils, ruler and so on. Try not to use multiple shades of pens, but at the same time make your work look professional. *Avoid using red and green as these are the colours that will be used for marking.*

Summary

Above all, you must remember that you personally have invested a tremendous amount of time, effort and money in studying for this programme and it is therefore imperative that you consider the suggestions given here as they will help to maximize your return on your investment.

Many of the hints and tips offered here are generic and will work across most of the CIM courses. We have tried to select those that will help you most in taking a sensible, planned approach to your study and revision.

The key to your success is being prepared to put in the time and effort required, planning your revision, and equally important, planning and answering your questions in a way that will ensure that you pass your examination on the day.

The advice offered here aims to guide you from a practical perspective. Guidance on syllabus content and developments associated with your learning will become clear to you as you work through this coursebook. The authors of each coursebook have given subject-specific guidance on the approach to the examination and on how to ensure that you meet the content requirements of the kind of question you will face. These considerations are in addition to the structuring issues we have been discussing throughout this appendix.

Each of the authors and Senior Examiners will guide you on their preferred approach to questions and answers as they go. Therefore, where you are presented with an opportunity to be involved in some activity or undertake an examination question either during or at the end of your study units, do take it. It not only prepares you for the examination, but helps you learn in the applied way we discussed above.

Here, then, is a last reminder:

- o Ensure you make the most of your learning process throughout.
- o Keep structured and orderly notes from which to revise.
- o Plan your revision – do not let it just happen.
- o Provide examples to enhance your answers.
- o Practise your writing skills in order that you present your work well and your writing is readable.
- o Take as many opportunities to test your knowledge and measure your progress as possible.
- o Plan and structure your answers.
- o Always do as the question asks you, especially with regard to context and communication method.
- o Do not leave it until the last minute!

The writers would like to take this opportunity to wish you every success in your endeavours to study, to revise and to pass your examinations.

Karen Beamish
Academic Development Advisor

how to pass the case study examination

How to pass the case study exam

Figure A2.1 shows the case study exam process.

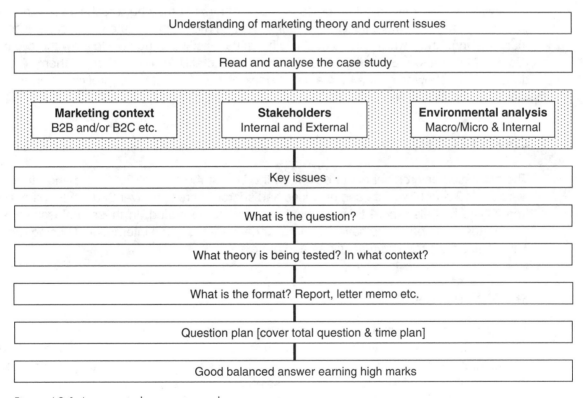

Figure A2.1 An approach to a case study exam

Understanding marketing theory

Take great care that you understand how to use the models and marketing theories. Figure A2.2 shows a generalized version of the Boston matrix. In the box marked 'Dog' it is noted that often a product is in the decline phase; that is to say the market growth is negative, find a textbook that indicates this possibility. Relative market share, to who? What 'market' are we talking about? Aston Martin does not compete with the Ford Ka. The implication of this is that we know and understand the segmentation structure for the market situation.

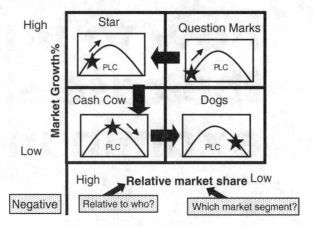

Figure A2.2 Adapted Boston (BCG) Matrix

The situation is more complicated for some case studies, for a range of product/market situations the Boston Matrix is of little use. The implication of the Boston matrix is that competitive advantage is correlated with market share, often true for FMCG products. However, for highly technical products in a B2B context, it may be a technological advantage that is the issue. The more flexible GE matrix may be more appropriate in this case. Know your tools (theory). Know which one to use, in what situations. Knowing how to draw the two models (Boston Matrix and GE matrix) does not give you the skill to use and apply them. A sculptor does not learn how to create by reading a book alone. You only gain proficiency in the use of tools (theory) by reading and then practising their application.

Current issues

The marketing environment is turbulent. In the UK, at the start of 2006 gold and other metals were at a 10 year high. Gas and oil prices had sharply increased over 2005. Exports of clothing from China had also more than doubled over the same period. In these professional exams candidates are expected to have a general understanding of the international business climate. This comes from reading magazines and papers.

What is a case study?

The case study is a brief overview of a business situation. The purpose of the case study is to allow you to demonstrate your ability to analyse a marketing situation. To do this effectively, for this integrative paper, you need to know, understand and have experience of the application of the relevant theory. This is an active process not a memory exercise. So, practice on a range of case studies is essential, two are given in this workbook. The specimen answers are available on the CIM website at www.cim.co.uk/learningzone. However do not be tempted to look at these too early. They are the 'winning post'. If you do not learn how to 'run the race' (analyse the case study, etc.) when you get into the exam you will not know how to win through. Simply memorising past case studies is not a strategy to pass this exam. You need to learn analysis and problem solving skills. This needs active practice, not just passive reading revision. On analysing the case study you may need to make realistic assumptions (in a 3 hour exam the case study has to be simplified to keep to a readable length). A wide knowledge of current marketing and business climate developments, demonstrated in the exam, will gain you marks. In any case, knowledge of theory, if you have no understanding of the continuously evolving international business climate, will not gain you career success.

After the general analysis there can be a diagnosis of the situation. What are the key issues? Read the questions carefully to see just what is required. What theory is being tested? What is the context? In what format is the answer required? Plan your answer before you start writing. The whole process, shown in Figure A2.3, will allow you to develop a balanced, insightful, approach.

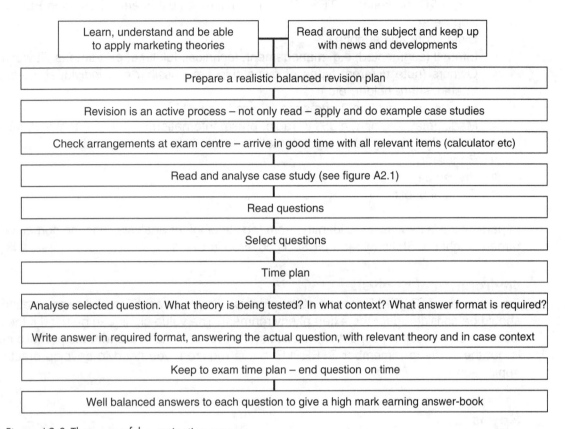

| Learn, understand and be able to apply marketing theories | Read around the subject and keep up with news and developments |

Prepare a realistic balanced revision plan

Revision is an active process – not only read – apply and do example case studies

Check arrangements at exam centre – arrive in good time with all relevant items (calculator etc)

Read and analyse case study (see figure A2.1)

Read questions

Select questions

Time plan

Analyse selected question. What theory is being tested? In what context? What answer format is required?

Write answer in required format, answering the actual question, with relevant theory and in case context

Keep to exam time plan – end question on time

Well balanced answers to each question to give a high mark earning answer-book

Figure A2.3 The successful examination process

Read and analyse the case study

With a highlighter pen read the case study. Highlight key words and make brief notes as to what are the key issues. What is the marketing context? Note this is not an issue of 'or'. A case study is not one dimensional. A case study can be international and service and B2B and B2C (e.g. a bank). Below is an outline of areas and factors that may apply:

- o B2C and/or
- o B2B and/or
- o Product and/or
- o Services and/or
- o International and/or
- o Not-for-profit/social and/or
- o Relationship marketing and/or
- o Consumer issues and/or
- o Green issues and/or
- o Limited budget and/or

The issues are covered in Unit 2 'The context of marketing'.

Stakeholders

Who are the key stakeholders? What are the issues relevant to them and the case study organization? Note just as with customers stakeholders can segment. Some typical examples of potential stakeholders are given below:

- Customers (B2B: segmented and/or B2C: segmented). Possibly customers' customers (e.g. P&G marketing to TESCO, then to ultimate customers – Push and Pull strategy)
- Suppliers
- Distributors and agents
- Internal (segmented, e.g. management, technical, full time, part-time, shift worker, etc.)
- Owners (note different types of ownership are possible e.g. individual, co-operative, trustee, share holder, etc.)
- Industry (competitors, trade associations, etc.)
- Media (may segment e.g. TV, radio, press. International, national, regional, local)
- Political (may segment: e.g. International (e.g. EU), national, local)
- Regulatory
- Pressure groups
- General public.

In particular it is necessary to identify, from the stakeholder analysis, who the communications' targets might be. Stakeholder analysis is covered in Unit 1.

Environmental analysis

Focused use of STEEPLE (or one of its variants), Porter competition and segmentation issues should be considered for the external environment. The value chain can be used if the internal issues are an important aspect of the case study scenario. As noted with the portfolio models it is not the ability to remember STEEPLE that is required, you need to develop practice in its application.

Key issues

A SWOT analysis helps focus the range of issues uncovered in the above analysis. This will then indicate the key imperatives that face the organization (e.g. gain new customers, introduce new products, move into international markets, etc.).

What is the question?

Specimen answers to past questions are not for 'learning' in parrot fashion. They are for you to be able to compare your solution to a situation. They are an aid to practice, not another textbook. This issue is important as candidates must answer the question asked in the exam, not the specimen answer from last time. Take care to answer the question fully. In an outline context of a marketing plan, for example, is the 'product' simply 'a product' or are there elements of service? If service is an element, the service-extended marketing mix should be used.

What theory is being tested? In what context?

In the December 2005 examination 'The Urban Culture Festival 2006' Question 1(d) tests candidates' communications skills with 'Draft a letter to potential sponsors selling the benefits of involvement with 'The Urban Culture Festival 2006.' " Apart from communications skills (in drafting the letter) a number of different theory elements are involved: this is a B2B style context, the case study has international aspects, the sponsors involvement will be to add value to their marketing communications (the letter will need to explain to sponsors how sponsorship could complement their other marketing communications activities).

What is the format?

If no instructions are given it should be assumed that report format should be used. Other formats used in CIM exams include memos, letters, budgets, schedules and briefing notes. These various formats are covered in Unit 9.

Question plan

In the analysis of marginal fail papers against good pass papers, it was noted that marginal fail candidates tend not to question plan. Students in the upper quartile of performance tend to question plan. A UK training manual for meetings had a cartoon where the caption was: 'Before opening your mouth, put the brain in gear': before your write an answer, think and plan. This is important as in the time stress of the exam it is easy to cover 5Ps, not 7Ps, as an example. If you have question planned, mark the Ps off as you cover them so you do not forget them.

Time

A common reaction, when looking through the above process, is that there is not enough time. There is enough time but only if you practice case studies and exam technique. It is better to practice now than fail an exam and then have all the time, expense and trouble of a resit.

The successful exam process

Figure A2.3 gives the outline of the successful exam process.

Before revision

Learn and understand the theory and content of the programme as you progress. An attempt to cram in knowledge in the last few weeks will not work. This exam requires understanding and application as well. This must be developed throughout the programme with the skills of case study analysis and answer writing. You need to set this all in the current business context so keep reading marketing magazines and business pages of newspapers during your programme, do not leave this to the revision time; this is too late. Before you start your revision, time plan to ensure you cover all the topics and practice all the skills that will be tested in the exam. Ensure that you keep a time/work/personal–life balance.

Revision and before the exam

Implement your revision plan. Make certain your plan contains active learning as well as reading (e.g. practising the application of STEEPLE). Continue with case study and exam question practice. If you have the opportunity (if offered by your tuition centre) do a mock examination. Ensure that you have your examination pack sorted (spare pens, highlighters, calculator, etc.). Know where and when the exam is to be held. Arrive in good time and allow for problems (e.g. difficult traffic).

Examination

As given in Figure A2.3 read and analyse the case study. Read the questions, analysing what is required. Select your questions. Time plan and keep to the time plan.

For each selected question do complete analysis. What theory is being tested? In what context? Keep to the required format and ensure that you make your answer context relevant (e.g. if you use an Ansoff matrix then make certain you put some key case study material into it). End the question on time. A common cause of marginal failure is not to leave enough time for the last question.

After the exam do not have a depressing 'post-mortem'. If you have another exam, focus on what you can do in the future. If it is your last exam, you have earned some R&R!

Summary

Examination success does not depend on two weeks cramming before the exam and memorizing past case study answers. What is required is the development of knowledge, understanding and application of marketing theory into the given case study context. This requires the development of skills in analysis and problem solving to recommend appropriate marketing actions. In this section a structured approach is outlined which will allow you to develop this skill and achieve success, not only in the exam but also in your marketing career.

Further study

In this workbook there is a selection of recent exam case studies. Further case studies are available on the CIM website. The more case studies you work through the more you will develop your skills.

Hints and tips

Do not 'zap through' to look at the specimen answers when working through past case studies. Work through the case study and develop your own answers. When completed, compare these with the specimen answers provided and the senior examiner's comments. Discuss your approach with your tutor and other students. Only by this process will you fully develop your skills.

Bibliography

Cameron, S. (2005) *The Business Students Handbook: Learning Skills for Study and Employment*, 3rd edition, FT Prentice Hall.

how to pass the integrative assignment

How to pass the integrative assignment

The process to compete a successful assignment is given in Figure A3.1.

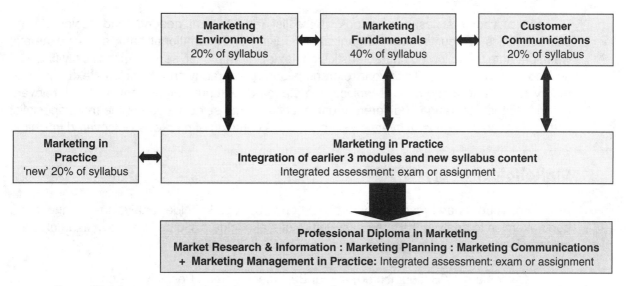

Figure A3.1 Integrated relationship between earlier Professional Certificate in Marketing modules and Marketing in Practice. Bridge to Professional Diploma in Marketing

Understanding of marketing theory and current issues

This is covered in Appendix 2 and is not repeated here.

General research into your selected organization

An important first task before you start to complete any of the detailed assignments is to prepare the ground and do some general research. Preliminary analysis and planning is needed for the integrated project. The preliminary research and planning papers may not form part of the answer but without the framework to assist with the creative process, the result is likely to be a badly constructed submission lacking in depth and strength to gain a good grade. The tools for this are covered in Units 1 and 2. Issues about academic reports and other formats are covered in Unit 9.

The contexts of marketing

What is special about your selected organization? What is the marketing context? Note: this is not an issue of 'or'. A company is not one dimensional. A company can have aspects of international and service and B2B and B2C (e.g. a bank). Below is an outline checklist of areas and factors that may apply:

- o B2C
- o B2B
- o Product
- o Services
- o International
- o Not-for-profit/social
- o Relationship marketing
- o Consumer issues
- o Green issues
- o Limited budget and/or

So, one of your first tasks is to look at the list (add to it, if needed) and decide on the characteristics of your selected organization. Taking an international bank as our example, we might note the following characteristics/contexts: international, service (specifically financial services), B2B and B2C. Thus your references and bibliography should include textbooks and theory relevant to these special topics. One standard textbook will not cover all the relevant ground for the vast range of different organizations. Some selective use of the more specialist texts is indicated. A general overview of the various contexts of marketing is covered in Unit 2.

Stakeholder analysis

As part of your general research, you should draw up a stakeholder analysis table and it is a good exercise to analyse the internal structure of stakeholders. Some illustrative examples are given below:

- o Customers: B2B (segmented) and/or B2C (segmented). Possibly customers' customers (e.g. P&G marketing to TESCO, then to ultimate customers – Push and Pull strategy)
- o Internal: management (technical). Full-time, part-time, shift worker and so on
- o Media: TV, radio, press. International, national, regional, local and so on
- o Political: International (e.g. EU), national, local and so on.

General issues of stakeholder analysis are covered in Unit 1.

Environmental analysis

Complete a focused STEEPLE (or one of its variants) analysis. Do not leave as 'Exchange rate: £ moving up, the £1 = $2 is a possibility'. Go on: *Exchange rate: £ moving up, the £1 = $2 is a possibility, implication in trading will be (a) better (UK company selling USA holidays) or (b) worse (UK manufacturer exporting to the USA).* A Porter competition analysis should be completed. The segmentation issues should be evaluated. A value chain analysis can be useful.

Key issues

A SWOT analysis helps focus the range of issues uncovered in the above analysis. This will then indicate the key imperatives that face the organization (e.g. gain new customers, introduce new products, move into international markets, etc.).

What is the task? What theory? What context?

Figure A3.2 outlines the integration of the various threads to produce a coherent submission. The organizational audit will give you the context for your organization. These general issues are covered in Units 1 and 2. This analysis will direct you into the right selection of theory (e.g. for a charity organization specialist texts on not-for-profit marketing). The review of the organization's marketing mix again provides a foundation for the specific assignments. The service-extended marketing mix is covered in Units 3–7. Over your studies on this and the other CIM modules, you will have developed your marketing skills and kept up with the current trends in the industry by reading the marketing and business press.

Guidance on report structure for submissions is given in Unit 9. Do not forget to acknowledge your information sources in your references and bibliography. The 'Harvard' system of referencing is recommended and guidance on its application is given in Unit 9.

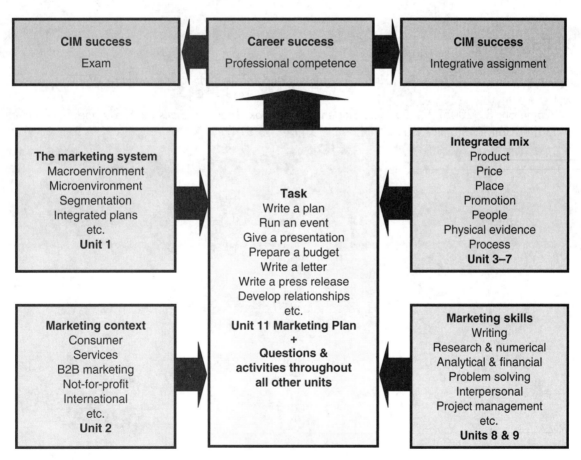

Figure A3.2 Integration of elements to complete a marketing task

Further study

Most colleges keep an archive of past projects. Look at past projects to get ideas to develop your own approach. These are not only useful for style and structure. Be selective and look at projects in your selected area. These may give you useful key references. Past projects in a library are just like journals and may be used as such. Remember it is essential to reference any material you directly use.

Hints and tips

Do not rush to start writing your report. Complete the analysis of your selected organization's marketing environment and read around the relevant theory. Remember to read articles or textbooks in your selected area (e.g. if your selected organization is a bank, look at some textbooks on financial services). Draw up a project time plan to allow you to do this preliminary groundwork. Remember to adapt standard report structures to the precise needs of the question and to keep close to the specified word count.

Bibliography

Anderson, J. and Poole, M. (2002) *Assignment and Thesis Writing*, 4th edition, Wiley.

Cameron, S. (2005) *The Business Students Handbook: Learning Skills for Study and Employment*, 3rd edition, FT Prentice Hall.

answers and debriefings

Unit 1

Debriefing Activity 1.1

Your result will depend on your chosen organization. However, consider you are the marketing manager for a local college offering the CIM Diploma. Customers may be defined as the people who pay for the course. The competition would include other local colleges/universities offering the programme; people might wish to study by distance learning; take another qualification, for example BA Marketing or follow another profession such as Public Relations (PR). All sources of competition need to be identified, not just the direct competition. Later in the unit, we will see how Porter's five forces of competition model can help.

Debriefing Activity 1.2

There is a fair range of stakeholders. Some are given below. You should use a structural approach.

- o Students (future, present and past)
- o Relatives and friends of students
- o Internal stakeholders (trustees, academic, administration, technical support, etc.)
- o Competing institutions
- o Suppliers
- o Business community (employers, trade associations, professional institutions, etc.)
- o Government (national and local)
- o General public
- o Media.

Note the key skill is to apply the concept to develop specific stakeholder segments relevant to the context. You should now review Question 3 June 2005 'Kernow Railways micro franchise'; 3a 'Identify FOUR key stakeholder groups of Kernow Railways' and 3b 'Describe how the stakeholder groups identified contribute to and benefit from the success of this franchise.' You should compare your analysis with the specimen answer on the CIM website.

Stakeholder analysis should be undertaken in four stages: (1) identification of the key stakeholders, (2) potential impact of the stakeholders identified on the organization, (3) the organization's aims with the stakeholder group (e.g. change of attitude from hostility to sympathy) and (4) potential actions that the organization might take to achieve these aims (e.g. communications activities).

Debriefing Activity 1.3

In the exams do use the diagrams and models as given, but adapt or annotate them to make them context-specific. Note that not all aspects of the model apply in a given area – be selective. Some elements of the model may apply in more than one way; adapt or annotate the model to show this. Models that are not made context specific do not earn high marks in the exam.

Care must be taken with the Porter model in that it does not take account of the dynamic nature of competition; it is a picture at a given time. Consideration should be given to how competition is evolving. The nature and character of the competition should be considered: very aggressive expansionist companies, such as Wal-Mart, have grown greatly where at the same time in the United Kingdom the Co-operative Society has seen a gradual decline. The model could be taken to imply that the relationships between suppliers and channels are threatening. In some circumstances this is true. However, in a relationship-marketing view, they might also be considered as potential partners. The health and capability of competing organizations can be assessed by considering their value chains.

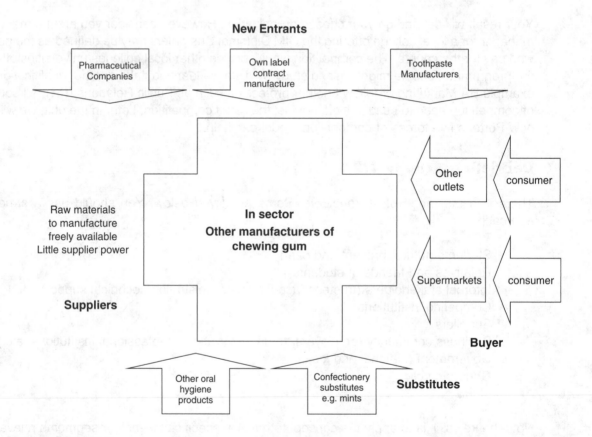

Evaluating the microenvironment is essential in providing the context for the organization's overall and, in particular its marketing mix, strategies. However, the marketplace is, in its turn, also influenced by the broader general business macroenvironment. The macroenvironment is considered in the next section.

Debriefing Activity 1.4

Some selected issues are shown below:

Social – Move to healthy eating, Atkins diet and concerns over food production.

Technical – Evidence regarding addictive foods.

Economic issue – Shifts in disposable income, changes in amounts people are prepared to spend when eating out.

Education – Better understanding of health and nutrition.

Political – Fast food; its source, manufacture and consumption have become politicized.

Legal – Raft of food laws, potential liability cases from overweight people.

Environmental – Customers' lack of care in disposing of containers.

Note again the skill is not to produce a generalized list but to develop a focused analysis relevant to the marketing context being considered.

Debriefing Activity 1.5

Element	Issues
Support activities	
Strategic stance and strategy	Niche strategy, geographic and potentially international expansion via web-based operations
Safety, environmental, quality and ethical policies	Normal office/warehouse issues in general, quality returns policy on defective records
	Data protection issues with computer database of customers
Physical and financial structure	Physical premises will need good office space and flexible warehousing along with good access for deliveries and despatches
	Communications must have broadband access
Information systems, structure and technology	Communications and IT systems will be vital
	Effective back-up is essential
	Loss of system/data would mean loss of business and seriously affect customer service
Human resources and organizational structure	Small business, so tight group of flexible staff
	Skill mix needed: financial, office, communications and IT, extra dimension could be passion for music
Technology development	The product is 'retro', so not much development there, but must track developments in communications and web technology in particular on-line security (e.g. virus protection, Internet payment fraud)
Marketing	Good MkIS (e.g. noting of requests and recording popular non-stock titles could indicate future list items), niche market so specialist press, selective PR and web-based communications strategy
Procurement	Seeking out specialist sources for records
	Note: IT, communications, physical distribution, marketing communications and so on are also significant cost drivers for the organization
Primary activities	
Inbound logistics	Records in
Operations	Picking of customers' required records and packing
Outbound logistics	Despatch by post or courier
Sales	Orders in (post, telephone and Internet). Order processing and payments
Service	Field service not a major issue in this context

315

Debriefing Activity 1.6

An abbreviated focused list of issues is given below:

- ○ Demographic data
- ○ Product and service usage history
- ○ Lifestyle
- ○ Satisfaction level.

Compare your notes with the specimen answer on the CIM website.

Debriefing Activity 1.7

Family life cycle – Large families have high use, single pensioner households much less.

Disposable income – The more affluent are more likely to buy premium brands.

Location – It can affect the nature of water. Hard water areas are different to soft water areas.

Washing method – Hand, top-loading, twin tub, automatic.

Nature of fabric – White cotton needs different treatment to wool and silk.

Place in the fabric care process – Pre-wash products, detergents, fabric conditioners, tumble dry and ironing products and 'refreshing' products.

This is a provisional list; some such as 'family life cycle' are direct 'lifts' from textbook lists; others such as 'nature of fabric' need a measure of creative interpretation.

Debriefing Activity 1.8

Outline analysis of 'Lake View Organic Farms'

Social/cultural	**Increased concern for environment, increased concern for healthy eating, high Internet access now**
Technological	Possibility of Internet marketing
Economic	Higher costs of organic farming, possible government subsidies
Education/training	Greater awareness of pesticide residues
Political	Generally supportive to green initiatives
Legal	Soil Association certification
Environmental protection	Green farming, need to reflect with green packaging and distribution
Direct competition	Other organic farmers
Substitute products	Non-organic produce
Buyer power	Supermarkets' high, decreasing margins. Easy for consumers to switch so overall high
New entrants	Not easy as Soil Association certification needed but imports possibly an issue
Supplier power	As producer not an issue
Logistics	Growing, harvesting, packaging, distribution
Financial issues	Co-operative ownership
Human Resources	No information in case study
Key stakeholders	Staff, co-operative owners, franchisees, supermarkets, customers
Segmentation	Restaurants, supermarkets, direct sales (size of family, location)

Debriefing Question 1.1

Outline analysis of 'The Urban Culture Festival 2006'

Social/cultural	Multiracial/multicultural city. 'Graffiti Gallery' not welcomed by all social groups.
Technological	website development
Economic	Higher costs (e.g. petrol) putting pressure on family budgets and thus might cause drop in sales if prices are increased
Education/ training	This is the first time a Marketing Executive has been appointed, some stakeholders will need training with regard to the value of marketing for the success of the festival
Political	Support of local political publics essential. Possible adverse reaction from some sectors to the 'Graffiti Gallery'
Legal	Appropriate entertainment licenses will be needed. Public liability insurance will be needed for some events
Environmental protection	With 100 000 people attending, special arrangements may be needed for transport (e.g. park and ride). This number of people will create a lot of litter; recycling should be provided (e.g. drink cans)
Direct competition	Other festivals in the region
Substitute products	Other forms of entertainment
Buyer power	Easy for people to switch allegiance from one annual festival to another, a very competitive environment
New entrants	Other regional organizations could start up rival festivals
Supplier power	Nothing indicated in case study
Logistics	Normal event management issues
Financial issues	With high fixed costs, good sales and marketing will be needed, with good budgeting and cost control
Human Resources	Recruitment and training of temporary staff
Key stakeholders	Customers (present and future), ethnic group organizations, internal participants, international guests, sponsors, media, general local community, local government (licenses, etc.) and local politicians
Segmentation	Ethnic/cultural groups, type of events, local customers, regional and international visitors

Debriefing Question 1.2

An outline analysis for 'SMS Cars Ltd'

Social/cultural	Patterns of car use. Appeal of entertainments for the launch event. How different venues might attract customers/potential customers?
Technological	Impact of Internet on information collection and marketing communications.
Economic	High cost of petrol makes fuel economy an issue (hybrid drive system could well be more attractive now)
Education/ training	Staff may need training on the issues in marketing and servicing the revolutionary hybrid drive system.
Political	At a local level for this case study context, so possibly not a major issue.
Legal	Data protection issues in the information collection and maintenance of a customer database.

Environmental protection	New hybrid drive system a significant step in reducing environmental impact of cars.
Direct competition	Other local franchisees for competing car companies.
Substitute products	Other forms of travel (e.g. bike, bus).
Buyer power	Large range of car offerings from competing companies, a very competitive market.
New entrants	New start-up dealerships.
Supplier power	Conditions placed on the franchisee by Ford and Hyundai as part of the franchise contract.
Logistics	Arrangements for test drives for new car sales. Arrangements for booking and completing servicing. Arrangements for booking, delivery and return of hire cars (e.g. out of hours rental car return).
Financial issues	High fixed costs in maintaining facilities and employing staff. The implication is that it is essential to maintain sales volume in a competitive market.
Human Resources	Staff training in new hybrid drive system.
Key stakeholders	Existing customers (with segmentation structure), potential customers, Hyundai management, employees, media, fashion show partners and travel partners (e.g. arrangements with local airport for car hire at the airport).
Segmentation	Demographics of existing and potential customers (B2C). B2B market for fleet sales and car hire.

Unit 2

Debriefing Activity 2.1

Key stakeholders – School managers (professional, board of governors).

Agenda – Want provision of services without effort, concern about potential financial impact of modifications to existing contract.

Parents' agenda – Views from 'food fad' (organic, free-range etc.) to could not care less 'let the kids have what they want'. Often the segmentation in this circumstance can be summarized as the committed to, those against and 'couldn't care either way' in the middle.

Children's agenda – Trendy tasty products.

Pressure Groups' agenda – Medical concern about early development of diabetes.

Potential points for parents' meeting discussion.

No product is healthy if consumed to excess; issue is a healthy overall lifestyle. A more balanced menu could provide meals with a higher nutritional value and avoid too many 'empty' calories (Right to safety*)

Possibilities of adding/introducing 'healthier' ingredients to the menu such as fresh fruits and vegetables, salads, organic and free-range meat. However, there may be resistance to restricting the number of occasions that items such as chips occur in the weekly menus (Right to safety, Right to choose*).

Dietary information on the menu to be made available to parents and children (Right to know, Right to safety (allergies)*).

Company helpline information can be made available on menus. Company website can contain this information for downloading. E-mail contact can be given to receive feedback (Right to be heard*).

* indicates possible links between 'Kennedy Rights' concepts and the case study situation, that is how the 'Kennedy Rights' concepts can be used to help identify and classify consumer issues in such a situation.

Debriefing Activity 2.2

Selected environmental issues to be considered:

Reduction of carbon dioxide (greenhouse gas) emissions. A key parameter for society is passenger mile fuel economy, which enables various means of transport (e.g. bus and train) to be compared. Overall, bus transport greatly reduces congestion and in London, travel times have been reduced after the introduction of the congestion charge. Increasing costs of fuel (recent oil prices) can make public transport more attractive. Social concern with pollution and congestion can influence enlightened companies to encourage green travel (e.g. participation in 'Park & Ride' schemes).

Internal Ps

Product – Service is product ... + ... service – are vehicles selected for green issues? (Type of fuel, fuel economy). Many cities in their consideration of new transport proposals are putting passenger mile fuel economy and environmental impact high up the agenda in the decision-making process.

Price – What are the increased costs (e.g. conversion of vehicles to bio-Diesel)?

Place – Network management – the right buses on the right routes (large empty buses are not green). In some situations, innovative solutions have been found such as 'Dial-a-Ride', where the bus only runs if there are confirmed passengers.

Promotion – Green media promoting green aspects such as 'Park and Ride'.

People – Internal marketing on issues such as fuel economy. Internal marketing issues to gain and maintain green culture in organizations.

Physical evidence – Recycled paper for tickets and other methods of providing tangible evidence of the intangible issue of care (for the environment).

Process – Efficient ticketing processes – slow processes do not only delay passengers but also waste fuel.

External Ps

Paying Customers – People want green services but not at increased costs.

Providers – Are the contractors to the bus company also green empowered?

Politics – Local politics such as gaining bus lanes.

Pressure groups – Working with pressure groups (e.g. local cycle groups).

Partners – Green link with railways for long distance Park and Ride schemes.

Problems – Negative: Concern about diesel engine emissions. Positive: partial solution to congestion.

Predictions – Uptake of public transport when compared to other forms of transport (e.g. modelling of uptake of 'Park & Ride' from experience in other cities).

The Ss of Green Success

Satisfaction of stakeholders – Politicians: progress to green agenda; Passengers: Improved service; Management: Improved profits, better efficiency (e.g. through more bus lanes); Employees: Contribution to a greener and better world; Public at large: Improved attitude to company and employees.

Safety – Green agenda addressed.

Social acceptability – Green Company appreciated by politicians, general public and financial stakeholders.

Sustainability – Better fuel efficiency and contribution to green, sustainable lifestyles.

Debriefing Activity 2.3

Issues in report writing are covered in Unit 9. Before you start writing, some review of the issues and context is invaluable. The client has some stakeholders (publics) who have or might have negative reactions to the proposed development. The PR activity will be to work to change attitudes and overcome objections. Potential stakeholders (publics) might include local press, local business, local pressure groups, potential employees, local politicians and the local public at large. If possible, visit one or two such outlets and read your local press to review any local commercial planning debates.

Issues that might be included are purchasing policies: will the company buy as much as possible of goods and services locally? Does the organization have green and ethical (e.g. fair trade coffee) purchasing policies? Will development have adverse environmental impact with late-night noise and litter? What are the company employment policies such as equal opportunity and/or trade union recognition? Overall, will the development have a positive economic impact or will profits and cash be channelled out to a distant international owner? Your report should identify the potential problems, issues and publics and propose approaches that might be used in a PR campaign to gain positive attitudes in the key publics and finally a successful outcome.

Debriefing Activity 2.4

Our address block with full contact information.

Date

Dear ((name))[*]

Your Personal invitation to Fantastic Fragrances Vibrant 2007 cosmetics launch

New Year, new you! Vibrant 2007 cosmetics will take you into the new season in style. There is a fantastic range of colours and, for a limited time, there is a chance for a free consultation and £5 off your next purchase. Act now; this opportunity is for a limited time only. Dial the hotline ##### or book online ###@####.## for your special appointment. Treat yourself for the New Year.

Yours sincerely,

Signature block

Different software packages use different symbols to enclose a mail merge insertion in a document. Another document would print the address on envelopes or address labels. Opinion will vary as to the tone to strike in such a letter. Here, links have been built to the national advertising that should have created awareness. The promotional offer is outlined with the key point for such promotions: an invitation to the customer to act NOW.

Debriefing Activity 2.5

Clean Sweep Collect Award

Date

Clean Sweep's Managing Director John Smith collected the coveted 'Investors in People' award at The Imperial Hotel. For the last 3 years, Clean Sweep has been providing top class cleaning services to local organizations. John Smith said, 'People are our greatest asset and this award is another milestone in the development of our services for local companies. With our development plans we will grow and provide more, much-needed local employment'.

Further Information about the award event and images are available at www.######

ENDS

Word count ###

For further information contact CIM Student – Telephone #### .../... e-mail ####@###

Before writing a press release, it is valuable to review the stakeholders and the objectives. In this case, the company wants to develop favourable awareness in the target customer organizations' DMUs (both existing and potential). This positive publicity might also facilitate the recruitment of potential employees. Circulation of the press release and press cuttings to employees should also help maintain positive attitudes within the organization. This outline is a little condensed due to space limitations; you should have a slightly fuller development. When managing PR events, it is good to talk to people and to agree the quotations you would like to use. It is good practice to clear the copy with key people before release.

Writing a press release featured in the June 2006 CIM case study 'SMS Cars Ltd': Question 3a 'Prepare a news release for the local newspaper describing the success of the launch event and promoting the new vehicle.'

Debriefing Activity 2.6

Internal relationships – Manager, other management, other Account Managers, support and creative staff.

Client relationships – Account Manager in client organization, other senior staff, finance for issues with invoices and payments (in the real world we need satisfied clients that pay in good time!). In the initial stages, visits to see key people and get a feel for the given client organization. Telephone and e-mail contacts to maintain communications. Linking in with agency events to host your client and develop relationships in an informal setting.

Media – Editors and journalists in the media relevant to the spectrum of clients.

Suppliers – Media space, printers, creative, courier services (for that last minute panic delivery) and so on.

Industry – Competitors (may want a job with them later), CIM professionals, education and training providers (in a fast-moving world continuing professional development is vital).

You may have identified other key stakeholders. The PR professional must develop relationships all the time. When the big issue comes up (e.g. a general product recall because of a quality problem), the trust must be there and the communications channels open. There is no time to do this in the heat of managing an issue.

Debriefing Activity 2.7

Intangibility – Possibly the most important of the issues. The need is to make the intangible tangible. Both the event managers and the participants want something that is memorable with a sense of occasion. In a life overfull with corporate activity something fresh and imaginative. The right ambience is vital to create that climate to build relationships and communicate.

Inseparability – Clients and speakers that do not arrive are not good news. Make certain that people can get to a proposed location.

Variability – The location that worked well for the way out 'dot-com' creation conference may not work so well for more conservative clients. People–people chemistry is complex.

Perishability – You are not able to store an event. The location cannot store hotel rooms. Time/day negotiations may enable you to find lightly booked periods where a discount might be available.

Service quality – A vital area. A valuable source of information is mystery shopping and having a look around the venue as an ordinary member of the public. Apart from the catering and the like, who will link with you in the management of the event (supply that extra extension lead that was forgotten etc.)? The best atmosphere and service can be ruined if the staff do not know the additional dimensions needed for presentations, demonstrations and so on.

The service extension to the marketing mix is fully covered in Unit 7.

Debriefing Activity 2.8

Before drafting this memo you should have considered who will receive it and what they want/ need from the communication. Your boss and management in general want feedback that the changeover is being properly managed. The restaurant managers need information about how the changeover is to be made without upsetting customers. The front-line staff will need to be informed and persuaded of the need to make the change. Some will be happy with the change others may not be so. A key stakeholder will be the existing loyal customers who have been used to smoking. The implication is that some persuasion should be contained in the memo.

MEMO

To: All Staff

From: CIM Student (note: in the exam you should not use your own name)

Date: ####

Proposed non-smoking policy

Increasingly restaurants have become non-smoking in line with the change over the last decade with the elimination of smoking on public transport. Soon the legal situation will change but it has been decided to effect the change now. In 2 months' time, all our restaurants will become non-smoking. To warn our loyal smoking customers we will be displaying a notice indicating the date of the change. This will give some time for these clients to become aware of the change.

On the day of the change, notices will be placed on the entrances to say 'This is a smoke-free restaurant'. New table notices will also be displayed: 'Thank you for not smoking'. Once this change has come into effect, it is considered that all staff will benefit from the improved working conditions. The majority of customers is expected to be very supportive of the change; and with early warning, the change over will not take our regular customers by surprise.

Signature block

Debriefing Activity 2.9

Selective use of the Carter/Terpstra model could be made. Some selected points are given below:

- ○ *Language* – Not all visitors may fully understand English. Documentation may need to be translated. Interpreters may be needed at meetings.
- ○ *Religion* – Hotel and restaurants should be informed of any special dietary needs (e.g. Kosher, Halal etc.).
- ○ *Values and attitudes* – Different cultures have different work patterns. Japanese technical staff tend to expect to work very long hours late into the evening. Such a schedule might not be so welcome with other cultures.
- ○ *Education* – Given visitors are trained, technical professionals are possibly not an issue.[*]
- ○ *Social organization* – In this context possibly not an issue.
- ○ *Technology and material culture* – Different cultures have different attitudes to technological change. However given these are technical visitors again probably not an issue.

     ◦ *Law and politics* – Given increasing concern over terrorism, care should be taken to assist visitors with potential visa problems.

     ◦ *Aesthetics* – For this technical context again probably not an issue.

* It is noted that models should not be over-worked. They prompt the marketer to ask if something may be an issue. The answer may be 'no' in some cases.

Debriefing Activity 2.10

The need is for the charity to give their key stakeholders the knowledge about the issues, to get action change to prevent smoking and ultimately change values and attitudes to smoking. The target audience for the letter are not marketing professionals, so jargon should be avoided. The group will be working locally in support of a national campaign but with limited local funds.

Your address

Date

Action group address

Dear Ms Smith

Potential activities for your Campaign

Not all people are aware of the dangers of passive smoking. You can generate this knowledge by gaining local media coverage with press releases and by participating in local 'phone-in' chat programmes where your experts can deliver the message 'smoking kills'. People could then gain further information (e.g. about help groups) from your website.

Changing the way people behave often needs a 'carrot and stick' approach. In the initial stages, some physical prompting may be needed. You could lobby local employers' organizations and provide speakers for their meetings to get local employers to ban smoking on their premises.

In the longer term, the campaign might move to changing people's attitudes to smoking. This is more difficult but involves getting people to consider that smoking in public to the annoyance of others is antisocial behaviour and not acceptable. National activities such as advertising can again be re-enforced at a local level with participation in local chat shows and letters to the local paper to fuel the debate.

Signature block

This outline is brief because of space limitations. One activity is given for each stage of the model. Your letter would have possibly identified more. A paragraph each for introduction and conclusion would be appropriate.

Debriefing Activity 2.11

The context of this situation is not only Performing Arts but of course services (entertainment) and probably a limited budget. Four illustrative slides are given below (Table 2.1).

Table 2.1 Regional theatre presentation

Slide number	Content of slide	Presentation notes
1.	Some regional Arts initiatives have failed to attract sufficient audiences in the past. Successful theatres provide a balanced portfolio to build a local loyal base, to attract new audiences and make Arts accessible and to not only provide performances but make the building the centre of the town and community	The opening and weekends are easy. Use and cash flow must also be generated by daytime use and full houses weekday evenings as well. Loyal supporters must be rewarded and a continual flow of new people is needed to maintain a good financial position. The diverse artistic needs of the local community must be satisfied
2.	The location should be marketed. Activities should not be limited to performances but also daytime use of restaurants and space used for art exhibitions. Loyalty to the theatre should be maintained with 'friends' schemes that will give significant discounts to regular users of the theatre	The need is to place the theatre at the centre of the town. The place to meet for lunch. Regional visitors should not consider their stay complete without a visit to the theatre. A key foundation is a loyal base of supporters who support the venture by regular visits. Loyalty schemes should be developed to build the theatre into the lifestyle of these core supporters
3.	A range of productions is needed to attract a diverse audience including Plays, Opera, Ballet, Lighter productions (e.g. musicals)	With a limited population, no single area will provide sufficient potential audience to fill the theatre every day of the week all year. One objective of the theatre is to make art available to regional audiences. Some of these may be minority interests and more popular productions not only bring in a different range of people but also provide surpluses for financing more experimental ventures. The whole community should find that during a programming period there is a 'must see' production for them
4.	Stars are needed to provide focal points. Regional arts must compete with over 100 channels of TV, classic productions available at low cost on DVD. The presence of 'stars' provides the sense of occasion to get people out of their suburban homes and visit the city centre theatre	Star personalities clearly provide the attraction to bring in the audiences. However, they also provide additional opportunities. Visiting stars are also local news and provide a focal point for local publicity to lever a restricted communications budget

You may have produced more slides. An introduction on why a balanced portfolio is needed. Then a body of around 5–7 on how this balanced portfolio of activities could be achieved followed by a concluding slide.

Debriefing Question 2.1

Lake View Organic Farms

SME (small and medium sized enterprise), limited budget, product, service (delivery), relationship marketing (customer retention), green and ethical issues.

The Urban Culture Festival 2005

The festival organisers have not for profit objectives (however events must cover costs), limited budget, services, event management, performing arts, e-marketing, relationship marketing

SME Cars Ltd

SME (small and medium sized enterprise), limited budget, event management, product, service, relationship marketing, database marketing

Unit 3

Debriefing Activity 3.1

Video recorder: 2000 maturity. 2006 decline.

Analogue TV: 2000 maturity. 2006 decline.

Cathode ray tube based TVs in decline.

Digital TV: 2006 in growth.

High-definition TV: 2007 in introduction, 2011 maturity?

Existing generation – DVDs: 2007 maturity, 2009 decline?

New format DVDs 2007 introduction/growth, 2012 into maturity or even possibly decline.

Below some selected issues are debated in this fast-moving sector. New technology will only succeed if it provides some real benefit to adopters. Will an innovative product be a technical curiosity or a 'must have' part of our new life styles?

Video cassette recorders, DVD players, DVD recorders and hard disc recorders: Why are hard disk drives appearing in DVD recorders? The hard disk allows you to instantly pause live TV or replay a football highlight – but the DVD is used to archive programs cheaply.

Analogue TV, Digital Terrestrial ('Freeview') and Sky Digital: What new types of set-top box are likely to appear with the increasing adoption of broadband Internet services in the United Kingdom? How is the market distorted by government intervention? 'Internet Protocol' (IP) set-top boxes are likely to appear alongside existing technologies to stream video on demand across the Internet. The plan to 'switch off' analogue TV signals is highly controversial, especially since TV is considered as a social service in the United Kingdom by Ofcom, the United Kingdom's communications regulator, and is currently available licence-free to those over the age of 75 to 'reduce social isolation'. The UK government has announced tentative plans to financially help vulnerable individuals to cross over to Digital TV.

Cathode ray tube TVs, plasma displays, LCD panels and projectors: Many early flat-panel displays used plasma technology. Why are most consumers leapfrogging this technology and going straight to LCD? Cross-pollination with the laptop computer business has significantly improved the manufacturing yields for high-resolution LCD panels, making them a low-cost flat-panel TV technology and leaving expensive plasma panels behind.

High-definition TV: What is holding HDTV back from becoming the standard format? HDTV broadcasts require a large part of the radio spectrum, limiting the number of channels you can broadcast in total. The picture benefits are most obvious on very large, high-resolution flat-panel TVs that are still relatively expensive. Recording HDTV programmes also requires very high-capacity storage devices like Blu-Ray disc recorders, still to be widely adopted by the market.

DVD and emerging formats such as HD-DVD and Blu-Ray: What factors are influencing the choice of DVD's successor? What happened when the competing DVD standards DVD-RAM, DVD+RW and DVD-R were introduced? The battle between HD-DVD and Blu-Ray is fierce, involving not just electronics manufacturers, but Intel, Microsoft and Hollywood studios – Digital Rights Management (DRM) technology to protect the content from copying is now as big an issue as the physical form of the media. When DVD was introduced, many consumers waited for multi-standard drives (that could play and record in more than one format) to emerge before buying their first DVD recorder – delaying adoption of the technology.

Microsoft Windows Media Centre edition, Microsoft Xbox 360 and Sony Playstation 3: What plans do Microsoft have for home entertainment systems? Is the PC or games console likely to emerge as an all-round entertainment device? Sony launched a version of the Playstation with video recording capabilities and a Blu-Ray disc drive in Japan during 2004. Known as the Playstation PSX it received an indifferent reception from Japanese consumers. Despite this, Microsoft continue to promote their media-centric operating system on PCs and the Xbox 360. In late 2006, Sony encountered problems with the production of Blu-Ray lasers and the European launch of its latest playstation was delayed.

Debriefing Activity 3.2

Here a top-of-the-range, built-in washing machine is considered:

Intangible benefits – confidence, well-being and status.

Tangible benefits – low cost in operation, low noise, easy fabric care, ease of use and so on.

Features – Stainless steel drum construction, anti-vibration mountings to reduce noise levels, intelligent microprocessor to optimize wash conditions for different loads and so on.

Signal attributes – stylish design to fit in with the modern kitchen. At the top of the range, expensive houses may have a separate laundry room.

Legal conformance – safety and electrical noise laws (must not cause interference with other electrical/electronic products).

Account conformance – not an issue in this question context.

Safety – apart from electrical legal issues, auto-locking door, so it may not be opened when in use and so on.

Environmental life cycle – Plastic parts should be clearly marked to assist with recycling. Full life cycle would also take into account the energy, water, detergents, and so on consumed during the machine's lifetime.

Performance – Benchmark washes with 'standard' dirt and stains to demonstrate efficiency.

Complementary products – water, electricity, detergent and other wash aids.

Range and depth – possible part of a full range of kitchen appliances. Depth – different colours to fit in with different kitchens.

Service – Initial installation and in-field maintenance.

The ideal machine would take dirty clothes, operate in total silence, use minimum resources (e.g. water) and return them ready to wear (who wants to iron?).

Debriefing Activity 3.3

You should observe that the market is segmented, with some older products aimed at a more confectionery market but with more recent introductions aimed at the 'oral hygiene' market, chewing gum becoming in effect a toothbrush on the move. This has provided market rejuvenation of what could have been perceived as old and tired confectionery. It is also noticeable that innovative packaging has a role to play in this sector. The eight-stage process assists in minimizing product failure. Clearly, a key stage is the fostering of innovative new product ideas in the organization in the first place. Marketing is a creative process.

Debriefing Activity 3.4

You should note a range of products including generic (often blue packs), own label and premium brand. Some major brands have more than one product such as Cherry Coke. There are also specially positioned brands such as 'sports energy' drinks at a premium price.

It is interesting that there appears to be less activity in the generic and own label brands in the chewing gum/oral hygiene market.

Debriefing Activity 3.5

There is a clear division between single-use products (tin of soup) and those which are used over a period of time. Taking a plastic tomato sauce bottle as an example, we can note

- On first opening a tamper evident seal has to be broken.
- The shape of the container and colour link to the branding.
- The flip top is easy to use and protects the unused product from contamination.
- The plastic squeeze-type bottle makes it easier to dispense the product. Glass bottles have a habit of not dispensing anything then suddenly dumping half a bottle on your meal.
- Both glass and plastic packaging are suitable for recycling.

Food packaging has come a long way from the brown paper bag.

Debriefing Question 3.1

Using the structure from figure 3.4 Architecture of product: Intangible benefit: place with a sense of occasion, Tangible benefit: easy access, comfortable surroundings to put delegates at ease, Features: specific issues such as room size, menu etc., Signal attributes: good standard of decoration & smart staff, Legal conformance: music licence, Account conformance: n/a, Safety: fire exits, Environmental life cycle: n/a, Performance: speed of service, complementary products: quality food etc, Range & depth; single location n/a, Service: assistance with event planning

Unit 4

Debriefing Activity 4.1

Interest rates have for the last few years been at a half-century low, making the finance of large loans more affordable. Shifting patterns of demand have encouraged prices in hot spots to move much faster than inflation, so in some depressed areas, prices have not moved as much, thus illustrating the law of supply and demand. In major cities, certain areas command a premium price, as they are perceived to have 'status'. Other factors can influence the decision, for example for families with children, a house in the catchment area for a 'good' school may command a premium. There are some side effects. The large rise in prices has provided the foundation for the purchase of second homes in holiday destination areas forcing prices up and excluding local people from the market (changes in pension rules may still add further fuel to the market for second homes); often these areas have lower wage levels than found in London. The mortgage sector is a jungle with people being encouraged to take low-start-cost mortgages without much long-term protection in the event of adverse interest rate movements. The endowment mortgage trap has caused problems for many people, with the linked investment policy not providing the anticipated funds to cover the mortgage. The danger is that short-term incentives might drive a long-term investment issue.

Debriefing Activity 4.2

New China Calculations

Costs	Fixed costs	Variable costs	Sales revenue	Profit contribution
Original evening calculations				
Overheads	200 000	8	25	17
Depreciation	30 000			
Total fixed	230 000			
Number of trading days	312			
Fixed cost per day	737.1795			
Breakeven as customers per day	43.3635			
Next year's analysis – Evening only trading				
Overheads	210 000	9	25	16
Depreciation	30 000			
Total fixed	240 000			
Number of trading days	312			
Fixed cost per day	769.2308			
Breakeven as customers per day	48.07692			
Alternative strategy				
Fixed costs a day	769.2308			
Divide above by 44 customers a day	17.48252			

Debriefing Activity 4.3

Some key cost drivers are given below.

There are two options: self-processing and use of a contractor. The cost of cameras and so on is the same in both cases. (Note: a working assumption is made here that traditional imaging is being used rather than digital. In case studies and questions, it is sometimes necessary to make reasonable working assumptions.)

Capital costs – Cost of the cameras, lights, and the like, possibly the purchase of transport along with costs of fitting out the premises.

Fixed – Rent of premises for studio, insurance for premises, car, photographic equipment and professional indemnity insurance (e.g. if wedding photographs are not of an acceptable quality). Cost of communications such as telephone rental and fixed ISP and broadband monthly subscriptions are to be included here.

Variable – Direct cost of travel fuel and so on, cost of materials (film, batteries etc.) and of film processing. Cost of specific communications such as telephone calls and postage for delivery of photographs are to be included here.

Debriefing Activity 4.4

Some key test parameters might be

- Costs by vehicle type per mile
- Costs by vehicle type by passenger mile
- Profitability by pickup location (e.g. airport may be more profitable than city centre)
- Unprofitable miles percentage (cost of travel to pick up dead time and travel costs)
- Time from call to pickup (customer service parameter), both overall and broken down by time of day, day of week
- Customer complaints per driver.

These are just some selected parameters that might help the company improve service and profitability.

Debriefing Question 4.1

First, it is noted that the question does not give you enough information. In this case, this was deliberate. In case studies, it is often necessary to make working assumptions. If you need to make working assumptions, give them in your answer. In real life, you may need to do this and often this is the starting point for some research to confirm the assumptions. In this case, the assumption is that each friend will be accompanied by another person (e.g. partner or friend). There is also an assumption that there are no additional costs for the additional people mid-week.

The revenue of the new scheme a year for each person will be £20 + (10 × 2 × £10) = £220

However, there is a loss on the old scheme of £15 × 2 × 6 = £180

The net gain of the new scheme is £220 – £180 = £40

The number of people needed on the new scheme is the cost (£5000) of setting it up divided by the revenue per card sold (£40): 5000/40 = 125.

We note that 400 of the seats are premium and only 30 per cent on average are free per night: 120 (400 × 0.30 = 120). This is less than the number of friends' seats needed for breakeven 125 × 2 seats per card = 250. Thus, research would be needed to see if the demand would be spread over all weekdays. This could be linked to a restriction that a second choice date needed to be selected or premium seats could be allocated on a 'first come first served' policy and late applications would be allocated standard seats (still with a price advantage). The key point is that simply calculating the numbers is not enough. It is essential to debate the implications for the marketing plans.

For the 'Friends' dinner for two', the project revenue is based on 10 visits with two people, with a profit of two pounds and a 50 per cent up take. The 'average' additional income will be 10 × £2 × 2 × 0.5 = £20

This give us a new revenue figure of £40 + £20 = £60

The new breakeven figure is now £5000/£60 = 83.3 (i.e. around 84 people).

The significance of this is that in such businesses marginal additional revenue is most important. Given the importance of having two tickets rather than one purchased, this might suggest that the dinner offer should be framed on the basis of a 'dinner for two offer'. Again, it is not just the figures that are important but then moving on to deciding the marketing implications and adjusting the offer accordingly.

Debriefing Question 4.2

A number of factors need to be considered. The marketing mix is used to structure this brief overview. It must be remembered that although we consider 7Ps in different units all elements interact; for example, if we need a higher quality product it is likely to have an impact on price.

Product: (remember product is product + service) Is it just to collect a 'takeaway' coffee to drink on the train or is it a café culture leisurely drink with table service? The higher the quality of the coffee, the higher costs involved (cheap instant coffee granules or fresh roasted and ground?). The more service that is provided, the higher the staffing costs may be. Remember that cost of coffee can be considered as variable cost, but once staff levels have been set they represent a fixed cost for the period and do not change with the number of cups of coffee sold.

Price: As discussed earlier in this unit, the issues to be considered are the estimated, fixed and variable costs for the various potential product/service offerings. Clients do not see price they see value (if they can get the same offering for less round the corner they may well go there) and it must be affordable (very expensive 'designer' coffee might not be appropriate for a student refectory with customers on restricted incomes).

Place: Again it is important to remember the marketing mix element 'place' is not just location. It is about convenience. A key issue to be decided will be hours of opening. Will early hours and late-night opening be rewarded with enough additional revenue to justify the extra staff costs? Here it is important to take the right cost elements into the calculation. Marginal cost elements are more appropriate for this issue than adsorption costing with fixed cost allocations (extra opening hours will not change the rent).

Promotion: Advertising and like promotional expenses are not variable costs. You place an advertisement and the costs do not change with the number of cups of coffee you sell. The increased fixed costs do have an impact on the breakeven estimates. Promotional prices (e.g. coffee and meal deal) are variable costs. The expense depends on the level of up take of the offer.

People: What will people be paid? Will premium rates apply to weekend working? How will the people be dressed, just clean overalls or specially designed uniforms to fit the ambience? Will performance bonuses be paid? Will the level of tips be an incentive to employees?

Physical evidence: Should the surroundings be just clean and generically functional or theme designed to provide that authentic Paris Café culture experience?

Process: Should this be collect yourself from the counter or full table service?

The need is to make estimates (supported by research) of how much people are prepared to pay for the level of product/service they require. Will there be enough customers to safely move the proposed operation past breakeven? Pricing is more complex than simply entering a few figures into a spreadsheet with the 'correct' answer appearing to four decimal places. The marketer needs to exercise a lot of skilled judgment in interpreting the implication of the figures. Spreadsheets of themselves do not make decisions. They provide vital evidence and do help marketers to evaluate the likely impact of different marketing decisions.

Unit 5

Debriefing Activity 5.1

With wet film, the need for a dark room and the use of dangerous chemicals deterred the vast majority users from processing at home. Now almost all computers will accept camera memory media and many common systems come with image-processing capability bundled in the start-up software package (so much so that the free digital camera is a frequent promotional option). Home processing is now an easy option. Standard colour printers do a fair job (there are problems with long-term colour stability). For people without computers, companies such as Kodak are producing home printers, where the camera or memory card can be 'docked' and images printed. Printing can be slow and media (photo-quality paper and cartridges) is surprisingly expensive.

A second option is the re-invention of the mini-photographic laboratory. Here people can plug in their memory media and print out on higher quality printers with better overall quality and lower print costs for longer print runs. For more specialist printing (e.g. large sizes (e.g. A1) and specialist media (e.g. your own customized mouse mat)), the services of the more specialist laboratory are still needed. However, with broadband access, people can send their files over the Internet, no need to go to the shop to hand over your film. The finished articles can then be returned by courier service or by post.

The new technology has changed the balance of outlet options for the consumer. Home processing is a realistic option. The mini-laboratories and central laboratories have had to rethink their distribution and business processes (for the central laboratory, inbound logistics become broadband delivery of files, rather than a van delivering rolls of film). The process of a local agent collecting films and customers having to return to collect their prints a day later is a non-starter. The agents appear to be out of the loop completely. Digital processes and e-communications are rewriting distribution of 'goods' and services. A similar revolution will be taking place in the distribution of film and music. Why should we trek into town or wait for snail mail to deliver a CD or DVD when we can download over broadband?

Debriefing Activity 5.2

Only selected issues are given below. You may well have considered additional aspects.

- o Weekly supermarket run replaced by Internet ordering and home delivery.
- o High-street travel agents are on the decline as more people 'e'-book travel and hotels directly.
- o Pirate (illegal) radio stations broadcasting alternative music can now become legal and reach a global audience by pod casting over the Internet.
- o New groups can distribute their music by a similar mechanism. They do not have to hope for a big record company to back them. Minority interest music can become freely available.
- o How long will the high-street video hire shop last with video on demand over broadband and a large selection of recent films available on a 'pay-per-view' basis?
- o Already music charts have a 'download' chart. This may ultimately be the death of the high-street 'record' shop. Moreover, it may change the way artists release material. Now if you only want four tracks from an album, you can choose to download only these tracks rather than buy the whole album.
- o Portable sensors monitoring key health parameters (e.g. blood pressure) can communicate to and from a domestic home base using wireless technology (e.g. Bluetooth) and link the patient to the surgery for remote diagnosis.
- o Specialist surgery is difficult to provide in lightly populated areas. Experiments are under way with medical robotics. A specialist surgeon in a major city may be able to complete a procedure remotely in a regional small hospital many hundreds of miles away. In part, the 'digital doctor' might replace the 'flying doctor'.
- o e-Banking is popular with customers (the bank that is always open) and with the banks (vastly reduced costs when compared with services provided at a high-street branch).

Debriefing Activity 5.3

Your list might include water, sewage, gas, electricity, home banking, communications (telephone and broadband), snail mail deliveries, window cleaning and other miscellaneous services such as pizza delivery.

Debriefing Activity 5.4

The usual place to start with outlets is to take the manufacturers' view. Marketers as 'advocates' for the customer in the organization should ask the question the other way round. Not 'Where do we want our products?' Rather 'Where would our customers like to be able to obtain them?'

Places where you might expect to find 'plug in' connections might include hotel bedroom, hotel business suite and so on. Increasingly, however, people do not want all that trouble and now seek out wireless connections in areas such as airport transit lounges, motorway service stations, Internet café, libraries and so on. The year 2006 has seen more advances using wider network capabilities so whole cities may become, in effect, one large wireless 'hot spot'.

Debriefing Question 5.1

A sound starting point would be to list all the things that will be needed on the stand; these could include brochures, toys for exhibition, hospitality supplies and so on. An irritating problem for international business is that US paper sizes can be different and those nice A4 sized brochures might not fit a standard US stand. With international point-of-sale activities, care needs to be taken over differing sizes and other standards (e.g. in the United States the voltage and frequency of electricity supply are different). In shipping the samples to the exhibition, care needs to be taken not only to allow enough time for the physical transport of the goods and exhibition materials but also for administrative procedures such as clearing customs. There is nothing more frustrating than to know that your display materials are in the country but held up by a glitch in the paperwork delaying customs clearance. Local sources can be identified for hospitality supplies.

A key problem is sometimes one is faced with a narrow time-window with often just one day to get all the materials on site and set up the stand. Exhibitions are a demanding activity. More cover on exhibitions is given in Unit 9.

Unit 6

Debriefing Question 6.1

Internal

B2B – potential sponsors.

Participants – local and international guest artists

Customers – people attending the range of events; in a full analysis include the segmentation variables.

Regulatory – licences for performances, health and safety at temporary venues and so on.

Pressure groups – concerns about the Graffiti Gallery, local residents groups concerned with noise and traffic problems, community groups wanting to participate (e.g. Caribbean Carnival)

Political – local politicians for general support and need to be convinced of innovative activities, for example 'Graffiti Gallery'

Suppliers

Media

Debriefing Activity 6.1

The assumption is that the museum is run by a local charity. A list of likely stakeholders might include charity trustees, staff, volunteers, donors to the museum, media, visitors, prospective visitors, public at large, local historians and researchers, students and supplier publics. It should be noted that this is a not-for-profit context.

Debriefing Activity 6.2

Full range from road signs, building signage, vehicles, own label products, documentation, trolleys, carrier bags, posters and other advertisements, and so on. The corporate imagery has to work across a broad range of objects from a large vehicle to a receipt.

Questions on the communications mix are common in the CIM exams, for example December 2005 'The Urban Culture Festival 2006' Question 3 'Describe the advantages and disadvantages of advertising using the following media specifically in the context of the Urban Culture Festival 2006: television, radio, cinema, magazines and other alternative media (please specify)', and June 2006 'SMS Cars Ltd' Question 5b 'Make recommendations as to how the promotional mix could be used to increase demand for the Vehicle Servicing Department.'

Debriefing Activity 6.3

Definition of requirements such as need for a scanner (problem recognition), reading literature and discussing equipment with friends (information search), evaluating how good the various functions are for her special graphic design needs which are different to spreadsheets (evaluation of alternatives), purchase, possibly from a local outlet but increasingly online. Information and influence will come from publications, friends and possibly college staff.

Debriefing Question 6.2

Comparing one medium against another is a type of question it is wise to be prepared for in the exam.

Radio advantages – can be regional or national; intimate medium; catches people on the move; some possibility of selecting targets with time of day and selection of station; can be relatively low cost.

Radio disadvantages – limited scope for creativity; only a short message; message does not last; cover of target segments may be patchy.

Press advantages – large range of titles; can target regional or national; may be able to select position of the advertisement (e.g. record offers in the music review section); lasts longer than a radio advertisement; can carry more information; some scope for creativity but colour may be expensive.

Press disadvantages – daily press still has limited life; easy to miss an advertisement; can be expensive; may need to use a range to get good cover of a target segment.

Debriefing Question 6.3

Analysis of morning paper

Cost per thousand of target audience is £1000 divided by circulation adjusted by the percentage on target:

$$£1000/50\,000 \times 0.4 = 0.05$$

The same calculation for the evening paper gives the following:

$$£750/30\,000 \times 0.3 = 0.083$$

The apparent higher cost of the morning paper (£1000 against £750) would appear to be justified by the likely higher 'hit' rate on the target segment. However, when the higher response rates for the evening paper are taken into account (with targets twice as likely to respond) this looks the more attractive option. Note that more information is really needed. Absolute number of responses and potential profit from these is needed to justify the advertisement, and in real life more research and analysis would be required. This type of question exploring different options is a common CIM exam topic, for example December 2005 'The Urban Culture Festival 2006' Question 2a 'Identify THREE sales promotion techniques that could be used to build audiences across the different events at the 2006 Urban Culture Festival', and 2b 'Recommend THREE public relations activities to gain maximum awareness amongst your target audiences.'

Debriefing Question 6.4

Advantage of publicity – this medium is free (this is not to say publicity is free as PR, writing press releases and support cost money), can be a mechanism to lever communications on a limited budget, can get cover where advertising is not permitted (e.g. BBC) and favourable comments are more convincing from independent third parties.

Disadvantages of publicity – no control over the copy, no control over when and if published, can have adverse effect if third party has negative messages about the product and/or organization.

Advantage of advertising – control of the copy, control of when and where published.

Disadvantage of advertising – can be expensive, may have less perceived authority than publicity.

Debriefing Question 6.5

Different cultures have different styles of meeting and greeting and forms of address from rather formal to informal. In some cultures it is acceptable to 'get down to business' immediately. With others, more attention to social preamble is appropriate. If entertaining over lunch, it is necessary to confirm special diet requirements, for example vegetarian. Alcohol consumption may not be appropriate and in modern business meetings, mineral water is often the preferred choice. Clearly, you should first be aware of the cultural background of your business guests and then be empathetic to their needs. An empathetic approach is more likely to build relationships and long-term profitable business.

Debriefing Activity 6.4

This debrief is written around the activities for a spring open day for college. Pre-event personal selling with visits to local schools, leaflets, advertisements in the local press; a major local college might use some local TV and radio advertising, posters, and gain publicity in the local press with special events; follow-up story for the local press. Note also the need for internal marketing to brief staff and existing students. Note the need to link with the college website. No one single activity is the solution; it is the integrated application of the communications mix that is required to achieve the objectives.

Debriefing Question 6.6

It is suggested that the structure from Figure 6.1 can be used as a checklist. A possible communications mix might be as follows:

Advertising – inclusion on all general advertising, for example in directories. Advertising in local marketing publications, for example CIM local events calendar.

Publicity – press release, possibly using an open day and a local marketing business celebrity to create news value.

PR – special events around the open day for employers who might sponsor students. Press releases and media packs.

Personal selling – visits to local employers to sell the programme on a one-to-one basis.

Point of sale – in service marketing terms, an attractive location to pay fees, not some hatch in the wall of a cold corridor. We would hope this is in place.

Sales system – no new, specific action, would be the college's normal system.

Sales promotion – possibly a discount scheme for larger employers who send more than five students onto the programme.

Direct marketing – mailshot to training Manager and Marketing managers in the local area.

E-communications – ensure specific pages were set up for the new programme on the college website. Establish links to other relevant sites.

Sponsorship – approach local organizations for a 'best student prize'; plan not only for the launch but for the future as well. Prize can be given at an event to generate more publicity. Sponsor a local CIM event at the college.

Debriefing Activity 6.5

Selected briefing points might include the following:

Identification of the targets – identification of the communications targets and their information needs (e.g. prospective students, employers).

Integration with the other elements of the communications mix – links to other media (e.g. telephone contacts).

Must have – data regarding the use of the logo and so on.

Must not have – making certain that copy and images will not offend people from differing cultural backgrounds.

Budget – in real life a budget would have to be considered and progress monitored against budget to avoid any overspend.

Schedule – a list of the key dates for the project.

Point of contact – in real life the person responsible for the project from the organization, linking in with the agency.

As mentioned earlier in working with agencies, one needs to take a professional critical view of the quality of work but this is very different to becoming an amateur graphic designer.

Debriefing Activity 6.6

Note the need to collect both quantitative data (how many visits were there and how long did they spend on the website, etc.) and more qualitative data such as ease of use and how good the imagery is in communicating. With prospectuses, was the index good? Was the information complete and up to date (e.g. did it reflect changes in the CIM syllabus)?

Debriefing Question 6.7

Segmentation review

Retail outlets for consumer sales

- o Large chains such as supermarkets, convenience stores (including independents with cooperative purchasing), forecourt sales and so on. 'Cash & Carry' wholesalers supplying the small independent outlets.
- o Small independent outlets such as independent convenience shops, independent garage forecourt sales.

B2B sales

As with many 'retail' products there is also a B2B market.

- o Large chains: hotels, restaurant chains (both owned and franchised), airlines, railways and so on.
- o Small outlets: independent hotels and restaurants.

Marketing communications:

Large customers

A major activity would be personal selling with a package of incentives such as point-of-sale material and joint promotions. This would also include personal selling to wholesalers servicing the small independent outlets.

Small customers

Activities could include advertising in the trade press, publicity (e.g. feature articles on new product launches), direct mailing and displays in the case of wholesalers. Promotional offers to their customers (e.g. reduced prices). Incentives to stocking (e.g. entry into a competition for the owner when stocking the product for the first time).

Unit 7

Debriefing Activity 7.1

Intangible benefit – reassurance, feeling of safety and peace of mind.

Tangible benefits – value for money, rapid installation, minimum disruption to house, and appropriate boiler and parts used in installation.

Legal conformance – conformance of installation to relevant standards for gas, water and electricity.

Safety – appropriate care taken with safety during installation and conformance of the installation to all relevant standards after work is completed.

Environment – care taken during installation to minimize impact with the old parts segregated for appropriate recycling.

Performance – apart from physical installation quality, minimization of disruption (do staff clean up after installation?).

Complementary products – full installation system and pre-existing services (gas, water and electricity, the need to check these are adequate, e.g. water pressure satisfactory).

Range and depth – full range and depth, so there is installation of other products plus other services such as maintenance and insurance.

At the end of this unit, return to this activity and consider how the service-extended marketing mix elements apply to this situation.

Debriefing Activity 7.2

Often in this type of situation, it is useful to draw up an event timeline of actions, in this case from leaving house to arrival at the destination hotel.

Travel to airport – was it a good experience with connections made on time or were trains crowded and dirty (different range of experience but same type of issues, e.g. was parking easy if you go by car)?

Checking in – was this easy and friendly or a nightmare hour in a queue, with difficulty getting the type of seat you wanted?

Duty-free experience – well stocked with friendly people or a limited range with poor service?

Flight – was the food good and well served or was quality poor and service slow and unresponsive? Were the seats good or from 'cattle class'? Was the flight departure and arrival on time?

Entry – were immigration and customs easy and pleasant or another hour of waiting?

Luggage reclaim – quick and simple or yet another hour's wait and a rugby scrum to recover your luggage only to find it was damaged (possibly just one better: that it was at Heathrow and you were at Gatwick).

Journey to destination – were taxis (or other transport) easy to find and quickly available or still yet another long wait?

Important to note that it is the total travel experience that we remember, not just the flight.

Debriefing Activity 7.3

Selective use of the model is appropriate, as issues like contracts of service will not be available to you, but taking the main headings from Figure 7.1.

Organization – what is the college style, is there a good structure and is the organization structure supportive of a good quality programme delivery?

Individuals – are the teaching staff appropriately qualified, with good personalities, highly motivated (and motivating) with appropriate supportive behaviour?

Customers – does the class form a learning culture; is this assisted by the college with the provision of appropriate student areas? Is the teaching one-way or responsive to students' needs (e.g. account taken of participants from not-for-profit organizations) and is there opportunity for participation in the process (e.g. presentations, role play and syndicate exercises)?

Feedback and control – you will not have access to staff appraisal systems but are there procedures in place for student problems and course issues to be identified and resolved?

Debriefing Activity 7.4

Environment – environment of the bank, style and decoration – a reflection of corporate values and identity.

Tangible clues – style and quality of documentation from chequebooks to bank statements, credit and other cards, style and design. Are appropriate safety features built in?

Facilitating goods – in our definition for a golf club this includes golfing accessories and things you use in playing the game. In this sense, banks do not sell chequebook covers, wallets or even books on personal finance. Not every part of a model is important in every case.

Debriefing Activity 7.5

Exam route – easy to prove the work is entirely the candidate's work. The same exam is taken by all centres and centrally marked, so it is relatively easy to ensure uniform standards. Overall, it is easier to control the administration of the systems. From the candidate's view, more exam stress and exam questions may appear remote from candidate's own marketing experience.

Assessment route – more difficult to audit that the work is entirely the candidate's unaided work. Differing organizations are used so it is more difficult to ensure uniform standards. Work is completed over a longer period so systems are more difficult to administer. For the candidate, there is not the stress of an exam, but there is a workload problem in completing and researching a report. With some flexibility of examples, the candidate may consider the experience more relevant to their work experience.

Debriefing Question 7.1

The application of the service-extended marketing mix is a frequently used format for questions in the CIM exams and it is wise to develop your skills to apply the mix in a variety of situations. Given the limited amount of time in the examination context, the full detail of the mix modules given in this and earlier units would provide too much detail so some selectivity is needed. Some selected key issues are given below. More development would be needed for a full examination answer.

Segmentation – for the local paper we might consider readers to be segmented by regular readers with home delivery and people who buy their copy from a news-stand. We should note that much of the revenue for a local newspaper (as for most press) comes from advertising and these segment into professional (local companies) and non-professional (small advertisements and announcements).

Product – the actual paper, its style layout and content (news and features). Note in 2004 the move from some of the broadsheets to tabloid format, number of pages and feature 'pull outs', and so on. Note that, increasingly, there is a newspaper website offering headlines and other features.

Price – needs to be packed with features to provide value with good advertising revenue that helps keep the cover price down for readers. Note that the advertising can be engineered to cover the total costs so that the paper can be given away.

Place – distribution via traditional shops with delivery, supermarkets and increasingly, to reduce costs, automated dispensers.

Communications – local paper so there is not a big budget but there must be a mix of communications for readers. These might include local radio, posters, bus advertisements, delivery vans and point-of-sale displays. A good website to contact the paper and get information would be appropriate. Use of the paper's own space to promote special features for individual advertisers (e.g. personal messages for Valentine's Day) will prove good. Sponsorship of events can generate value for both readers and commercial advertisers (e.g. local half marathon). Note a key public here is news provider for the professional PR people for local organizations and 'part-time' PR managers (e.g. club secretaries, who act as an important news source for the paper).

People – the commercial staff should be friendly and professional. However, key for this is that the editor and the feature writers should be local mini-celebrities. You just have to read Jill's column if you want to know about local dance events and the like.

Physical evidence – good quality invoices and press packs for commercial advertisers and layout of the city centre shop.

Process – automated dispensing machines to reduce selling costs while providing good cover for all readers; for advertisers, the ability to place advertisements by any suitable means, increasingly electronic by e-mail (e.g. providing copy by file attachments).

Note that in any given situation, one element of the mix may need more development than another. Given that a paper is all about communications, it is not surprising that there needs to be a little more attention to this element of the marketing mix. The above treatment is in outline. You may have some other elements that you think are important. The above treatment is about 350 words long. In an exam situation, it is difficult to write much more than 1000 words for a single question. It is essential to be concise, focused and provide complete cover of the issues (it is too easy to develop too much at the start and not to leave enough time for the last aspects of the question).

Debriefing Activity 7.6

No specific debriefing is possible, as the experience will depend greatly on the country you were in. The whole marketing mix, what is sold, how it is paid for (more use of credit cards in the United States), the nature of the outlets (out-of-town 'mega' store or traditional village market), the promotional messages, the people, the physical evidence and the process (in the United Kingdom the price shown is what you pay, in other cultures it is the point at which you start to negotiate) can all be different.

Debriefing Question 7.2

This is a selective review of the issues that might be considered by an international airline.

People

Legal – A high security area so flight crew must have documented security clearance. Standards of competence (e.g. pilots) must be subjected to re-evaluation. Health checks are required for pilots.

Individuals should be educated to the right level and have an engaging personality to provide good in-cabin service. For an international airline, language skills are important. Staff should be sensitive to the cultural diversity of the passengers. Behaviour must be friendly and professional. Appearance is important as dress style etc. may be part of the branding experience (e.g. Emirates).

Customers – A key issue is that passengers should make themselves aware of the safety provision in the aircraft (e.g. position of exits). Other customers: an occasional issue is that 'standard' class is full but there is still spare space in the premium classes. It is to the advantage of the airline to fill all seats, an empty seat does not make any profit contribution. However, care must be taken in selecting passengers for a free up-grade to business class.

Physical evidence

Environment – Considerable management and design effort is devoted to giving the interior of an aircraft a style that is the signature of the airline.

Tangible evidence – The standard of the food is evidence of the standard of the service. This is one of the ways in which premium class is differentiated from standard class. Given the differing cultures of the passengers the food provided needs to conform to a range of religious and cultural needs. The provision of in-flight information in the major languages also provides evidence of the airline's care in providing an empathetic experience.

Facilitating goods – Providing travel items such as flight bags with the airline logo.

Process

This has been an area of great activity with the application of ICT such as direct e-booking, e-ticketing, self check-in and so on. However, once on the aircraft the emphasis is on a high standard of personal service, particularly for premium-class seats. The process may be highly regulated (e.g. safety, security and passport checks). The new use of ICT needs customer involvement. Overall, the customer gains from the extra convenience. The airline gains from reduced costs. The price is total dependence on ICT and although failure of the computer systems at check-in are rare, major disruption is caused when it does occasionally occur.

Unit 8

Debriefing Activity 8.1

The key decisions to be made – Is there a sufficient demand in the location to support the programme? Are there the resources to provide a quality programme? For this analysis, we will only consider some selected issues largely from the external environment.

Segmentation issues – How many potential students are there in the local area? What is the detailed segmentation structure (e.g. full-time, part-time, mature, etc.)?

Mix issues – Product demanded (e.g. full-time, part-time, intensive weekend or distance learning), price (e.g. who will pay, student or employer, etc.?); place (time of sessions, location of sessions, e-based access); promotions (What media might be appropriate? Are suitable mailing lists available? What is the communications task? Do students know about the CIM qualifications or is this to be part of the communications task?); people (Are suitable tutors available?); physical evidence (Are premises suitable? Can good quality documentation be provided?); process (Do students want a personal-based process or more e-based distance learning, etc.?).

Debriefing Activity 8.2

This is a mixture of quantitative and qualitative data.

Quantitative data – How does the market segment? What is the size of the segments? How much chocolate do individuals eat? Where do they purchase it? And so on.

Qualitative data – How do people feel about chocolate? How does the product fit into their lives? What do they think of the present brands? Some years ago, a company thought that existing brands were 'feminine' and introduced a more chunky bar that had more of a 'masculine' positioning. The product was very successful.

Debriefing Activity 8.3

What segment(s) to target? What services to offer? What pricing structure? What location? What opening hours? Where to communicate (e.g. poster locations)? What style for the salon interior? Just some of the decisions to be made.

Debriefing Activity 8.4

Only some selected sources are included here. You may well have identified more in your discussions. Sampling errors: in the past telephones were owned by more wealthy households. It is easy to think that now this is easy and telephone surveys will be representative. However, the 'no answer' situation is a problem. People in full-time employment may be less likely to respond. The selective response is a key issue and should always be checked out. People are also not honest; what they say is not what they do. Of course, we are concerned about the Third World, but not enough to pay more for 'free trade' coffee. Framing a truly neutral question is a little more difficult than it might at first appear.

Debriefing Activity 8.5

Considering this type of issue is often useful both in real life and in the exam situation to use some structure. Here we shall adopt the marketing mix as the framework.

Products – Are there any new introductions? Are new technologies being built in, new benefits provided, additional segments being targeted and so on?

Price – What are the pricing structures on offer? Are credit terms and others being offered as well?

Place – Are new outlets being used or new distributors appointed?

Promotion – What are the new messages and platforms? Is new media such as the Internet being used (e.g. for technical support data)? What literature is available?

People – Who is on the stand? Are they all the same as last year or are there a fair number of new people? Who are they and do they represent new initiatives in the way products are being promoted?

Physical evidence – Is the stand bigger or smaller than last year? Has much money been spent on the design and fitting of the stand? What impression does the stand give about the competitor and their products?

Process – Any new communications processes being used?

Debriefing Activity 8.6

Information would include sales of products, effect of promotional offers, loyalty card usage, damaged, out-of-time and returned goods, number of customers, spending patterns of customers and so on. Note qualitative information can be obtained from analysing internal video recordings.

Debriefing Activity 8.7

A major problem is the degree to which crime is reported. Much crime can go unreported to the Police (e.g. people do not think it is worth the effort or, in the case of violent crime, victims are frightened). The analysis of crime figures can be distorted by changes in the readiness of people to report crime. After an awareness campaign, is an apparent upturn in crime real or just the result of changing people's readiness to report it? Changing the classification of a crime can make it difficult to look at crime figures over a period of years. These and other issues can make the analysis of figures difficult, as it is difficult to find a firm basis for comparison.

Debriefing Question 8.1

This type of question is frequently asked in CIM examinations. A context-specific response is required, not a general 'fit any situation' list. Some selected points are included below.

Information that would be useful in this situation with suggested methods of obtaining it: Quantitative analysis of readership by segments and features read (by questionnaire); comparison with actual demographics of locality (secondary research, e.g. census data); Qualitative information – how people view the paper (focus groups). Note: an informal view could be formed by analysing internal information such as letters to the editor and customer comments by telephone. This type of information may be biased towards people with more spare time and not fully representative of the main group of readers.

For B2B advertisers, an analysis of who spends what and when from internal data; some field research on how clients evaluate the success of their advertisements.

How information could be used to better market the paper and increase its profitability? Better targeting and focus on features appreciated by readers should bring in new readers and get occasional readers to become more loyal. Improved media packs resulting from the information would assist client organizations in planning their advertising better and making more use of the paper. Indirectly the increased circulation would increase the value of the advertisements and so build up more use and also allow higher prices to be justifiably charged for a given amount of space.

Unit 9

Debriefing Activity 9.1

Diane Peters,
25 Montreal Drive,
Southside,
NEW TOWN,
Home County
XY23 9GH
Home: 01653 249687
Mobile: 0776 2349875
dpeters@internetprovider.co.uk
15th January 2006

Ann Smith,
Marketing Manager,
New Theatre,
South Street,
NEW TOWN,
Home County
XY23 ZA19

Dear Ms Smith,

Reference AS/23/2006 – Marketing Assistant Vacancy at New Theatre

I am writing in response to your advertisement for the above position and wish to submit my curriculum vitae for your consideration.

My professional qualifications include the Advanced Certificate in Marketing from the CIM, which I have completed recently, and hope to continue with my studies in this area to gain diploma level. Although I have always enjoyed marketing, my CIM studies have really put a different perspective on them, enabling me to consider the tasks within an organizational framework and to fully appreciate the impact that good marketing can have.

Having always had a real passion for the Arts, in all their forms, I was delighted to be offered a year's contract assisting with marketing at The Sibelius Concert Hall last year, which I found stimulating and enjoyable. Whilst there, amongst many and varied tasks, I was responsible for helping to maintain their customer database and helped to modify this invaluable marketing communications tool.

In my spare time, I am a keen actress, being a member of The New Town Players Amateur Dramatic Society, and I am committed to the Arts in all their forms being promoted to as wide an audience as possible.

I enclose my curriculum vitae and references for your perusal. Please do not hesitate to contact me if you require any further information. I look forward to hearing from you.

Yours sincerely,

Diane Peters, BA (Hons).

The covering letter is to 'lift' your CV so it is the one that gets fully looked at, with the content of the CV in the personal selling process, sending the message 'interview me, I can perform well in this job'.

Debriefing Activity 9.2

Header will contain all the relevant to and from information. Footer will contain the disclaimer information.

Dear Jill,

Thank you for your enquiry regarding the CIM course at New Town College regarding career prospects in Marketing and PR.

Marketing is a broad-spectrum industry that could involve a huge variety of tasks, one of which could be PR. Public Relations is solely concerned with the public image of a company or individual, so may include supervision of the company/individual profile through the media and the control of brand image through publications and publicity material. In addition, a general Marketing qualification such as the CIM courses on offer at New Town College would also train you in product positioning, market research, pricing, promotion as well as customer and B2B relations.

Thus, you can see that the job prospects are perhaps more open to someone who has a general Marketing qualification but has then perhaps chosen to specialize at a later date within the field of PR. It is by no means necessary that a PR executive has a specific PR qualification, yet they must demonstrate all the key marketing skills, whereas a marketing job would include aspects not included within a specialized PR course.

May I recommend that you peruse the college website (www.newtowncollege.ac.uk) to see the components within the CIM courses on offer in more detail. Please do not hesitate to contact me if you require any further details.

Best regards,

John Carter

Marketing Manager, New Town College

Debriefing Activity 9.3

Note the variety of local news from 'good news' stories about people with awards and problem issues such as a local company with a redundancy problem. Reflect on the issues a marketer faces on a day-to-day basis managing the press contacts, with both 'good' and 'bad' events to manage over the entire year.

Debriefing Activity 9.4

The stakeholder analysis should have been completed, it is similar to that completed with the 'CIM Student Award' case study. The message in this case is more about your local learning centre and the exciting novel activities in its programmes: learn, gain skills, succeed and have fun and excitement with new friends.

In at the deep end for local business students!

A group of students from the University of New Town Business School are braving the perils of life at sea. They are visiting the local Maritime Training Unit, where their team-working skills will be tested to the limit as they battle to repair a leaking ship in a force-nine gale! Well, they will of course be safely ashore at the time; but the simulator, which is used to train naval recruits, is renowned for its realism. The students themselves are from a variety of backgrounds but none of them have ever been to sea before, let alone battled the elements under such extreme conditions. This promises to be the ultimate training for the cut-throat business environment they are hoping to join on completion of their postgraduate course at the University. Will the students recognize the value of working as a team or will it be every man (or woman) for themselves?

Contact block would give university contact information and full details of time and place for this event.

Notes to editor: might contain more information on course and the simulation exercise.

Attachment block: links to relevant web pages with images of students and the simulator facilities.

To gain media cover, you need to gain the interest of an editor with many press releases on their desk or on their computer. There are only a few local features each night on the local news so it has to be something special to gain cover. This event was featured on regional TV. It was newsy (it coincided with the recent release of the film 'Titanic') and had the potential for spectacular and different images.

Debriefing Activity 9.5

Only a simple outline is given here. The 'timeline' would include these things: investigate stand options, book stand, approach members to help on the day, design and agree copy for posters and handouts, and get them printed, brief team, run event and review for next year.

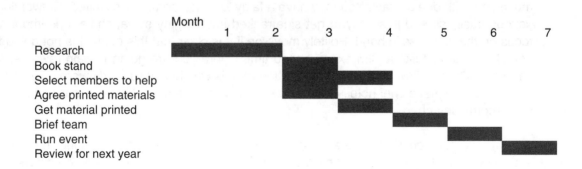

Activity 9.5 Simple chart for CIM event

Debriefing Activity 9.6

The key issue is that communications are vital. Therefore, an understanding of the audience's needs is vital. Then you should consider the techniques. Was the pace right? Was the tone interesting? Was the topic kept alive? Could you hear all the presentation? Was eye contact maintained with the audience or did the presenter mumble into the lecture notes? Could the slides be read (say above 18 points) or were they a 10-point dump from a book? On the other side (the danger for the computer buff), were the PowerPoint slides too 'busy'? We learn not only from what we do but also from observing what others do.

Debriefing Activity 9.7

Conflicting expectations of internal stakeholders are a common problem for the front-line marketer. They are damned if they do and damned if they don't. If they publish the press release as instructed, it has no news value and gets no media cover. The marketer is at fault, as they have not encouraged the media to have 'the right attitude'. If they write a 'newsy' story that gets printed, the 'heavyweight' academics feel that their worthy, but totally news-lacking, work is not given the right gravitas. The key conflict is that the organization wants to 'get the message over'. The media wants a good news story and for good measure, some exciting images (an ancient professor in front of a computer does not work).

The first need is to understand the different perspectives. The Dean is concerned about the world of other academics. The key element will be to diplomatically acknowledge that this public is important but this particular activity was aimed at different audiences that are also important and do not read these 'heavyweight' titles. Assertive qualities are important to a marketer.

Debriefing Activity 9.8

Checklist for person attending a conference for the first time

Before the conference: First decide what your objectives are (e.g. to gather information, develop new sales leads, make new professional contacts, etc.). Have a look at the checklists of delegates and speakers (often these are given on the conference website and updated regularly). Identify key people that may be of interest. Research their organizations (organizations' websites are most useful). Some organizations (e.g. Universities) hold pages on individuals that can provide more detail. Make certain your business cards are up to date and that you have a plentiful supply.

At the conference: Identify your targets (usually name badges are worn). Try not to spend too much time with one contact. You may have a fairly long list, and time is limited. Networking is a serious business and it is easy to get sidetracked into lengthy social chats. It is important to focus on the business in hand. Politely move on if it is clear that this contact is not going to be useful. This is just like a CIM exam; spend time where you are going to gain rewards. Make certain you have follow-up contact information (that is why business cards were invented). It is often helpful to make brief notes on the back of the business card. That way card and notes do not become detached.

After the conference: Complete any agreed follow-up (e.g. arranging a second meeting). File your new contacts. This may just be a simple card filing system or they may be entered into a computer contact management/diary system. The important thing is to be able to find the contact information a year later when a new issue arises. Check if there is any further information in the post-conference publications (e.g. conference proceedings).

Debriefing Activity 9.9

Key contact data such as name, address, e-mail address and so on, and then key words of interests, so selective follow-up can be undertaken at a later date. This might not only include academic interests but also sporting and so on, as this may help build the relationships (e.g. invitation to a sporting event).

Debriefing Question 9.1

Some selected points in brief note form are given below:

Formal business letters – Formal invitations to speakers, formal confirmation and approval of contracts and so on. Advantage: Good quality and can convey corporate image. Weakness: Slow, expensive, unless premium paid no proof of delivery, not as easy to archive as electronic media.

Business e-mails – Detailed follow-up to speakers, day-to-day communications with team, day-to-day follow-up with contractors and others. One of the most popular and useful forms of business communication. Advantage: Fast and inexpensive, good audit trail, easy to archive, large attachments are possible, marginal cost very low. Weakness: Too easy (think before you hit the send key), some people still not 'e' literate.

Memorandum – Formal communication of information to team members and others. Advantage: Little over an e-mail in modern business practice. Weakness: No proof of receipt, expensive, hard-copy filing slow and expensive when compared to electronic files. In general, there is little that can be done with the hard copy office memo that could not be done quicker and easier with the office e-mail.

Business reports – Formal reports might be appropriate for maintaining a record and communicating information (e.g. review of the conference after the event). Advantage: Provide a formal record. Can be distributed as e-mail attachments cutting down costs and speeding up distribution. Weakness: Take time and effort to write well.

Press releases – To the media before, during and after the event. Press releases are usually sent by e-mail so journalists and editors can directly download the text and then edit it as required for their publication. Advantage: Easy to distribute. Weakness: Often ignored with vast flow of 'spam' on an editor's screen. Though press releases are short, it takes experience, time and effort to write a good one.

Fax – Used for sending copies of documents. Increasingly less frequently used since e-mail is more convenient and less expensive. Advantage: Audit trail. Weakness: Can be slow, line costs for international transmission can be high. Documents can be scanned and sent as e-mail attachments at lower cost.

Face-to-face conversations – Good with team members and provides 'live' contact. In the age of the e-mail and teleconferencing, people still need face-to-face contact to build relationships. A key activity in networking.

Formal meetings – Good to share information and agree decisions. Advantage: Good face-to-face contact. Can be motivating. Weakness can be de-motivating if badly run. Follow-up with minutes with action points circulated is essential.

Telephone calls – To speakers, suppliers and team. Advantage: Instant feedback, some of the advantages of full face-to-face contact. Weakness: No formal record (follow-up with a confirming e-mail), can be a time waster (a little social discussion builds relationships, too much wastes very expensive time), interrupts people's work flow (voicemail can help here). Expensive compared to traditional landlines.

ICT – Websites can give information to all involved in the conference (speakers, delegates, suppliers, conference team members). Databases, spreadsheets and formal project management tools not only are useful planning tools but also communicate project activities to participants.

Unit 10

Debriefing Activity 10.1

The outline spreadsheet gives an overview of a possible schedule and provisional budget. This is divided into money and a marketer's time.

The proposed strategy is to place advertisements in the local evening paper with posters and a press release.

Outline communication schedule for franchise road show

	week 1	week 2	week 3	week 4	week 5	week 6	week 7	week 8	week 9	week10	Budget days	£
Research media											1	
Research mailing lists											2	
Write copy for local flyer											0.5	
Write copy for advertisements											0.5	
Write copy for press release											0.5	
Clear copy for above											0.5	
Place advertisements											0.5	
Release press release											0.25	
Advertisements appear												480
Mail out to financial advisers											2	300
Road show event												
Follow-up with contacts made											2	
										Totals	9.75	780

Spreadsheet 10.1

Budget-type questions occur regularly in the CIM exams. In December 2005 'The Urban Culture Festival 2006' the question was 1(a) 'Calculate the expected revenue, costs and profit from holding the celebrity Gala Evening at each of the two venues, stating any assumptions.' In June 2006 with the 'SMS Cars Ltd' case study the questions was in two parts 1(a) 'Calculate the total direct cost of both venues for the launch event and fashion show. Show your calculations and state any assumptions.' and 1(b) 'What other costs might there be for this type of event?' It should be noted that these are core questions and it is not possible to avoid budget / finance questions in the CIM exam.

Debriefing Question 10.1

The fixed cost is given as £15 000 and the marginal income per ticket £22. In this simple model there are considered to be no variable costs.

Breakeven number of tickets = [Fixed costs]/[Income per ticket] = £15 000/£22 = 681.8 or around 80 per cent

This breakeven value may be considered rather high and the venture risky. A 50 per cent breakeven would appear to give more security. For 50 per cent breakeven:

Fixed costs = [850 × 0.5] × [New selling price]

Rearranging the equation

New selling price = [Fixed costs]/[850 × 0.5] = £15 000/425 = £35.29

This is rather a large price increase, and more consideration would need to be given if such a price would be acceptable to people. Further consideration for setting the price is given in Question 10.2. If you have access to a spreadsheet, you should set up a simple financial model and look at how the breakeven moves with changes in price and costs. Remember in the exam you will have to use a calculator.

Debriefing Question 10.2

Selling price = £250

Cost of packing, postage and insurance (ppi) = £24

Cost of silver for model = £170

Labour cost of manufacture = £25

Set-up costs (fee to artist, manufacture of mould) = £3950

Breakeven calculation at selling price of £250

Set-up costs = No. of units sold × [Selling price–Variable costs]

Set-up costs = No. of units sold × [Selling price–(Cost ppi., etc. + Cost manufacture + Cost of silver)]

Rearranging the equation

Breakeven no. = Set-up costs/[Selling price–(Cost ppi., etc. + Cost manufacture + Cost of silver)]

Breakeven number = £3950/[£250–(£24 +£25 + £170)] = £3950/[£250–£219] = £3950/£31 = 127.4

Breakeven price calculation with sales volume set at 100 models

Set-up costs = No. units sold × [Selling price–(Cost ppi., etc. + Cost manufacture + Cost of silver)]

Rearranging the equation

Breakeven price (100 models) =

[Set-up costs + Sales no. × (Cost ppi., etc. + Cost manufacture + Cost of Silver)]/Sales no.

Breakeven price (100 models) =

[£3950 + £100 × (£24 + £25 + £170)]/100 = [£3950 + (100 × £219)]/100 = [£3950 + £21 900]/100 =

£25 850/100 = £258.5

Calculation for breakeven size at price £250 and volume 100 models:

Let Size = the fraction of the size needed for the new lower-cost model

Set-up costs =

No. Units sold × [Selling price–(Cost ppi., etc. + Cost manufacture + {Cost of silver × size})]

Rearranging the equation

No. Units sold × {Cost of silver × Size} =

[Number of units sold × [Selling price–(Cost ppi., etc. + Cost manufacture)]–Set-up costs =

100 × (£170 × Size) = 100 [(£250–(£24 + £25)]–£3,950 = (100 × £49)–£3 950=

£17 000 × Size = £4 900–£ 3 950 = £950

Size = 0.95 or 95 per cent (by weight)

By dimension

$(Dimension)^3 = 0.95$

(A model twice the height would weigh $2^3 = 8$ times as much–length to weight is a cube function

Dimension = $0.95^{(1/3)}$ = 0.983

The height of the model could be reduced by about 2 per cent to get the required cost for a breakeven number of 100 models.

This is only one solution. Instead of reducing the size, it might be possible to make the model slightly hollow on the inside. Marketing debate would be required to decide which is the more acceptable solution for customers. Calculations feed numbers into the debate; they do not of themselves provide total marketing solutions.

Debriefing Activity 10.2

A	B	C	D	E
1	Original values			Comments
2	Selling price		250	
3	Cost of packaging, postage etc		24	
4	Cost of silver for model		170	
5	Labour cost of manufacture		25	
6	Set-up Set up costs		3,950	
7	**Calculations as completed in Question 10.2 but with ability to change values**			
8	Cost of silver percentage	110		
9	Breakeven @ Selling Price	250	**282.14**	[D6]/[D9-(D3+(D4*0.01*C8)+D5)]
10	Breakeven price @ models	100	**275.5**	[[D6+C10*(D2-D3-D4-D5)]/C10
11	Size (weight ratio) @ Models	100		
12	Size (weight ratio) @ price	250	**0.8636**	[[C10*(C9-D3-D5]-D6]/C10
13	Converted to dimensions		**0.9523**	D12^(1/3)
14	As percentage (weight)		86.364	
15	As percentage (dimensions)		95	
	Cost of silver [C8] increased by 10%			

Spreadsheet 10.2

The spreadsheet shows the calculation for a 10 per cent increase in the silver price. In this case, the breakeven volume at a selling price of £250 climbs up to 282. If we want breakeven at 100 models, the price would have to rise to £275.50. If we were to reduce the cost by reducing the size of the model, we would have to reduce the weight by 86 per cent (95 per cent by size).

If we replace the value of 110 per cent for the cost of silver to 90 per cent (10 per cent reduction in cost of silver), the calculation then gives breakeven volume at a selling price of £250 down to 82; in case of breakeven at 100 models the price could drop to £241.50. If we were to hold the cost to £250 and have a breakeven of 100 then the weight could increase by 106 per cent (102 per cent by size).

A modest spreadsheet model can quickly give answers on the impact of potential changes in pricing strategy. It does not make the decision but it does greatly inform the decision makers during the decision-making process. Moreover, after the launch the impact of environmental changes can be evaluated.

Debriefing Question 10.3

Four areas should have been considered in your question plan:

o   A media plan with objectives
o   Justification of the timing
o   A budget within the limit of £20 000
o   Justification of the media selected.

Review your question plan and discuss with your tutor.

Unit 11

Debriefing Activity 11.1

One professor of Chemistry gave a very short mission for the department 'The preservation and extension of the boundaries of Chemical knowledge.' The preservation was of course the teaching activities and the extension of the research activities. There are various opinions, but a short single sentence that sums up the organization in terms relevant to all the stakeholders has much to commend it. This can be expanded to provide some depth, interpretation and amplification with a few additional paragraphs. The key point is it must be relevant to all the key stakeholders, not just the owners. 'We want to make as much money as possible while keeping costs as low as possible': this is not inspiring to the customers; they want to charge high prices, or the staff and they want to pay us less and cut the pension rights. Look at your examples and see if they work for all the relevant stakeholders.

Debriefing Activity 11.2

'To gain the CIM Diploma in 2 years, etc.' We can have standards and timescales in our personal life.

Debriefing Question 11.1

Outline marketing communications plan for launch of 'Be Happy'.

[Note this plan is in outline and where appropriate commentary has been added in square brackets.]

Aims and objectives

To provide communications support for the launch of 'Be Happy'. To create x per cent awareness after the launch.

Key communications stakeholders

Key stakeholders will be customers, users (many fragrance purchases are gifts), media, pressure groups (not animal tested, do not want adverse publicity), internal stakeholders, front-line sales consultants (people who sell the fragrances in department stores, etc., may be employees of the perfume company or of the store, depending on the specific arrangements within the store), marketing managers of key outlets [Boots etc. control much of the UK market so need a push strategy to persuade them to stock the new fragrance].

Segmentation and platform

A light fragrance for day use for the young working professional woman who is aspiring to a balanced 'wellbeing life-style'.

Communications before launch

Personal selling to key account Marketing Managers to get into the stores with suitable local support for the launch.

Direct marketing with invitations for key fashion journalists to the major launch event [their diaries fill up quickly].

[There are many other actions such as booking advertising space, agreeing the copy, etc. but not included in this outline plan.]

Internal marketing to the sales consultants so they are ready to sell the product on launch.

Regional briefing 'away-days' to build product knowledge and establish commitment to the launch.

Communications during launch

[Note the overall need is to take prospective customers through the AIDA process. The invitation is to use Figure 6.1 as a prompt list. The word 'prompt' is used rather than 'checklist' since the latter appears to imply that marketing is like painting with numbers. It is not. Creative solutions are needed. The communications mix options are advertising, PR, Publicity, personal selling, point of sale, sales systems, sales promotion, direct marketing, e-communications, sponsorship and exhibitions. All except sales systems might have a place.]

Advertising

TV – advertising around appropriate lifestyle programmes to create awareness with customers.

Press – fashion magazines are given the lifestyle platform by selected lifestyle magazines. To create awareness but with 'scratch and sniff' it could also be used for sampling.

Leaflets – to be used where appropriate and at point of sale.

Posters – in key locations such as airports.

Public relations

Launch event for the major account customers and the Press.

Publicity

Launch event and press releases on the background and the development of the perfume for fashion and lifestyle magazine cover.

Personal selling

Training of the front-line sales staff to close the sale. Note the chance to sample when clients buy other products.

Sales promotion

Launch 'gift pack' with free make-up bag or other such item [BOGOF not appropriate in this area. May be attractive to the customer but also needed to prove commitment to the outlets; if you do not prove your commitment with this type of support they will not stock the line.]

Direct marketing

May be an opportunity for personal invitations from local client databases for regional in-store launch events. [Regional use of RM concepts and local client databases built up by the sales consultants.]

E-communication

Good website for general information. Selected areas for pressure groups (e.g. assurance product not animal tested) and protected area for the press for download of images for editorial and online press release access.

Exhibitions

Possibly not much, but might be opportunities in selected areas such as suitable 'life style' exhibitions.

Sponsorship

Investigate the possibility of sponsoring some suitable lifestyle programme. Might link to some arts theme such as a travelling exhibition.

Schedule

In real life, a chart or computer-based project system would be used. In the exam, a simple chart might be appropriate. [Remember this type of issue might have a question asked along the lines of 'Discuss the project management of the communications for a product launch.']

Budget

Again, in real life a detailed budget spreadsheet would be developed. In the exam setting, a potential question would give you some media costs and ask you to develop a media spend budget with justification.

Control and feedback

Simple, direct measures such as sales against budget. The tracking of awareness and customers' attitudes to the product. Not only tracking the advertising but also the PR events (e.g. did they achieve their objectives?).

Clearly the above is only an outline and you may have taken some different views about the emphasis you might place on one element of the mix. Remember there is only one right answer – one that succeeds in the marketplace. If there were truly one right answer, we would only end up with one style of advertisement. The best plans all involve an element of creativity.

Have a look at the specimen answers for questions on the CIM website (www.cim.co.uk) to compare with your solutions. Discuss your approach with fellow students and with your tutor; if you get time, read the marketing press to see what launches are in progress and see the industry view of what campaigns have worked and which are the ones that have been successful and discuss the issues with your fellow students. Just reading a textbook will not develop the practical skills to pass the CIM exams or succeed in your marketing career so look for examples of good and bad practice all around you.

Debriefing Question 11.2

If it is assumed that there will be 28 screenings over the two weeks, then to gain full capacity, 2 800 people will be required to attend the film festival. This will require an increase of 432 per cent in audience numbers, a significant challenge. This must be achieved with a limited budget.

The outline plan below contains some 'original' solutions. You may not agree with them. You may have much better ideas. Marketing is creative and there is more than one way to make a success of the film festival. The general outline below follows the 'standard' framework for a business plan. Comments and justification are given in square brackets in italics. Given space limitations a briefing note format is adopted.

Mission

'World Cinema to reflect world culture'. To bring to the Urban Culture festival the best of world cinema.

Aims to provide a quality cultural experience.

To maintain close to full occupancy.

Objectives

To reach 85 per cent occupancy over the 2-week programme [as a plan is developed and refined objectives could include number of customer (by segment) and target spends].

Environmental analysis

STEEPLE

Social: Multicultural environment and more knowledge of 'Bollywood' are increasing awareness and interest in world cinema.

Economic: Although the offer gives 'value for money', this still represents a fairly expensive evening for an average family. Assume limited room for increased spending by 5 days a week commuter customers. [*You might start to consider if additional money might be found from sponsors to keep ticket prices down.*]

Education: Front-of-house staff will need to be educated to provide informed advice to potential customers.

Political: Some care may be needed as some films may have a politically controversial content.

Legal: Should not be a major problem.

Environmental: Not a major issue in this context.

Competition analysis

Direct: Local cinemas.

Substitute products: Other entertainment opportunities [Note we have to take care not to damage other events in the Urban Culture Festival programme].

New entrants: Nothing in the case study to suggest this might be a major problem.

Buyer power: Lots of other offerings so a very competitive environment. Need to link in with other events under the 'Urban Culture Festival' brand.

Supplier power: In general, obtaining films should not be difficult. No other major issues.

Internal analysis

A value chain analysis could be completed but there are not major operational issues for the film showing. An analysis for a catering establishment is given in Unit 1.

SWOT analysis

Strengths: Vibrant festival providing a good context for the film programme.

Weakness: Rather low audience uptake in the past.

Opportunity: Expanded capacity with the two screenings a night.

Threats: Entertainment is a competitive environment. Easy via the Internet to rent/buy world cinema on DVDs.

Market segmentation [outline only, not complete]

Various ethnic communities

Regular 'arts' cinema attendees

Normal cinema attendees

Infrequent cinema-goers

Education [given the international context may be of interest to local education groups, for example language classes]

Marketing mix

Product

A balanced programme of films well linked and integrated into the Urban Culture overall programme will be required.

Prices

There is a possibility of offering different prices for late and early evening film screenings. Consideration might be given to family and group discounts.

Place: Precise hours of screening. There is the possibility of afternoon screenings for education groups.

Promotion

It may be assumed that programme details will be included in the general publicity for the Urban Culture festival. It must also be noted that only a very modest budget is available.

Posters and leaflets should be available in the cinema and the participating restaurant prior to the film festival. Limited advertising in the entertainment pages of the local paper. PR: press releases to gain interest in notable films in local press, radio and TV. For education groups some direct marketing would be appropriate. Information on the programme should be included on the cinema and festival websites. Direct marketing and personnel selling should be employed to find local sponsors for the Film Festival.

People: Some training to front-of-house staff to give informed advice on the international programme.

Physical evidence

Tangible clues: Some attempt to provide decorations and so on in keeping with the film showing (e.g. poster/arts display).

Facilitating goods: A chance for creative marketing thoughts, for example CDs of world music.

Process: A friendly personal experience with a feeling of the international cultural experience.

Action plan and budget

In real life more research would establish the action plans and budgets (e.g. a break-even analysis, etc).

Control

Normal standard control points such as sales against budget, customer satisfaction measures, and so on.

The above is only an outline but shows how the process of writing a marketing plan is both analytic (e.g. STEEPLE analysis) and creative (consideration of potential new products).

The Chartered
Institute of Marketing

Professional Certificate
in Marketing

26 – Marketing in Practice

Time: 14:00 – 17:00
Date: 8th December 2005

3 Hours Duration

This examination is in **TWO** sections.

PART A - Is compulsory and worth **40%** of total marks

PART B - Has **SIX** questions; select **THREE**. Each answer will be worth **20%** of the total marks

DO NOT repeat the question in your answer, but show clearly the number of the questions attempted on the appropriate pages of the answer book.

Rough work and notes must be written into the answer book or on supplementary sheets and must be clearly identified.

Professional Certificate in Marketing

26 - Marketing in Practice

PART A

The Urban Culture Festival 2006

The Urban Culture Festival (UCF) takes place annually and is a celebration of art, entertainment and culture from cities around the world. It started ten years ago as a result of various ethnic groups wanting to express their own cultural heritage in a large multi racial city. It comprises musical events, dance, art, theatre and even street performers and graffiti (e.g. words or drawings, especially humorous, rude or political, on walls, doors, etc, in public places) artists in a variety of city locations.

The festival has grown and now attracts participants from around the world and with increasing numbers of visitors each year, approximately 100,000 people attended last year's festival.

The 2006 event is set to be the biggest yet, with over 120 different events. The growth of the festival has led to your appointment as Marketing Executive, the first time that anyone has had this job, and your brief is to inject some much needed marketing throughout the festival.

Highlights of the festival

Launch Reception

The traditional start of the festival will be attended by over 250 people, including artists, musicians, local civic leaders, celebrities plus guests from around the world. This event reflects the diversity of urban culture and is where Japanese graffiti artists mix with hip hop DJs, and where African poets mix with Bhangra musicians.

Caribbean Carnival

This is a colourful procession and open-air free concert, which was watched by over 20,000 people in 2005.

Asian Dance

An Asian dance company is booked to appear at a local theatre which can accommodate 500 people. In 2005, only 200 people attended, at a ticket price of £10.

Graffiti Gallery

This free event aims to show that graffiti is part of urban culture and an art form in its own right. It is the first time that it is has been included in the festival, however, this decision has upset many people who consider graffiti to be destructive.

Film Festival

Each night for two weeks a different film, from a different country, will be shown at a small cinema which can hold 100 people. Last year, 647 people attended, paying £5 per film.

The Celebrity Gala Evening

This is the highlight of the festival. Last year all of the tickets, each priced at £25, were sold in advance. This year the organisers of the festival are considering either raising prices for the Gala Evening, or moving to a larger venue. You are to help in making this decision. The two venues are City Hall and The Warehouse.

City Hall

In 2005, this prestigious central location was used. It is close to the railway station and is in a pleasant, pedestrianised area of the city. It can hold 2,350 people and would cost £5,000 to hire for the evening. Fifty staff will be needed at a cost of £7 per hour for 4 hours each. Average revenue from food and drink sales is £2 per person, a mark-up of 100%.

In 2006 hourly rates for staff are expected to increase by £1 per hour, adding to costs but the organisers feel that the venue would still be sold out if ticket prices rose by 20%.

The Warehouse

This venue is a large, converted warehouse situated in the dockland area of the city, a trendy rebuilt area popular with young people for living and socialising. This venue costs twice as much to hire as the city hall but can hold 3,200 people and the organisers are confident that 95% of tickets can be sold in advance at a price of £25.

Profit from food and drink will be around £1.25 per person (at the same mark up as the City Hall). Staffing costs will be 10% higher than the City Hall.

Remaining tickets will be available on the night for £30 each and it is hoped that all will be sold.

Marketing opportunities

1. Sponsorship

As a high profile event with a whole host of subsidiary events, there are many opportunities to sell sponsorship packages to local and national businesses. This has never been attempted before.

2. Website

As Marketing Assistant, one of your responsibilities is to oversee the development of a website www.ucf.org that until now has been very basic.

The above data has been based on a fictitious situation drawing on a variety of events and do not reflect management practices of any particular organisation.

PART A - Compulsory

Question One

a. Calculate the expected revenue, costs and profit from holding the Celebrity Gala Evening at each of the two venues, stating any assumptions.

(16 marks)

b. Identify the **NON-FINANCIAL** factors that should be considered before selecting one of the venues.

(8 marks)

c. Considering financial and non-financial factors, which venue would you recommend for the Gala? Justify your decision.

(8 marks)

d. Draft a letter to potential sponsors selling the benefits of involvement with UCF 2006.

(8 marks)

(Total 40 marks)

PART B - Answer THREE questions only

Question Two

a.   Identify **THREE** sales promotion techniques that could be used to build audiences across the different events at the 2006 UCF.

(10marks)

b.   Recommend **THREE** public relations activities to gain maximum awareness amongst your target audiences.

(10 marks)

(Total 20 marks)

Question Three

Describe the advantages and disadvantages of advertising using the following media specifically in the context of the UCF 2006:

-   television

-   radio

-   cinema

-   magazines

-   other alternative media (please specify)

(Total 20 marks)

Question Four

Compare how the **THREE** elements of the service marketing mix (people, process and physical evidence) might differ in application between the UCF and a financial services provider.

(Total 20 marks)

Question Five

a.   Identify **THREE** key issues that the organisers of the UCF need to consider with regard to receiving and hosting artists and visitors from different national and cultural backgrounds.

(10 marks)

b.   Explain how you could use networking and personal selling skills to attract and retain sponsors for this and future Urban Culture Festivals.

(10 marks)

(Total 20 marks)

Question Six

a.   Identify how the website can be used to support the UCF before, during and after it takes place.

(12 marks)

b.   Recommend and justify **ONE** online and **ONE** offline technique which could be used to increase the number of 'hits' on the website.

(8 marks)

(Total 20 marks)

Question Seven

Produce an event plan for the 2007 UCF, using a suitable event planning model.

(Total 20 marks)

The Chartered
Institute of Marketing

Moor Hall, Cookham
Maidenhead
Berkshire, SL6 9QH, UK
Telephone: 01628 427120
Facsimile: 01628 427158
www.cim.co.uk

The Chartered
Institute of Marketing

Professional Certificate in Marketing

Marketing in Practice

SENIOR EXAMINER'S REPORT FOR STUDENTS AND TUTORS
DECEMBER 2005

**SENIOR EXAMINER'S REPORT
FOR STUDENTS AND TUTORS**

MODULE NAME: Marketing in Practice

AWARD NAME: Professional Certificate in Marketing

DATE: December 2005

1.   **General Strengths and Weaknesses of Candidates**

Strengths
- Time management continues to improve with each sitting
- The improvements in answers to the compulsory numerical question seen in the last paper have been maintained
- Candidates appear to be understanding the questions better than previously
- Candidates understand and can apply the criteria for venue selection

Weaknesses
- Many overseas candidates still struggle with the basic calculations required in the compulsory question
- Many candidates failed to pick up maximum marks for letter format
- Many candidates failed to distinguish between the promotional element of the marketing mix and sales promotion
- Understanding and application of the service mix (people, process and physical evidence) still not embedded
- Some examiners reported problems with the legibility of some handwriting

2.   **Strengths and Weaknesses by Question**

Question 1

a) Most UK and some overseas candidates managed the financial questions well, understanding the requirements of the question and applying the appropriate figures to correctly calculate income, expenditure and profit for both venues. However these calculations still presented substantial problems for a substantial number of overseas candidates. Few stated any assumptions as requested although most did show their workings so marks could be given for parts of the answer that were correct.

b)c) A well answered question with most answers based correctly on the ASFAB acronym. Either venue could have been recommended as long as there was a justification to support.

d) A surprising number of candidates could not set out a letter correctly. Many then went on to repeat the UCF case material in the letter content rather than identifying the benefits of association with the UCF to potential sponsors as requested. Such answers gained few marks. Very few letters contained a robust or persuasive 'call to action' with most being passive such as 'if you are interested please call'.

Question 2

a) Many candidates, particularly overseas, were confused between sales promotions which were asked for and promotion in general. Those who answered using 'promotion' provided information that was therefore not appropriate and consequently lost marks.

Candidates who did apply sales promotional techniques generally did well with answers covering:
- discounts for multiple ticket purchases
- BOGOF
- discount vouchers for tickets for other events
- discounts for early purchase
- free gifts for early purchase

However, too many answers failed to include any time related restriction to these techniques thereby effectively making them no more than price discounts, indeed several candidates suggested 'discounted prices' as a sales promotion which gained no marks. Competitions were a regular suggestion but this was generally not linked to increasing overall ticket sales but used to raise awareness. Most suggestions gave tickets and gifts away without linking to increasing sales.

b) Most candidates were able to suggest three public relations activities however there was a lack of creativity in these suggestions. Press releases, press conferences and artist appearances on television or radio were most common. Very few made reference to targeting the media that was read, seen or listened to by the target audience for the UCF. Those who did typically gained full marks. Too many candidates suggested advertising as public relations activities.

Many answers used public relations techniques that were not really suitable for this particular scenario such as sponsorship and exhibitions and failed to show how these would raise awareness which was the topic of the question.

Question 3

This was probably the most popular question in the paper and provided a clear framework for candidate answers. Most answers provided two to four short bullet point answers each for media advantages and disadvantages. Maximum marks were gained where answers were suitably contextualised to the UCF case. An example would be the benefits of advertising in magazines read by the UCF target audience. What almost all answers failed to do however was to identify how easy it was for each media to be targeted at different segments such as those that the UCF wished to target.

Weaker answers failed to contextualise and simply listed the generic advantages and disadvantages of each media. Furthermore, saying that one media is expensive or not expensive is not in itself enough as this needs to be quantified more by stating if this is based on opportunity to see or some other benchmark. There was confusion over the role of disc jockeys on radio from many overseas candidates who suggested that they would be promoting the UCF rather than an advert.

Question 4

Not a particularly popular questions and one that was generally poorly answered. Few answers actually compared how the service mix elements of people, process and physical evidence were similar or different between the UCF and a financial services provider such as a bank. There was also some confusion as to what each mix element was made up of with many answers placing staff uniforms in to the people section instead of physical evidence. Few answers picked up the role of buildings in physical evidence despite this topic being a part of the compulsory question when deciding which venue, City Hall or the Warehouse, was the more appropriate for the Gala Evening.

Question 5

a) This questions covers syllabus 3.6 'explain how an organisation should host visitors from other cultures and organising across national boundaries'. As such examiners were looking for answers that might cover language, religion, business and social customs. These could be expanded upon to touch on dress codes, ways to greet, eye contact and invasion of personal space. Some strong answers not only identified three key issues but also made suggestions as to what actions were needed to be taken to ensure that everything ran smoothly. Most answers covered these and other issues well.

b) This question covered syllabus 2.7 'use networking skills in the business world' and 4.2 'evaluate promotional activities and opportunities. It was not a particularly easy second part of the question and most candidates struggled to provide strong answers. Some of these provided a number of suitable points that would attract and retain sponsors in the form of a best practice list such as the need to set up meetings, to be on time, dress appropriately and quickly establish a rapport. They also covered the application and interpretation of body language and use of supporting materials such as brochures. These are all good points that would have found favour with the examiner and show how this question could have been answered successfully in many different ways.

A few strong answers suggested creating a target list of organisations and undertaking research to see if their customer base matched that of the UCF. Few discussed methods of lead generation although many did touch upon the first communication which could be by letter as in question one, or by telephone or face-to-face. Most answers failed to suitably describe the role of personal selling or take sponsors through the personal selling process.

Many candidates failed to answer this question fully by covering networking or personal selling but not both.

Question 6

a) A popular question with most candidates realising that what was required was a bullet point list under the headings of Before, During and After the UCF. This allowed the examiner to award marks under each heading for quality and quantity of suggestions. Candidates who answered in an essay style generally failed to distinguish what time period they were referring to and so reduced their chances of gaining maximum marks. Generally speaking candidates managed to provide suitable answers to this question.

b) Answers to this second part of the question were generally a little short in length thereby not reflecting the possible eight marks available. Off-line answers sometimes failed to understand that the purpose was to drive traffic on to the UCF web site. On-line techniques focussed on pop-ups and banner advertising.

Question 7

This was the least popular question although those who did answer it typically produce well structured answers around the SOST+6Ms model. It was also noted that candidates often appeared to be short of time on this question.

3.   Future Themes

Candidates should re-visit the Marketing in Practice syllabus and ensure that they are familiar with its content. Note that the first four elements build upon and reflect the work candidates would have undertaken on the other three modules, e.g. Element 1: Gathering, analysing and presenting information, draws on the Marketing Environment syllabus. Therefore, candidates should ensure that they have covered the three modules before attempting Marketing in Practice. Element 5: Administering the marketing budget (and evaluating results) is not covered elsewhere but is assessed as part of the compulsory question so candidates and tutors should ensure that they spend a suitable amount of time covering this element. One of the best ways of doing this and preparing for the whole examination is to practice on past papers of which there are now a good number plus read examiners feedback and review the specimen answers.

The Chartered
Institute of Marketing

Professional Certificate in Marketing

Marketing in Practice

Time: **14.00 – 17.00**

Date: **8th June 2006**

3 Hours Duration

This examination is in **TWO** sections.

PART A – Is compulsory and worth **40%** of total marks

PART B – Has **SIX** questions; select **THREE**. Each answer will be worth **20%** of the total marks

DO NOT repeat the question in your answer, but show clearly the number of the questions attempted on the appropriate pages of the answer book.

Rough work and notes must be written into the answer book or on supplementary sheets and must be clearly identified.

Professional Certificate in Marketing

Marketing in Practice

PART A

SMS Cars Ltd

You work as a Marketing Executive for SMS Cars Ltd, a private company that holds the franchise for Ford vehicles, which are produced in Europe (the UK), and Hyundai, which is a South Korean manufacturer. The company has seven sites in the south of the UK and is family-owned by Harry Stephenson, who set up the business 30 years ago, and his two sons Jack and Nick.

There are four areas of the business that require your marketing skills: vehicle sales, self-drive vehicle hire, vehicle servicing and replacement parts supply.

VEHICLE SALES

New Vehicle Launch Event

Hyundai is launching its latest concept car, called the 'Portico', on 1st July 2006, and SMS Cars Ltd has been asked to organise a launch event in their area. The Portico is a family car for the future that offers six seats plus a large cargo space. The rear doors open backwards, providing very easy access to the back seats through a large, pillar-less entrance. The vehicle also comes with the option of either a 24-valve V6 petrol engine or the revolutionary Hyundai hybrid drive system, which features two electric motors driving the front and rear wheels.

Your Managing Director wants to combine the launch of the Portico with a fashion show as an added attraction, to create maximum interest and impact and to impress the four senior Hyundai executives from South Korea who will be attending as guests of SMS Cars Ltd for two days. Potential buyers will be able to view and sit in the new vehicles, talk to sales staff and enjoy some food and drink. A 30-minute fashion show in the same area will then take place, followed by more opportunities to review the new range of cars.

A local fashion store has agreed to provide the men's and women's clothing ranges, in return for SMS Cars Ltd promoting their clothes and store at the launch. A local art and design college has agreed to provide 10 fashion students as models for the clothes, and 5 hair and beauty students to help with the models' hair and make-up.

It has been decided not to hold the launch in one of the showrooms but at an historic location, by invitation only. Two possible venues have been suggested.

Durley Hall

The 800 year old stately home of Lord Darcy, set in beautiful gardens with lakes and water features, is located in an area of outstanding natural beauty and is accessible by narrow country lanes. The house and gardens are usually open to the public for £5 per person during the day. However, for this early evening event, a charge of £2 per person is payable by SMS, plus £300 for the space to contain the car launch and fashion show. As there is no indoor area for the launch and the weather in July can be unpredictable, a marquee would need to be hired at a cost of £450. Outside caterers would also be needed and a firm has quoted £6 per person.

National Motor Museum

The museum has a collection of more than 200 vehicles spanning over 100 years, including Grand Prix racing cars and cars featured in movies such as 'James Bond' and Mini Coopers from 'The Italian Job'. There is motorway access within two miles of the museum, which is very important with hundreds of people visiting in the summer. The museum is open to the public during the day but can be booked for corporate events in the evening. The launch and fashion show can be held indoors in one of the well-equipped, purpose-built exhibition halls, so there is no need to hire a marquee and the staff are very experienced at hosting corporate events such as this. There is a standard charge of £1500 for the venue. In addition, hirers must use the in-house catering service, which will cost £8 per person.

There are a number of other direct costs, which would be associated with both venues:

- hire of the catwalk (for the models to walk along): £200
- hire of a music system and disc jockey: £250
- printing the invitations plus the cost of envelopes and postage: £2 per invitation
- expenses for the fashion models: £20 each
- expenses for hair stylists and make-up artists: £15 each

You plan to send out 800 invitations and expect 10% to respond confirming their attendance. It is also expected that, as this event will appeal to both men and women, 75% of those who respond will take up the offer of attending with a friend or partner. Both venues will provide entry for SMS Ltd staff and the models at no charge.

OTHER ASPECTS OF THE BUSINESS

Vehicle Servicing and Mechanical Repair

Each site has a vehicle workshop which will service and repair any make of car. Charges for labour are higher than many of your competitors, making these workshops expensive. This makes it difficult to attract and retain customers and you have been asked to see how marketing can help increase income.

Replacement Parts Delivery Service

The company sells replacement parts for Ford and Hyundai vehicles from each site. For trade customers, such as other vehicle retailers and mechanical and bodywork repairers, the company offers a new 'Express Delivery Service', where replacement parts can be delivered to the customer's premises, often within a few hours of an order being received.

Self-drive Vehicle Hire

The company has a fleet of 25 cars available for hire from any of its sites. Three different models are available but the amount of time they are actually out on hire (utilisation rate) varies from model to model.

Model	Description	No of Cars	Week rate	Utilisation in past 12 months
Ford Ka	Mid-sized 3- or 5-door	10	£150	60%
Ford Fiesta	Mid-sized 4- or 5-door	10	£180	45%
Ford Mondeo	Large 4-door saloon	5	£300	30%

The Managing Director would like to increase hire prices by 10% for the next 12 months. However this is predicted to result in a drop in vehicle utilisation of 5% for the Ford Ka to 55%, 5% for the Ford Fiesta to 40% and 2% for the Ford Mondeo to 28%, unless there is some promotional activity.

The above data has been based on a fictitious situation drawing on a variety of events and do not reflect management practices of any particular organisation.

PART A – Compulsory

Question One

a. Calculate the total direct cost of both venues for the launch event and fashion show. Show your calculations and state any assumptions.

(16 marks)

b. What other costs might there be for this type of event?

(4 marks)

c. Produce a report for your Managing Director (MD) that recommends which venue to select. Justify your recommendation, explaining what criteria you used to come to your decision.

(12 marks)

d. What marketing objectives would you set for this event, and how would you evaluate its success?

(8 marks)

(Total 40 marks)

PART B – Answer **THREE** questions only

All questions relate to the SMS Cars Ltd case study

Question Two

a.   Write a letter to current and potential customers inviting them to attend the launch event. Include a method of reply to confirm their attendance.

(10 marks)

b.   What guidance would you give to SMS Cars Ltd staff working at the launch event on how to receive guests and attend to their needs?

(5 marks)

c.   What factors must be considered when important guests from other countries are coming to such an event?

(5 marks)

(Total 20 marks)

Question Three

a.   Prepare a news release for the local newspaper describing the success of the launch event and promoting the new vehicle.

(10 marks)

b.   You have been asked to represent SMS Cars Ltd at a business networking event run by your local Chamber of Commerce*. Your Manager has suggested that you use this as an opportunity to raise the profile of the organisation and to promote the launch of the event. What personal objectives would you set yourself to ensure that you achieve your aims? What networking skills would you use?

(10 marks)

(Total 20 marks)

*   Chamber of Commerce – an organisation of business people designed to advance the interests of its members

Question Four

Produce a short report, for consideration by the Marketing Department, which:

a. identifies what information SMS Cars Ltd would want on their customer database in order to segment the marketplace effectively and assist with future marketing activity.

(12 marks)

b. explains how this information could be gathered.

(8 marks)

(Total 20 marks)

Question Five

Produce a briefing paper to be forwarded to the Manager of the Vehicle Servicing Department which:

a. describes how the **THREE** elements of the extended marketing mix (people, process and physical evidence) can be used by the Vehicle Servicing Department to improve customer service.

(8 marks)

b. makes recommendations as to how the promotional mix could be used to increase demand for the Vehicle Servicing Department.

(12 marks)

(Total 20 marks)

Question Six

You have been asked by the Managing Director to examine the implications of an increase in hire prices on business activity.

a.   Copy the following table and calculate the annual income for each model of the self-drive vehicle fleet for the past 12 months and state any assumptions

	Max. 12-month income (weekly rate x 52 wks)	Multiplied by utilisation rate	Number in fleet	Total income last 12 months
Ford Ka				
Ford Fiesta				
Ford Mondeo				

(6 marks)

b.   Copy the following table and calculate the annual income for each model of the self-drive vehicle fleet for the next 12 months after the 10% increase in hire prices

	Max. 12-month income (weekly rate x 52 wks) +10%	Multiplied by utilisation new rate	Number in fleet	Total income next 12 months
Ford Ka				
Ford Fiesta				
Ford Mondeo				

(6 marks)

c.   What conclusions can you draw from your findings?

(8 marks)

(Total 20 marks)

Question Seven

Produce a short report to be circulated to Departmental Managers which explains how ICT can enhance the marketing mix (product, price, place and promotion) to generate sales and encourage customer loyalty to all departments of SMS Cars Ltd.

(20 marks)

The Chartered
Institute of Marketing

Moor Hall, Cookham
Maidenhead
Berkshire, SL6 9QH, UK
Telephone: 01628 427120
Facsimile: 01628 427158
www.cim.co.uk

The Chartered
Institute of Marketing

Professional Certificate in Marketing

Marketing in Practice

SENIOR EXAMINER'S REPORT FOR STUDENTS AND TUTORS (EXAMINATION) – JUNE 2006

SENIOR EXAMINER'S REPORT
FOR STUDENTS AND TUTORS

MODULE NAME: MARKETING IN PRACTICE

AWARD NAME: PROFESSIONAL CERTIFICATE IN MARKETING

DATE: JUNE 2006

1.   General Strengths and Weaknesses of Candidates

Strengths
- Time management and format (reports, letters, news releases) were generally good
- Numerical questions were generally answered better than previous sessions
- More candidates are contextualising their answer to the case study as required
- Candidates understand and can apply the criteria for venue selection

Weaknesses
- Candidates, particularly from some overseas centres still struggle with the basic calculations required in the compulsory question
- Too many candidates failed to pick up maximum marks for letter format
- Few candidates were able to write good news releases
- Application of ICT to the marketing mix was generally weak

2.   Strengths and Weaknesses by Question

Question One

Strengths:
- Most candidates were able to calculate the direct or common costs for both venues as being £2325 being made up £200 catwalk hire, £250 music/DJ, 800 invitations to be printed and posted at £2 each totalling £1600, expenses for 10 models at £20 each totalling £200 and expenses for 5 hair and make up artists at £15 each totalling £75.
- Candidates correctly calculate the number of guests attending (80+60=140) and could then successfully calculate the variable costs of the two venues.
- A good range of other costs were identified for 1b) such as transportation of staff and vehicles to the venue and staff overtime costs
- Overseas candidates also mentioned security, decorating the venue and providing gifts for all who attended as is customary in some countries.
- The strongest answers to 1c) applied the ASFAB criteria to BOTH venues as a comparison before coming to a recommendation
- Evaluation of event success (1d) produced some reasonable answers around sales made over a period, test drives booked, awareness and perception change measured using questionnaires.

Weaknesses:
- Many candidates, particularly from some overseas centres, mis-calculated the number of guests attending the launch which subsequently led them to incorrectly calculate the variable costs for both venues (see Specimen Answer for details)
- Very few answers provided any assumptions and most of them were information given in the case e.g. SMS Ltd staff enter at no charge
- Candidates cannot change the nature of the question by their assumptions (e.g. assuming that all 800 guests invited attend and calculating costs accordingly)
- Weaker answers to 1c) only discussed one (the recommended) venue or failed to apply any form of venue selection criteria.
- For 1d) many candidates simply ignored this part of the question.
- Very few candidates produced SMART objectives for the event. Most realised that objectives should be SMART and explained what each letter stood for however, this gained no marks as it was the application of this principle that was being assessed.

Question Two

Strengths:
- A very popular and generally well answered question with most candidates able to lay out a letter in an appropriate format and include the key dates, times and facts.
- Some excellent letters sold the benefits of the Portico and the event
- There were a range and combination of appropriate response mechanism used to confirm attendance
- Many strong answers to 2b) covered greetings, body language, appearance, product knowledge and handling questions

Weaknesses:
- Letter content was often variable with many letters barely mentioning the new Portico vehicle or its unique features which was the purpose of the letter and the launch event.
- Other letters failed to cover launch date, time and location or mention the fashion show or that food and drink were available.
- Answers to 2c) generally listed cultural differences without putting these differences into the case context.

Question Three

Strengths:
- Most answers were able to lay out the news release although the content was variable.
- Answers to 3b) were better on identifying networking skills focussing on interpersonal and communication skills.

Weaknesses:
- This was by far the least popular question especially with overseas centres.
- 3b) was poorly answered with candidates generally not providing any personal objectives for attending a networking event. These could have been, to create a professional image of myself and of SMS Ltd, to raise awareness of SMS Ltd and the product launch or to identify opportunities to promote other SMS Ltd services.

Question Four

Strengths:
- This was the most popular question with many candidates identifying personal and demographic information
- Many provided comprehensive lists or fields of data that would be useful to a car dealership in targeting future marketing activity e.g. family size might suggest a family car and income would suggest a certain price range

Weaknesses:
- Many answers failed to identify vehicle ownership and transaction history as information for the customer database. This would identify heavy, light and lapsed users etc. and could be drawn from car sales, servicing, replacement parts or car hire invoices.
- Some candidates, particularly overseas effectively wasted time by describing what a database was and the intricacies of segmentation which were not asked for and gained no marks. Candidates must answer the question set to gain marks.
- Answers to 4b) often lacked context and application to the case with many explaining the differences between primary and secondary data and all the various methods of collecting the information irrespective of whether or not they were an appropriate method in this case.

Question Five

Strengths:
- Most candidates provided reasonable and practical suggestions for the extended P's that were applied to the case.
- Most candidates were aware of the various aspects of the promotional mix and could provide appropriate suggestions in the context of the vehicle servicing department.

Weaknesses:
- Some answers lacked depth and practical suggestions containing general aspirational statements that staff should give good customer care and processes should be efficient without stating how.
- Usual confusion about uniforms being part of people instead of physicals and a general uncertainty of what are the processes as part of the mix.
- A few answers still discussed the marketing mix instead of the promotional mix

Question Six

Strengths:
- Not a popular question however it had the highest average mark of all six optional questions.
- Most candidates were able to complete the tables provided and gained maximum marks for parts and b.

Weaknesses:
- Some candidates still could not process a simple group of numbers even with the format and calculations provided.
- Most answers failed to draw many reasoned conclusions from the tables such as whether the increases in hire rates were warranted and impact on vehicle utilisation.

Question Seven

Strengths:
- Some strong answers that applied various ICT's such as website, e-mail, texting and automated call answering.
- Some excellent suggestions around virtual car and showroom tours, on-line payments, car hire and servicing booking options.

Weaknesses:
- Answers that totally ignored ICT in providing suggestions for the mix.

3. Future Themes

In light of the answers given to this paper, the following are areas that will need to be assessed again in future papers:

- Writing SMART objectives (not just knowing what the letters stand for)
- Budgeting including addition, subtraction, multiplication and percentages
- Writing news (press) releases that editors will want to use – centres must ensure that this part of the syllabus is being taught
- B2B activities including networking and personal selling
- Writing business letters that contain that right level of detail and persuade the reader to take action
- Application of the service P's (people, process and physicals) to a given situation

Please review the specimen answers for further details on how to tackle this module.

appendix 6

curriculum information and reading list

Aim

The Marketing in Practice unit is concerned with the application of marketing in context and also forms the summative assessment for the Professional Certificate. It aims to assist students to integrate and apply knowledge from all the units at the Professional Certificate level.

Students will not be expected to have any prior qualifications or experience in a marketing role. They will be expected to be conversant with the content of the other three units of the Professional Certificate before undertaking this unit.

Related statements of practice

Hb.1 Contribute to project planning and budget preparation.
Hb.2 Monitor and report on project activities.
Hb.3 Complete and close down project activities on time and within budget.
Jb.1 Collect, synthesize, analyse and report measurement data.
Jb.2 Participate in reviews of marketing activities using measurement data.
Kb.1 Exchange information to solve problems and make decisions.
Kb.2 Review and develop one's skills and competencies.
Kb.3 Embrace change and modify behaviours and attitudes.

Learning outcomes

Students will be able to:

5.26.1 Collect relevant data from a variety of secondary information sources.
5.26.2 Analyse and interpret written, visual and graphical data.
5.26.3 Devise appropriate visual and graphical means to present marketing data.
5.26.4 Make recommendations based on information obtained from multiple sources.
5.26.5 Evaluate and select media and promotional activities appropriate to the organization's objectives and status and to its marketing context.
5.26.6 Calculate and justify budgets for marketing mix decisions.
5.26.7 Develop relationships inside and outside the organization.
5.26.8 Apply planning techniques to a range of marketing tasks and activities.

5.26.9 Undertake basic marketing activities within an agreed plan and monitor and report on progress.

5.26.10 Gather information for, and evaluate marketing results against, financial and other criteria.

Knowledge and skill requirements

Element 1: Gathering, analysing and presenting information (20 per cent) (Marketing Environment)

1.1 Identify sources of information internally and externally to the organization, including ICT-based sources such as intranet and Internet.

1.2 Maintain a marketing database, information collection and usage.

1.3 Investigate customers via the database and develop bases for segmentation.

1.4 Explain information gathering techniques available.

1.5 Source and present information on competitor activities across the marketing mix.

1.6 Investigate marketing and promotional opportunities using appropriate information gathering techniques.

1.7 Gather information across borders.

Element 2: Building and developing relationships (20 per cent) (Customer Communications)

2.1 Describe the structure and roles of the marketing function within the organization.

2.2 Build and develop relationships within the marketing department, working effectively with others.

2.3 Explain the 'front line' role: receiving and assisting visitors, internal and external enquiries.

2.4 Represent the organization using practical PR skills, including preparing effective news releases.

2.5 Explain the supplier interface: negotiating, collaborating, operational and contractual aspects.

2.6 Explain how the organization fits into a supply chain and works with distribution channels.

2.7 Use networking skills in the business world.

2.8 Explain the concept and application of E-relationships.

2.9 Describe techniques available to assist in managing your manager.

Element 3: Organizing and undertaking marketing activities (20 per cent) (Marketing Fundamentals)

3.1 Describe the scope of individuals' roles in marketing: meetings, conferences, exhibitions, outdoor shows, outlet launches and press conferences.

3.2 Identify alternative and innovative approaches to a variety of marketing arenas and explain criteria for meeting business objectives.

3.3 Demonstrate an awareness of successful applications of marketing across a variety of sectors and sizes of business.

3.4 Explain how marketing makes use of planning techniques: objective setting, co-ordinating, measuring and evaluating results to support the organization.

3.5 Appraise and select a venue based on given criteria and make appropriate recommendations.

3.6 Explain how an organization should host visitors from other cultures and organize across national boundaries.

Element 4: Co-ordinating the marketing mix (20 per cent) (Marketing Fundamentals)

4.1 Select a media to be used based on appropriate criteria for assessing media opportunities, and recommend a media schedule.

4.2 Evaluate promotional activities and opportunities including sales promotion, PR and collaborative programmes.

4.3 Explain the process for designing, developing and producing printed matter, including leaflets, brochures and catalogues.

4.4 Analyse the impact of pricing decisions and role of price within the marketing mix.

4.5 Describe the current distribution channels for an organization and evaluate new opportunities.

4.6 Describe how organizations monitor product trends.

4.7 Explain the importance of the extended marketing mix: how process, physical aspects and people affect customer choice.

4.8 Explain the importance of ICT in the new mix.

Element 5: Administering the marketing budget (and evaluating results) (20 per cent)

5.1 Demonstrate an ability to manipulate numbers in a marketing context.

5.2 Explain the process used for setting a budget and apportioning fixed and overhead costs.

5.3 Explain how organizations assess the viability of opportunities, marketing initiatives and projects.

5.4 Prepare, present and justify a budget as the basis for a decision on a marketing promotion.

5.5 Make recommendations on alternative courses of action.

5.6 Examine the correlation between marketing mix decisions and results.

5.7 Evaluate the cost effectiveness of a marketing budget, including a review of suppliers and activities.

Related key skills

Key skill	Relevance to unit knowledge and skills
Communication	Contribute to a group discussion
	Synthesise information
	Make a presentation
	Produce a written communication
Application of number	Interpret numerical data
	Calculate and justify budgets
	Use data to evaluate the effectiveness of marketing results
Information technology	Collect, analyse and interpret data from various sources
	Derive new information
	Maintain and use a marketing database
	Use IT to manipulate and present information
Working with others	Develop relationships and use networking
	Apply planning techniques
	Undertake marketing activities and review progress

Key skill	Relevance to unit knowledge and skills
Improving own learning and performance	Apply planning techniques to agree targets and plan how these will be met (methods, timescales, resources)
	Select and use a variety of methods for learning
	Manage time effectively
	Seek feedback to monitor performance and modify approach
	Review progress and provide evidence of meeting targets
Problem solving	Explore a complex problem, identify options and justify option selected
	Plan and implement the option selected and review progress
	Apply agreed methods to check the problem has been solved and draw conclusions

Assessment

The CIM will normally offer two forms of assessment for this unit from which study centres or students may choose: written examination and an integrative assignment. The CIM may also recognize, or make joint awards for, units at an equivalent level undertaken with other professional marketing bodies and educational institutions.

Recommended support materials

Core texts

Dibb, S., Simkin, L., Pride, W. and Ferrell, O. (2005) *Marketing Concepts and Strategies*, 5th European edition, Boston: Houghton Mifflin.

Syllabus guides

BPP (2005) *Marketing in Practice Study Text*, BPP Publishing.

Curtis, T. (2007) *Marketing in Practice*, Oxford: BH/Elsevier.

Supplementary readings

BH (2006) *CIM Revision Cards: Marketing in Practice*, Oxford: Butterworth-Heinemann.

BPP (2005) *Marketing in Practice: Practice and Revision Kit*, London: BPP Publishing.

Gabay (2003) *Teach Yourself Copywriting*, 3rd edition, London: Hodder and Stoughton.

MacKay, A. (2004) *The Practice of Advertising*, 5th edition, Oxford: Butterworth-Heinemann.

Temple, N. (2003) *Writing Copy for the Web in a Week*, London: Hodder and Stoughton.

Wilmshurst, J. and MacKay, A. (1999) *The Fundamentals of Advertising*, 2nd edition, Oxford: Butterworth-Heinemann.

Overview and rationale

Approach

The Marketing in Practice syllabus, first launched in September 1999, requires a broad and practical demonstration of marketing, rather than any depth of understanding at a strategic level. The unit will test students' ability to draw on a wide range of subject matter and put forward practical, well-argued recommendations.

Marketing in Practice is the province of the well-rounded and versatile Marketer, and aims to replicate the challenges, diversity and pace of a typical first marketing role. From an educational standpoint, it seeks to integrate the full Professional Certificate syllabus, and as such is best suited towards the latter phases of course delivery of the Professional Certificate, or, alternatively, it can be run throughout the year alongside the other three units.

This unit offers the opportunity to put into practice the entire Professional Certificate syllabus, integrate key skills, and draw on students' experience. It should be lively and fun for all involved. It rounds off the Professional Certificate and so provides a springboard for the Professional Diploma, which builds on the knowledge and skills at this level and goes on to develop students for a role in operational marketing management.

Syllabus content

As stated above, this syllabus aims to integrate fully the other three units at this level, and assist the student to put new learning into practice. Its integrative nature is broken down further in the next section.

Delivery approach

Element 1: Gathering, analysing and presenting information
Points to stress here are the need for business decisions to be based on information, sources of information that can be accessed, and the need to evaluate the information. There is a strong practical element, and information-gathering techniques are examined. Segmentation is also touched upon – not in any great depth but as a practical tool to use in marketing situations.

This should be used to reinforce learning from the Marketing Environment unit (Professional Certificate) and students should be encouraged to share practice from their own organizations.

Element 2: Building and developing relationships
This section is concerned with the people aspect of marketing. Commencing inside the marketing department, it then looks across the organization, before examining relationships outside – whether with suppliers or further down the supply chain.

This integrates well with Customer Communications (Professional Certificate). Tutors should combine the human aspects with the procedural and contractual to give a realistic view of the real world. This element very much lends itself to a highly interactive approach. This area also supports the Marketing Management in Practice unit at Professional Diploma.

Element 3: Organizing and undertaking marketing activities

Research has shown that many marketing assistants have responsibility for organizing a variety of events, from sales meetings to full blown conferences, and from exhibitions to corporate hospitality. Students should be encouraged to share experiences to compare and contrast different approaches. Again, there is a strong practical element, and it is essential that students have a grasp of costing and can evaluate the success of activities undertaken.

This builds on knowledge from both Marketing Fundamentals and Customer Communications.

Element 4: Co-ordinating the marketing mix

'Co-ordinating' is a key word – this is not strategic management of the mix. For example, students at this level would not decide pricing strategy, but may be asked to report on the effects of a pricing decision. They may not deal with strategic advertising, but may control local advertising.

Similar demarcations apply across the mix. In line with research findings, there is a heavy emphasis on promotional activity, but all 7 Ps and their application should be explored, building on the input in Marketing Fundamentals. Budgeting and dealing with information are also important features in this section. This topic is developed further in Marketing Planning (Professional Diploma).

Element 5: Administering the marketing budget (and evaluating results)

This need not strike fear in tutors or students; practical and tactical are again watchwords for this section. Company accounts, discounted cash flows, etc. are not needed at this level. There is however a need for an appreciation of costs, how they are apportioned, and how cost effective are marketing activities. As such, basic manipulation of figures is essential. The acid test of a student's ability is whether or not the following questions can be answered: 'How much does it cost?', 'How do we split the costs?', 'What will the result be?', and 'Is it worth doing?'

This element intends to provide a basic understanding of finance in business to underpin progress to Marketing Planning (Professional Diploma), and the critical element of 'control' at Professional PG Diploma.

Additional resources (Syllabus – Professional Certificate In Marketing)

Introduction

Texts to support the individual units are listed in the syllabus for each unit. This Appendix shows a list of marketing journals, press and websites that tutors and students may find useful in supporting their studies at Professional Certificate.

Press

Students will be expected to have access to current examples of marketing campaigns and so should be sure to keep up to date with the appropriate marketing and quality daily press, including:

- ○ *Campaign* – Haymarket
- ○ *Internet Business* – Haymarket
- ○ *Marketing* – Haymarket
- ○ *The Marketer* – Chartered Institute of Marketing
- ○ *Marketing Week* – Centaur
- ○ *Revolution* – Haymarket.

Websites

The Chartered Institute of Marketing

www.cim.co.uk	The CIM site containing case studies, reports and news
www.cim.co.uk/learningzone	Website for CIM students and tutors containing study information, past exam papers and case study examples. Also access to 'the marketer' articles online

Publications on-line

www.revolution.haynet.com	Revolution magazine
www.brandrepublic.com	Marketing magazine
www.FT.com	A wealth of information for cases (now charging)
www.IPA.co.uk	Need to register – communication resources
www.booksites.net	Financial Times/Prentice Hall Text websites

Sources of useful information

www.acnielsen.co.uk	AC Nielsen – excellent for research
http://advertising.utexas.edu/world/	Resources for advertising and marketing professionals, students, and tutors
www.bized.com	Case studies
www.corporateinformation.com	Worldwide sources listed by country
www.esomar.nl	European Body representing Research Organizations – useful for guidelines on research ethics and approaches
www.dma.org.uk	The Direct Marketing Association
www.eiu.com	The Economist Intelligence Unit
www.euromonitor.com	Euromonitor consumer markets
www.europa.eu.int	The European Commission's extensive range of statistics and reports relating to EU and member countries
www.managementhelp.org/ research/research.htm	Part of the 'Free Management Library' – explaining research methods
www.marketresearch.org.uk	The MRS site with information and access to learning support for students – useful links on ethics and code of conduct
www.mmc.gov.uk	Summaries of Competition Commission reports
www.oecd.org	OECD statistics and other information relating to member nations including main economic indicators
www.quirks.com	An American source of information on marketing research issues and projects
www.statistics.gov.uk	UK Government statistics
www.un.org	United Nations publish statistics on member nations

www.worldbank.org	World bank economic, social and natural resource indicators for over 200 countries. Includes over 600 indicators covering GNP per capita, growth, economic statistics, etc.

Case sites

www.bluelagoon.co.uk	Case – SME website address
www.ebay.com	On-line auction – buyer behaviour
www.glenfiddich.com	Interesting site for case and branding
www.interflora.co.uk	e-commerce direct ordering
www.moorcroft.co.uk	Good for relationship marketing
www.ribena.co.uk	Excellent targeting and history of comms

© CIM 2007

Index